AVERTING THE AP

AVERTING THE APOCALYPSE

AVERTING THE

APOCALYPSE

☀ SOCIAL MOVEMENTS IN INDIA TODAY ☀

Arthur Bonner

DUKE UNIVERSITY PRESS • Durham and London 1990

© 1990 Duke University Press
All rights reserved
Printed in the United States of America
on acid-free paper ∞
Library of Congress Cataloguing-in-Publication
Data appear on the last printed page of this book.
Maps by Christopher L. Brest

Contents

AVERTING THE APOCALYPSE

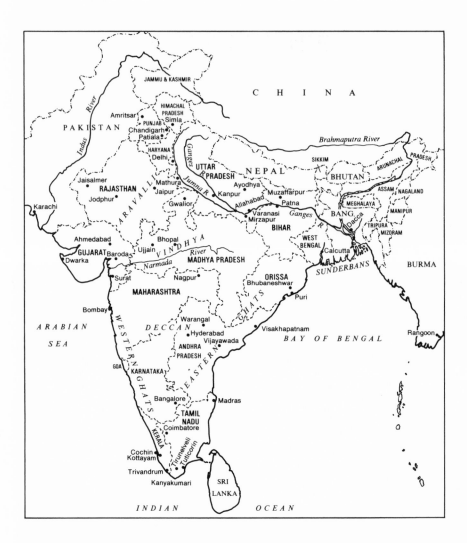

1 ❂ A Longing for Freedom

The most revealing recent image of our global society was the picture of Chinese students in Beijing's Tiananmen Square rallying around a copy of the Statue of Liberty—a gift of the French sculpted to welcome to New York immigrants from many nations and cultures. The fact that the scenes were seen simultaneously on television screens in every part of the world, and that people of many different cultures and economic conditions reacted to the poignancy of the events, reinforced the universality.

Throughout the world there is a longing for democracy in the American and French revolutionary sense of men and woman able to control their own destinies and of open debate and freedom from fear. People everywhere saw parts of themselves in the pictures from Beijing.

Existing systems—whether the capitalist system in Western society, the Marxist system in Eastern Europe and China, or the caste system in India—are decaying. There is a universal pattern of conflict, taking different forms according to local conditions. The growth of social movements is an indication of this decay and conflict.

When the leaders of social movements speak of conflict, they do not mean the destruction of authority. They realize power is needed to regulate complex systems. For them confrontation is designed to expose invisible power: to force ruling groups to innovate and admit persons and issues previously excluded from the decision-making process.

Social movements have many names: the women's movement, the ecology movement, the peace movement, the democracy movement in China, the ethnic nationality movement in many parts of the Soviet Union, the antiapartheid movement in South Africa, the civil rights movement among blacks in the United States, and the wide variety of movements for better health and safety and a more equitable distribution of economic resources. The variety is misleading, for they all share a resistance to modern processes that have led to economic stagnation, ecological crisis, deepening deprivation amid increasing prosperity, and alienation manifested by racism, alcoholism, and drug addiction.

Alberto Melucci, a professor of sociology at the University of Milan in Italy, describes social movements as "laboratories in which new experiences are invented . . . to challenge the dominant codes of everyday life." He says they are different from traditional forms of collective action in that they have no universal plan of history:

> Contemporary social movements operate as signs, in the sense that they translate their actions into symbolic challenges to the dominant codes. . . . Collective action is a form whose models of organization and solidarity deliver a message to the rest of society. . . . Contemporary social movements stimulate radical questions about the ends of personal and social life, and in so doing, they warn of the crucial problems facing complex societies.

Social movements are radical but without the Marxist obsession with class and the struggle over production and distribution of goods. Activists are equally concerned with how society or a group generates and distributes information about itself and the surrounding structures.

In the West this is often carried too far: activists are so concerned with the larger problems of peace, the environment, and intellectual freedom that they are out of touch with—and at times antagonistic to—the bread and butter issues of factory and farm workers.

This is not true in India, where the social movement is concerned entirely with the poor. Its actors strive for immediately realizable benefits: a better place to live; improved medical care; more food and nurseries for children; and they don't expect this generation to be deprived for the promises of the future. The key word is empowerment: the poor must have rupees in their pockets so they are no longer bound to the local moneylender and landlord. The poor must also learn to shed the inferiority born of centuries of caste oppression and the belief in *karma* (inherited fate). Empowerment means ending hierarchies and bringing everyone into the decision-making process. A major characteristic is the high percentage of women as members and leaders. With their criticism of patriarchal oppression, women heighten the suspicion of hierarchy.

Sunita Narain: An Environmental Activist

Sunita Narain, coeditor of a four-hundred-page report on the state of the environment in India and codirector of the Center for Science and Environment in New Delhi, typifies the difference between the Indian approach to the environment and that of the West: Indian activists are concerned with the equitable use of the land, not with the mere preservation of beauty.

When I called on her at her office in New Delhi, she said she was twenty-five and had been in the environmental field for seven years and with the center for five years:

"In his early book, *Hind Swaraj*, Mahatma Gandhi said it took Britain half the world to feed itself. He asked: 'If India became like Britain, how many worlds would it need?' We quote that often. We don't have the rest of the world to rape, so we rape our own countryside. If you set up a paper mill, it wastes the entire forest around it, and the forest moves farther and farther away so now paper mills are going to the Northwest or the Andaman Islands to get supplies. The forests are disappearing, with a tremendous impact on the lives of the poor who live around them.

"For a long time people blamed the destruction of the forests on tribals or other village people who lived in or near the forests: especially blaming slash-and-burn cultivation. But that's unfair. When tribals and villagers used the forests, they made sure they were not destroyed: They collected only twigs, small branches, and dead wood. It's not they who have destroyed the forests; it's the market economy.

"We need to develop forests for three reasons: firstly, the ecological security of the watershed area: that is, to prevent erosion and the ensuing floods. Secondly, to meet the basic needs of people for things like fuel, fodder, thatch, and poles. Thirdly, to meet the cash needs of the people: that is, growing trees to earn money. Once the needs of the people are satisfied you can also use trees for commercial purposes, like making paper.

"So far our common resources of water, land, and forests have been controlled by the state structure, and they've made a complete mess of things. We've got water, but we haven't developed a system to trap it as it falls. There's too much centralization. People expect the state to provide them with water rather than have their own village *tank* (a word derived from Portuguese: any artificial pond or lake), making sure every family gets a share from it.

"In times of drought, when people are threatened with starvation because they can't buy food, we spend millions of rupees to employ them in building roads, so they'll have some cash. The money could be better used for projects to harvest water, like small check dams and tanks.

"Given the fact our society is caste ridden and corrupt, the question is: How can we transfer control to the people? We must rebuild village communities and also give women a voice in the management of these communities. Women are the vital element. When you talk about basic needs, you're talking about women. Unless you give women a voice, you'll never give the environment a voice. You can understand this if we start with the fact that the basic needs of a family are often seen only in terms of cash, which is held by the man, not the woman. But the man's priority can be completely different; he sees fuel as non-cash, something that's gotten free from the environment.

"Fuel is always the last thing bought with the family's supply of cash. Men will buy food, clothing, and maybe a radio, but they're seldom willing to spend money for fuel. It's a woman's job to go out and forage for it. If the surrounding trees are cut, the woman has to walk farther and farther and spend hours a day just to get fuel to cook a meal. A man is perfectly willing to cut and sell a tree to get cash, but a woman wants the trees nearby so she can collect twigs and leaves. Thus it's often the woman who cherishes and protects the environment, not the man."

The Paradox of Mahatma Gandhi

In India, as in the West, political theories based on charismatic leaders and institutionalized parties no longer have meaning. The belief that a particular individual can recognize and fulfill an historical process has been shown to be the starting point for political programs that, at best, have kept the poor in chains and, at worst, have led to violence and totalitarianism.

While social movement actors in the West quote the thoughts of Mahatma Gandhi and regard his nonviolent principles as meaningful for the nuclear age, Indian activists do not look to him for moral inspiration. The West sees Gandhi in terms of his abstract teachings, while modern Indians who are determined to change society see him in terms of his life.

He conceived nonviolent noncooperation as a process for breaking the material and metaphysical chains of slavery, but he tied himself so closely to the interests of the ruling castes that he could not possibly put his beliefs into practice. As he confessed shortly before his death, the nonviolence practiced in India was mere pacifism willing to coexist with the traditional oppressive power structure.

It was through the instrumentality of Gandhi that power was transferred in India in what Antonio Gramsci called a "passive revolution." By this he meant a process presided over by established elites who use what are propagandized as revolutionary changes to maintain and consolidate a supremacy based on a narrow consensus that ignores most of the population except as cheering crowds in the background.

Gramsci, a man with a twisted spine that left him less than five feet tall and continually racked with pain, became the leader of the Italian Communist Party after World War I. He was arrested by the Fascists in 1926 and spent the rest of his life in prison, dying in 1937. Eric Hobsbawm in Britain called him "an extraordinary philosopher, perhaps a genius, probably the most original thinker of the twentieth century in Western Europe."

Most of Gramsci's thoughts are embedded in notes he wrote in the form of long letters from his prison cell. He never lived to work them into an ordered form. Although a Communist he, in effect, destroyed the theoretic basis of Marxism by asserting that cultural factors more than a preexisting economic formation are the basis of a "class" and that a class has to be constructed to be a politically active agent.

He also developed the concept of the "hegemony" of a civil society. By this he meant the predominance, obtained by consent rather than force, of a class or group over other classes. Hegemony is attained and exercised, according to Gramsci, by the many ways in which the educational, religious, and other institutions of society join, directly and indirectly, to form a common social-moral language separate from, although interlinked with, the coercive dominance of rulers.

Gramsci's theories help to explain the social movement process. Metamorphosis might be a better word: activists seek both continuity and change. Gramsci said society does not have one hegemonic center, but many. Social activists are trying to reshape all of the centers to develop a new, broad-based hegemony. Dropping the cant words, they seek participatory democracy based on consensus, even if given reluctantly, and not on pure force.

Examining the Process, Not Searching for Solutions

There is no way of knowing if social movements in India can be translated into a coherent political formation able to solve the country's many problems, so what follows is not a search for solutions. A journalist is primarily eyes and ears. This book is the product of a series of visits with actors in the social movement in the undramatic course of their daily lives as they experiment with projections for a more humane future. Neither is what follows a discourse on the convoluted politics of India, although contemporary realities will not be ignored: the experiments of social activists can be understood only in terms of the disintegrating social and economic structure that surrounds them.

Often described as the world's largest democracy, India in fact is a fledgling democracy on the order of Nigeria, the Philippines, or any of a score of Asian and African countries. Political practices that evolved in Europe over a matter of centuries were a response to a specific climate; it was unrealistic to expect the European plant to flourish in a different environment. As Satish Saberwal of Delhi's Jawaharlal Nehru University writes:

> Institutions designed after Western prototypes and implanted in the modern period are not layered deep in the Indian tradition. One should not take it for granted that the elements needed to sustain institutions of Western design would ordinarily be available to those located in every part of the Indian social and cultural milieu; and when persons formed in the less helpful of those milieus have to operate and, more generally, cope with these institutions, difficulties of some seriousness may reasonably be expected to arise. Political actors in contemporary India are heirs . . . to a variety of political traditions coming down from the precolonial period. . . . Such multiplicity of codes . . . tends to exact a heavy price.

Unlike European democracy, with its centralizing and codifying traditions of Greco-Roman society and the Roman Catholic Church, democracy in India is heir to what Saberwal describes as "interlinked webs of kinship, affinity, and clientship" that, especially under the Rajputs in the north, "functioned around a hierarchy of rulerships." The exercise of power in India has not been through strong dynasties and abstract principles of law or rights but through kinship, marriage, and ties between patron and client. This tradition of a multiplicity of claimants to power at all levels of society accounts for, in modern times, the constant splintering of political parties and the rapid changes of personalities in state and central governments.

India lacks what de Tocqueville envisioned as an abstract force more binding than the outward institutions of power:

> A government retains its sway over a great number of citizens far less by the voluntary and rational consent of the multitude than by that instinctive, and to a certain extent involuntary, agreement which results from similarity of feelings and resemblances of opinion. I will never admit that men constitute a social body simply because they obey the same head and the same laws.

The defeat of Rajiv Gandhi—sardonically styled "The Promise that Failed"—and the Congress Party by alliances of disparate personalities and cliques in the November 1989 election was a result of this clawing for power. It did nothing to advance solutions to the nation's economic and social distortions. To the contrary, the emergence of the Hindu *Bharatiya Janata* (Indian People's) Party (BJP) as a major power broker presaged many years of bitter struggle over the body of secular democracy.

There are too many institutions in place to permit the dissolution of the existing union. Rather, the question is: What kind of an India will survive into the twenty-first century? Will it, like other fledgling democracies, be held together only by strong men or strong parties?

Indians themselves ask: What went wrong with the promised tryst with destiny?

2 ✿ A Missed Tryst

India and Pakistan were supposed to to become independent simultaneously on August 14, 1947. However, astrologers discovered the 14th was inauspicious, so secular India postponed its freedom until one minute after midnight, and ever since it has observed August 15 as Independence Day. The first sentence of Jawaharlal Nehru's speech welcoming freedom is etched in the nation's memory: "Long years ago we made a tryst with destiny and now the time comes when we shall redeem our pledge, not wholly or in full measure, but very substantially."

He spoke of ending "poverty, ignorance, disease, and inequality of opportunity" and recalled one of Mahatma Gandhi's memorable phrases: "The ambition of the greatest man of our generation has been to wipe every tear from every eye. That may be beyond us, but so long as there are tears and suffering, so long our work will not be over."

More than two generations later, most of the population forms an underclass characterized by malnutrition, disease, illiteracy, squalor, high infant mortality, low life expectancy, stunted growth, low capacity for work, and an unjust distribution of resources that forces millions into urban slums that are growing three times faster than the population as a whole. The government admits 40 percent of the population is below the poverty line, defined as an average per capita intake of 2,400 calories in rural areas and 2,200 in urban areas. Many believe the official figures are juggled and that at least 50 to 60 percent are below the poverty line.

Gandhi's Dream Abandoned

Despite his bow to Gandhian pieties, Nehru summarily abandoned the Mahatma's dreams of a decentralized village economy based on India's abundant manpower and followed Lenin and Stalin in the belief that Five-Year plans and capital-intensive heavy industries were the road to utopia. The result was the same: planning burgeoned into a sluggish bureaucracy and a maze of approvals that impeded industrial expansion, discouraged competition, and provided no incentives for cutting costs or improving quality.

Economic growth has averaged 3.5 percent a year. With a population growth rate of 2.1 percent, per capita income has risen a mere 1.4 percent a year. At less than $300, annual per capita income ranks among the lowest in the world. But even this does not reflect the depths of deprivation. A landless laborer who works only part of the year considers himself fortunate if he averages five rupees a day or about $130 a year.

The highly praised "Green Revolution" (the heavy use of improved seeds, fertilizers, and pesticides along with large applications of water) made India self-sufficient in wheat and rice, but these cereals are consumed almost entirely by those with above-average incomes and most of the higher income from increased yields went to large and medium landholders who could afford greater investments. The rich got richer and were better fed while the poor suffered. While the production of cereals increased from 70.9 million tonnes in 1961–62 to 173 million tonnes in 1988–89, production of coarse grains and pulses—the main source of protein in the vegetarian diet of most of the poor —declined slightly from 11.7 million tonnes to 11 million tonnes. With increasing population per capita availability of pulses decreased from sixty grams per day in 1951 to a meager thirty-six grams in 1989, and since about 1983 the retail price of *dal* (the generic name for a variety of pulses) has doubled to an average of ten rupees a kilogram (2.2 pounds).

India has sent satellites into space and maintains a permanent station in the Antarctic. It brags of 150 institutions of higher learning, but education alienates graduates from their culture so that, with the concomitant shortage of employment matching their technical skills, 10,000 emigrate every year to Europe or the United States.

Only 5 percent of the population is covered by adequate water and sanitation facilities. No Indian city, including the four largest—Bombay, Calcutta, Madras, and Delhi—has a complete sewage disposal system. Out of 142 cities with a population of 100,000 or more, seventy-two have no sewage system at all, which means sewage either soaks into the soil and pollutes groundwater or flows through open drains into streams and rivers and pollutes them. Seventy percent of available water is polluted and over 80 percent of illness is related to this unsafe water.

In the capital city of Delhi—favored above all others—only about 440 million gallons of water are available against a demand of 700 million. A cholera epidemic in the Delhi slums in 1988 killed 260 persons. This in a city that is home to the National Institute of Communicable Diseases, the Central Health Education Bureau, the National Institute of Public Cooperation and Child Development, and three medical colleges.

Because of erosion due to deforestation at the rate of 3.2 million acres a year, the Central Soil and Water Institute estimates India loses more than 5 billion tons of soil a year. Erosion is so great that the Brahmaputra, Ganges, and Jumna rivers carry five times their normal level of silt, as a direct consequence of which the states of Uttar Pradesh, Bihar, and West Bengal are devastated by annual floods that kill hundreds of people and destroy or damage tens of thousands of homes and farms.

Efforts to channel the water for productive use have been frustrated by official incompetence. In 1986 Prime Minister Rajiv Gandhi complained that $15.4 billion had been spent since 1951 on plans for 246 large irrigation projects but only 65 had been completed, and out of the original forecast of 50 million acres of new irrigated lands, only 15.6 million acres were receiving water.

Before independence India was characterized by an abrupt divide between 5 percent of the population who lived in luxury and 95 percent who shared various degrees of marginalization. The 5 percent is still there: wealthier and more powerful than ever. In addition, planned development and regulated private enterprise have created a previously nonexistent middle class, comprising about 10 percent of the population, conspicuous by its Eurocentric attitudes toward what makes life worthwhile. In Delhi alone about one thousand dealers sell auto air conditioners, stereos, and musical horns, along with special car scents at $20 a bottle.

The politically strong new middle class has spurred a vast expansion of colleges and universities to the neglect of schooling for the poor and dispossessed who make up the remaining 85 percent of the population. Adult literacy in rural areas, where 85 percent of the poor live, is 36 percent, and since the dropout rate is over 70 percent at the primary stage, most quickly revert to functional illiteracy. In the long run this is suicidal. No society in history has improved its quality of life without banishing illiteracy.

The Caste Syndrome

Power remains visible in the hands of a caste elite whose authority is far different from the class system of the West. Caste is not easily explained. When Europeans first encountered the gross manifestations of untouchability, unapproachability, and unseeability, caste seemed to center around ideas of ritual purity and pollution. Closer acquaintance demonstrated what might be polluting in one part of the country was not in another. Moreover, as increased mobility and the growth of towns and cities made it impossible to enforce the rituals of purity and pollution, caste remained entrenched. Most sociologists now adopt the view that caste can be best understood as status groups: individuals who share a certain consciousness of being a separate community with a distinctive life-style. The groups are ranked in terms of relative honor: a caste is defined by its status in relation to another caste.

No other society has elaborated status groups to the extent of India. There are tens of thousands of castes. These are often called subcastes, but that term is inexact: a misnomer to take cognizance of the difference between the Indian terms *Varna* (literally, color: commonly translated as caste) and *jati* (literally, occupational group: commonly translated as subcaste).

The Varna category is made up of the three highest all-India castes, *Brahmins* (priests), *Kshatriyas* (warriors), and *Vaishyas* (merchants)—the *Dwijas* (twice-born)—and an amorphous fourth group known as *Sudras* (agricultural workers). All others were *Antyaja* (outcastes or untouchables).

The British first described untouchables as the depressed castes but then invented a category known as the Scheduled Castes and Scheduled Tribes, so-called because of the schedules, or lists, of groups singled out for positive discrimination. Gandhi called untouchables *Harijans* (Children of God). Nowadays, activists among them reject euphemisms and call themselves *Dalits* (broken people).

Castes are separated by language and region and further particularized into clans and lineages. An upper caste man, although a member of a single Varna, such as a Brahmin, will see himself in different lights in different situations. At the minimal level he will be part of a marriage circle restricted to a particular set of Brahmins. While looking for a job, he might project himself as a member of a larger group of Brahmin marriage circles. While taking part in state politics he may see himself in an even larger group of Brahmins speaking a particular Indian language. Finally, as a foreign-educated, English-speaking professional, he may see himself only as a Brahmin.

The higher elements in any Varna series blend with what Western cultures perceive as class and modernization: an acquired status based on wealth, education, and employment. This is crucial to an understanding of continued inequality in India. Where previously structural distances were maintained through interdictions on marriage, commensality, and social exchange, the ascending status distances are now maintained and reinforced by such things as the degree of command of a foreign language and foreign technology.

The Flexibility of Caste

A collective status is not immutable: large clans and tribes have risen in caste ranking to become rulers, priests, warriors and, in modern times, commercial entrepreneurs. This is known as Sanskritization: a process of moving up through imitation and accommodation of the rituals and ceremonies of the dominant castes. Only ranking changes, not the hierarchical structure, so that a member of a twice-born caste retains his social superiority even if he is poor, since the status of an individual is channeled through his hereditary group. A Sudra who becomes a government official will always be looked down upon as a Sudra while a Brahmin who works as a cook is still a Brahmin and may still be addressed as *Panditji* (honorable learned person).

Sanskritization can be seen as part of the psychology of victimization. An historical and cultural heritage that denies equality simultaneously implants a sense of guilt. An untouchable who attempts to achieve a higher status acknowledges the chains that bind him to a position of inferiority; he internalizes his degradation and imitates his oppressor to feel less insecure or alienated.

Broadly speaking, Indian society can be divided into two parts. One is the Brahminic, comprising the three twice-born castes plus large regional Sudra and even untouchable castes that have become relatively wealthy and better educated and have adopted Brahmin social structures. Before the arrival of the British the Brahminism of the three twice-born castes was a thin veneer comprising no more than 3 percent of the population. Now, Brahminism, seen as an amalgam of caste, class, and consumerism, comprises about 15 percent of the population.

The remaining 85 percent can be described simply as non-Brahmins: a heterogeneous mixture of what are called the "other backward classes" plus Dalits, tribals, Muslims, Christians, and Sikhs. Although the non-Brahmins, in Indian fashion, see themselves entirely in terms of their separate castes and religions, and for that reason remain politically and socially divided, they are homogeneous in terms of class and deprivation.

What is generally depicted as Indian culture is actually the Brahminic. Some scholars have divided religious beliefs into the Great Tradition and the Little Tradition, as if Brahminism was the central, unifying theme of Indian civilization and local traditions mere carry-overs from some distant, discredited past. The opposite is closer to the truth: the many varieties of Indian beliefs and practices are the hallmark, or Great Tradition, of Indian culture, while Brahminism represents a persistent attempt to impose the values of a self-defined elite.

Caste As Racism

The parallels with racial exclusivity are everywhere apparent. The group nature of caste, perpetuated by tightly knit marriage circles, makes it easier for economic and social opportunities to be appropriated by those who collectively occupy a privileged position in relation to those who have collectively been fixed in a deprived condition for centuries.

Birth into a twice-born caste, clan, and family decides what school a boy will go to, whom he will marry, whom he will consult about his career, whose career he, in turn, will help, whom he will vote for, and, finally, how his estate will be divided and who will inherit it.

Poverty is subjective: a person may be poor because he has a categorical identity that limits his ambitions. Thus caste explains the persistence of the underculture of poverty and deprivation. It negates, to a large extent, the upward mobility expected in a society with legal guarantees against discrimination on the basis of birth, caste, religion, or sex.

The use of English as the language of government, business, and universities raises another barrier that only the most brilliant or favored lower caste man can surmount, and then only at a high cost to his self-esteem. An upper caste youth raised in an English-speaking, consumerist environment is among peers as he gets his degree and finds a job. A lower caste man, especially an untouchable, has to shed the values and traditions of his family and leave his childhood friends behind. This psychological stress, along with poor primary and secondary school preparation, leads to the high dropout rate that characterizes the performance of lower caste men in colleges and universities.

The ultimate blow falls when a lower caste man, through skill and tenacity, earns the degree that is his entry ticket to government. He is now a painfully conspicuous minority. He may be the only one of his kind in a large office and finds he must be careful not to antagonize the upper castes who surround him. While a high caste government official is viewed as acting perfectly normal when he helps his fellow caste members, a low caste official may be regarded as showing undue favoritism.

The syndrome is familiar to those acquainted with racism in the United States. Blacks who have "made it" are reluctant to help other blacks lest they be accused of identifying with black culture rather than the white culture into which they have gained what may be only token entry.

A Metaphor for Oppression

The correlation between casteism and racism can be best understood through the analysis of the Tunisian-born French sociopsychologist Albert Memmi, who goes beyond skin color and uses racism as a metaphor for oppression. He sees four essential elements: stressing real or imaginary differences; assigning values to these differences; generalizing from them and claiming they are final; and using them to justify aggression or privilege. According to Memmi:

> If the difference is missing, the racist invents one; if the difference exists, he interprets it to his advantage. . . . The difference is assigned a value in such a way as to discredit the defendant and reflect credit on his accuser. . . . One thing leads to another until all of the victim's personality is characterized by the difference and all of the members of his social group are targets for the accusation. . . . In the extreme, racism merges into myth . . . by which the victim is stripped of value. Broadly speaking, the process is one of gradual dehumanization. The racist ascribes to his victim a series of surprising traits. . . . Slowly he makes his victim a sort of animal, a thing or simply a symbol.

This has been happening in India for more than a thousand years and despite legislation to outlaw untouchability, caste/race discrimination still exists, as noted in the Seventh Report (March 1985) of the Commission for Scheduled Castes and Scheduled Tribes:

Judging by the present level of the socio-economic development of the Scheduled Castes, it becomes clear that the benefits of infrastructural development are not yet to reach them in any perceptible measure. . . . The Commission . . . observed the pitiable living conditions of the Scheduled Castes whether they were in the rural areas or in urban locations. In villages, they invariably live in separate localities often at some distance from the main village. They do not have basic amenities like safe drinking water, electricity or health facilities etc. Their *bustees* (shantytowns) are mostly not connected with the main road.

Democracy, with its rule by power blocks rather than consensus, can be hard on minorities whose identities single them out, such as blacks in America and Algerians and other Muslims in France. With education and increased communications, the higher and emerging middle castes have become institutionalized and politicized, forming broad caste associations and even joining other castes to present a united front in state elections.

Colonial Continuity

In the colonial concept forced social change is justified as a "civilizing" mission to modernize backward societies. The term "backward" derives from a lineal theory of historical and economic progress, shaped by nineteenth-century concepts of Darwinian evolution, that links the European industrial revolution with consumerism and the expansion of market economies. The proper uses of natural resources emerged in the context of "growth" in Western colonizing societies and then, in economic theory, were raised to the level of universal applicability.

A corollary is the curse of what is known as the "Orientalist" construction of Asian history. Orientalism assumes Western institutions are "natural" and all else merely the "other," somehow distorted or malformed. This leads to the reductionist approach of the World Bank and various foreign aid programs: it is only necessary to examine the parts of non-Western societies, make repairs and adjustments according to Western blueprints, and all will be well. The endless failures of these programs and the continued dependence of Third World governments are explained away as poor education or the backwardness of the "other" rather than an indictment of reductionism itself.

Elite inheritors who had internalized Western concepts were encouraged and funded by the World Bank and others to continue the colonialist civilizing mission under the rubric of development. Unrestrained by the informed opposition that serves as a check to governmental authority in the West, this Eurocentric elite became an even more predatory breed of colonizers, free to commercialize the previously nonmarket economy and to commandeer the natural resources the "backward" rural poor needed for their daily existence.

The pejorative label collaborator may seem too strong, since it was used in Europe to describe someone who helped the hated Nazi invaders, which the British in India never were. Nevertheless, Indians who faithfully served the Raj (British rule in India) were undoubtedly collaborating with racists who treated all Indians with contempt and who came only to extract wealth to be remitted home.

The English-speaking elite who dominated the Indian National Congress saw themselves as the natural successors to the British, ruling over a metaphysical entity comprising "unity in diversity." Nehru, in his *Discovery of India*—a rambling excursion through Indian history written during five months in prison in 1944—rhapsodized on this eternally existing nation: "Some kind of dream of unity has occupied the mind of India since the dawn of civilization."

In Nehru's eyes, Chandragupta Maurya, who repulsed a weak Greek invasion by the successors of Alexander in the fourth century B.C., "raised the old and ever-new cry of nationalism and roused the people against the foreign invader." A century later, when the Emperor Ashoka extended his suzerainty to southern India he was, in Nehru's words, fired by "the old dream of uniting the whole of India under one supreme government." Later, Nehru pictured the sixteenth-century Muslim Emperor Akbar as "the great representative of the old Indian ideal of synthesis of differing elements and their fusion into a common nationality. He identified himself with India and Indians took to him although he was a newcomer."

Nehru made it appear that the British had merely restored the continuum of five thousand years of civilization and that transforming the colonial state into a nation-state was a mere matter of nomenclature. This is a caricature.

India's Diversity

In Europe new civilizations and conquering peoples eliminated or absorbed earlier inhabitants, but the successive waves of peoples who invaded India simply found places within the indigenous structure. India, unlike any other country, accepts a variety of cultural forms and considers them immutable. It is a civilization where 1,650 languages and dialects are claimed as mother tongues and where there is no national dress, cuisine, painting, dance, music, or life-styles.

Out of the babel of mother tongues, sixteen are recognized as official languages for public purposes, with Hindi and English as the link languages. It is claimed Hindi is the language of central and north central India and is spoken by 45 percent of the total population of the country, thus justifying its use as the premier link language. The remaining 55 percent say the predominance of Hindi is exaggerated by treating separate languages, such as Rajasthani, Bhojpuri, and Maithili, as mere dialects of Hindi when in fact they are not homogeneous and have their own cultures and literature.

Other large language groups, particularly those in the south numbering in the tens of millions, resist the imposition of Hindi, arguing their children are at a disadvantage if they must learn two languages to compete on an all-India level with Hindi-speaking children who have to learn only one.

The British were replaced by collaborators who—determined to perpetuate strong central rule—retained and enlarged an elite civil service once proudly known as the "steel frame" of colonial statism. Recruits to what is now called the Indian Administrative Service (IAS) are selected through exacting examinations, with English as the mandatory language. One of these officials, when assigned to a state government, may be appointed as a district (the equivalent of an American county) collector. As such, he will be the highest civil authority and also have control of the police and, as a magistrate, hold judicial authority too.

Parallels with British colonialism must be made with caution. What is exhibited today is not a replication of foreign rule but rather an unequal social system that existed for centuries before the British imposed their rule. Only the shell of the British civil service remains in place: the contents are thoroughly Indian, reflecting a profound distrust of grass-roots initiatives. It was just the opposite with the British, who delegated large amounts of power to local officials so they might redress local inequalities and improvise according to the situation they found on the ground. Now district level IAS officers with their immense authority are often tools of local politicians and oligarchies. The result is a system that severely limits access to power by the largely illiterate and impoverished majority and invites selective application of the laws, with the privileged exempt from punishment or check.

"Waiting for the Apocalypse"

The failure of modern social legislation and democratic institutions has led to a sense of impending doom. As Satish Saberwal notes:

> There is a sense of crisis in and about Indian society. The difficulty is not specific, local and temporary; it is general, widespread and persistent. It is evident in the difficulty we have over such elemental issues as unemployment, population growth, sanitation and control over violence; in all . . . political parties, legislatures, bureaucracy, [and the] judiciary; in key societal institutions like the university and trade unions. The list can go on.

Deepening despair gives rise to cynicism. For many years a leading opinion-shaper was Sham Lal, the editor of the *Times of India*. Now retired, Sham Lal's social criticisms are confined to occasional book reviews. In 1988 he dismissed a book by Rajni Kothari, India's foremost spokesman for democratic reform, as "tired rhetoric." Kothari, in *State Against Democracy*, had called for a greater devolution of power and a rethinking of national priorities. Sham Lal commented:

> Only an unshakable faith in the nation's democratic destiny can sustain the hope that the institutions at all levels can be rebuilt [in] a new design in which redistributive justice plays the key role. . . . As things fall apart and the center is unable to hold, we can perhaps console ourselves that the myth that a new grass-roots democracy will emerge from the ruins of the old elite democracy. That should make at least the waiting for the apocalypse somewhat less painful.

Cynicism seems justified. The streets of Bombay, for instance, give little reason to expect that poverty, illiteracy, and caste/racist superiority will ever be eased sufficiently for India to keep its tryst with destiny.

3 ❀ The Rich and the Poor

Bombay is the richest city in India and the busiest port. It has the wealthiest stock exchange and the largest concentration of textile mills and is the center for films, fashion, and advertising. It once embodied the dreams of Anglicized Indians of a cosmopolitan society where people stood in queues, and it was a pleasure to motor along Marine Drive, savoring the wide view of the Arabian Sea.

It now is an urban nightmare. The population grew from 4.15 million in 1961 to 8.2 million in 1981 and is expected to reach 11.1 million in 1991, with virtually no increase in municipal services above the 1960s level.

Bombay, which began as seven swampy islands, is now a single island fourteen miles long and three miles wide, joined by bridges to Greater Bombay to the north and northeast. More than 90 percent of all jobs in Greater Bombay are located on the island and, of those, 90 percent are on the southern tip. It has a population density of about 100,000 a square mile: about four times that of New York. Tokyo and Bombay have about the same population, but Tokyo has 5,600 acres of parks and Bombay only 290.

Like Manhattan, Bombay is an island where the wealthy feel they must live. Modern Indian Moguls, wallowing in unreported and untaxed incomes, are willing to spend the equivalent of a half million or even a million dollars (at least half paid under the table to escape notice) to live in a new apartment tower. Also like New York, Bombay is a city where rent controls, in force since 1947, have halted the construction of middle- or low-income housing and, due to a lack of repairs, led to the rapid decay of buildings lashed by the fierce monsoon rains. A single room in a *chawl* (tenement) sells for fifty thousand rupees ($3,500).

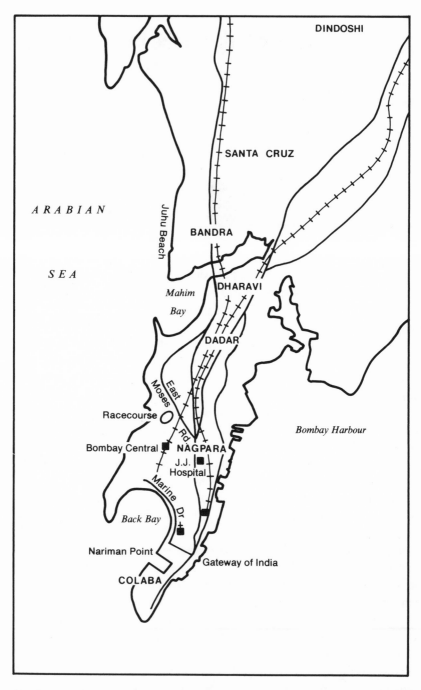

Bombay

An apartment in a new multistory house, with three or more hours a day commuting, goes for half a million to a million rupees ($35,000 to $70,000).

Six luxury hotels (patronized mainly by rich Indians) were opened in 1987, while half the population lives in bustees or on the sidewalks. When a tenement collapsed in January 1988, killing twenty-six people, it was estimated that 16,000 buildings were in a similar perilous state.

No other city has a slum as large as Bombay's Dharavi, where more than half a million people are crammed into tin shacks on four hundred swampy acres. The residents include educated, salaried office workers who cannot find affordable housing elsewhere and are so embarrassed by their surroundings they try not to let friends know they live in Dharavi.

Except for the most wealthy areas, piped water to houses is available for only an hour or so twice a day, while in the bustees a hundred families may be served by a single tap. The sewage system serves little purpose because half the population is not connected to the outlets. And with an insufficient force to dispose of garbage, and piles of trash strewn about by rag and paper pickers, it is believed Bombay supports 250,000 stray dogs.

At times the smell of urine is overpowering. Some owners try to protect the sides of their buildings by decorating them with religious pictures. For instance, a wall in the Bombay Central area had images of the gods Ganesh and Hanuman, the Virgin Mary, Sai Baba (the founder of one of the most popular Hindu sects), the untouchable leader Bhimrao Ramji Ambedkar, a Christian cross, a trident and drum (symbols of the god Siva), the number 786 (considered auspicious by Muslims), and the mystical Hindu symbol *Om*.

Sidewalks, dug up for some municipal purpose, are never fully repaired, and a pedestrian has to make his way around and over piles of dirt and stone amid pools of muddy water. Even if the sidewalk is restored, there is little room to walk between the goods that merchants display outside their stores and the hawkers who have set up shop at the curbside.

The Crush of Commuters

One million commuters ride trains designed to carry 1,200 passengers but which, in peak rush hours, carry 3,500. Another 3.8 million use the buses. A Bombay bus, in service for sixteen hours, will carry 18,000 passengers. During a comparable period a London bus will carry only six hundred passengers and a New York bus about four hundred. Actually, many Bombay buses fail to make it through the day: antique, overworked, and ill-maintained, they fail in midjourney.

A journey by taxi is not much faster than by bus. Bombay's streets account for only 8 percent of its land and are further narrowed by hawkers. Since motor vehicles must compete for the remaining space with bullock or hand-pulled carts, there are traffic jams every few blocks.

While their vehicles belch noxious exhaust into the already polluted air, the drivers vent their anger by blasting their horns. This, when combined with the high-pitched film songs blaring from store loudspeakers, produces a noise level that has been tested at between fifty-seven and ninety-five decibels, far higher than the fifty-five-decibel limit suggested by the World Health Organization.

Life becomes worse during the three months of the monsoon. Once in 1987 an awesome twenty-two inches of rain fell in twenty-four hours. Slum dwellers buy large plastic sheets to cover their shacks and commuters, who leave one or two hours early to get to work, are crammed dripping wet into the trains and buses: long experience has taught them to expect delays because of flooded tracks or potholes six to nine inches deep that suddenly appear on the streets.

During the monsoon the drinking water, doubtful at the best of times, is further infected by sewage flooding into the pipes, and hospitals and clinics prepare for a 50 percent increase in the incidence of cholera, typhoid, and diarrhea.

The poor who seek hospital treatment face another ordeal. Bombay boasts nearly one-third of its municipal budget is spent on health services, but one-third of that goes to three teaching hospitals that concentrate on specialty surgery. While these services are available to the rich or influential, patients in filthy and inefficient wards are guinea pigs for doctors training to practice abroad or to establish private clinics for the affluent. Forty percent of Bombay's population is below the age of twenty, but the city spends less than 10 percent of its health care budget on maternity and child welfare services.

Working Space Is Living Space

Walk through any slum in India and you will hear hammering, cutting, sawing, or the thump of shuttles coming from almost every hut: any conceivable item of metal, leather, or cloth is a cottage industry.

This busy sound of industry is also a mark of caste. In India it is the despised Dalits who work the hardest and often are the most enterprising. Stephen Fuchs, a German anthropologist, described the wide variety of Dalit castes that can be found throughout India: stone, salt and lime workers, miners, well diggers, fishermen, boatmen, palanquin bearers, basket and mat makers, vagrant artisans, traders, bards, genealogists, drummers, musicians, actors, jugglers, acrobats, songwriters, temple servants, painters, sculptors, astrologers, palmists, exorcists, mendicants, domestic servants, watchmen, messengers, weavers, leather workers, washermen, toddy-tappers, liquor sellers, scavengers, field laborers, barbers, potters, blacksmiths, carpenters, masons, and oil pressers.

It would be an error to call the artisans of the Bombay slums entrepreneurs, since they rarely have surplus capital to invest, but they do have enterprising spirits. Some acquire a battered sewing machine and become sidewalk tailors; others get a few tools and establish themselves as cobblers and makers of cheap sandals. Some have a hand-turned iron crushing machine to squeeze juice from long stalks of sugar cane.

Others set themselves up in tea stalls or sell cigarettes, *bidis* (grains and dust of tobacco wrapped in a dry leaf: the cigarettes of the common man), and *pan* (a mixture of betel nuts, lime, and tobacco or various spices wrapped in a bit of leaf of the betel palm). Women sell vegetables in residential areas or bananas or other fruit to office workers. With tens of thousands of commuters who cannot afford restaurants, the permutations of selling food are endless. One way to cater to them is to buy a butane gas stove and set up a sidewalk *chat* (fast food) stall, selling three or four vegetable dishes dispensed in disposable bowls made of leaves stitched together, eliminating the need to wash dishes where water is scarce.

The Pavement Dwellers

The poorest of Bombay's poor are those who have only their labor to sell. Many willingly bind themselves to contractors who can assure them a better-than-average chance for getting work. The contractor gets a commission on each man supplied, or he may collect a fixed sum and pay the laborer a bare minimum. This type of work is most often found on construction sites or in railroad yards or truck depots, where groups of men are needed at fairly regular intervals and employers want to avoid responsibility under the minimum wage or health and pension laws.

Other men become porters, headload carriers, handcart pullers, and cycle rickshaw peddlers, while women become domestic servants. Normally, domestic servants would be expected to belong to the mainstream labor force, but it is common for a housewife to hire a servant for only a few hours a day to clean a house or prepare vegetables for cooking, thus absolving herself of responsibility for providing living space and other benefits.

The most visible of the urban poor are the pavement dwellers, a descriptive phrase that distinguishes them from those who, in the West, would be called homeless. In a city with an equitable climate—where even during the monsoon the strong sun will soon appear to dry things out—living without formal shelter can be a deliberate, rational decision ensuring access to earning opportunities and reducing the expenditure on housing to zero.

A linkage between living space and work place explains why the poor live amid some of the most expensive real estate in the country. Congested wholesale markets, dockyards, railway stations, and commercial business zones offer the best opportunities to sell labor in a highly competitive environment. Many earning opportunities are location specific: a shoe shine boy, for instance, can capture a strategic point if he sleeps as well as works there. Or someone trading in goods sleeps where he sells to safeguard his inventories.

Handcart pullers, who move heavy loads through the narrow streets on long wooden carts, need a place to keep carts. Since there are no parking places in a congested bustee, it is more rational to keep one's cart in a commercial area that is not congested at night. By living there as well, a man protects his vehicle from theft and is available at first call in the morning.

Most pavement dwellers live in shelters of cloth and plastic stretched over bamboo frames, using the wall of a building as support on one side. As a civil nuisance, they are all too visible. However, as human beings—as Sheela Patel discovered—they are invisible.

4 ❀ We, the Invisible

We have to break through the perception the poor are dirty and illiterate and don't know what they want," Sheela Patel said. "Housing is a basic requirement and not welfare. We want to create an atmosphere in which people can articulate what they want, how they want it, where they want it, and what they're able to do themselves."

Sheela, a small, freckled-faced woman radiating energy, graduated in 1974 from the prestigious Tata Institute of Social Science in Bombay with a master's degree in social work. Although not a Christian, she was hired as a counselor in child guidance at the Nagpara Neighborhood House, an American Protestant missionary institution, and spent ten years there, becoming progressively restless.

"Counseling was along traditional American lines," she said. "You do nice things to help an individual fit into a social mold and never question these norms. I gave it up and went into general administration and became the assistant director. They allowed me to bend norms to allow impoverished people the opportunity to improve themselves.

"On both sides there were pavement dwellers. When their houses were demolished, they would usually lose things, and I allowed them to leave their belongings in my room. The minute the truck came, half the women would run out to deal with the police and the other half would run up to my office. At one point the demolition was very brutal, so I took a case to court. Then, very gently and sweetly, I was told I should do this in my personal capacity and not as assistant director.

"I thought I would be a little adventurous and try something new. I had a lot of support from my friends. I don't mind taking responsibility, but I need to be part of a team. In 1984, when I was thirty-two, I quit my job, and we started this organization."

"Conscientization"

She referred to the Society for Promotion of Area Resource Centers (SPARC), a group of social workers and researchers concerned with poor migrants in Bombay. She described their aim as "conscientization," which she defined as "helping people learn to fight for themselves rather than creating a traditional program that would perpetuate dependency." She said SPARC got grants from the central and state governments as well as from international agencies in Germany, Switzerland, and New Zealand.

SPARC's office is a former garage at the rear of a municipal clinic in central Bombay, with pavement dwellers on all the surrounding streets. SPARC discovered it, dirty and caked with mud from past flooding, and persuaded local officials to let them use it for a nominal rent. They cleaned it and furnished it with only a telephone and a desk: all work, including frequent meetings with planners and community groups, is conducted sitting on the cloth-covered floor. The leveling process reflected an organizational attitude: Sheela, although she has the title of director, said she was not the leader and all decisions were reached by consensus after group discussions. She said SPARC was an organization of women working for women: as one of its publications phrased it:

It is women who have to turn a shelter into a home; who must set up all the family's survival systems—the water source, the cooking fuel, the health care, education of the children; it is women who suffer the most hardships vis-à-vis the lack of proper latrines, bathing areas, water supply, the distance of markets and ration shops; it is she who is blamed when the child runs outside the pavement house and is hit by a truck; if her son joins the local gang of thugs, thieves, smugglers or drunks, or if she or her daughter is raped when they go out, in unlit darkness, to relieve themselves; it is she who must bear the wrath of demolition squads who arrive when her husband is away at work; and after the demolition, it is her sari, tied to bamboo poles, which will shelter the family from the sun.

SPARC is a reaction to social pressures that made migrants the fodder for demagogues.

For more than a century Maharashtrians nurtured their ethnic pride by recalling the exploits of Shivaji, the seventeenth-century warrior who made the Marathas the dominant force in India until internal quarrels left them prey for the expanding British Empire.

In the early 1960s Bal Thackery, whose previous claim to fame was as a newspaper cartoonist, created the *Shiv Sena* (Army of Shivaji), with the slogan "Maharashtra for the Maharashtrians." Thackery gained the support of textile mill owners as a counter to Communist trade unions and was thus able to ensure jobs for "Sons of the Soil." In 1968 the Shiv Sena emerged as the second largest party in the Bombay Municipal Corporation. By 1985 it had grown to be the largest single party in the corporation.

The Pavement Dwellers' Case

Earlier, in 1981, trying to out-do the Shiv Sena's demagoguery, A. R. Antulay, the Congress Party chief minister (the equivalent of a state governor in the United States) of Maharashtra, proclaimed he would deport 100,000 slum dwellers. As a starter he had rows of pavement shelters demolished and thousands of their occupants loaded into buses and trucks to be dumped just outside the city or at points along the Maharashtra border. The evictions took place during blinding monsoon rains: the newspaper pictures were pathetic. Civil rights activists soon persuaded the Supreme Court in New Delhi to restrain temporarily the demolitions. The order was periodically extended as the "Pavement Dweller Case" slowly made its way through the courts.

On one side human rights advocates argued the homeless were not trespassing because the pavements were public property: saying they lived there out of necessity, not by choice. They pointed out article twenty-one of the constitution guaranteed citizens the "right to life" and said this must include the right to livelihood: without guaranteed employment, shelter, and wages, people have a right to seek work and housing where it is available. In rebuttal lawyers for Maharashtra and Bombay argued the authorities were not stopping the pavement dwellers from living, only from living on public property. Furthermore, they maintained the right to life of pavement dwellers could not be at the cost of another section of the public, such as pedestrians who were forced to walk on the dangerous roads because the sidewalks were otherwise occupied.

When the Supreme Court rendered its judgment in July 1985, it turned out that the pavement dwellers both won and lost. The court accepted the major argument that the right to life includes the right to livelihood and that people lived on the sidewalks because they lacked alternatives. The judgment said, in part: "Those who have made pavements their homes exist in the midst of filth and squalor which has to be seen to be believed. Rabid dogs in search of stinking meat and cats in search of hungry rats keep them company. The people work and sleep where they ease themselves, for no conveniences are available to them."

Nevertheless, the court upheld their eviction as long as "prior notice" was given and the demolitions were carried out in a "humane manner." The question of where they should go was left unanswered.

Getting the Facts

Sheela Patel and her associates decided the first thing was to get some facts. "Pavement dwellers are highly visible on one hand, but they're invisible as human beings who have a history and a story, just like ourselves," Sheela said. "There have been lots of reports on slum dwellers, but almost nothing has been said about pavement dwellers."

They enlisted the support of other social scientists and community workers and in September and October 1985 conducted a census of over six thousand households comprising nearly 27,000 individuals living in the "E" ward of central Bombay. Their report, the largest such study ever done, was called *We, the Invisible*. It found:

1. Forty-three percent were wage earners, significantly higher than the national figure of 38 percent.

2. Slightly more than 53 percent earned less than twelve rupees a day ($1 at the then prevailing exchange rate), with the earnings of women about half that of men.

3. More than ninety occupations were elicited. Thirty-three percent were unskilled labor, including construction workers, dock workers, and headload carriers; 21 percent were small traders of edible goods or petty consumer items like purses and cheap clothing; 14 percent were self-employed, such as barbers, tailors, and paper and rag pickers; 12 percent (mostly women) were domestic servants; another 12 percent were skilled workers, including metal workers, weavers, and plumbers; and a final 14 percent were in miscellaneous occupations such as small traders and the lowest grades of city employees.

4. Slightly more than half the earners said they spent either no time at all (their work was home based) or reached their work place by walking less than half an hour. Only 16 percent used the mass transit system to get to their jobs.

5. With all the publicity about migrants from other states flooding into the city, the census showed nearly 34 percent were either born in Bombay or within the boundaries of Maharashtra. Most of those from other states were landless and unskilled manual laborers: more than half had no assets whatsoever in their native place and another 27 percent owned a hut and nothing else. In sum, migrants were not pulled to the city by promises of an easier or better life; they were pushed by the lack of development and growing impoverishment of the countryside.

The Bombay Municipal Corporation waited until well after the monsoon to resume demolitions. Then, in March 1986, the flimsy homes of three hundred families living on East Moses Road, near the exclusive Mahalaxmi Race Course, were dismantled, and the residents and their belongings were dumped on an arid, rocky site known as Dindoshi, more than twenty kilometers to the north. In the next three months 1,500 families from slums throughout Bombay were dumped at Dindoshi, creating an instant new slum.

SPARC workers, while making the census, had established a relationship with groups of women in several pavement colonies. They wondered if there was a way to meet the city's need to regain control of the streets while also meeting the needs of those who lived there.

The Qualities of Deprivation

"One of the qualities of deprivation is no one gets lead time to plan or sort out options," Sheela said. "If a company wants to move from Bombay to Madras it takes five years to plan for the shift. Pavement dwellers also need time. Their survival system depends on being part of a structure in a certain place. The poorer the family, the greater the sophistication of its infrastructure. It's all on a day-to-day basis: I borrow money from you in the morning and give it back at night. They don't have a day care system, but they do have an intricately worked out system to take care of other children in case of need. If you uproot someone you have to reestablish that infrastructure."

To explore alternatives SPARC took groups of women to several possible sites to see if there was a supply of water and whether there was alternative work for traders, laborers, rag pickers, domestic servants, and everyone else. Once people were involved, their individual needs came to the surface. For instance, would a recent migrant renting space in a pavement colony be entitled to a hut of his own in the resettlement

community? Would a woman with three children, who had been abandoned by her husband and was now living with her father, be entitled to
a hut of her own? And what of a widow who had a place large enough to
rent out a part to a tenant? Should she get only a hut for herself and
thereby lose her livelihood?

SPARC also involved women in planning their new homes. The mu-
nicipality promised each family a plot measuring fifteen by ten feet. An
average sari is fifteen by five feet, so SPARC showed the women a sari
was the equivalent of the length of the plot and two widths was the
breadth. Other units of measurement were obtained from the waist cord
used for tying a woman's trousers, about fifty-four inches, and the
mangalsutra (wedding necklace, the equivalent of a wedding ring in the
West), about twenty inches. Using such templates, women could envi-
sion the size of a new home and how they would have to arrange their
new living space.

For several months all seemed well. Some city officials worked
closely with SPARC and even attended meetings with the women of the
pavement communities. Then it suddenly collapsed: a different politician was given responsibility for relocating pavement dwellers, and soon,
without notice, a demolition squad showed up and the entire cluster of
two hundred families with which SPARC was working was dumped
with the rest at Dindoshi.

Sheela was caustic: "The basic requirement of moving people from
the pavements should have been to improve the quality of life. Instead,
it became a wonderful opportunity for anyone with some education or
influence to legalize illegal things. Some people got lots of places for
houses, and some got nothing. People who live in pavement houses
have three sides, with a wall at the back. In Dindoshi they got 150
square feet but not enough material to build on it, and so the dealers in
secondhand material in the new place made a lot of money out of it.

"Toilets were built after the houses had come up and they're badly
made: the bottom leaks. There are now 3,500 families in Dindoshi and
277 toilets. Each family has about five people, so there are about sixty-
three persons per toilet. People shit all around them, and it dries in the
sun, but that's better than the toilets.

"The people were supposed to pay rent, but the officials let a year
pass before they announced each family would have to pay thirty rupees
a month, or almost four hundred a year. Where would they get so much
money? A moneylender will charge enormous interest or will say, 'I'll
give you two hundred and you go away.' Few could find new occupations

in the area, so with one thing or another 70 percent of the original settlers from our group have left."

I said that was a disappointing conclusion to a story that had started so well. I asked if she and other SPARC workers were disappointed.

"We made a promise to stay with the people, and now we've set up a center in Dindoshi," Sheela replied. "We have worked with women to improve bus transportation, get ration cards, and find schools for their children. We shouldn't be in a hurry. At first the Municipal Corporation did all kinds of things to get us out of there, but now they've accepted there's truth in what we say about people building their own community organizations. They're working on our suggestion for the women to build and take care of the drainage channels between two houses. We also want their help so the women can plant and care for trees to absorb the water that comes out of houses. We want space where women can undertake income-producing work on a collective basis and other space for a communal center to train people for new work. We've formed a women's cooperative, and we encourage women from other groups to join it. We hope to set up two community centers and an information system, and we're trying to get several women employed in distributing milk.

"For us, housing is not a structure, it's a movement: it epitomizes a transition in the way people think. Our objective is not to become a construction company. I will not get the finance, fight with the government, and get you a new job. We say, 'How can we creatively develop finance that you can generate and which is your right under the national scheme.' We're negotiating with banks for people who are forming societies to build houses three years from now, and we'll ask the bank to do that investment.

"We also say, 'If you build a house, you can lower the cost by having an input in design, materials, and labor.' We're trying to negotiate with the government for land where we can set up a building center to take technology being developed all over India to change large bunches of people.'"

Town Planning for the Poor

SPARC is also involved in planning for the future of the vast slum at Dharavi, where more than $26 million has been appropriated by the central government and international agencies for low-income housing and "slum upgradation." Spanning the marshy regions of northeast and northwest Bombay, Dharavi now has as many as eight hundred inhabitants an acre, so planning involves what to do for the people already living there.

"SPARC is trying to create a dialogue between the government and the people," Sheela said. "It's a peculiar thing; we're almost tutoring both groups. Government is too arrogant; it presumes to know everything, while people don't believe the government is up to anything good. Most poor people live in sprawled-out houses, not tall apartment buildings that are expensive to build and harder to maintain. The government is planning high-rise buildings with four one-room apartments per floor. You know what will happen: rich people will buy the four rooms, knock down the walls or put in doors, and have the kind of space they're used to. We say build structures this can't be done to; help people to protect themselves.

"We say Dharavi should be developed so the children of those now living there can benefit. There are plans for wide roads and fairy gardens. A small access road where large trucks can't go is good enough for the kids to play in: just have limited access to mass transportation. You don't have to displace twenty families for modern swings that rust in this bad weather and can't be maintained. We say people have the right to decide; don't choose options on their behalf."

I prompted Sheela to talk about women:

"People ask, 'Are you working first with women or first with the poor.' We say this is a nonchoice: if your objective is to find solutions for those who are worse off, you'll have to work with women. As long as the family is the basic unit for socialization, it will be the primary support system. As an organization we will not facilitate individuals or small groups. We believe in empowering collectives. If we look at the basic socialization of men and women, women are supportive and self-sacrificing."

I was surprised. I said some feminist groups thought such terminology reflected male chauvinist attitudes.

"In this way we find ourselves differing from many feminists," Sheela said. "We're not competing with men or want to be better than men. We believe a woman's ability to be cooperative is better than the aggressive environment a man may create."

There was another woman working for slum dwellers and also working in the most crushing environment of all for women: the brothels of Bombay.

5 ✹ The Rescue of Bishnu and Uma

One evening in Bombay I was talking with Pellisary Antony Sebastian about his human rights activities when he was called away by another social activist, Anna Kurian. She wanted his help in prosecuting brothel keepers who had bought two kidnapped Nepali girls, Bishnu and Uma.

Sebastian and Anna are conscience-keepers: they refuse to give way to the tendency of professionals and other educated Indians to avert their eyes when confronted by suffering and injustice.

As far back as November 1936, in a speech at the inauguration in Calcutta of the Civil Liberties Union (CLU), Nehru mentioned how hard it was to sustain resentment: "We sometimes protest, we sometimes express indignation, but the fact remains that some time after, we get used to it and we do not feel very strongly about it."

Even the formation of the CLU was nothing more than a pious gesture, since efforts for individual justice were overshadowed by the freedom struggle. Then in 1948 Nehru suggested it be disbanded as unnecessary in free, democratic India. His advice was not accepted, but still the group withered away amid the optimism of "nation building."

The feeling that all would soon be made right ended with the suspension of civil liberties and the detention of tens of thousands of innocent persons during the 1977–78 State of Emergency declared by Indira Gandhi, who succeeded her father as prime minister. When the Emergency ended, and Mrs Gandhi was temporarily swept from power, the human and civil rights movement was reborn.

Now every major Indian city has at least one, and sometimes two or three groups of activists, ranging from Sebastian's Committee for Protection of Democratic Rights in Bombay, with its wide range of publications and handbooks for activists, to the Naga People's Movement for Human Rights, which has published several reports on police and army atrocities against tribals in the states of Nagaland and Manipur.

But, as Nehru said more than half a century ago, Indians "get used to" violations of civil rights. Memories of the injustices of the Emergency have long since faded and the reports of human rights groups hardly rate a half column in local newspapers. Injustice in one region often is not mentioned at all somewhere else.

Sebastian for the Defense

When Sebastian (among Indians, male first names are often ignored) was a child, he was crippled by polio and now wears braces on both legs and makes his way about with the aid of crutches. Undaunted by his infirmity, he became an attorney. He lives in a room, barely wide enough for a bed and bureau, on the ground floor of the YMCA in the Colaba area, where the island narrows down to a point.

"As soon as I got my degree I went into public interest work," he said as we sat facing one another on chairs squeezed into what little space remained in the room. "In 1978 I read that fourteen people had died in a hospital of gas gangrene and many others lost their limbs. It happened when a woman with gas gangrene was admitted to the general ward, where there were many others with external injuries. Gas gangrene is caused by a virus in horse dung. People go barefoot and pick it up. It's highly infectious. The affected limb must be amputated, and if a person with gas gangrene comes to a hospital, he should be quarantined and the hospital should be evacuated. The operating theater should be closed down for one month, and the entire hospital should be fumigated before it is reopened.

"I decided to find those who lost their relatives or their limbs and persuade them to sue the hospital and the doctors. But the hospital wanted to cover it up and refused to give us information, and many relatives could not be found: patients had come from far away and left the world without leaving any trace behind. We found some relatives, but they were illiterate and didn't believe they could sue the government. They also thought people who offered to help might be attempting to dupe them.

"Ultimately, we found a young engineer whose father had died. His mother was also educated and his sister was in school, but on the day they were supposed to come to court they didn't turn up, so we could not prosecute either the hospital or the doctors, even though the case involved criminal negligence."

Why Passivity?

I said foreigners could not understand this passivity and the refusal of Indians to demand justice. I had in mind an anecdote about American troops in Calcutta during the World War II famine of 1943, in which millions of Indians died. A soldier, seeing starving people on the streets and food in store windows, is reported to have remarked, "If I were them, I'd smash the windows and help myself to all that's there." I also thought of a comment by Sarojini Naidu, the preindependence woman poet and politician: "Oh, the patience of India! How I hate her patience!"

"It's true, they don't fight," he said. "Throughout their lives they've been taken for a ride. No one has really helped them, and, in this case, they might have thought we too would take them for a ride. I learned from that experience we must approach people who are already organized and aware of their rights, and so I associated myself with various civil liberty organizations, trade unions, and student organizations in Bombay and elsewhere."

Sebastian has no pretensions; he is available to all who may seek his help. As we were talking, he was called to the lobby by Anna Kurian to discuss the kidnapping of the two Nepali girls. Women are not allowed to visit lodgers in their rooms, so Sebastian had to meet her in a combined lounge and game room, noisy with the shouts of boys playing table tennis. At that time I had heard of Anna but had not met her. After she left, Sebastian, in response to my questions, clarified the antiprostitution laws:

"Prostitution is not illegal in itself. The law is aimed at people who live on prostitutes and who do allied things like kidnapping and keeping them in custody. At an initial stage force is used to tame them and attach them to the profession, but after one or two years they get accustomed to the life. If a woman does this of her free will and collects some rewards, in the form of money or whatever, that may not be unlawful.

"You'll see hundreds and hundreds of brothels in the red light districts of Bombay. The government tolerates this and will act only if there is prostitution in other areas and the residents complain their rights are being invaded. If the police do raid a place on the complaint of someone or other, and recover a boy or girl, they'll not punish the keeper, even though the sentence can go up to imprisonment for life. The law is merely an expression of the appearance the state wishes to make. It does not represent reality on the ground. There's hardly any public pressure for enforcement, although no one says it's good."

A few days later I called on Anna for the first of several long talks. She is a short, stocky woman in her early fifties, with short black hair and plastic-rimmed glasses, usually wearing subdued, chiffon saris. With her husband, an advertising executive, and two grown children, she lives in a large apartment with high ceilings and tiled floors in the once-fashionable Colaba area. She is in perpetual motion, talking rapidly, taking telephone calls, and rushing off to meetings.

She is a graduate of the College of Social Work of the University of Bombay and was employed there for a while after getting her degree. In 1982, amid the rising controversy surrounding slum and pavement dwellers, a director of the college asked Anna if she could help a colony of construction workers building a huge complex of commercial and residential skyscrapers at Nariman Point, near the tip of the island. As a sort of talisman, they had named their slum Sanjay Gandhi *Nagar* (Colony), after the younger son of Indira Gandhi, then the most influential man in India. At their request Anna formed the *Nivara Hakk Suraksha* (Organization to Protect the Right to Shelter) with herself as its treasurer. The organization is the leading advocate for slum dwellers.

Shabana's Fast

She told about the most famous incident in the struggle for housing for the poor: the time when Shabana Azmi, India's most honored film actress, went on a fast:

"The government said all slums established after 1980 were illegal and could be demolished without provision for alternate housing. The Sanjay Gandhi colony was established long before that, but the government said it would only recognize a colony if its people were on the election rolls before 1980. How can they get registered if a colony is constantly demolished and built again?

"I was always concerned about children. This country is in their hands, and my children will face their children however they grow up. I found not even a quarter of a cup of milk will go into the stomach of a slum child. So I opened a school, first for the children of that slum but then others came. We started them on the learning process and gave them lunch and a place to do their homework.

"Then, in 1986, a demolition squad came and tore the slum down, including the school. We had spent 50,000 rupees ($3,500) in setting it up: now it was all gone. There were 180 children and it was near exams, so we put out mats and the newspapers carried pictures of children sitting on the footpath doing their homework.

"On April 1 we decided to recapture the site and several writers and directors from the film industry joined us. There was a *lathi* (a long, brass-tipped bamboo stick) charge, and we all got arrested. The government released us and said it wanted time to reconsider, but nothing happened. Then we said we would start a fast at the site. That night Shabana telephoned. She said, 'Anna, I'm coming tomorrow.' She canceled a trip to a film festival in France and came in the morning."

Shabana Azmi is not a doll-like woman. She has a somewhat large nose and mouth and small chin, but she projects a quality that makes her more lovely than any woman who appears on the screen with her. Her father, Kaifi Azmi, is a Communist poet, and Shabana is best known for her films of social consciousness, but she never before had used her fame to play a real-life role. When she appeared and sat down near workers with dirty, ragged clothes and calloused hands, her picture and the fate of the Sanjay Gandhi colony became front page news throughout India and in many Asian and Middle East nations where Indian films have a large audience.

"Shabana said she would only drink water," Anna continued. "We took a carpet from my husband's office, and we made a nice tent. The film producers came to me and said, 'She's a precious thing. We'll buy five acres of land and give it to the people.' But Shabana said, 'No. That's not the idea. The government has to act; these people have a right to a roof over their heads.'"

Shabana's fast lasted for only two days. City officials, after insisting the Sanjay Gandhi residents had no right to alternative housing, found about three-and-a-half acres for them in Dindoshi. One day I went with Anna to the site, a dreary, barren place where small hills of solid rock had to be chopped away to level the ground. There was a problem involving an adjacent colony that wanted to run a water pipeline across part of the Sanjay Gandhi allotment, and Anna went to the police to register a warning of possible violence if the adjacent colony did not run its pipe around the Sanjay Gandhi site.

Helping Prostitutes

One evening, when Anna finally had free time, we went to a private club and sat on a terrace overlooking the sea to escape telephone interruptions, and she told me about the rescue of Bishnu and Uma:

"In 1974, when I was with the social service department of the YWCA, we worked with the Women's Branch of the Criminal Investigation Division (CID), trying to help prostitutes, but had little impact. For example, a girl of seventeen, who had a baby, was in a brothel. One day she ran away, leaving the baby behind, and came to us for help. We went with a senior inspector of women police to reclaim the child but the brothel keeper refused to give it back. The inspector smiled, saying, 'Come on, give, give, give.' Here was a minor and a child and the police acted so pleasantly! The keeper said, 'She created a problem. I lost money, so I will keep this child.' Finally, the police did get the child back, but they took no action against the brothel keeper. All the racketeers are known to the CID, and the CID gets a portion of all the illegal business going on in this city. This is a well-known fact.

"No one is interested in helping prostitutes. There was a meeting at the YWCA of a women's organization organized to protect women who were raped or beaten. I said, 'You're making a lot of noise about rape: What do you say about young girls who are raped eight or nine times a night?' They had no answer. Some people say, 'My wife and daughter are safe on the streets because of these prostitutes.' But I said: 'Because I have to be safe, do other women have to suffer? I would like to establish a society where we all can be safe.'

"Some people talk of licensing prostitutes and making them submit to a medical examination. Someone said on television when a commodity is offered to the public, the seller should see it is safe and pure. He was saying women are commodities. If you have to control smallpox, do you license it? Or TB? People who talk that way don't want to treat a woman as a human being who has to be looked after and helped.

"It Is Written on My Forehead"

"Girls are tricked or forced into prostitution. Retired prostitutes are sometimes procurers in villages who know everybody. Say a girl is in trouble with a stepmother: they tell her she can go to Bombay and look after herself. The village girls don't even know how far Bombay is; they think they can get work and come back quickly. A former police commissioner told us if a woman comes to Bombay with a baby in her arms, the procurer will find her at a railway or bus station and take her to a brothel. There, the child will be left even without water until the woman yields. After a while, they get the idea: 'Look, it is written here on my forehead. I have to do this.' If we suggest they leave, they ask, 'Where will I go? My family won't take me back. You don't know what life means. My life is over.'

"When they're first brought to a brothel, they'll not be able to go to the toilet without being watched: a eunuch goes with them to guard them. Once their keepers are sure the girl will not escape, they're allowed freedom to go for shopping or to see the quacks who are called doctors.

"Recently, some police have become more cooperative when women try to escape. A while back, a young woman ran out of a house and took shelter in a police van. She told a police officer she had a B.A. and was brought here from Madras to take a job and then forced into a brothel. 'Please set me free,' she said. Her parents were informed and came to take her back, but they did not press charges. They said the publicity would ruin their family's name.

"It may be easy for older women to escape, but what about the girls who are eight, nine, or ten years of age? They don't know what's happening. They're used in a terrible manner and will die in three or four years. Brothel keepers get so much money from them they never want to let them go. If there's a raid by police, the children are hidden in a closet or up in a loft until the police leave."

An Answered Prayer

Anna said Bishnu, fourteen, and Uma, thirteen, an orphan living with Bishnu's family, were kidnapped from their Nepali village by a man and his wife who knew their family and who promised the girls they would see a wedding ceremony in Katmandu, Nepal's capital. Fortunately, Bishnu's father, Jan Bahadur, was both a retired policeman and a member of an evangelical Christian group. There is a long-established trade in Nepali girls kidnapped for the Bombay brothels, and when the girls disappeared, Jan Bahadur and his eldest son set out immediately to search for them, armed with a letter of introduction from his minister to an evangelical group in Bombay, where one of the woman volunteers knew Anna and asked her to help.

"Luckily, they had pictures of the girls, and we gave these to the police," Anna said. "I also told Jan Bahadur and his son to walk around the streets. The next day his son was standing someplace when Bishnu was being taken in a *tonga* (horse-drawn carriage). She saw him and shouted, 'Brother, brother' in Nepali. He took a taxi to follow but, when they came to a red signal, the tonga passed through while the taxi halted. He tried to chase on foot, but the people with Bishnu got away. The brother told us, and I went to the CID, and we searched houses in the area but could not find her.

"Jan Bahadur and his son continued to stand in the streets. Jan Bahadur was desperate, and he silently prayed, 'God, give my daughter in my hands. I cannot find her.' He prayed for ten minutes, standing there. Bishnu was sleeping nearby. She heard a voice saying 'Bishnu, Bishnu, get up, your father is here.' She got up and looked out the window, and there was her father. She called out, 'Father, father.' He looked up and saw her at a window and signaled to her with his fingers at his lips to keep quiet. He wrote down all the signs he saw in Hindi. He didn't understand English, but he drew the letters like pictures. Then he went to the Nagpara police station and told them. They raided the house, but the brothel keepers had learned what was coming and were hiding the children in secret places. 'Go there, Go there,' they ordered the children. But Uma saw Jan Bahadur with the policemen and caught hold of him.

"They still could not find Bishnu. More policemen came with guns and began to ransack the place. One policeman saw a girl being led away by one of the brothel keepers. 'Where are you going?' he asked. He had a copy of the photograph and looked at it. The girl seemed familiar. He asked her, 'What's your name?' She replied, with a very small and frightened voice, 'My name is Bishnu.' 'What's your father's name?' he asked her. 'Jan Bahadur,' she said."

Prosecuting the Brothel Keepers

As the search for the children went on, the man who had kidnapped the girls was captured when he returned to Nepal, but his wife escaped. Simply rescuing Bishnu and Uma and arresting the kidnapper was not the end of the case for Anna Kurian. Many years had passed since the incident of the brothel keeper who refused to return her baby to the seventeen-year-old girl who ran away from a brothel. The police did not prosecute, but now there was a new law on the books, and Anna was determined to test it.

In 1956, not because of pressure for action from within India but because the government had signed a 1950 United Nations convention against prostitution, the rubber-stamp legislature of the time approved a law called the Suppression of Immoral Traffic in Women and Girls Act. The shortened title—SITA—is ironic, since Sita is the name of the goddess who symbolizes purity and fidelity, and yet SITA, in effect, gave social sanction to prostitution and only penalized the commercial operations of pimps and madams.

In 1986, after publicity about the terrible misuse of a kidnapped Nepali girl, Parliament passed another law called the Prevention of Immoral Traffic in Persons Amendment Act (PITA), which included substantial fines and imprisonment for procuring, seducing, detaining, or living off the prostitution of a child or minor. There is also a provision that two women police officers must accompany raiding parties to question inmates and remove those who desire their freedom. In their absence a woman member of a recognized social welfare organization is authorized to conduct the interrogations. It was PITA that gave Anna the right to involve herself in the search for Bishnu and Uma.

"Jan Bahadur said he saw more than a hundred children while he was standing in the streets," she said. "Maybe he was exaggerating, but there are many, and the police do nothing. They don't disturb the brothels because the brothels nourish them. But now, because of our pressure, the police for the first time have filed a case against the two owners of the house who had bought Uma and Bishnu from the kidnappers. We only have to stand as an advocate to see punishment is done."

The man who will see justice is done is Pellisary Antony Sebastian. That was the reason for Anna's call on him that night at the YMCA: to ask him to stand as an advocate.

A single blow for human rights will hardly make a difference. Bombay, with its slums, crime, and prostitution, has become what Shanghai was before World War II, the most degraded city in the world. It is, as Sister Rita found, the center of a slave market that extends throughout India.

6 ❀ Sister Rita's Report

Prostitution is devoid of truthful love," Sister Rita writes in the beginning of her book, *Trafficking in Women and Children in India*. "The hallmark of respect for persons is to protect them against destruction and exploitation. This is totally absent in the sexual exploitation and sale of women." She also asks a question: "Are women in India considered human beings: full persons in their own right?" In effect, her answer is, no.

In the West the thousands of streetwalkers in London and New York in the last century were a response to poverty and lack of opportunity. Similarly prostitutes in contemporary Bangkok, when interviewed, say they volunteered to sell sex because they wanted more money; instances of coercion among the tens of thousands of Thai prostitutes are rare. But the opposite is true in India: although some women and girls may have taken the first step because of poverty or to escape a bad family situation, all will live brief, tormented lives as slaves.

Sister Rita Rozario, who joined the order of Good Shepherd Sisters in 1954, is about five feet tall, with gray hair and a low, somewhat harsh voice. Although she speaks with obvious conviction, she has the placid manners of a once-cloistered nun. She was born in Bangalore, in Karnataka, to parents who had migrated from Kerala; her mother tongue is Malayalam. She studied in Bangalore and Bombay and has a master's degree in social work. She learned about the condition of prostitutes when her convent, making use of her technical training, established a screening and diagnostic center in Bangalore for the placement of women and children in orphanages and rescue homes.

Sister Rita comes from a family of musicians. In 1967, after Vatican II brought major changes in Roman Catholic institutions and a search for new ways of service, she was asked to explore the use of classical Indian singing, dancing, and instrumental music in the service of the church. She later returned to social work and got permission to replace her habit with a plain, pale beige sari. In 1983, after a pilot study in Bangalore, she began her major investigation. I met her in a quiet Good Shepherd Convent tucked behind a church in northwestern Bombay.

"After the French Revolution, our mother-founder started this order for girls molested by men," she said. "In 1854 a few sisters came here for the same work but found a greater need for education and other work. The issue of sexual exploitation is hush-hush in Indian society. A girl has to be a virgin to be married, so if a child is sexually exploited, parents don't want their next-door neighbors to know about it: they won't report it to the police or anyone. The early history of our congregation was not spoken of to outsiders, and when my work was first mentioned in newspapers, people wondered why a nun should take up this issue."

"Each Night Is a Torture"

Sister Rita drew up formal questionnaires and found recruits to help her survey, at random, a variety of red light districts, streets of singing and dancing girls, and railway and bus stations. Sister Rita, who speaks and understands the major south Indian languages, conducted most of these interviews herself, putting aside the large cross she normally wears on her chest and changing into a drab sari for ten- or fifteen-minute conversations at bus stops and tea shops while pimps and guards were out of earshot.

"A man warned me: 'Sister, this is a volatile group. They're riot-prone and can hurt you. I advise you not to go.' But I was concerned about the women. I don't use the word profession: I say women in prostitution. Whatever they do, these are women who need our care. They took great risks to tell me of their plight in the hope others would not suffer their lot. They said, 'Each night is a torture.'"

The survey contacted 1,100 respondents in fourteen states and two union territories, of whom 89 percent were prostitutes or otherwise sexually exploited while the others were madams, pimps, women rescued before their sale or exploitation and customers and others on the fringes of prostitution. Of those identified as engaged in prostitution, 66 percent were below the age of eighteen at the time of their initiation and another 29 percent were younger than twenty-one. Of those where information was available, 72 percent had no education.

The most revealing results dealt with how prostitutes are recruited. Among those where information was available, 14 percent were kidnapped and sold; 26 percent were conditioned by religious ceremonies or customs; and 19 percent were either lured into false marriages, raped, and forced into prostitution or deserted by their husbands and then forced into prostitution.

Instances of voluntary servitude, such as a case where an eldest daughter took to prostitution to maintain her parents, were rare. There are several peculiarly Indian situations leading to prostitution. One is the process known as *chooth* (leaving). Child marriages are common (more exactly, engagements: consummation is supposed to be postponed until the girl reaches puberty, but instances of girls of five, six, or seven raped by their husbands are fairly frequent). When a couple married in infancy grows up, they often find they are unmatched. Sometimes the groom's family tries to escape and sometimes the girl's family also asks for chooth—freedom to leave. In either case money has to be paid, especially if the girl wants to leave her husband. In desperation she may seek the help of anyone willing to pay chooth and take her, or she may run away, becoming an easy target for procurers looking for recruits for what they pretend is employment as a waitress or household servant.

In reply to a survey question about the methods used to subjugate them, the girls and women told of being starved, cut with knives, branded, gang-raped, tied up for long periods, beaten, whipped, gagged, fed intoxicants or drugs, burnt with cigarettes, locked in dark rooms, threatened with weapons, or told their children would be harmed. Age made no difference: a ten-year-old girl was found in Kerala with burn marks on her body.

Twenty-six percent of those for whom information was available or applicable named their parents and guardians as the ones responsible for their subjugation. Eighteen percent named other kith and kin, such as an aunt, uncle, brother, elder sister, husband, or grandmother. Eight percent named friends and acquaintances, such as boyfriends, father's friends, future mothers-in-law, and enemies of the family. Fourteen percent were strangers who called themselves benefactors, and eight percent were public servants or professional people such as businessmen, policemen, doctors, medical students, employers, landowners, priests, and teachers. Only twenty-six percent were initially degraded by persons involved in the flesh trade. In short, almost three out of every four sexually exploited women were betrayed by persons who should have cared for them.

Prostitute Slave Routes

The survey traced several routes for trafficking in women, generally ending in Delhi or Bombay, the two largest demand centers. There is also a regular exchange of slaves between the two cities, either to give customers a feeling of "fresh goods" or to remove a girl who has made too many friends and may be planning to escape. At any one time an estimated twenty thousand women are being transported by a network of traffickers and pimps, often the same network that deals in drugs. The slave bazaar is so well organized a woman can be kidnapped in Bangladesh and moved across India for sale in Pakistan. Some women are auctioned like cattle at transit centers located just outside big cities. The price depends on the time, place, and condition of the "goods." A fair-skinned Nepali girl sells for more than a darker girl from the south, and, in either case, the younger the girl the higher the price.

A Kerala girl, meant to be exported, was sold at a twice-a-month auction just outside Bombay for sixty thousand rupees ($4,200). The highest reported price at this auction was for an educated Muslim girl sold to an industrialist for seventy thousand rupees ($4,900).

A long-established circuit involves the cities of Kanpur, Allahabad, Varanasi, Agra, Lucknow (the so-called KAVAL cities) in Uttar Pradesh. A newspaper report estimates ten thousand children below the age of sixteen are kidnapped every year from bus stands and railway stations or otherwise lured into slavery. Sister Rita's survey interviewed one well-spoken sixteen-year-old girl who said she stationed herself at such places and offered to care for children of harried mothers, only to kidnap them at the first opportunity. The victims are sold to gangs: the strongest and most sturdy for child labor, those with physical and mental handicaps for begging or as helpers for bootleggers, and the good-looking for the flesh trade. The on-the-spot price for a kidnapped or lured-away child ranges between one and two thousand rupees ($70–$140). They are quickly moved far away for resale at a much higher price.

Of the estimated fifteen thousand prostitutes in Uttar Pradesh, it is believed twelve thousand, or 80 percent, are from Nepal. The recruiting is done by Nepali women who are themselves prostitutes or brothel keepers, known as *didis* (elder sisters). They cross from India to their home regions and persuade parents to hand over their daughters for from 80 to 150 rupees, ostensibly to work as a servant, with the added lure of a promise the girl will be able to send back as much as a hundred rupees a month. In most cases the parents are fully aware the girl is being taken away for prostitution and the promise of additional money is seldom kept.

In underworld slang the girls, ranging in age from ten to sixteen, are called *petis* (boxes). The didi collects at least four petis (never three, which is an unlucky number) and takes them to a point near the border where two or three pimps supervise the onward journey to Lucknow or Kanpur: ready, if necessary, to bribe the border police. If the didi is a brothel keeper, she initiates the girls into the trade, usually using simple cajolery. If not, the didi sells them to a "trainer" for from one to five thousand rupees ($70–$350). He keeps a girl in a small room, beating and raping and burning her with cigarettes for three or four weeks, by which time she is completely broken and ready for sale again in Bombay, Delhi, or Calcutta for between ten and twenty-five thousand rupees ($700–$1,750).

If she survives, she will be sold or traded at least another ten times. In ten or fifteen years she may be back in the KAVAL cities running her own brothel and making the trip across the border as a didi to repeat the cycle.

Another route begins in West Bengal, where there are millions of impoverished Muslim migrants from Bangladesh and Bihar, and ends in Kashmir, where women and girls are sold to the Muslim men for between five thousand and twenty thousand rupees ($350–$1,400). A fifteen-year-old daughter of a laborer in West Bengal was lured to Kashmir on the promise of a holiday and sold for 1,600 rupees ($112) to a man who married her for the use of himself and his brothers. In another incident a nine-year-old girl was sold for marriage to a forty-year-old man. In a third a woman and her seven-year-old child were sold as farm laborers to a fifty-year-old man with nine children. She was told if she tried to escape her daughter would be raped.

Hyderabad, the capital of Andhra Pradesh, also has a large Muslim population. Girls are sold through brokers or unscrupulous *gazis* (judges) for marriage to rich Arabs who come on three-month tourist visas. The middlemen receive from 5,000 to 30,000 rupees ($350–$2,100) as the bride price. In one notorious case a girl, thirteen, was married to an Arab who was eighty-five. When the visas of their putative husbands expire, the wives are divorced through the Muslim custom of simply reciting "I divorce thee" three times. The families who sell their daughters have little left after meeting the demands of the brokers.

Prices Paid for Female Slaves

A fifteen-year-old girl in Assam was auctioned by her maternal uncle for nine thousand rupees ($630); a tribal woman in Bihar was bought for two thousand rupees ($140) as a bride price and later sold in West Bengal; Muslim girls in West Bengal were sold at auctions at prices ranging from 2,500 ($175) to 20,000 rupees ($1,400), the highest figure going for a girl destined for an Arab country.

Four tribal girls from Maharashtra, sold by the lot in Delhi, went for forty-six thousand rupees ($3,220). A girl bought in Tamil Nadu for five hundred rupees ($35) was sold in a transit auction for fifteen hundred rupees ($105) and resold in Bombay for three thousand rupees ($210).

A newborn baby in Bangalore was sold for three thousand rupees ($210), and a "good-looking" tribal girl in Karnataka sold for ten thousand rupees ($700). A man who brought his young bride to a religious fair in Uttar Pradesh was arrested, along with three pimps, after he sold her in a nearby red-light district for six thousand rupees ($420).

A girl in Madhya Pradesh (age not given) was bought for five thousand rupees ($350) and soon resold for eight thousand rupees ($560); a fourteen-year-old tribal girl was sold in Madhya Pradesh for four thousand rupees ($280); another fourteen-year-old tribal girl was kidnapped from Madhya Pradesh and sold three times to different brothel keepers in Calcutta for prices ranging from three thousand to seven thousand rupees ($210–$490) and within a few months was brought to a hospital almost dead from mistreatment. Sometimes no money at all changes hands: girls have been bartered by fathers for alcoholic drinks, and a stepmother exchanged a daughter for a sari.

The Dark World

Girls whose fathers are too poor to feed them, or whose husbands are too drunk or irresponsible to care for them, frequently set out in a desperate search for work and are soon pounced on by the always-lurking procurers. They are sold for as little as five hundred rupees ($35) but sometimes bring their pretended benefactor as much as two thousand rupees ($140).

There is a ready market for them in Tamil Nadu among the owners of cheap liquor shops, who buy girls to encourage customers to drink. They are also sold to pimps or madams who claim prostitution rights to areas around major temples, where there are always tourists looking for pleasure as well as religious merit. A flesh merchant with five to ten girls may have rights to about three miles of streets. The owners work together: if the girls cause trouble, or are suspected of being too friendly with a customer or one another, they are sold to the pimp or madam in another area.

Among the dire fates is the *irunda ullagum* (dark world) of the national highway between Madras and the pilgrimage center of Madurai. Girls meant for use by truckers are sold for between one and two thousand rupees ($70–$140). Customers pay as little as five rupees (35 cents), of which three is for the pimp or madam, one is *mamool* (bribe; literally: custom, tradition) for the police, and one is for the woman. If a woman fails to bring in twenty to twenty-five rupees ($1.40–$1.75) a night, she is beaten, starved, or branded. Once, a young woman desperately seeking to earn the minimum ran onto the road and was killed by a passing truck. Her death rated a brief newspaper notice.

The Hell of Kamatipura

In the Bombay red-light areas "special" Nepali girls sell for fifty thousand rupees ($3,500), while "ordinary" Nepali girls can sell for as little as four thousand rupees ($280). "Average" girls from Tamil Nadu sell for 2,500 to 3,000 three thousand rupees ($175–$210).

The number of prostitutes in Bombay is estimated at 100,000, 20 percent below the age of eighteen. The victims are bought by *seths* (moneylenders) and sent to brothels or, if they are between seven and twelve, kept in the seth's home and brought to a brothel only on the express demand of a customer. The seths keep a record of the money spent to buy a child and for her upkeep. When she gains puberty and is sent to a brothel, she may have to sell herself for the next five or six years to clear what the moneylender considers a justifiable debt.

Clients are charged between twenty and fifty rupees ($1.40–$3.50) a visit, depending on their status and that of the girl. A big-spending petty trader, carried away by whiskey and music, may throw away 250 rupees ($17.50). Visiting Arabs are made to pay whatever the *gharwali* (madam) can extract: sometimes as much as three thousand rupees ($210). The most insistent demand of Arabs from the Gulf states is for immature girls whom they can sodomize.

The money goes directly to the hands of the gharwali: the prostitutes are never allowed to touch it. In most brothels the gharwali keeps half the earnings, except for tips, and charges the women for food, water, electricity, and whatever else she needs, including abortions or other treatment by the quacks who call themselves doctors. During the first few years of their enslavement, when the gharwali is recovering the price she paid for the slave, the women are not paid anything.

Half the prostitutes of Bombay are concentrated in the Kamatipura area, five minutes' walk from the Bombay Central railway station. Eight to ten live and work in a small room with a loft to take customers but with no running water or sanitary facilities.

Eventually, diseased and disfigured, they are thrown away to fend for themselves. If they are lucky, they own a *palang* (string bed) to sleep on in a Kamatipura alley. To earn money for food, they walk the streets and ask for two rupees (about fifteen cents): for many, the streets are also where they die.

Prostitution, the Police, and Politicians

The *Economic and Political Weekly,* in an article discussing the lack of enforcement of antiprostitution laws, reported the Vigilance Cell of the Crime Branch of the Bombay police collected thirty to fifty rupees ($2.10–$3.50) per month per brothel as a bribe, depending on the earnings of the keeper. In addition the police demanded an extra five hundred rupees ($35) if they discovered the brothel keeper had forced a new minor into prostitution. The article estimated the monthly income of the Vigilance Cell at about 100,000 rupees ($7,000). It can be surmised some part of this was forwarded to higher police echelons and to local politicians.

During election campaigns brothel keepers are expected to make additional contributions, in return for which they are granted favors in getting things like a better supply of water or improved sanitation. If the keepers take a girl to the municipal hospital, other payments must be made to clerks and medical attendants.

The amounts available for bribes can be seen in the profits estimated from a six-story apartment house raided in the Santa Cruz area of north Bombay. Two hundred and ten women were found in twelve two-bedroom flats. Since Santa Cruz is a residential area, the rates charged customers were higher than in the red-light areas of central Bombay: ranging from 500 to 700 rupees ($35–$50).

The nightly income was estimated at 120,000 rupees ($8,400), with about half going to the building owners, giving them a monthly return of 1,800,000 ($126,000) on an investment of 2,000,000 rupees ($140,000) in construction costs. It was assumed the owners, behind a front of lawyers, were *Dadas* or Dons, as the leaders of Bombay's underworld are called.

The law forbids earning from prostitution, but for someone able to pay bribes and hire lawyers and strong-arm men to keep the prostitutes in check, the law is easily evaded. When questioned, the prostitutes are trained to say they are individual contractors who pay part of their earnings to others for rent, food, and other expenses. Since prostitution, in itself, is not illegal there is no one to punish.

The law concerning minors is also easily avoided. After a year in a brothel a girl of fourteen or fifteen is so worn she can easily pass for the minimum age of eighteen. It is possible to disprove this by taking X rays of bone structures, but the well-bribed police and hospital attendants never have this done.

The Concept of Shakti

Sister Rita's report and the many newspaper stories about the buying and selling of women and girls raise two questions: why are women so utterly victimized, and why do they allow themselves to be so mistreated? The answers to both questions must be sought in the myths and folk attitudes of Indian culture.

Shakti is a concept unique to Hinduism. It signifies female power that has a dangerous or threatening aspect when not modified by male power. In Hindu mythology *Kali* is the embodiment of shakti. She represents irresistible power and chaotic energy—both the Eternal Mother and the Terrible Mother—and is depicted performing a victory dance after killing a demon. She wears a necklace of arms and heads, and her blood-red tongue hangs out as she displays the head of the demon: she is on a rampage, killing and destroying everything in her path. Siva, her husband, is sent to restrain her and lies at her feet. Kali, entranced by her killing, at first does not notice Siva and is about to step on him, but when she realizes he is her husband, she ends her rampage. Thus her husband regains control of her, and the earth is saved.

Throughout Hinduism the benevolent feminine deities are those who are married and who have transferred control of their sexuality to their husbands: the male subordinates female shakti power in marriage.

This leads to the idea men have the right, in fact a duty, to dominate women.

The ideal woman of Hinduism is Sita, the heroine of the early first millennium epic *The Ramayana*. Sita is a silent, uncomplaining sufferer who willingly follows her husband, Rama, into exile and undergoes all kinds of hardship until she is captured by the demon king Ravana. She resists Ravana's advances, starving herself and remaining pure in body and thought, yet when Rama, in great triumph, rescues her, he announces he is suspicious because she had lived with another man. Sita does not complain about this lack of faith or criticize Rama in any way: instead, at his demand, she walks into a fire as a test of her purity and emerges unscathed, earning the title "Stainless One."

Women Turning Against Their Kind

As a woman gets used to accepting less food, clothing, and education, her culturally ordained low status is reinforced, and women turn against their own sex.

Chetna (awareness) is a woman's organization in Gujarat that does extensive work in health education. In one of its monthly publications it told a story illustrating the attitude of women toward women:

We found one of the best ways to impart training on weaning foods is to adopt the babies of health workers who come for training and have them follow the course of foods we suggest at appropriate ages. Invariably, all babies thrive. Recently, one such baby girl of a deserted mother fell seriously ill during training. Our trainers rushed her first to the local public health center and later to a general hospital where she was given appropriate care and ultimately recovered. Raliatben, the baby's maternal grandmother, said disparagingly: "Whoever heard of such fuss being made for a girl child. If she dies, she dies."

With all this, prostitutes' resignation to fate is easily understood. As girls, they grow up with a sense of helplessness, and a few threats, or the experience of gang rape, will extinguish what remains of their resistance. The slavery of prostitution is something the elite image makers of India prefer to hide. Sister Rita conducted and published her survey hoping to shape a new Indian social conscience: shame is a spur to reform. This is also the hope of a doctor in Bombay who has studied other aspects of prostitution, including eunuchs and slaves of god.

7 ❀ Devadasis and Hijras

Religion in India can be used for social reform—Gandhi is the best example—and also can be used to justify conduct society disapproves of, for instance, the *devadasi* (slave of god) cult and the *hijra* (eunuch) cult.

While enrolled at the Aurangabad Medical College in Maharashtra, Ishwarprasad Gilada was elected secretary of the All-India Medical Students Association, and in 1981, when he was twenty, he went to Geneva as a student representative to the Thirty-Fourth Assembly of the United Nations World Health Organization.

After he got his degree, Gilada joined J. J. Hospital, one of Bombay's three huge municipal hospitals, to work with lepers and patients with sexually transmitted diseases. When I met him, Gilada was living in a colonial-style bungalow hidden in a grassy compound on the sprawling hospital grounds. Lean, about five-feet-six, with a neatly clipped beard, heavy eyebrows, and black eyes, he seemed younger than his thirty years.

As an outgrowth of his experiences at Geneva, Gilada formed the Indian Health Organization. He gathered doctors and medical students for a succession of flood and disaster relief projects and to treat victims of Hindu-Muslim rioting in 1984 and 1985. But the organization's primary work has been with prostitutes. The group's research, and Gilada's own experience, support Sister Rita's findings on the betrayal of women by those who should protect them.

"I see at least two cases a week of girls raped by fathers, brothers or uncles," he said. "About 8 percent of child prostitutes are victims of incest. There was one case of a sixteen-year-old sold to a brothel by her father after incest. We found another case of a nine-year-old abused by a policemen. A fifteen-year-old girl brought to our clinic with symptoms of sexually transmitted disease had been raped by a self-styled social worker and then sold to a brothel keeper.

"Young girls are given hormonal preparations or indigenous medicinal vaginal sticks to induce early puberty, so they can start earning more money. But they earn money before they reach puberty. Many Arabs from the Gulf states tell pimps they want a young girl. They think if the girl is a minor there are fewer chances they'll contract a venereal disease. Some sodomize the girls. Either you sodomize her or you force her into vaginal intercourse. The child can't do anything. She's only nine, ten, or eleven years old and there's no check by the government; it's going on openly. The girls are dead by the time they're thirty."

Tulasa's Tragedy

Gilada estimates 15 to 20 percent of Bombay prostitutes are lured away or kidnapped outright from Nepal. The most notorious case was discovered in December 1982 when a prostitute named Tulasa was brought to Dr Gilada's clinic suffering from severe vomiting: she had tuberculosis, meningitis, and three types of sexually transmitted diseases. As she recovered, Gilada learned her story.

When she was thirteen, she was kidnapped from her village home, taken to Katmandu, then to Lucknow in Uttar Pradesh, and finally to Bombay where she was sold to a Nepali brothel keeper for five thousand rupees ($350). She was resold to another brothel keeper for seven thousand rupees ($490) and sold again for 7,500 rupees ($525). She was shuttled between luxury hotels and dingy rooms and used by five to seven men a day. Once, when the police discovered Tulasa in a raid, they took her away and demanded seven hundred rupees (about $50) from the brothel keeper to get her back: after bargaining they settled for five hundred ($35).

Tulasa was not yet sixteen when she was brought to the hospital, so grievously injured she could not walk. She remained there for a year and a half, until she was transferred to a newly established rehabilitation home in Katmandu. The Nepali police captured her two kidnappers, and they were sentenced to twenty years in jail, but in India not a single person was punished.

However, Tulasa's tragedy did have one beneficial result. The PITA antiprostitution law was enacted to punish brothel keepers who profit from the misery of minors primarily as a reaction to the Indian Health Organization's publicity about Tulasa.

The Goddess Yellamma

Gilada believes ten thousand girls are inducted every year into prostitution through the devadasi and related cults, of whom three thousand eventually are sold to the brothels of Bombay. There are many versions of the legend of Yellamma, the cult's goddess. Generally, they tell of the sage Jamadagni whose wife, Renuka, was so pure-minded she could carry water in a pot made of sand. One day, returning from a stream with the pot balanced on her head, she saw *Gandharvas* (earth spirits, minor deities) swimming in the water. A thought crossed her mind that life would be more enjoyable with a handsome Gandharva, and, with that, the pot made of sand dissolved and the water poured away.

Jamadagni, sitting in a trance, had the power to know all that happened. He took the stray thought as infidelity and ordered his sons to chop off their mother's head. The two eldest refused, but the youngest, twelve-year-old Parasurama, did as he was told. After decapitating his mother, he asked his father for a boon, which was granted, that his mother be restored to life. Jamadagni told Parasurama to bring his mother's head. He could not find it, but a woman of an untouchable caste — Yellamma — was passing by, and he cut off her head instead. Jamadagni placed Yellamma's head on Renuka's body, and she came back to life.

There are as many interpretations of the Renuka-Yellamma legend as there are varieties of the story. Since devadasis are invariably drawn from Dalit castes, the most obvious seems that it takes away the stain of sex with an untouchable: their heads (symbolized by Yellamma's) may be low caste, but their bodies (symbolized by Renuka's) might be used by upper caste men without defilement.

Dedicating Girls to Yellamma

Devadasis appear to be vestiges of fertility rites and temple prostitution. The modern cult is primarily a way to recruit prostitutes from Maharashtra, Karnataka, and Andhra Pradesh. In 1983 Gilada and another member of the Indian Health Organization, Dr Vijay Thakur, a psychotherapist, conducted a study at the Saundatti temple in northern Karnataka, near the border with Maharashtra. They found 88 percent of the girls dedicated as devadasis were below the age of eleven. Some were pledged in their mother's womb: if a first child was a girl, and the mother became pregnant again, she would promise her daughter to Yellamma if the newborn turned out to be a son.

Some families have a tradition of dedicating their eldest daughter, or at least one daughter, to Yellamma to assure the family's well-being. A Yellamma girl, though from an untouchable caste, is considered auspicious and is welcome in higher caste homes to bring good luck on births and marriages. A girl might also be dedicated to avert illness during an epidemic or starvation during a famine, or because of mental retardation or a skin rash that could indicate leprosy. By dedicating them to religious-sanctioned prostitution, a family is relieved of the responsibility for their care and simultaneously earns money from their sale.

Traditionally, dedication ceremonies are held at the Saundatti temple on the auspicious full moon day of the Hindu month spanning January and February. A woman personifying Yellamma goes into a trance and points to a girl as her own. One with matted hair—not long and straight in Indian fashion—would be an obvious candidate, since matted hair is an attribute of Siva.

However, women's advocates call it a sham, saying the woman in the purported trance may likely be a Yellamma gharwali seeking recruits for her Bombay brothel, with the selection of child-candidates arranged in advance by families willing to sell a daughter for five hundred to five thousand rupees ($35 – $350): matted hair can easily be managed with the aid of oil or grease.

Fighting the System

Devadasis are drawn primarily from south and central Indian untouchable castes whose traditional occupation was the disposal of dead animals, tanning skins, and the manufacture of shoes and other leather articles.

In the late 1960s, when Dalit activists demonstrated at the Saundatti temple to stop the dedication ceremonies, they were dispersed by the police, with many beaten and jailed. But then in the late 1970s elite-led women's organizations took up the issue as part of a modern agenda to rid Hinduism of practices derogatory to women. While Dalits could be ignored and even put in jail, educated women commanded attention and respect.

After a Delhi-based group calling itself the Joint Women's Program organized a series of meetings and press conferences and managed to get articles printed in several widely circulated women's magazines, the Karnataka legislature outlawed the devadasi cult and established a program to attempt to rehabilitate women freed from the practice. Two years later devadasi and related religious-sanctioned prostitution was outlawed in the adjoining state of Andhra Pradesh.

But, in keeping with the disjunction between promise and reality evident in India, Drs Gilada and Thakur say the ceremonies continue at Saundatti and smaller temples in Karnataka and Maharashtra.

The Making of a Eunuch

The Saundatti temple is also used to sanction one of India's most bizarre sex cults: the hijras. Gilada discussed his examinations and interviews with hijras:

"In India, homosexuality is not permissive: you'll never see gay clubs or gay bars here. There are some homosexuals who meet in a garden or other quiet places, but there are no public displays. However, in India, when something is not permitted in one part of society, it can go on in another part in the name of religion. The hijras worship the goddess Bahucharamai and are very organized and literate: they're rarely troubled by the authorities.

"They're divided into three categories. Those who are castrated are 50 to 60 percent; transvestites who are not castrated but wear saris are 30 to 40 percent; transsexuals who, after castration, get a vagina constructed with plastic surgery are perhaps as few as 2 percent.

"There are several ways hijras are recruited. They may have been sexually assaulted in their childhood and become confused about their sexual role. Or they may develop a psychology or conviction that many people in society are attracted to a boy because of his manners and not the male sex organ. When they grow up, they run away from home, knowing they must keep their homosexual attitudes a secret and that if their family arranges a marriage for them, they won't be able to maintain marital harmony. Once they leave home, they can't find any other place to receive them and make their way to hijras. After a year or two they're under pressure to get rid of the male sex organ. They hope this will change their voices and get rid of facial hair, giving them femininity.

"The castration is done by a *daima* (senior eunuch) at a big ceremony with food and liquor. The candidate is intoxicated with alcohol, and the entire genitals are cut off with a saw: the penis as well as the testicles. Hot oil is poured on the wound to prevent bleeding, and a hot rod is inserted to prevent closure of the urethra. A new rod is inserted every day; it also takes care of infection. The daima looks after the eunuch for six to eight weeks, giving him hormone pills and injections to try to make the change complete.

"We estimate there are three thousand hijras in Bombay. There may seem more because they're so prominent: they go in clusters and easily stand out as males wearing saris and women's make-up. They tend to separate into three groups. About a third are homosexual prostitutes. Others, mainly the older ones, have petty jobs as cooks, maids, or guards in brothels. The third are those who are most familiar to ordinary Indians. They dress in saris and appear at a house on the occasion of a marriage or birth, dancing, singing, and making rude remarks. People believe they draw evil spirits or bad thoughts on themselves, so the occasion will be a happy one. They'll not leave until they're paid a substantial amount of money."

As we ended our talk, Gilada said he would soon leave J. J. Hospital and set up a private practice to treat sexually transmitted diseases: working three or four hours to earn a living and spending the rest of his time trying to increase awareness about the conditions of prostitutes.

"We have to stop the kidnapping," he said. "If we give prostitutes medical attention and demonstrate we care for them, we can get a proper history and create a social awareness of the suffering of women forced into prostitution. Now, there's a stigma; people give for the blind, lepers, and handicapped but not for prostitutes.

"Some people have joined us but not in the proportion I thought when we began. For instance, I thought most women's groups in Bombay would support us and would start their own actions. But when we made a small survey of some feminist organizations we found they believed prostitution was in the interest of women; that it gives an outlet for male instincts and serves as a protection for other women."

A purely materialist determination—a belief that I am sufficient unto myself, free to pursue my own ends—was never as compelling in India as it was in the West. However, this changed under the pressure of Eurocentric ideas and economic modes: there was an appropriation of resources for individual use. A command of English meant recruitment into the bureaucracy and a steady income, unlike the uncertainties attached to agriculture. As educated boys became valuable assets and dowry became groom price, women were further devalued, leading to the burning of brides and the use of amniocentesis to abort females in the womb.

8 ☀ Female Feticide

Amniocentesis was developed in the mid-1960s to detect fetal abnormalities through an examination of about fifteen cubic centimeters of amniotic fluid drawn through a needle inserted, with the aid of ultrasound scanning, into the sac covering the fetus. The operation is usually performed during the fourteenth or fifteenth week of pregnancy.

It was apparent from the start that amniocentesis could also be used to determine the sex of the fetus, but obstetric textbooks brushed this aside. Said one: "Amniocentesis . . . should not be offered for such trivial reasons as choosing the sex of the offspring." Trivial in the West but not in India where there are proverbs like "Bringing up a daughter is like pouring water on sand" and "Bringing up a daughter is like watering a plant in another's courtyard."

The Rajputs of northern India have long been notorious for killing female babies. As early as 1789 the British tried to end a practice among Rajputs in eastern Uttar Pradesh. There are still Rajput villages in the desert areas of Jaisalmer in Rajasthan state where not a single female has been born in more than a hundred years. The custom is for the *dai* (midwife) to place a bag of sand in the baby's mouth just after birth. The Rajputs are exogamous—brides must come from another village—so the total absence of daughters is countered by bringing girls from outside.

Elsewhere female infants have been killed by smearing opium on a mother's nipples or by smothering them by putting the placenta over a baby's head. In Tamil Nadu the Kallar community of landless laborers in the Madurai district have a custom of using a crushed paste of oleander berries: when put into a newborn's mouth, the girl dies within an hour.

The Kallars are an exception: female infanticide is a feature of Brahminic communities where dowries dominate social life.

Sons and Daughters

Throughout India women perform *vratas* (fasts, vows, and visits to temples) to obtain sons and to ensure a long life for sons already born. They also perform vratas to secure the best husbands for their daughters and to ensure a long life for these husbands. A son born after a daughter is seen as the fruit of the mother's vratas, and the daughter herself is seen as having brought good luck in the form of her newborn brother. In many wedding invitations the groom's name is prefixed with a phrase meaning "one with long life." The prefix added to the bride's name means "one who aspires for blissful married state."

The Indian telegraph system has a method of sending cheap, standardized messages of congratulations or condolence; the messages are coded by number, and the sender merely has to telegraph the number to have the complete message delivered. For Hindi telegrams the message for a son translates: "Congratulations on the birth of a son." The message for a girl reads, "Good luck for the new arrival." She will need all the luck she can get.

India is one of a handful of countries where female infant mortality exceeds that of males. Studies of rural districts in Punjab show a juvenile (below ten years) sex ratio as high as 1,170 males for every thousand females, which means one out of every seven or eight girls has been removed from the population through either direct or indirect infanticide.

The life expectancy at birth for women in Uttar Pradesh is about forty-six years, with rural life expectancy less than forty years. A study in Patna, in Bihar, found that for every baby boy abandoned by parents there were five baby girls. Reports from various parts of the country have shown twice as many boys are taken to hospitals for treatment of common diseases as are girls.

Social scientists who surveyed three villages in Uttar Pradesh in 1981 found women wanted medical treatment for their daughters but "because of their low status in the family" were overruled by household males:

In one case, a girl had fallen from the roof and became unconscious. On the advice of the village doctor, the wife asked her husband to take the girl to a city hospital, but her husband flatly refused and said it was not serious. The wife submitted to her husband's decision without protest, but continued to weep bitterly. The husband, unperturbed, said to the doctor, "Kindly do whatever you can. I shall not go to the city. If nothing can be done, let her die. I have many daughters." The couple had three daughters, and they belong to a high caste family. Fortunately, the child survived due to the prompt treatment of the village doctor.

Half Man and Half Woman

Myths and scriptures ascribe a high status to women: learning is symbolized by the goddess Saraswati and wealth by the goddess Laxmi. Siva is represented in one of his forms as *ardhanarishwara* (half man and half woman). A wife is the moral and religious half of a man: he is not complete without her. There are four *ashramas* (stages) in the life of a twice-born male. The first is the *brahmacharya* (celibate, learning) stage. Through marriage he passes to the second stage, *grihastha* (householder). Thus marriage is a necessity, although a male of advanced spirituality may prolong the brahmacharya stage throughout his life. This is all but impossible for a woman because of the parallel need to control the female shakti principal.

Here, despite the equality of ardhanarishwara, a woman must be kept in a state of perpetual subordination, as illustrated by Manu, the ancient lawgiver, who wrote that an unmarried woman is dependent on her father, after marriage on her husband, and, when widowed, on her son. Indians developed an elaborate system to ensure this dependency. To control her sexuality and ensure her virginity, a girl had to be married before the puberty ceremony was performed for her. Keeping a grown girl in the house was both irreligious and scandalous. This had the further advantage of transferring her from one control to another while she was too immature to have a sense of her own identity. It also ensured that she would be totally respectful to her in-laws.

Indian women accept that it is their duty to sacrifice their health for the well-being of their families and feel they have failed if they become sick. A family never sits down to a meal at the same time: women are expected to cook and serve the men of the family first and then the boys. By the time these have finished, the women may be left to subsist on rice that has stuck to the bottom of the pot, flavored with a bit of salt and green chilies or, in northern areas, with dry flat bread and some pickles.

Worshipping Husbands As Gods

There is another Hindu concept: *pati parameshwar* (to worship one's husband as god), an ideal espoused in many Indian myths as well as the code of Manu: "Though destitute of virtue, or seeking pleasure elsewhere or devoid of good qualities, yet a husband must be constantly worshipped as a god by a faithful wife."

There is a folk saying that woman should be like water, which takes the shape of the vessel in which it is poured and yet does not leave a mark on the receptacle. Another says she should be pliable like mud that is cast into the shape chosen by a potter. Both make clear that a girl, leaving the control of her father, is simply transferred to a new situation of male dominance in her husband's family. Unlike in the West, marriage does not free an Indian woman to assume her own identity.

If little girls express resentment because a brother has been favored with a sweet, they may get a better share, but along with it they may be reminded the capacity to adjust is of prime importance for girls. A girl who continues to cry when she is hungry is considered fussy and teased for her lack of restraint. Girls are told they must learn to bear pain and deprivation, to eat anything that is given to them, and to develop a quality of self-denial to ready themselves for the reality they will confront in the house of their mother-in-law.

In 1985 women students at the Madras Law College went on strike because males were molesting them in what Indians call "Eve teasing." College officials were shocked, saying: "As women they should learn to give in, otherwise they would disrupt the existing harmony." The officials said the women should have taken joint action with male students, appealing to them for protection and security.

The Comparative Freedom of Non-Brahmin Women

All castes practice arranged marriages, but among Brahmins the status of the groom's family is at least as important as the merits of the groom, while among non-Brahmins, the merits of the groom is the deciding factor.

Among Brahmins the groom has the right to reject a proposed bride, but the bride has no similar right. Non-Brahmin brides do have this right.

Brahminic women, if mistreated, have to suffer in silence or, if life becomes utterly unbearable, commit suicide. If a non-Brahmin woman feels neglected or harassed, she can go back to their parental house in protest and seek help to retaliate.

A Brahminic wife may not criticize her husband even for infidelity, but if she is unfaithful she may be divorced and her family boycotted, if she is not simply killed outright. To the contrary, non-Brahmins do not give social approval to extramarital relations and a wife, if she has some means of support, can seek a divorce or may return to her parents. In any non-Brahmin divorce action, if the fault of the husband is proved in a caste or village council meeting, a woman can claim compensation.

In Brahminic circles a husband may seek a divorce on any pretext, but divorce from the woman's side is almost nonexistent. If by some chance a woman does obtain a divorce, she will be excluded from all social and cultural functions of a family and a village. (It should be remembered that Indian villages are segregated according to caste, generally with a clear space separating Brahmins and non-Brahmins, so that each, in effect, has a separate village although both sections will have the same village name.)

Widowed or divorced Brahminic women rarely are allowed to remarry, particularly when they have children. Non-Brahmin women have no hesitation about remarriage and, where there are children, are actually encouraged to find another husband. Male Brahmins smoke and sometimes drink, but not females. There is no such discrimination among non-Brahmins. Brahminic women are supposed to close their ears to any discussion of family business or other affairs, but non-Brahmin women are party to all that goes on around them.

Outlawing the Misuse of Science

In 1971, as part of its population control program, India's Parliament passed the Medical Termination of Pregnancy Act, legalizing abortions before the twentieth week. About the same time a few Indian doctors learned of the brave new world of amniocentesis, making it possible to abort only females.

The original name of the man who organized a successful campaign to outlaw this misuse of science in Maharashtra was Ravindra Pathak, but Pathak is a Brahmin name, so when Ravindra became a social activist, opposing caste and all it stood for, he dropped his last name. However, there are hundreds of thousands of Ravindras and people kept asking him for the rest of his name, so now he calls himself

Ravindra RP (with no punctuation)—"R" for his mother, Rukmini, and "P" for his father, Pandharinath.

I first met the reborn Ravindra RP at a small, crowded office at the Shrimati Nathibai Damodar Thakersey Pharmacy College (another problem name: it's so unwieldy the school is simply called SNDT College) in Bombay, where Ravindra teaches pharmacology. He is thin, with white burn marks on his hands and lips, and speaks so rapidly I had to listen intently to keep up with him.

"The fight against amniocentesis was a case where many things came together," he said. "In 1974, when I was twenty-four and a student at Nagpur (in Maharashtra), Jayaprakash Narayan gave his call for Total Revolution, and I joined his youth movement. After taking a master's degree in 1977, I thought if we wanted a nonviolent way of life, the best course would be to work on alternate technology. I went to the Gandhi *ashram* (traditionally, a religious community) at Wardha near Nagpur and worked with rural technology, like biogas and solar energy, and was involved in campaigns against industrial pollutants and how hormones have a destructive effect on women. Later, I came to this school, and when the amniocentesis issue arose, I had the ideological and technological background to take it up. In addition, my wife—we became friends at Wardha and then married—works full-time in the women's movement."

The Lure of Amniocentesis

By the middle 1970s several doctors were quietly using amniocentesis for sex determination. Then Dr Prithipal Singh Bhandari, in Amritsar in the state of Punjab, and his wife Kanan, a gynecologist, went public by advertising: "Invest 500 rupees now, save 50,000 later." The advertisements were taken as a legal contract, and when aborted fetuses turned out to be male, several clients sued for damages. Reacting to the front-page stories, feminist and human rights groups demanded the practice be banned. But the controversy merely served to spread the good word, and by 1986 Bombay had 274 clinics conducting tests for rates of between 150 and 500 rupees ($10.50–$35).

Since the amniocentesis centers seldom perform abortions and, conversely, since abortion clinics have no way of knowing the sex of a fetus has been predetermined, there are no statistics to track abortions as a direct result of sex determination. However, an early survey by the All-India Institute of Medical Science found forty-eight out of fifty mothers who opted for abortions did so after amniocentesis showed they were carrying a female child.

There have also been a few newspaper case histories. A mother, promised anonymity, told a reporter she had two daughters: five and seven. Her husband took her to an amniocentesis clinic when she was in her seventh month with her third child. The test showed it was female, and he demanded she submit to an illegal abortion. When she resisted, he beat her, saying she had challenged his manliness by continuously producing girls. She finally agreed to an abortion that cost two thousand rupees ($140). She was again pregnant. When the reporter asked if she would agree to another test, and another abortion if the fetus proved to be female, she replied, "Yes, that is part of my life: it is my karma."

"I did a study and found amniocentesis had arrived at even small towns," Ravindra said. "They would barely have a place for a decent meal, but three amniocentesis clinics had come up. In 1985 we formed the Forum Against Sex Determination and Sex Pre-selection to bring people together. We wanted to avoid what happened earlier when interest flared up, with a lot of newspaper publicity, and then died down. We decided not to raise it solely as a feminist issue. The moment you do that half the people turn away. We said it was a misuse of science and technology and was such a basic issue it affected our entire society. This is a country where a girl gets married at thirteen or fourteen and is a mother at seventeen. The incidence of anemia is high, so if a woman like that is made to undergo abortions two or three times there will be a serious threat to her health. We talked with doctors about the medical dimension, with lawyers about the legal dimension, and human rights groups on the social dimensions.

"In 1985 we had a parent-daughter march. In 1986 we had a cultural festival with three hundred children from slums, tribal areas, and from well-to-do families, with music, dances, and dramas with girls playing what are supposed to be masculine roles, fixing electricity and starting a car, and boys doing cooking. There were hundreds of letters to editors as all the vocal community supported a legal ban on the misuse of amniocentesis. Then some political people supported us: opposition members of the Maharashtra Assembly moved a private bill asking for the ban. Mostly, such bills don't become law, but they attract attention. In 1986 the state government formed a committee that commissioned a study of the state of the technology."

The study was conducted by Dr Sanjeev Kulkarni of the Foundation for Research in Community Health, who was able to get the records of fifty gynecologists. Eighty-four percent said they were doing the tests, and 64 percent admitted they did so only for sex determination. The Kulkarni study also revealed over 95 percent of the women who came for the tests knew the purpose was to discover the sex of the fetus and that most of them were forced into it. The report persuaded the state legislature in December 1987 to ban misuse of the technology.

Will the Ban Be Obeyed?

Ravindra believes evasion of the ban will not be widespread in Maharashtra. But he concedes there's reason to be suspicious: "Laws to protect women in India have never been enforced, and there will always be some bad people," he said. "Any doctor who has a syringe and enough skill to puncture the amniotic sac can do it. A doctor who does the test in some distant village sends the fluid anywhere for analysis. When the result comes back, the abortion can also be done anywhere. What's more, the test leaves no noticeable marks on a woman's body, so how can you prove an abortion is being performed because the family does not want a daughter?

"However, we can't compare this to what happened with the prohibition of liquor, for instance," Ravindra continued. Doctors are honorable members of their profession and for a small financial gain, they're not likely to break the law. If they do, and are caught, their licenses may be suspended or canceled. Other doctors must have a license to establish a laboratory to examine the fluids. Furthermore, the law prohibits a doctor who legally uses amniocentesis from supplying information to a patient as to the sex of a fetus.

"One doctor told us, 'I always felt guilty while I was doing this so I was happy when the government invoked the ban.' Many others said they were in a rat race. Patients said if they didn't do the tests they were inefficient, so they were forced into it. Also, there was the thought: 'Everyone else is making money, so why not me?'"

Ravindra and others are campaigning to have the Maharashtra ban become a pattern for a nationwide ban on the misuse of amniocentesis. Their chances for success seem minimal. Sex determination has the support of the rich and powerful. A reporter who visited the best-known test center in New Delhi, the Loomba Genetic Center, found among those being registered for amniocentesis were the daughter of a minister of the central government and wives of two high IAS officers. The demand from India's elite is so great the Bhandaris of Amritsar, whose practice in Amritsar is larger than ever despite the early adverse publicity, have opened a branch center in New Delhi.

Support was ratified when Vasant Sathe, the central government's minister for energy, asked: "What is the justification for banning sex tests when abortions are allowed?"

Opponents of a legal ban say outlawing amniocentesis will only drive it underground and lead to unsanitary operations without the expensive ultrasound equipment needed to ensure the fetus is not injured by the needle. Some doctors are already using the ultrasound equipment by itself. They say they can see the clear outline of a penis and testicles within the second trimester with 70 percent accuracy.

The rich and powerful are flocking to a new clinic in Bombay that claims the ability to weed out daughters even before conception. Dr Gita Pandya of the Foundation for Research in Reproduction and Reconstruction has obtained a franchise from Dr Ronald Ericsson of the United States to use his process for filtering out the Y (male) chromosomes from X (female) chromosomes by passing sperm through a protein-based liquid, usually albumin. The theory is that the XY sperm that produces males swims faster and lives shorter than the XX sperm. The husband provides a semen sample at the clinic, and the sperm is made to swim through the gradient. The XY chromosomes are harvested and artificially inseminated in a woman who has just begun ovulation. Only 20 percent of the inseminations are successful. When they are, Dr Ericsson claims a success rate as high as 80 percent in producing a child of the required sex. Others doubt his claims.

Dr Pandya charges four thousand rupees ($280) a consultation, plus a series of extra fees, making the service beyond the reach of most Indians but still much cheaper than the fees charged by Ericsson clinics in the United States or Europe. Eighty-three percent of those who used the service were businessmen, and another 17 percent were from government or other professional ranks. Seventy-six percent had many girls in their family.

Brides Are Not for Burning

The battering of women has long been recognized as a sordid feature of Indian society. If there is a complaint of a husband beating his wife, the police tend to ask, "Why does he do so?" The implication is she must be provoking him. In Uttar Pradesh a nineteen-year-old was married to an alcoholic mechanic who regularly beat her. One Saturday night he ordered her to remove his shoes. When she refused, he beat her and burned her to death. They had been married just nine months. In Madras a drunken husband who worked as a headload carrier found nothing to eat when he returned home. When his wife could not produce money so he could eat out, he beat her so severely she died on the way to a hospital.

There are also familiar newspaper stories of young women meeting violent deaths in Brahminic communities, but here suicide is often given as the cause. Typically, a recent bride, tormented by her in-laws, is said to have killed herself by jumping in a well or by using the kerosene readily available in an urban kitchen to immolate herself. Or, if not a suicide, it is called an accident: an inexperienced cook stood too close to a cooking fire, her synthetic sari caught fire, and she died before anyone could help her.

In the late 1970s, when news spread of the feminist movement in the United States, modern Brahminic women began to form organizations to raise their consciousness. They soon began to publicize what had long been a shameful secret: many of the deaths passed off as accidents or suicides were, in fact, murders.

Dowry given at the time of marriage is often only the beginning. The husband and his family, threatening to abandon the bride, may demand more cash, jewels, or gadgets: well aware that a married woman thrown out of her house is degraded in the eyes of both her family and her community. If the threat of abandonment does not work, the bride is continually harassed, beaten, and even killed.

The new women's groups found the phenomena so common they gave it a generic label: dowry deaths. In 1978, 327 suspected incidents were investigated nationwide. By 1985 the figure had risen to 990. But because the murders occur indoors, without witnesses to contradict husbands and in-laws who swear the fiery death of a woman was a pure accident, it's believed all official reports are gross underestimates.

Even the police in Delhi who, under the eye of a large and alert press corps, are considered more responsible than police elsewhere, registered only forty-three cases of bride burnings in 1985. But in the same year a study of just one hospital in Delhi showed 381 young women were admitted suffering from severe burns in 1985.

As newspaper stories of suspected dowry deaths increased, and public service ads appeared in newspapers showing a female doll being set afire with the heading "Brides Are Not for Burning," Parliament reacted with the customary spate of reform legislation.

Under the latest legislation both the giving and taking of dowries are cognizable offenses, with the threat of imprisonment of up to two years. In addition, cruelty to women, including coercion for dowry, is also a criminal offense. Finally, every unnatural death of a woman in the first seven years of her marriage must now be investigated both by the police and a magistrate. Despite the difficulties of obtaining sufficient evidence for convictions, dowry death laws are being enforced in high profile cities like Delhi and some state capitals. Several husbands and other relatives, including mothers-in-law, have been sentenced to terms of as long as life in prison.

All else is the usual exercise in reformist futility. Lavish weddings, with huge displays of costly dowry items, can be observed by the thousands in the traditional spring or fall wedding seasons: including receptions attended by the highest government and judicial officials.

Marriage: A Marketplace and Circus

Most women try to achieve economic security in the form of gold and jewelry in case they are thrown out or deserted by their husbands. And, despite the heated cries against the dowry system, many women insist on large dowries. They see it as a similar lifeline: conferring status on them and ensuring they will find acceptance and good treatment from their in-laws. Opponents say such women are under the spell of a consumer society where status comes with an automobile, a color TV set, and the number of kitchen gadgets a woman owns. They say dowry lowers the status of a woman by proclaiming a man's worth is measured by his job, family status, wealth, and appearance, for all of which his bride's family must pay.

What makes a marriage work, they say, is respect for the dignity of a woman for herself alone: that marriage depends on love, warmth, understanding, and sharing, not on a car or TV set. They also say the dowry system has turned marriage into a combination marketplace and circus. Not only must the bride's family give a dowry, it also has to bear the wedding expenses, which the groom's family would have done in village society. Previously, marriages were held at home with guests limited to the extended family and business friends. Now, the groom's family insists on a ceremony at a five-star hotel with guests invited by the hundreds, even thousands for the very rich. Where marriages were once simple rituals of knotting together a sari and *dhoti* (a man's long white waist cloth) or walking seven times around a sacred fire, now there must be dances and even, the height of Eurocentrism, a three-tier wedding cake.

Lavish weddings are ghoulish amid the tragedies of bride burnings and suicides. In 1988 alone there were three appalling incidents. In Kanpur, Uttar Pradesh, three sisters hanged themselves with their saris, leaving a note saying, "Dear Mummy and Daddy, we are doing this on our own. Please forgive us." In New Delhi two young doctors at the same hospital killed themselves by injecting lethal doses of drugs, saying they could no longer bear seeing the pressures exerted on their fathers. In Kerala four sisters hanged themselves and left a note: "Our parents are not yet able to pay fully for the dowry of our sister who was married sometime ago. Having sold their gold and land, we are not sure that they will be able to provide anything for our marriages. Hence the decision to end our lives."

The Failure of Education As a Reform

While the age of marriage has been steadily going up, along with the length of time spent in school, two other traditional teachings are retained: status ranking and the conviction that a girl should be subservient to her husband and thus should not be more highly educated than he is.

High schools, colleges, and even advanced studies are seen merely as respectable parking places for a girl until a suitable groom can be bought. Since ranking is according to caste and not individual merit, the determination of her proper level of education is related to the level of the males of her jati.

This is a major factor in the dropout rate of Brahminic girls: their education is ended at a point lower than the general education of males. To phrase it differently, she is not educated for her own sake but to give her the maximum advantage in the marriage market.

This does not mean she is ultimately destined to be a housewife. She may be educated to a point where she can find a job. But, again, this is not for her sake, but because she will be married to a male and live in a consumerist urban setting, where two incomes are a necessity and where women are free to work because of the availability of servants.

All this is part of the concerns and life-styles of the Brahminic elite, presided over by the goddesses Laxmi and Saraswati. In contrast, when Prema Purao began to help the thousands of poor Bombay women make a success of life, she found the more relevant goddess was Annapurna, the giver of food.

9 ✺ The Goddess of Food

Other than being the mother of a son, the most positive image of women in India is symbolized by Annapurna, the supplier of food who never says no. Gathering, cooking, and serving food gives a woman value and prestige, defines her kinship roles, and contributes to her self-esteem.

Annapurna has the inevitable Indian ambiguity: on one hand, the goddess symbolizes woman as the provider—the source of nourishment. On the other, she glorifies privation and sacrifice as the basis of feminine moral character—a disposition where a woman has to think first of others and ought not to care what remains for herself.

To modern Western women this may seem negative, but in the reality of the unceasing struggle for existence it is entirely positive: Annapurna also represents courage and the will to live and to help others to survive too.

"Women are my weakness, and I don't like pity," said Prema Purao. "Women are good fighters. I tell them to come forward. If any husband is a drunkard and starts beating his wife, my God, we'll go there and strike him and beat him and do whatever we can. I'm nonviolent: I don't want to go with a knife. But we feel if problems come, women must be in the front now. She shouldn't say, 'I'm a woman, how can I do this?' If a man can do it, so can a woman."

Prema Purao is about five-foot-seven—tall for an Indian woman—with gray hair and steel-rimmed glasses. I called on her at her center in the Dadar section of Bombay. She has been a fighter all her life. As a child, she joined her older brother in the movement for Goan independence and participated in terrorist activity. She was captured when she was twelve: too young to be sent to jail, she was externed to India. In 1945 she came to Bombay to work in the Communist trade union movement and, in the mid-1950s, married Dada Purao, who pioneered the formation of unions of bank employees. Prema was secretary of the union.

"At that time for a man to marry a girl who had left home and traveled all over the country was unthinkable," she said. "My husband always told me, 'You're an independent woman. You can choose whatever you want to do.' He used to help me and is still helping me, even though he is no more." As she said that, she looked up at a large picture of him on the wall.

"First We Must Give Bread"

"I'm not attached to any party now," she said, "but I'm still a political person." Actually, she is criticized by Communist ideologists who say she undermines the class struggle by making it possible for women to adjust to the existing power structure. Prema disagrees: "It's not enough to organize a union. First we must give bread."

In 1974 she formed Annapurna as an organization of women who prepared meals for men employed in the textile industry. Once the mills employed 35,000 women, but the aging factories, starved for capital for modernization, could not meet competition from Pacific rim nations and newly independent countries, and Indian factories closed. In addition, with modern labor laws, employers had to give women maternity leave and other benefits, so they were no longer a cheap source of labor and were fired. Now there are fewer than 2,500 women employed in the mills.

"These women had a relationship with textile workers, who originally were their colleagues," Prema explained. "When textile workers come from their villages to a big city like Bombay, they leave their families behind and rent a bed in a chawl. But they still need food, and hotel or restaurant food is too expensive. They want home-style cooking. So here were these women out of jobs who wanted work and workers who wanted to eat.

"I became aware of this system during the textile industry strike in 1973. It lasted forty-three days. The men had no money to pay for their food, but they still returned to their chawls to eat. The women pawned their *mangalsutras* and utensils to raise money to feed the workers. I saw these women, quietly enabling men to continue their struggle, but their own problems were never taken up."

The Chawls of Bombay

The chawls of the textile workers—built generations ago by millowners —are long, three-story structures with rows of ten by fourteen cubicles along a narrow central hall. Some of the cubicles are rented by a complete family, but others have three tiers of beds on either side. The beds are occupied in shifts, often with two men to a bed, so a cubicle sleeps twenty to thirty men.

The women in the chawls, who are in a small minority, can be either married, widowed, or single. To support themselves, or help support their families, they cook meals for the men without families: working a fourteen-hour day to accommodate the three shifts of the mills. Usually, a woman has to rise at five in the morning and queue up at a single tap to get water, and, as frequently happens, if water is available only once a day, they must fill buckets for the entire twenty-four hours. They try to limit their shopping to every two or three days, some of which can involve more long queues for kerosene or other rationed essentials. She might have a daughter or daughter-in-law to help her, or, if she has enough customers, she will hire a girl to help with preparing vegetables, grinding spices, and cleaning the metal dishes.

Before Prema Purao organized Annapurna, much of a woman's profits was eaten by interest. Private moneylenders charged 10 percent interest a month. A grocer is paid at the end of the month, when the workers receive their wages and settle their bills. The grocers account for interest by charging higher prices, and the mostly illiterate women have no clear idea of the extent of their debts or how the final sum is reached. Moreover, once a woman accepts credit from a grocer, she is bound to him and cannot shop around for cheaper prices.

Prema learned of two women driven to desperation. One was a young, good-looking woman who had built up a large debt she could not repay. The grocer said unless she had sex with him, she would get no more grains, and she had to comply. Another woman, faced with a huge debt, thought her only solution was to run away: where, she did not know.

"I thought I had the capacity for work and should use my skills in organization, communications, and dialogue to help women," Prema said. As secretary of the bank employees union she knew how banks worked and how to negotiate with them. In July 1969 Indira Gandhi had nationalized commercial banks as a populist measure to win support from the left to offset pressure from conservatives within the Congress Party. The stated aim was to have the banks lend money to the poor to become self-sufficient.

"I don't call them poor: they're skilled workers and can work and give you service," Prema said. "I thought, why can't we use the nationalized banks for these women? The money belongs to us. I took fourteen women to a bank, and they got loans with just their names and thumb impressions. Then slowly, slowly it came up. People tried to discourage them. 'This is a government bank,' they said. 'You'll have to pay high taxes,' they said. But they saw no one came to check, and no one did them harm. We trained those fourteen women, and now they're our leaders. The banks have issued 25,000 loans, and the interest is only 4 percent a year: the women used to pay 120 percent a year."

Prema produced a thick binder of computer printouts showing the names of women who had received loans. She succeeded beyond all expectations by turning it into a group effort. Although each loan was sanctioned individually, applications are made by a group of women who decide who will get money and for what purpose. Then, if one defaults, the entire group shares responsibility. From a banker's point of view this solves two difficulties: the feasibility of a project is evaluated by persons familiar with the type of activity, and there is a character check on the borrower.

For the women the psychological benefits are as valuable as the access to low-interest loans. Through the group bonding, they can break out of the isolated, home-bound existence that makes Indian women so vulnerable—gaining confidence by sharing their problems and helping others who encounter difficulties. Previously, women in the chawls were competitors: if a man refused to pay his bill on a spurious complaint about the quality of the food, another woman would be eager to snatch him away. Now, if a man defaults, no one else will feed him.

The Goal: Status and Independence

"My main goal is women must have status in society," Prema said. "During a strike in 1982, men lost their jobs, and we had many cases of drunken husbands. So we started a center for job training for women and also a shelter for mistreated women. The local leadership tries to solve problems, but if that's not possible, we call the people to the center and have negotiations and dialogue.

"Women must stand on their own and bring others forward. People ask me, 'Why don't you get an academic to work in the office?' I say I don't need them. Illiteracy is not a big problem. Slowly, they can learn to write and read. Literacy must come from them: we must not impose on them. We adopt one hundred daughters a year, sending them to school and giving them materials. They ask, 'What we will do after education?' We give them self-employment."

Prema showed me around other parts of the small building occupied by Annapurna. In one area young girls were making *chapatis* (thin, round bread baked on a hot plate). It's time-consuming work, and many working women nowadays prefer to buy ready-made chapatis. Prema said they supplied chapatis to three hundred families a day—with customers more than satisfied with food they trusted rather than the often adulterated and unsanitary products of the bazaar. In another area homemade pickles, another staple of Indian meals, were for sale. Groups of Annapurna women, trained at the center, were operating canteens at J. J. Hospital, the Bombay Telecommunications Center, and the Bombay airport.

I wanted to see how the meal service operated in a chawl, and Prema arranged for a guide and gave us the Annapurna station wagon (used to deliver food products and pick up supplies) for a few hours. My guide was Parag Raje, twenty-five, who, I soon discovered, was a university graduate and the son of a Communist leader but disenchanted with party politics. I asked why the Communists were not able to build sufficient strength in Bombay to resist being swept away by the ethnic demagoguery of the Shiv Sena.

"It's not enough to fight against something," he said. "The Communists should have had a constructive alternative. If they had entered the economic field in the 50s and 60s, they would have had strong economic institutions by now. If they organize cooperatives for men and women below the poverty line, they'll be able to build a mass base and a cadre and watch their creation flourish."

Building a Cooperative Community

I said that seemed what Prema is doing: building a cooperative community. He agreed: "A woman should aim to build her own structure and achieve economic independence. If her husband is a drunkard and she walks out of her house, where can she go? She'll be forced into a brothel. But if a mistreated woman enters a group and realizes she's not alone, she gains more courage. Only an organization can insure success."

We came to a long, tall, brick chawl, the sides streaked with black.

Even though it was only three stories, each floor was a double height to allow for ventilation in the swarming interior. We climbed a flight of stairs and walked down the corridor to the small, neat room of Urmilla Kaldankar. Parag said she had been with Annapurna for fifteen years and was now, although illiterate, an area director, responsible for about 2,500 members in a radius of about two miles, with four local directors under her. She was also a member of the central managing committee.

"Everyone is from her own class," Parag said. "There are no fancy society ladies telling the women what to do." At my request he asked how the meal system worked and translated her reply:

"Each boarder pays 250 rupees ($17.50) per month for two meals a day, seven days a week. That includes nonvegetarian food. A woman will have as few as fifteen or as many as forty customers. In this area people are well paid. In other areas they can only afford less than two hundred rupees [$14] for their food."

Parag said the men pay twelve rupees (84 cents) a month for a bed for one shift. A confirmed, rent-controlled tenant like Urmilla, who has been in Bombay for thirty-five years, pays twenty to twenty-five rupees ($1.40–$1.75) a month for a whole room. But it would not last: if a room became vacant it could sell for 100,000 rupees ($7,000). He also expected Annapurna would be evicted from central Bombay: "The municipality wants to tear down the chawls for apartment houses only the rich can afford."

Sweets for a Guest

Urmilla had built a loft in the upper part of the room as a separate bedroom, and we sat on chairs next to a small table in the kitchen and dining area. Urmilla worked full time for Annapurna and no longer served meals to lodgers. Parag said she was born in a Maharashtrian village and migrated with her husband when he became a mill worker. She did not work in the mills herself but did piece work at home. Now she was a widow with three daughters, one of them in college. Urmilla gave me a small, round ball of sweet confection: the traditional method of greeting someone who visits a house for the first time. Sweets are a sign an event or visit is auspicious.

"Once these women were afraid to cross the threshold of the house," Parag said. "Now they're not afraid to speak into a mike at a large gathering. A woman knows if anything happens, the organization will back her. There was one woman who was stopped at the corner by a moneylender and was threatened. She called Urmilla who went up to the man and said, 'She's a member of Annapurna: You don't touch her.' Her harassment stopped from that day onward."

When we arrived, Urmilla's middle daughter, a girl of about sixteen, was dressed in the ankle-length gown women use for sleeping and working around the house in the morning. She went up to the loft and returned dressed in a blouse and jeans to return with us to the center, where she worked in the accounts area. I asked Parag to ask Urmilla when her daughter would be married.

"She says she was married when she was thirteen," he translated. "She says, 'I had this suffering but my daughters will not.' She says they must be sixteen or seventeen before they are married."

And would Urmilla arrange the marriage?

"She says her daughter will find her own husband," Parag translated. "She says they'll only see if it's a good choice. If not, they'll openly advise the girl he's a bad man, and if she still can't find someone, they'll arrange the marriage. That's how things are usually done by families who have lived a long time in Bombay. That's how we're progressing."

Why So Many Beggars?

We left and drove to a separate office maintained by Annapurna to handle its financial affairs. Once, when we stopped at a traffic light, a woman with a baby in her arms knocked on the car's window, begging for money. I asked Parag why there were so many such beggars in Bombay.

"There are 350 million people below the poverty line in India so a few thousand beggars on the streets of Bombay are not many," he replied. "Annapurna has said, 'Give us a home and vacant land. We can teach beggars to grow vegetables or have some other money-earning activities.' We don't want to limit our scope just to cooking. These women are our sisters from the villages. Maybe one of our women recognizes a beggar. She says, 'You played with me many years ago. What has brought you to this?' The woman replies, 'You married an industrial worker. My husband was a drunkard.' Or there was a famine or floods and they lost everything. We're also asking the government for land in the north where women can cook cheap, clean meals on a large scale. We can even start something for middle-class office-goers and the working housewife: a good nutritious meal to take home. All these schemes are there."

Like Prema Purao herself (her family was Brahmin), Parag was an example of a counterelite activist: idealistic yet pragmatic. Although he did not sympathize with the narrow Communist Party activities of his parents, he still shared their disgust at India's oppressive class and caste system. His university degree was in economics and banking, but instead of using it to get an easy job, he was working with Prema in the financial organization of Annapurna.

We climbed the steps to a wide and comfortable office, with women at typewriters and clerks behind glass windows. All of the staff, except for one middle-aged man who was the chief accountant, were women. Since illiterate village women are terrified at the thought of going into a crowded banking office, where they would be ignored if not insulted by the largely male clerical staff, Annapurna had arranged for bank officers to come to this office to pass on the group loans. Parag showed me around. The women were given passbooks showing the amount of their loans. Payments were indicated by colored stickers, with different colors for different amounts: by counting the stickers the women knew how much they had paid.

"Bank officers would not go to the doorsteps of these ladies and have dust on their shoes," Parag said. "They can give a large loan to some private businessman and have a happy day. But we see that millions of rupees go to thousands of women: that way you can uplift not just one but many." He picked up a loan application with a picture of a woman attached.

"Look at this, a fruit seller," he said. "She's finding a way to work and live. She'll be part of a group of ten to forty women. There'll be a meeting, and the name of each one will be spoken out loud, and then there will be a discussion of priorities: who needs it the most. We get 99 percent recovery. The other 1 percent is when a woman dies.

"When someone comes for a loan, the Annapurna leader will know what her work is. She might have a debt of five hundred or one thousand rupees ($35–$70) to a grocer or moneylender. That's a very big amount for this woman. The Annapurna group leader goes along with that lady to see that first she clears away her debt and is free from this capitalist system.

"Then she feels, 'Annapurna has taken such an interest in me, why should I not repay the loan?' A poor woman is more honest than the biggest industrialist. He'll declare bankruptcy and escape his debts in millions, but the poor woman feels if the bank gives me the money and I don't repay it, the bank will bring the police and arrest her."

"She pays regularly to her group leader, who has learned how to keep books and gets a small fee for herself. The group leader brings the payments to the center. If a woman with a loan wants to check up, she ὶ come here with her passbook to see if all her payments have been cre ited correctly."

Caring for Women

As we left, I noticed a woman sitting on an imitation leather coach in the reception area. She looked so disconsolate I asked Parag who she was.

"She's one of our members," he replied. "We've given her shelter here for fifteen days. Her husband is a drunkard and keeps beating her. We've tried to reform him and have even contacted the police but without success. She has four children, and her husband beats them too. They're small and scared, and their development is not normal. When they see their mother beaten and slapped they become very frightened. We have put them in a boarding school and have allowed her to stay here and do some work in the office.

"In a majority of cases, after fifteen days or so, the husband cools down. He says, 'I'm very sorry, give me a chance to reform.' People say a woman should divorce her husband and leave her house, but a divorce will cost a lot of money and after that who will sustain her? Is she going to beg on the streets? If we can't keep a woman here, we take her to some friend's or relative's place where she stays for a few days. The husband sees the wife is not helpless and someone is backing her.

"And now there's a group feeling. A woman cooks seven days a week: How is she going to get rest? In the old days she had to do it on charcoal and suffered from TB. Now, if she wants to see a doctor, she'll ask a neighbor, 'Please take my customers for one week, I'll get a rest.' She knows her customers are being looked after by her elder sister, as she calls her. The neighbor says, 'All right. I'll rest another time.'

"What if women, in the dead of night, hear screams from another room in the chawl? They used to say no one must interfere. Now, these Annapurna women are bold enough to say, 'You may quarrel, but why are you beating her? There should be no violence.' Formerly, even the wife would turn them away, saying, 'You're outsiders. You may help me today but forget me tomorrow. I'm better off beaten but still have the security of my husband.' So she accepted this injustice and beating silently, but now she has a permanent organization to help her for more than just a few days. She tells her husband, 'See, you don't beat me. I'll call my friends to protect me.'

"There's a saying a woman is a woman's greatest enemy. People believed women were divided and couldn't be friends with another woman: they would only quarrel. Now, we've shown women can organize and cooperate, and they're their own greatest friends. First we teach her to be strong enough to live. Then she can be strong enough to fight."

With Prema Purao and Annapurna, I completed my wanderings in Bombay. Next, I visited surrounding areas where other activists were working with those at the very bottom of Indian society: the tribals.

10 ✺ Tribal India

Article forty-six of the fundamental rights section of the Indian Constitution reads: "The state will promote with special care the educational and economic interests of weaker sections of the people, and in particular the Scheduled Castes and Scheduled Tribes, and shall protect them from social injustice and all forms of exploitation."

Yet life for the scheduled castes remains deplorable and is even worse for the scheduled tribes: 85 percent of tribal families are below the meager official poverty line. Most of the mills, factories, and mines of postindependence industrialization have been built in what were once the tribal lands of central India. The displaced tribal men and women were hired to build the projects—being paid near starvation wages and living in shacks with few medical or educational facilities—and then were replaced by more skilled, or more politically favored, outsiders when the construction phase ended.

Since tribal homelands were concentrated in hilly areas where rainfall and river flows were the greatest, they were also displaced by the huge new dams and canals. Their victimization was documented in a report of the Commission for Scheduled Castes and Scheduled Tribes, which found out of 1.7 million people displaced by 119 government projects, nearly half (.8 million) were tribals.

Where and How They Lived

There are 212 scheduled tribes in India, constituting 7.5 percent of the population. They once inhabited 20 percent of the country's geographical area: the mountains and foothills of the Himalayas in the north and northeast, the Vindhyas of central India, the mountains and hills of the

Western and Eastern *Ghats* (Steps) running down both coasts, the mist-shrouded hills of the south, and the deserts and Aravalli mountains of Rajasthan.

A tribesman could use whatever he could cultivate, mainly through the slash-and-burn method with shifting plots, and everyone had a right to a house in the community center and to gather food, fuel, building materials, medicinal plants, and a few marketable commodities from the forests. It was a segmentary society, based on a nuclear family with no clear central authority: operating, instead, through an informal balance of power. A strong or charismatic figure might emerge from time to time, especially if there was a threat from another tribe, but there was no way to resist the encroachments of colonialism.

When the British, in the middle of the last century, began to count and classify Indians, they described these isolated peoples as tribes, on the analogy of the tribes of North America, Australia, and Melanesia.

There undoubtedly were many tribes in India in the remote past, just as there were in ancient Europe. But no tribe remained in India, in the historic sense of the three Latin, Etruscan, and Sabine tribes of Rome or in the anthropological sense of a self-contained unit with a common government and territory. Instead, there were peoples who had been stripped of all power and who had retreated to the forests and mountains to retain their last shreds of freedom.

Unlike Christianity, which converted and helped to assimilate the tribes of Europe, Brahminism is a colonizing rather than an integrating creed.

The people who called themselves *Aryans* (nobles) and who migrated to India in about 1500 B.C., termed the original inhabitants *Dasas* (bondsmen or slaves), *Dasyus* (bandits), or *Mlechhas* (unclean people), and described them as "black-skinned, wild-eyed, stub-nosed, and of faltering speech."

The Aryans wanted nothing to do with them. Instead, in a process of selective incorporation over thousands of years, they assimilated only the chiefs, priests, and traders as Kshatriyas, Brahmins, and Vaishyas and ranked the rest as Sudras and untouchable outcastes.

While no Indian tribe managed to maintain its pristine identity, those who retreated to the forests at least avoided the humiliation of untouchability. This was because Brahminism is based on the permanence of societal distinctions and sees nothing incongruous in different life-styles. It had no conscious impulse to assimilate or reform the tribals as long as contact was casual: the shy and powerless tribals were ignored or taken for granted as part of the strange and dangerous world of mountains and forests.

The Displacement of Tribal Peoples

This relatively frictionless coexistence was possible only so long as there was no population pressure, and hence no need to deprive the tribals of their lands.

Indian history is marked by repeated invasions and internecine warfare which, with the dislocations of agriculture and frequent famines, led to near-zero population growth. There was always more land than people to cultivate it, so the tribals were left alone in their mountains, forests, and deserts.

The isolation ended with the Pax Britannica: railways and roads cut into the hills, and law and order was extended to previously unadministered areas, giving entry and protection to traders and moneylenders who exploited tribal ignorance of a money economy and then seized their lands for the repayment of alleged debts.

Since the tribals had no title deeds or records of having paid land revenue, their lands were also seized by the British as unoccupied government land. The tribals, without knowing what had happened or why, were told they were encroaching on the land where they had lived for countless generations.

In many regions tribals lost their economic independence within the space of twenty years. Displaced and unemployed, they became a huge pool of migrant labor for the quickening pace of colonial exploitation. Thousands were enticed to semislavery in the new tea gardens carved out of the jungles of Assam and the lower Himalayas. Others became "bonded laborers," working as virtual slaves to repay debts to contractors building the new railways, roads, and factories, or serfs for *Zamindars* (former tax collectors given permanent rights to huge estates).

Removed from their native hearths and gods, most tribals became indistinguishable, in dress and physical appearance, from the untouchables whose lot they now shared. They also adopted certain Hindu beliefs and practiced forms of worship akin to Hindu rituals.

Nevertheless, many still do not subscribe to Brahminic social values: they have no caste distinctions; they recognize the equality of sexes; they prefer marriage by mature young men and women; they have freedom of divorce; they encourage widows to remarry; and they have no dietary taboos.

They are also known for their gentleness and honesty—at least among those least exposed to modern "civilization." They are an appealing people, and for this, as well as their exploitation, many social activists, like those in Thane District north of Bombay, have taken up their cause.

11 ❀ A Truck and Some Cows

In 1967, when I was about twenty," Ramesh Chote said, "I read in a newspaper of the rape of a tribal woman in Thane District. Afterward, they made a fire, beat her, and burned her alive in front of all the tribals. She was still crying, but people were afraid to help her."

Small, sturdily built, with graying hair, Ramesh was dressed in jeans and a sweat shirt when I arrived at his scantily furnished, untidy apartment in a northern residential area of the city. He said his wife had objected to the amount of time he spent on social activities and had divorced him.

"I went to see if the report of what happened to the woman was true, intending to remain only a few days, but I stayed for two months," he said. "I wanted to stay forever, but a retired judge working for tribals advised me to get my degree so I would have something real to contribute."

Ramesh became a civil engineer and joined Kaluram Dhodhade, one of the rare tribals to achieve leadership in his own right. Kaluram founded the *Bhoomi Sena* (Land Army), which seemed in the early 1970s to mark a significant breakthrough in grass-roots mass mobilization.

Thane is a hill area and once was heavily forested. Tribals still comprise about 25 percent of the district's population. Most are landless while others seldom have more than five acres. In 1970 Socialists, in an effort to publicize the failure to enforce land ceiling laws, organized a symbolic "land grab" of part of a two thousand acre estate registered in the name of a religious trust, a common device to evade the ceiling laws. Theoretically, the income belongs to a temple deity, but, in fact, a dominant family or caste profits from perpetual tenancy rights.

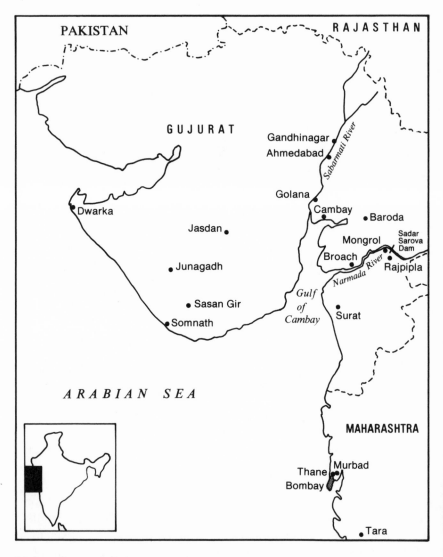

Maharashtra and Gujurat

The Rise and Fall of the Bhoomi Sena

As often happens with activists, jail was a school for Kaluram Dhodhade, who was among 150 persons arrested and sentenced to fifteen days.

"Kaluram discussed with other inmates what they should do when they came out," Ramesh said. "Someone mentioned setting up a boarding school for poor children. Others wanted education against high food prices. Kaluram said tribals were primitive and knew nothing of schools and prices. They only knew to eat the roots of trees. He said, 'We will take up bonded labor and land alienation.'

"When he was released, he organized the Bhoomi Sena and began to collect affidavits from tribals whose land had been taken over by moneylenders. No one wanted to go against the landlords because they were from the Congress Party or had connections with the Congress, but Kaluram decided to take direct action. About six hundred tribals took their sickles and cut the crop on the land of a moneylender. After the police ended that action, he announced a larger action. Then, with all the attention of Bombay newspapers, the government was compelled to act. A subdivisional magistrate brought his court to the villages and ruled in favor of all but one of eight hundred cases that he heard. By 1972 most of the alienated land was restored to tribal ownership."

The Bhoomi Sena's success was its failure. Elite volunteers, promising to bring managerial and technical efficiency to the Sena's affairs, established a trust to get government loans. It encouraged tribals to borrow as much as 10,000 rupees to dig wells that often proved dry and the borrowers had to default. The ultimate failure rose out of an effort to make bonded laborers self-sufficient.

"Some tribals had land for raising good quality grass," Ramesh said. "There's a big demand from dairies that sell milk to Bombay. The tribals needed money to start planting, so they would borrow fifty rupees. Then when the grass was dry and two or three meters high, they cut it and took it in bullock carts to the grass trader's house. It might be worth a thousand rupees but he paid only fifty. He said, 'Whether it is one bullock cart or ten, it is my property.' If the tribals refused to deliver the grass, the moneylender would send a truck and men to beat them and force them to load the truck and then take it away."

When the trust arranged for loans for tribals to start the planting season, the traders retaliated by refusing to buy the grass and, moreover, got other traders to boycott the tribals. Some traders purchased grass from as far away as Gujarat and Rajasthan. The trust then took loans to establish its own marketing organization, hoping for the added benefit of eliminating the middleman. Commodity trading is a risky business in any market. The trust had a series of losses, and by 1975 it was bankrupt. With that, the Bhoomi Sena disintegrated, and the traders regained their control of the grass markets. Even worse, the landlords slowly took back almost all the land that had been returned to the original tribal owners.

A New Generation of Activists

For a few years Ramesh was a consulting engineer for projects in Africa, and then in 1985 he opened an office in Bombay. His specialty is design, testing, and construction for below-level foundations and piling and irrigation. He also works, at cost, for social groups needing drafting or design work. Once or twice a week he returns to Thane to help out and to encourage a new generation of activists who have resumed where the Bhoomi Sena left off. He suggested I look at the work of Vivek Pandit.

We took the Bombay electric commuter railway north to the end of the line and then a dilapidated bus through farmlands and clusters of new factories and cheap, barracks-like apartment buildings and walked along a dirt road for the final five kilometers to Vivek's home and office.

"I remember 1968," he said, "when you could see dense forests all around here. This was supposed to be a reserved forest area, but the Congress Party is corrupt. One or two years before an election the politicians give timber traders permission to clear, say, one acre. They clear five acres and sell the lumber on the black market. Part of the profit goes to the Congress election committee in the area."

Vivek, an intense man in his early thirties, had little time for me. His group, the *Shramajivi Sanghatana* (Workers Organization or Trade Union), demonstrated their militancy by greeting one another with a raised right arm and clenched fist and by shouting *"Zindabad"* (Victory).

Freeing Bonded Laborers

Ramesh took me to a nearby dairy center with facilities for artificial insemination, the storage of milk, and the distribution of fodder. Two huge black-and-white Holstein bulls were tethered nearby. There was also a cooperative brick kiln and a training center for masons and carpenters. Some of the students were using bricks from the kiln to build a circular, open-sided meeting hall and small residential quarters for young men and women who would be trained for farm, forest, and health work. Ramesh said two smaller centers were being established in other areas.

He had to return to Bombay after lunch. My new guide was Sangita Koparde, twenty-two, dressed in a simple *kameez-salwar* (a long, loose shirt worn over loose trousers, gathered at the waist and narrowed at the ankles). She told me about the dairy project:

"It grew out of a realization we needed to rehabilitate a large number of released bonded laborers. In 1984 we had an awareness camp, and four bonded laborers came and declared themselves free. To get more information Vivek asked people to go to their relatives in different villages and ask the names of landowners with bonded laborers and how many did they have. Some of our volunteers also went near a village, and people came out a back path to give information.

"Vivek met the laborers and told them they could be free. Tribals are convinced they must repay whatever they have borrowed, but Vivek changed their minds. He said, 'There's this law that makes it illegal to have bonded laborers and the government is on our side. You can be a free citizen.'

"We were helped by a man who once was a *tahsildar* (a government officer in charge of a *tahsil*, a subdivision of a district or county) and became a member of our organization after he retired. Only a tahsildar or collector (the administrator for an entire district) can release bonded labor, and he showed us how to go about that. We collected affidavits, and 177 families were released.

"But the government evaded its legal responsibility to rehabilitate them, and we realized small measures—like giving loans to buy a bullock cart—would not help for long. We considered various projects and then got the idea of a dairy. We figured it was not only an income project, but if they can't sell the milk, their children will drink it. We have distributed cows to 160 families: they bring the milk to our three centers, and we have a small pickup truck that collects it and sells it to a government outlet.

"The women who take care of cows don't have any skills: they've never had money to own animals, but they've seen milking done. They get five to seven liters of milk a day, which gives them 19 to 26 rupees ($1.33–$1.82) income. We soon will be getting good Jersey cows and hope to get as much as twenty liters a day. We'll distribute these to families who take pains to do good work."

Psychological Rehabilitation

It seemed complicated, but there was an even greater test of tribal skills: a quantum leap in responsibility.

"Government officials laughed when we proposed a project for the tribals to own their own truck," Sangita said. "They had never heard of tribal families owning a truck. But the tribals asked for it; now they have their truck cooperative and are doing fairly well. Some already knew how to drive, and now they have also learned simple motor mechanics. We realized if you just say to a family, 'You're released,' they'll still have the mentality of bonded labor. We have succeeded in psychological rehabilitation. They were afraid even to look at their keeper or the police. Now, they're united, and they confront them."

Sangita said there were about thirty families involved in the brick kiln cooperative and twelve in the truck cooperative. They received a 50 percent subsidy under the Integrated Rural Development Program (IRDP), a government program to promote self-sufficiency among families below the poverty line. They also received a 40 percent subsidy under another government program to rehabilitate released tribal bonded laborers. Vivek's group helped them to borrow the remaining 10 percent from a bank.

A Guard Against Goondas

We returned to Vivek's office, where a thin mattress was spread on the floor for me to sleep on that night. The next day there was a village meeting, and I squeezed into a jeep with Vivek, Sangita, and several others. A guard, whom I had seen earlier at the office, was the driver. He was armed with a small revolver.

Sangita said a group of thugs employed by landlords angry at the activities of the Workers Organization had surrounded and stoned a meeting earlier in the year. Fortunately, there was a small police guard, and Vivek and others managed to get away safely after nightfall. The police later imposed a collective fine on the village of the landlords who had sent the *goondas* (from which the English word goon is derived). Ever since, Vivek had a guard when he visited villages.

It took us almost two hours to reach the village where about two hundred men and women raised their arms and shouted "Zindabad" as we walked to blankets spread on the ground for us to sit on. After long speeches in Marathi the meeting ended with a prize distribution for planting the most trees. Vivek awarded first prize—a metal cup—to a woman who had planted five hundred trees under the community program and another two hundred on her own. I was appointed to award the second prize, also a metal cup, to a woman who had planted just the official five hundred trees.

Sangita said the Workers Organization planted acacia, bamboo, and eucalyptus trees on 350 acres this year, hoped to plant another five hundred acres next year, and expected 90 percent of the saplings to survive. We drove off, stopped for a late lunch at a small town, and went on to Vivek's office where Sangita and I had another talk.

"We keep growing," she said. "When we took up the fight for minimum wages, laborers joined us, and now we're also working with a farmers cooperative for cultivating watermelons and vegetables. Some own land and some don't, but they all work together and share equally. There were ten women at the start: last year there were almost ninety.

"Our main task is making government people do their work properly and fighting corruption. We discovered a bank assistant manager who took eight hundred rupees from each beneficiary of a loan. We went to the manager and said we would expose this to Bombay newspapers. That was the only threat we needed: he said he would see to it people got their money back."

I asked Sangita how a young woman from a sophisticated city like Bombay had come to work in a rural tribal area.

"I studied at the College of Social Work," she replied. "In the second year we must choose between rural or urban work. I heard about Vivek and came to work with him. Much of India's problems can be traced to rural areas, but few people are willing to go there to work. There are many organizations. Some of them are just fighting and opposing things, but if you just fight and don't gain anything it's useless. There has to be constructive work. After I got my degree I came back here."

"How do your parents feel with you giving up better opportunities to come here?" I asked.

"My father was in politics with the Socialist Party," she replied. "Now, he also realizes it's useless if you're just fighting for your party. Besides, he knows it's better for me to do this than get involved in brown sugar (drugs)."

I never did exchange more than a few words with Vivek or his wife, who is also an activist. The next day I went by a series of local buses to eastern Thane to meet Vijay Sathe who was giving new life to the revolutionary tactics of Mahatma Gandhi.

12 ✹ Creating a New Revolutionary Class

With few exceptions Gandhian centers in India are little more than museums of memorabilia, but the methods and philosophies Gandhi developed, when stripped of religion and asceticism, are the everyday tactics of India's social movement.

Satyagraha for Gandhi was not simply a method for temporary gains but a blow to the heart of the master-slave relationship. To be free, Gandhi said, a person must first overcome his fear of death and embrace psychologically liberating work. His first major expression of the concept that the slave creates himself was in *Hind Swaraj*, with a reference to Britain's East India Company, the trading organization that conquered India and for which ordinary people used the respectful title *Bahadur* (literally, a brave or distinguished man):

> The English have not taken India: we have given it to them. . . . Recall the Company Bahadur. Who made it Bahadur? They had not the slightest intention at the time of establishing a kingdom. Who assisted the company's officers? Who was tempted at the sight of their silver? Who bought their goods? History testifies that we did all this. . . . It is truer to say we gave India to the English than that India was lost.

In explaining what became of the mythopoetic 1930 march to the sea at Dandi to make salt in defiance of British sovereignty, he wrote: "This band of satyagrahis . . . is not staging a play. . . . Nothing will be better than if this band of satyagrahis perishes. If the satyagrahis meet with death, it will put a seal upon their claim."

The revolutionary potentialities of Gandhi's philosophy went untapped as the freedom movement concentrated on the immediate task of independence. Now another generation, with modern secular philosophies but often armed with the tactics that Gandhi devised and used so effectively, is determined to displace the "Brown British" inheritors.

Antonio Gramsci, shut away in a Fascist prison, saw the potentiality of what Gandhi was doing. He used the Indian freedom movement of the 1920s and 1930s as an example of what he meant when he said there is no preexisting "class" shaped by economic conditions and that intellectuals have to construct a class as a specific agent for historical change.

Gramsci said in a society where most of the people are apathetic and ignorant, a small group can use the institutions of a civil society —the schools, churches, media, and similar organizations—to exercise hegemony. Here, the word hegemony means the perception that the structure of society is legitimate. He said intellectuals must try to create a new democratic hegemony based on the best interests of all of the people.

Indian social movement activists are trying to challenge the hegemony exercised by the small Brahminic caste/class by giving the "subaltern" classes—that is, the oppressed and excluded elements of society—an understanding of why they are in that condition and what they can do to remedy it.

In this they break with the "welfarist" approach. They are convinced the process of forging a grass-roots movement with local leadership is more important than immediate economic gains.

Living with an Uncertain Future

It took almost all day by crowded, creeping local buses to reach Vijay's home and office on a muddy alley behind the narrow main street of Murbad, a large market town in eastern Thane. He was a smiling, happy man: thirty-one, short and stocky, wearing glasses, with a round face, uneven teeth, a thin beard and mustache, and a shock of gray hair. I asked him how he got started.

"I got a master's degree from the College of Social Work in 1979. I was educated because people were indirectly helping me by growing food and constructing buildings. If people are well-off on one side, it means people on the other side are suffering a lot. I felt my education should be used to the maximum extent by downtrodden people.

"After I got my degree I started teaching a course in urban community development. One day seven or eight of us analyzed the situation. We realized when people have no other way to survive they migrate to the cities and live in slums. In 1980 we took the initiative to start social work here, and once I lived with the people I realized who was exploiting whom, and I was convinced, no matter what the difficulties were, this is where I must be."

Vijay's organization is called the *Shramik Mukti Sanghatana* (Workers Liberation Organization). It works in more than forty villages and has three middle-class activists—Vijay, his wife, and another man—and four full-time and five part-time tribal activists who have been recruited and trained from local people.

"We're not interested in overthrowing the government," Vijay said. "We only want this bureaucracy to be responsive to the people. To govern you must have one system or another. If everyone is asleep, there will be evils no matter what government is in power."

The work was originally a demonstration project of the College of Social Work. Vijay met his wife, Indavi Tulpule, when she came as a social worker. In 1985 when the school's support ended, the group was determined to survive on its own. I asked him how they supported themselves. He said he first got a law degree to have a source of income, but it did not work out: "They tried to contact and bribe magistrates and clerks and told their clients how to speak perfect lies. That was against my principles. And there was another thing: who pays your fees? Only someone who has money."

He and his partner, whom I did not meet, received two thousand rupees ($140) a month under a program of the Indo-German Social Service Society to train youth leadership. They decided they needed only 750 rupees apiece and were giving the remaining five hundred to support someone who was handicapped. Vijay said his group had counted 450 handicapped people in the area where they now work. He said Indavi received a monthly grant of eight hundred rupees ($57) from Oxfam, but that would end in two months. The Indo-German grant would end in one year:

"We live with an uncertain future. We have a son and don't know what will happen to his future. Of course, we realize if there is a total depression in the countryside, we may get some job or other in the city. Meantime, we only want money for our basic needs: food, clothing, and shelter. We don't want anything to be put in a bank."

Vijay said the sanghatana helped people with personal problems, like writing letters and applications, borrowing money, and treating sickness. On a village level they worked for better water supply, education, and afforestation: each member of the organization is pledged to plant five trees a year. They also staged athletics for tribal children and festivals to preserve tribal culture.

What interested me more than all that was what I had heard about his use of Gandhian tactics to challenge the government. For Gandhi satyagraha was a series of small steps. First the group and the leader discuss their goals. When these are clear, the opponent is notified and asked to sit down for a dialogue. If this is denied, a wider circle is notified of the issues in dispute, and public support and sympathy is sought. If there is still no resolution, a short strike or other public demonstration is organized. Finally there is the withdrawal of all cooperation with the opponent. At all points in the struggle the satyagrahis must meet in a body to discuss what is happening and be prepared to reach a reasonable compromise.

It was late afternoon when I arrived, and Vijay and his wife were busy. After a brief talk, I was shown to a small empty room where a blanket was spread on the floor for me to sleep on. It was not until late the next day (fortunately I had brought along a book to fill the empty hours) that Vijay was free to discuss his tactics.

The First Dharna

"For a long time, we had been registering complaints with the tahsildar, mainly land alienation cases, but he took no action. We had a *dharna* (a protest by sitting down before a government office or some other center) in front of the tahsil office in January 1986 and another in August, when we presented a list of 448 pending cases. We also posted a public notice that if no action was taken in three months we would stage an indefinite dharna and sent copies to officials in Thane and Bombay.

"On the appointed day 225 men and women marched in procession to the tahsil office and sat down. The police warned we would be arrested if we tried to enter the office, but we said every person had a right to inquire about his or her case. We sent in small batches with instructions to stay there if there was no action, but not to shout slogans inside the office or abuse government officials. I was arrested with the first batch. In the afternoon two batches of women and children went in, including Indavi. One woman sat in the tahsildar's chair and was slapped by a policewoman. By then the number inside and outside had grown to 450. We were all arrested and released a few hours later.

"The district collector (the next highest officer) called us and promised he would clear all the cases in one month. He did clear about 350 cases, but the main questions remained unanswered. For instance, there's a provision of the tenancy law that a hut has to be recorded, given a number, and entered on land records. We represented fifteen tribal hamlets with 350 families whose names were not recorded. We said the government should declare these hamlets as *gaothan* (village community land) on which any tribal can build a house.

"There's also a provision of law for restoration of tribal land that says once a decision has been made in favor of a tribal, the land must be handed over immediately, even if the nontribal occupant files an appeal. It also says if the land is not transferred for some reason or other, the tribal must be compensated for the period of the delay. There were eight pending applications on this issue, some dating back seven and eight years.

No Songs, No Slogans, No Drums

"Simultaneously, our work was going on. People came every day, and we had periodic camps to listen and record complaints. We decided to notify the public about what was happening and chose an auspicious day, August 15th, the anniversary of the day we got our independence, to show who really has independence: only big people—landlords, moneylenders, and politicians—are free. When we notified the police we intended some action, the district superintendent passed an order not to take marches, not to sing songs, not to shout slogans, not to beat drums—in all, not to disturb the public peace.

"We selected the twenty most important pending applications and twenty tribals, ten women and ten men, who were alert and not afraid. We made signs: 'When am I going to get my ration card?' or, for a bonded laborer, 'When will I be freed?' and they hung them on a string around their necks. There's a procession on Independence Day, with school children, officials, the police, and the general public. When our twenty tribals joined the procession, a police inspector said, 'This is not good.'

"We asked him, 'Is it good that a bonded laborer has filed his application for release one year ago and nothing has been done?' We went over all our twenty examples and asked, 'If this placard is not good, tell us what is good?'

"We said, 'There is no *morcha* [demonstration], no beating of drums, no shouting of slogans; people have kept mum; they're just walking on the road. You arrest all of us or have the tahsildar tell us, "Put away your flash cards, I'm going to do your work.'"

"The inspector said, 'Don't talk of arrests. I have just one request. The crucial ceremony will be raising the flag. If you can take off those cards for five minutes during that ceremony, there will be no trouble.' We agreed to do that—it was not a prestige point for us—but the tahsildar was so upset he canceled all the programs."

The Second Dharna

"In November, when the number of cases had risen to 924, we gave notice we would launch indefinite dharna on December 15. We summarized the cases under separate headings—work is required under the Rural Landless Employment Guarantee Program; declaration of gaothan; ration cards; identity cards required under the employment guarantee scheme—and sent a complete list to all officials. Nothing happened.

"We built a *pandal* (a multicolored cloth raised on poles to form a wide, flat-roofed shelter) in front of the tahsildar's gate that could accommodate about 350 people. There was a problem feeding all those people. There was a drought, and tribals could not get food from their hamlets. We appealed for contributions by going from house to house and shop to shop carrying big boards with a summation of our cases. When people realized the issues, some gave cash, others food and tea or oil for cooking and wood for fuel.

"On the second day the commissioner in Bombay asked us to go there for a discussion the following Monday. It was then Friday, so it was clear we would have to sit there for at least five days. On the third day the subdivisional officer (SDO), a position below the district collector but above the tahsildar, invited us. Myself and my wife and six tribals who had come forward as animators during all the previous activity formed a committee and went to see him and reviewed our cases one by one for more than four hours. For instance, there's a provision the tahsildar must supply ration cards within seven days after receiving an application in writing. We showed him cases of applications pending for three months and even one year.

"The SDO said, 'Please, you take away this dharna and I will see to it that your work will be done.' We said, 'We can't believe you. Last year, the collector ordered these things, but they were not done.' He said, 'I'm making a personal request: please withdraw this dharna.' We said, 'Even if we believe you, we don't know if all the others will.' We went and put the question to a vote, and the people unanimously took the decision: 'Nothing doing. No withdrawal until the work is cleared.'

"On the fifth day the committee went to the commissioner in Bombay and repeated the long story. We quoted examples for each topic and submitted a memorandum describing our efforts to get the work done: all of the notices we had sent out, the people we had approached, and our dharnas. He said, 'It's very tragic the tahsildar has failed in his duties, but now believe me: all this work will be cleared within two months.'

"This was our first meeting with the commissioner in Bombay, and we thought we should give him some respect. We said we would compromise on all pending applications except the demand for work, under the Rural Landless Employment Guarantee Program. This says if a poor rural person applies for work, he must be employed within fifteen days, and if he does not get work, the government must give him compensation of two rupees for every day he does not get work.

"We said we wanted work or nonemployment compensation from tomorrow and we also wanted identity cards that the workers need for jobs at government projects. There could be no compromise on these two points: the supply of land records could wait a few more days, but one cannot keep on starving. He said fine, and we left. On the sixth day he sent about 450 identity cards plus work orders so on the seventh day we withdrew the dharna."

The long story, interrupted by dinner and my questions for clarification, seemed to end on a note of triumph. I said the people must be happy. He agreed:

"We got a big victory when the huts were entered in the land records. People now feel secure, and if they die, their children will inherit the house. And everyone has received a ration card. In all, 85 to 90 percent of the cases were cleared. However, the demand for compensation for failing to return tribal land within the stipulated period is still pending. The old tahsildar has been transferred and the new one will take his own time even to understand the problems, so we'll give him a few months. If he doesn't act on the compensation cases, we'll resume the dharna on a small scale with one or two families.

"The entire system is bad. Even if a tahsildar is from the tribal community, he doesn't work for tribals. Many people are coming up in a hurry and are not concerned with others. We want a real change. Everything we do is a tool for awareness. Whether we win or lose in court is immaterial. We judge success by the extent we awaken a tribal or other poor person and educate him about his situation and give him confidence to tackle his problems himself: to take precautions and not be deceived again.

"We had a tribal who fought a land battle against a richer tribal for three years, going through appeal after appeal before he won. Now whenever there are problems in his village he comes to tell us and asks for guidance. He's been awakened. People believe they'll live and die the way they are born. It's a pattern of faith and superstition: Rama [God incarnated] came, Shivaji came, and Gandhi came. Like that, they think, 'Someday a great leader will come and lift us up and lead us to liberation.' They look up for heros and saints and don't look down among themselves. But a good tribal, who can organize in the same way I do, can do ten times as much good as I can."

Early the next morning as I was about to leave, I searched for Vijay to say goodbye and found him in the back washing the breakfast dishes under a tap. I said to Indavi this was the first time I had been in an Indian house and seen a man washing the dishes while a woman was available to do the work.

Vijay's brother-in-law was also there. "Vijay has no ego," he said.

I returned to Bombay and then continued south to the village of Tara where I met a man who helped explain why there is such a disjunction between the ideals of the Indian independence movement and the present realities of rural life.

13 ✸ The Mutiny of the Innocents

For a few days just after World War II the entire British naval installation in Bombay fell into the hands of mutineers. It was like October 1917 and St. Petersburg: a mutiny in the fleet and armed sailors ready to march to support the revolution. But India had no Lenin. The mutiny was suppressed and is now an inconvenient memory for the inheritors of British rule.

Balai Chandra Dutt, the man who inspired the mutiny, recalled the events in a small book, *Mutiny of the Innocents*. Dutt retired after a career as an advertising executive and lives sixty-five kilometers south of Bombay near the Yusuf Meherally Center, a rural outreach branch of the Yusuf Meherally Center of Bombay, named after one of the early leaders of the Congress Socialist Party, leftist wing of the Indian National Congress. BC, as he is called, invited me to stay at his house and told the story:

"We were totally ignorant about India and the character of the fight our leaders were waging. We were young ratings (enlisted men) who had been in service and suffered from discrimination on the battlefield: white against black—we saw it everywhere. We thought if we took over the navy our leaders would be happy to give us directions to finish off the British Empire."

They were wrong: the Indian National Congress wanted freedom without a revolution. Yet the most frequently heard slogan was *Inquilab Zindabad* (Victory for the Revolution). It was first shouted in Bengal at about the turn of the century, when Calcutta was the capital of British India and the province (including what is now Bangladesh). Terrorists inspired by Irish and Russian revolutionaries raided armories for guns and killed and wounded British officials.

The 1930s, when the Bengalis were eclipsed by the rise of Gandhi and the shift of the capital from Calcutta to New Delhi, saw a constant tug of war between Gandhi and Subhas Chandra Bose, the charismatic Bengali who had little patience with nonviolence. Bose, eager for a revolution, saw World War II as an unparalleled opportunity and secretly left India for Berlin. The Germans, who had barely heard of him, sent him by submarine to Tokyo, where Bose proposed to form a liberation army from among Indian prisoners captured during the Japanese advance through Asia. The Japanese allowed him to recruit prisoners for what he grandiloquently called the Indian National Army (INA), a poorly armed force that took part in skirmishes in Burma.

"Whose War Did I Fight?"

BC Dutt is also a Bengali. At seventeen he lied about his age, became a signalman in the navy, and at the war's end was stationed at a shore installation in Bombay. One day a friend returned from Malaya and handed him, for transmission to others, a package of photographs and literature about the INA. It was treasonous for a serviceman to possess INA literature, but Bose had been one of Dutt's boyhood heros and to be given such a mission was both an honor and a challenge. As he recalled in his book:

> I was twenty-two. I had come through the war unscathed. . . . I had served alongside British sailors and others from the other Commonwealth countries in different theaters. They knew what they were fighting for. . . . Whose war did I fight? . . . It was up to us, I felt, to prove that we were as much sons of the soil as the nationalist Indians who were fighting for the country's independence.

He sought like-minded enlisted men and soon a conspiratorial cell grew to about twenty men with another dozen sympathizers. Their first exploit was timed for what was celebrated as Navy Day. On the night before, they tore down bunting, burned some flags, and painted foot-high slogans on walls: "Quit India," "Down with the Imperialists," "Revolt Now," and "Kill the British."

No one was caught, but security became stringent, and it was difficult to repeat the performance. However, two months later, when the commander-in-chief was scheduled to visit the base, they managed to paint "Quit India" and "*Jai Hind*" (Long Live India) at the foot of the reviewing stand. Circumstantial evidence pointed to Dutt, and he was arrested when a search of his locker uncovered copies of a leaflet and other incriminating documents. The British did not know what to do with him: they were already prosecuting leaders of Bose's INA (who had surrendered when the war ended) and did not want another public demonstration of Britain's weakness. Despite intense questioning, Dutt only told the British what they already knew, and he was returned to his unit prior to discharge.

He had been detained for seventeen days, and there had been rumors of torture. Sympathy for him was so widespread he found other ratings openly reading literature about the freedom movement: some even publicly donated money for the defense of the INA soldiers. Dutt had no experience with crowds and spoke little English or Hindustani, as the lingua franca was called, and he receded to the background.

The Union Jack Hauled Down

On the morning of February 18, 1946, the men at Dutt's base began a hunger strike on the issue of bad food. Sailors at another Royal Indian Navy (RIN) base heard a rumor that British Tommies had shot and bayoneted some of the hunger strikers. They surged out to one of Bombay's main commercial streets, shouting "Inquilab Zindabad," stoning shops with foreign names, and pulling down the American flag at the United States Information Agency library. One British-owned newspaper ran a banner headline: "RIN Ratings Run Amok."

With that Indian officers joined their British counterparts in flight for safety, and within forty-eight hours 20,000 enlisted men had hauled down the Union Jack on seventy-four ships and twenty shore establishments, including four major bases. They had also formed a fluctuating coordinating committee, ranging from twelve to thirty-six men, all below the age of twenty-six.

They assumed leaders of the independence movement would welcome them with joy, but when they asked for advice, they were told to "remain calm" and to formulate their demands for consideration by the "proper authorities." Privately, Vallabhbhai Patel, who ranked with Nehru as second in command of the Congress Party, called them "a bunch of young hotheads messing with things they had no business in."

When a message was sent to Gandhi, he replied that if they were discontented they should resign, as if it were possible simply to resign from military service.

The British—seeing Congress leaders had no intention of helping the mutineers—mobilized to regain control. They tried using Indian troops, but one unit only fired blank bullets. More significantly, a Gurkha unit—soldiers who never before had disobeyed a British order—refused to participate at all. Then, on February 22, when British tanks clattered through the streets, civilians pelted them with stones and raised barricades to impede their progress. The mutineers hesitated to start a battle in which civilians would be killed and asked Vallabhbhai Patel for advice. He told them to surrender and promised no one would be punished. They took him at his word, and surrender flags were raised at dusk on February 23. In the following weeks British security men combed the naval installations and hauled off thousands of young sailors. Most were returned to their homes, but about five hundred were sent to prison as ordinary criminals: there is no record of how long they languished behind bars.

Nearly two million young Indians were in uniform, and the mutiny demonstrated little was needed for them to turn their guns against the British. Dutt's memories are bitter: "Most of them wanted the total overthrow of the Raj, the means did not much matter. . . . Other segments of society were similarly inclined. The leadership would not have it. They nipped what the young thought was the revolution in the bud."

A Pointing Finger

That was their innocence. Despite the revolutionary implications of Gandhi's philosophic concept of slaves risking their lives to break their chains, the Indian National Congress represented an elite who did not trust the passions of the poor. As Gramsci perceived in 1924, while editor of the Italian Communist Party newspaper *Ordine Nuovo* (New Order) in Turin, enlisting intellectuals as leaders of the poor has its perils:

> What a tragedy it would be if the groups of intellectuals who come to the working class and in whom the working class places its trust, do not feel themselves the same flesh and blood as the most humble, the most backward, and the least aware of our workers and peasants. All our work would be useless, and we would obtain no result.

For the intellectuals who led the Indian freedom movement, the common people were merely a superstitious mass invited to have *darshan* (sight) of the miracle-working Mahatma. Commenting on Gandhi's one-day visit to Gorakhpur in eastern Uttar Pradesh in 1921, during which he addressed a meeting estimated at more than 150,000 persons, Shahid Amin writes:

The Gandhi-darshan motif in nationalist discourse revealed a specific attitude towards the subalterns—*sadharan janta* or ordinary people as they are referred to in the nationalist Hindi press. To behold the Mahatma in person and become his devotees were the only roles assigned to them, while it was for the urban intelligentsia and full-time party activists to convert this groundswell of popular feeling into an organized movement.

The Gorakhpur tour was part of the first nationwide satyagraha—the Noncooperation Movement of 1920–22. Gandhi abruptly ended it following an incident at Chauri Chaura, in what is now Uttar Pradesh, where twenty-two policemen were burnt alive by a mob. He called it an "index finger" pointing to a possible future:

It shows the way India may easily go if drastic precautions be not taken. If we are not to evolve violence out of nonviolence, it is quite clear that we must hastily retrace our steps and reestablish an atmosphere of peace, rearrange our program and not think of starting mass civil disobedience until we are sure of peace being retained in spite of provocation.

Elitist distrust of the poor and determination to shape their own "passive revolution" (to recall Gramsci's phrase) led to the rejection of the initiatives of the mutineers.

When the mutiny was suppressed, BC—who had played no active role in the actual uprising—was discharged and put on a train to Calcutta. He promptly returned to Bombay, where an editor, appreciative of the items BC had passed on during the mutiny, helped him to start civilian life by making him a reporter. He then joined an advertising firm, and thirty-two years later, in 1983, he retired.

After dinner that night I said I could not understand how a country that gained its freedom under the banner of Gandhian nonviolence could spend 27 percent of its revenues for defense, with constant denunciations of Pakistan as a dangerous neighbor. I reminded BC that in his book he had written about the unity between Hindu and Muslim sailors: how the coordinating committee included servicemen from both religions.

"I can't understand why we should spend all our resources in trying to eliminate people who are part of our own culture," BC said. "Suppose we don't spend the money to defend ourselves from Pakistan and China? Will they take over India? If so, what will they do with it? When the Chinese invaded India in 1962, I was in Bangalore, and after a few drinks, I said, 'Open the door and let them come—whoever takes over India is dead.' This was repeated to the police, and they didn't see the humor or realism in it. When a friend warned me I might be arrested as a subversive, I went for advice to a Communist friend who had been arrested so many times he always had a bag packed in case they came for him. He told me to hide somewhere and find someone with influence to get me out of this. I took his advice and found a man, then in retirement, who had been warden of a prison where Nehru had been kept by the British. He passed the word on and later told me it would be safe to return home."

It was pleasant to find age had not dimmed his mutinous spirit. Now he had a new cause: planting trees—and we agreed to explore that subject the next morning.

14 ✹ Save the Western Ghats

According to myth, Ganga the river goddess was reluctant to come down to earth because of her immense power: it would be too destructive. She only agreed when Siva, who lives in the Himalayas, agreed to tie her down by using the locks of his hair. The locks are the forests and, too late, Indians are rediscovering the truth behind the myth.

The nationwide tree cover should be 33 percent, but satellite pictures show it is less than 11 percent. With the destruction of forests that held back the heavy monsoon rains, annual flood damage rose from about $96 million in the 1960s to more than $700 million in the 1980s, while the area affected increased from fewer than 8 million acres to more than 17 million acres.

One way Indians express themselves on public issues, generating media attention while reaching out to the illiterate poor, is by means of a *padyatra* (literally, foot journey or pilgrimage). Nowadays, the form is trivialized by politicians, but it is still respected as an act of self-sacrifice for a good cause.

Environmentalism in India is not an attempt to preserve picture postcard scenery but part of the overarching effort to help the poor: the worst victims of the rape of nature.

On November 1, 1987, two teams of activists set out on a padyatra called "The Save the Western Ghats March." One group started from the northern end of the mountain chain, on the border of Maharashtra and Gujarat, and the other from the tip of India at Kanyakumari. A hundred days later the two groups met midway at Ponda in Goa.

I joined the northern group as they entered Goa shouting slogans like "Save, Save, Western Ghats" and carrying placards with slogans like "Green is Beautiful." It was an area of open-pit copper mines: ugly slashes in the laterite soil spilled waste down the hills, fouling streams and polluting groundwater with toxic acids. In each town schoolchildren and their bands joined the march and later heard brief lectures on the need to preserve every tree and plant.

The marchers had not just walked and shouted slogans: when they stopped for the night, they questioned villagers about their fuel and water supplies and gathered statistics on how the destruction of the environment had changed lives.

The southern part of the Western Ghats receives more rain than the northern portion, and this was reflected in the statistics. In the south villagers had to spend an average of fifty minutes and travel an average of half a kilometer for water. In the north the average time was almost an hour and a half and the average distance almost a kilometer.

Most poor people in India use wood or cow dung for fuel. The average distance traveled each day for fuel in the south was a bit more than two kilometers and about four kilometers in the north. The time spent in the daily search ranged from ten minutes to ten hours in the south and from thirty minutes to nine hours in the north. Demonstrating the increasing burden of environmental decay, the time spent in collecting firewood or cow dung had doubled over the previous ten years.

The villagers also told of the deterioration of good farming land and a decline in animal husbandry due to a lack of fodder. Almost 62 percent of inhabitants of the northern villages and a bit fewer than 60 percent of those in the south said they had to migrate in search of a livelihood.

Serendipitous Encounters

At Ponda, where the marchers and others gathered to discuss their findings, I was introduced to Surekha Dalvi, a person who could tell about the destruction of the Western Ghats by wandering charcoal makers. Since social activists are little publicized in India, I depended on serendipitous encounters to discover them. Surekha said she lived at the Yusuf Meherally Center at Tara and invited me to visit her. She was not there when I arrived, but the serendipity was still working: I met BC and had a chance to talk with him about the mutiny and his new avocation of planting trees.

Tara is on the western side of the Western Ghats, not far from the sea. As he put on rubber boots for a walk through muddy soil, BC explained why trees were so important:

"Tree cover means when the rain falls it must not hit the land directly: it must be broken by leaves and branches. Afforestation is more than just planting a tree, it's a minimum three-to-five year project. It begins with the type of tree you choose, how you plant it, and how you take care of it. Every tree has a different effect on the soil: if you mix the types of trees, they'll equal out in survival. You must also choose trees that won't need any watering at all, and you must select the proper people to do the planting. This business of students coming over a weekend to plant trees is total nonsense. It may be good experience for them to get an awareness of the ecological disaster facing our country, but they don't know how to dig a pit for the plant. And once a tree is properly planted, you must protect it for three years from animals and people. A tree has a longer youth than a man-child: it needs longer protection to survive."

First, he showed me around his property, which he had originally bought as a vacation home, with a huge variety of shade, ornamental, and fruit trees. He said he expected 98 percent of his plantings to survive. Nearby there was a nursery with 10,000 seedlings growing in small plastic wrappings. Then we got into a station wagon and were driven south for a few miles. As we turned off onto a dirt road and followed the Patalganga River, I asked him about a wide stretch of the opposite bank that was colored a brilliant blue.

"It's chemical waste. Twenty square miles around here have been designated an industrial area, and it has attracted 50,000 people who care nothing for the environment. Ten years ago I could catch enough fish in an hour to last me for days: they've all disappeared. Ten thousand people used to get their drinking water from here. Now, quite often, the water department can't supply water because the river is polluted."

Troubles with Tribals

Our driver let us out by some empty fields seven kilometers from the center. He would go back and return for us in three hours: vehicles were too scarce to sit unutilized. As we trudged up a series of steep hills, BC explained his latest project:

"The Wasteland Development Board gave us money to plant trees but not the land. We wanted a place where outsiders would not interfere. Once you start somewhere, people from the city come and bring clothes for the men, saris for the women, and shoes for the children and think they've done a great thing. They don't realize they've done immense harm. The tribals say: 'Look, these people have given us something but those others gave us nothing.' Their greatest joy is in drinking. There are two villages near here where we did everything except allow them to drink. We gave them houses, clothes, and drinking water, but they wanted enjoyment: that we did not give them, and now we're their greatest enemy."

He called over a man plowing some land and spoke to him, pointing to a hill about a half mile away.

"I planted 26,000 saplings there last year and only 16,000 have survived," BC said. "They let animals in to graze and trample the plants into the ground. We pay this man to work for us. I've told him many times to build a brush fence to keep the animals out, but he says 'yes' and does nothing. I told him if he doesn't start work on the fence today, I'll get someone else.

"Tribals are still not used to working. It will take at least one more generation before they can organize their lives. You can find one fellow with a muzzle-loading gun or a bow and arrow: there's no forest left and he'll have to walk five kilometers before anything that can be called game is seen. If one goes, half the village will follow: they'll walk the whole day and night and shoot one rabbit and that will make them very happy."

Placating Snakes

We reached the top of a hill where men and women were scattered on a steep slope, chopping holes into the ground, while a half dozen young girls jogged toward us with shallow baskets of saplings on their heads. As we sat on a tree stump, an old woman with sagging breasts barely concealed by a sari end thrown over her shoulder approached and made a short, staccato speech.

"We fail to appreciate how their minds are working," BC said. "The woman is complaining we haven't done the proper worship ceremony and the snakes will come and bite them. She says we must break a coconut, pour the milk on the ground, and distribute the kernel to everyone on the job.

"Women walk seven kilometers to cut one tree and another ten to sell it in the market. It takes them ten to twelve hours plus their labor, and for that they get about ten rupees. We told them, 'You dig pits for trees near your houses, and we'll pay you ten rupees a day.' We talked to them day and night: it didn't make an impression. Their time frame is different from ours. They don't understand why they should work from eight to four. They'll be motivated if they see they're getting something right now, but something they might get after some time won't appeal to them. We're paying them for this work so they do it, but they have no concept of the future benefits of these trees."

He said they were planting several varieties of acacia and other trees that needed little water and were not palatable to cattle. Close to the village they were planting custard apple trees and cashew and blackberry bushes. We walked to the village on the top of a hill. I was surprised to see red tiled roofs on some of the mud and wattle huts. BC said the government had a program to distribute tiles; they were needed because the area was exposed to the full drenching rains of the monsoon. There was also a school built with cinderblock walls. BC said it was a waste:

"Technically all villages in Maharashtra must have schools, so they built one here, but the teacher comes once a month, signs the papers, and goes to the *Zilla Parishad* [district office] to pick up his salary. Who's going to check? The office is five kilometers away as the crow flies: no bureaucrat will walk up these hills."

After BC discussed the day's work with a full-time worker from the center who was supervising the project, we walked to the waiting station wagon and drove back to his house.

By any standard BC is a liberal and an idealist. After his fight against British racism in his navy, he joined the Socialist Party and was a founding member, in 1961, of the Yusuf Meherally Center in Bombay and its branch at Tara in 1967. But he is from an earlier generation of liberals, concerned with abstract ideals and progress rather than the daily lives of the poor.

Surekha Dalvi is of the new generation of counterelite activists, for whom the poor are not generalized abstractions but real men and women who, despite foibles and deficiencies, must be taken seriously and listened to as the only ones who can solve India's rural ills.

15 ❀ The Wandering Charcoal Makers

When Surekha Dalvi was twenty-two and still in college, she went to Tara to conduct nonformal education classes for children. She tells a story of a beautiful bird that was her "eye-opener" on the conditions of tribal people:

"A five- or six-year-old boy brought a lovely bird. It was dead, and I told him to throw it away. The next day he brought another dead bird, the same kind, and again I told him to throw it away. The third day he came with another bird, and I was very angry with him. I said, 'Look, this a lovely bird: why did you kill it and keep it?'

"He asked me if I would give him food. I couldn't understand the connection between food and that bird. He said, 'My father and mother have gone away for a job for the last six days and I have to go to the forest and catch birds. I eat them.'

"I had only thought how beautiful the bird was, how lovely. But the boy was thinking how much meat he would get from it. We went to his parents and asked why they were not giving food to their boy. They said they had taken a loan of fifty rupees and had to go to do this man's work. I said, 'You've worked six days now, so you're free.' They said, 'No, we have to work for one month.' When I told my friends in Bombay, they couldn't believe such things were happening only sixty-five kilometers away."

Surekha was now thirty-two: small, with a pug nose, short black hair, brownish-black eyes, wearing large glasses, and no earrings. She wore a brown print kameez over a plain, deep-maroon salwar. Her serious demeanor and dress were relieved by frequent, appealing smiles. She said in 1984 about seventy-five people had formed an organization called *Nirmiti* (Creation) as a private registered trust able to receive government funds:

"People used to come here and do charitable work, distributing clothing and conducting a nursery school, but we think the most important problem is economic: you must help people to stand on their own feet and get whatever government funds are available. The government's money is the people's money. Tribals can't cultivate land because they're poor. We help them get loans for oil engines to irrigate their fields, if they have any, and tools for farming. Suppose land is robbed from a tribal and should be restored: if we fight for it, they can succeed."

The Quality of Self-Restraint

The working group consisted of Surekha, Ashoke Saswadkar, a thin, bearded man who spoke little while I was there, and another man, Anil, who was away at the time. They also had six full-time local workers. When I asked how they supported themselves, she said they received contributions from friends and lawyers in Bombay:

"None of us gets a salary, we take what we need. A single man may get one hundred rupees, a married man with children more." Surekha lives in a small room at the Meherally Center. She said she and her husband Rajiv decided one of them should work to pay expenses: he has a law practice in Bombay and comes on weekends to visit her and participate in the work. By mutual consent they have no children, so Surekha can give full time to Nirmiti.

Indian philosophy and culture attaches great value to the attitude and quality known as *samyama* (self-restraint). An individual who, like Surekha, dresses simply and eschews the benefits of her background and education, is accorded respect. Surekha never acted as someone special, but that, in itself, is samyama.

She suggested we start with two nearby projects. We walked down the blacktop road, turned right through a village with brick houses, crossed about a hundred yards of empty ground, and climbed a hill. As usual, to reach a settlement of tribals or untouchables in India, you have to pass through the caste area closest to the road and go to a segregated area on less favorable soil.

Surekha said this was a settlement of Katkaris, listed by the government as a most primitive tribe. We came to a mud and wattle house with a skinny brown dog with long ears stretched by the entrance and, nearby, a woman scrubbing a brass plate with ashes from a fire: the customary substitute for soap. A picture of Ganesh, the elephant-headed god, was on a wall just inside the entrance, with a blood-red hibiscus flower as an offering on a shelf before it.

We kicked off our sandals as a woman greeted us and hurriedly spread a blanket on the floor for us to sit on. It was needed: the floor was covered with goat droppings. The goats themselves were in a pen that took up about a quarter of the house. Surekha said they were supplied under the Integrated Rural Development Program. She said the woman who greeted us had taken a loan, at 50 percent subsidy, and had received ten female goats and one male. This would give her an income of two hundred rupees ($14) a month from the sale of milk and grown kids. Surekha said that was a good income, even subtracting the loan installments over a period of three years.

We walked farther up the hill to a larger house with a porch and a string bed covered with a large piece of printed cotton, where a large man dressed in tight shorts with no shirt offered us seats. Surekha said he was a Katkari with the title of police *patel* (chief). She explained the British had declared the Katkaris of this settlement a "criminal tribe," and the patel's function was to report to the police when any tribal left or if any strangers entered it. But she said the reporting system was no longer enforced, and the Katkaris migrated at will. After chatting with the patel, Surekha told another story of an incident that shaped her life, saying it happened in this settlement.

A Mass Arrest

"One day, after we had started adult education and medical aid in various villages, we came here and found all the males were gone. When we went to inquire at the police station, the inspector said, 'Who are you? We don't know about social workers.' He told a constable, 'Throw these people out or arrest them.' We went to another social worker who had more experience, and he went with us again. Rajiv—this was before our marriage—had a press card. He showed it and said his father was a lawyer in Bombay. The inspector said, 'You should have told me this before.' He said the tribals had stolen some coal from a school five years earlier and were sent notices but had not attended the courts regularly. A nonbailable warrant was issued, and they were arrested.

"We went to the court and asked a lawyer for help. When he asked for money, we said we were social workers and had no money, but he said, 'First you bring me the money, and then I'll take action.' After that, both Rajiv and I decided we would complete our legal education to help the poor, especially the tribals. I got my degree in 1983. Now, the police are helpful: if they plan to arrest some tribal, they ask if I can come on a certain day to aid in a matter."

We left and followed a steep, rocky path to a high ridge and came to a village where women called cheerfully to Surekha, asking her why it was so long since her last visit. She said the village had 175 families of Thakurs, who were a more advanced tribe than the Katkaris, and that most owned some land, but it was cultivable only in the rainy season.

"People from the valley come up and use their land and water to grow vegetables for the Bombay market," she said. "Besides, the tribals don't have the money to cultivate their land or to transport the produce. About half of them go down to the coast as fishermen."

We came to a large, thatched-roof house where blankets were spread for us on a wide veranda. Surekha said a dozen families had formed a cooperative to farm seven-and-a-half acres and had asked for an engine and pipes to irrigate it. The pipe was donated, but they were only given the pump on hire.

"There are many groups in the village, and now the quarrels have gone," she said. "They work together for six months, each with his separate plot. They divide the water fairly, and they compete among themselves to see who can grow the best vegetables. It's a good business: each man has a net profit of 2,500 rupees ($175) at the end of the season."

It was too early for produce, but anyhow we went to look at the plot. When we returned, one of the men produced a wad of bills. Surekha said they were taking advantage of her visit to make a payment on the engine's rental. They also discussed other business. One man was drunk, talking loudly and interrupting others. They waited until he was finished, never reprimanding him or showing any sign of resentment.

After about an hour, when they finished their business and the drunk had left, we were given a small meal of rice, curried vegetables, and a few pieces of leathery chicken. Earlier, I noticed three men in clean shirts and trousers—obviously not villagers—entering a house across the way. I asked Surekha who they were:

"They're forest officers. It's common for them to come to a village and say they'll act on an application only if the people give them food like chicken and mutton and also liquor. But they don't do that in villages where we're active: they bring food and ask the people to cook for them. The people say those forest officers had liquor today, but they paid for it.

"Everyone steals from the poor. This is the only village within a four kilometer area, but it had no shop. We proposed the name of a tribal to establish a shop with a 50 percent subsidy under IRDP. We got all the sanctions, and the only thing left was for the bank to give the money. I had some other work and couldn't go with the man. The bank manager took his thumb print on blank paper and told him he could get the money if he came back in a month with a photograph. When he went back, they said to him 'You go see that man over there.' He was the middleman. He gave the tribal fifty kilos [110 pounds] of sugar and sixteen kilos [35.2 pounds] of peanut oil to start the store. After six months a notice came saying he had taken a loan of 4,500 rupees [$315], and they wanted it back.

"We were surprised. We went there, and the bank manager said he had taken all the money and showed the filled out form and this thumb print. We found there were many others with such loans. Local leaders, bank managers, politicians are all in a big racket. Once, someone showed me a letter saying there was a cooperative dairy in a village, and all the people had given eleven rupees as membership. But it was a fake: some politicians or local leaders had formed the society many years ago and were taking government loans in the name of these people."

The Charcoal Makers' Village

That was enough climbing and talking for one day. The next morning Ashoke joined us for a visit to a place where migrant charcoal workers had been resettled. We took a local bus, changed to another bus, walked across a railroad track, and up a small hill. Surekha said the settlement had seventeen families and was part of the village of Gagode, also called Vinobanagar after Vinoba Bhave, the originator of the *Bhoodan* (Land Gift) movement. Gagode was Bhave's birthplace. The Bhoodan organization had donated sixty-five acres to the village, but Surekha said the land was barren.

We entered a large, tin-roofed building that served as a school and village hall; it even had a television set, supplied under some government scheme. There was no school that day (I did not ask why), but about a dozen preschoolers were finishing a midmorning meal of boiled green peas. Surekha said Nirmiti worked in fifteen villages, most of which had schools for children three to five years old, teaching them songs, stories, the alphabet, and what she called "manners."

While Ashoke remained at the school to discuss business with community leaders, Surekha took me on a tour. "The government wants to stop the migration of the Katkaris, but to do that you must provide them with work and other income-generating activities," she said as we walked across a wide playground before the school. "The government has good plans, but the middlemen always take half the money. With our help the people get all the money."

Under one subsidized project Nirmiti had arranged for the Katkaris to build brick houses for all seventeen families, with the men paid for their labor. The houses measured only twelve by twelve feet, but the living area had been enlarged by thatched shelters in the front, and there was space in the rear for kitchen gardens of vegetables and fruit trees. Surekha also showed a goat project and a subsidized village store and said some men had started a brick kiln: they had learned the essentials working for private contractors.

"When they went to pay their first installment, the bank manager said that was the first time tribals had come themselves to repay a loan," Surekha said.

We came to a house with a noisy cackling from inside the extended front portion: it had been converted into a chicken coop. The birds, in neat mesh cages, were large, with bright eyes and perky heads: a sharp contrast to the usual scrawny village chickens. They were the project of an old woman with tattooed cheeks and arms who followed us, speaking excitedly to Surekha. When I asked her name, Surekha translated:

"Bhimi, mother of Mahedu." Like most village women, she defined herself in terms of her son. But Mahedu was not an idle figure; Surekha said he took the eggs to market on the back of his bicycle. She said Bhimi had received 140 chickens, of which 97 survived. They produced seventy to eighty eggs a day, which sold for forty-five to fifty rupees ($3.15–$3.50).

"That's a good income," she said. "In three years the loan will be paid off, and she'll be self-sufficient. It's a good business for women: they're at home full time and are careful to feed and water the birds. They also use the money to look after the whole family. Men wander all the time, get drunk, and squander a family's resources. We have fourteen applications for new poultry projects but approval only for ten; we'll select families who don't drink."

Where Do They Go? What Do They Do?

It began to sprinkle and soon, as often happens during the monsoon, the rain was falling in solid sheets lashed by strong winds. We ran to the shelter of the school where Surekha joined the business discussion. Since it was still raining hard when they finished, we had time for Surekha to tell me the story of the charcoal workers:

"We believe 40,000 Katkari men and women and 60,000 children are engaged in making charcoal and that two million tons of timber are converted every year. When we first came in contact with them four or five years back, we found they were only available for four months. We asked where they went, and they said they didn't know. They said contractors arrived at their settlements with trucks, gave them advances of one hundred to four hundred rupees, and took them away with a few belongings. It was impossible for us to do anything for them, such as starting schools, because they were always shifting here and there. They didn't even have *pukka* [permanent] houses in their settlements: they left a house for eight or nine months and came back to rebuild it out of sticks, mud, and thatch.

"We gave them postcards and said, 'Just write your postal address, and we'll find you.' We got one reply from far away and went to look for the family. As we later learned, a contractor buys the right to cut wood over a large area from some landowner. There the Katkari families are spread out, far from any village; some are in locations 2,000 feet high in the mountains.

"But we didn't have to search for them there. Each area has a market on a different day of the week. The contractor arranges credit for the women to get a supply of rice, grains, and a few other things at these markets: he doesn't give them a single *paise* [one-hundredth of a rupee] in cash; everything is charged against their advance.

"We asked where the local weekly market was held and found that family and others. They said they cut the trees, chop the wood into pieces, dig the soil for the kiln, cover the pile with mud—leaving vents to control the flame—watch the kiln day and night, put out the fire with water, and finally bag the charcoal. It's a skilled job: if they don't watch carefully, the wood will burn to ashes. They suffer burns and cuts, but there's no compensation for accidents.

"The whole family was paid five to ten rupees for a fifty kilo bag of charcoal, with no separate payment for women and children, who also had to work. Then, when it came to settling accounts, they were charged at a high rate for their weekly supplies. They also were charged for having an axe sharpened, for the cane baskets used to carry charcoal, and even for the transport to and from the work site. It ends up with a Katkari rarely able to take home two hundred to four hundred rupees for the eight or nine months' work. Most of the time the contractor claims they owe him money and only gives them *baksheesh* [a gift] of a few pots or pieces of cloth. They then worked for local farmers during the rainy season. Since they had no cash, they had to borrow money from the farmers until the season ended, so once again they were in debt.

"Bonded labor was outlawed by a ruling of the Supreme Court. We went to the government and said, 'These are bonded laborers. You can see clearly they have no choice of where they will work.' We said they had been declared a primitive tribe and were entitled to relief under the Bonded Labor Rehabilitation Scheme. The government said it didn't know about this and had no provision for alternative employment. But they did know: there were records of Katkaris doing this going back a hundred years.

"We estimated the contractors were getting 200 percent net profit on their investments. We formed a trade union, the *Kolasabhatti Kamgar Sanghatana* [Charcoal Kiln Workers Organization], and asked that a minimum wage be fixed for them. In November 1987 the High Court directed the Maharashtra government to fix a minimum wage within two months. But the government meantime had banned the charcoal business because of environmentalist complaints that it was destroying the Western Ghats. After delaying for some time, the government said the question of a minimum wage no longer applied since the work had been prohibited."

"You can't win," I remarked. "Every time you move the government finds a way to sidestep you."

Surekha agreed: "They went ahead and banned the business without caring for the tribals thrown out of work. Now we're trying something else: we've asked the government to give them work under the Rural Landless Employment Guarantee Program. We've also just had a fight for higher wages."

The Workers Fight Back

Earlier Surekha had said the main objective of Nirmiti was to create awareness among the Katkaris and to help them stand on their own feet. She nodded in the direction of a man in his twenties: thin, of medium height, with bright eyes, who had been talking animatedly during the business discussion.

"His name is Dharma," Surekha said. "He's illiterate but aware. He supervises the work in the settlement and shows visitors around. He's an ordinary laborer at a brick kiln and doesn't ask any pay for his work in the village.

"The government has banned the charcoal kilns, but the business is still going on. If a truck carrying charcoal is stopped, they claim it's old stock going to market. Last year the Charcoal Kiln Workers Organization had a meeting and voted to demand twenty rupees a bag for the charcoal. No one dared ask the contractors for that much, but Dharma said, 'The business is going on illegally so the contractors are in a difficult position, and we can benefit from it.'

"He went to the workers and told them to cut the wood but not to fire the kilns, and they all agreed. The contractors brought politicians and others to threaten them, but they stood united with Dharma. Finally, they realized they had to settle and asked us to go with them to talk with the workers. We had a conciliation meeting, and the contractors agreed to fifteen rupees. They had never paid so much: sometimes they paid as little as five rupees."

There was a moral to Surekha's story: tribals still fighting for justice at the birthplace of Vinoba Bhave pointed to the failure of charismatic leadership.

16 ✹ The Failure of Charisma

The challenge posed to the social movement is how to end the traditional Indian longing for charismatic leadership and create a broad, secular movement that includes the poor as active participants.

Charisma, in its original sense, means to be graced by God with a special talent for preaching or healing. The term has been desanctified in the West into a label for someone with great popular appeal, but in India, where God, *avatars* (a deity reincarnated), and saints are not easily displaced, it retains its divine implications.

Thus, Mahatma Gandhi's appeal was patently charismatic: he said his goal was *Ram Rajya* (Kingdom of God) and claimed to be guided by "an inner voice." When Gandhi was assassinated in January 1948, many of his closest followers, like Tibetans after the death of a Dalai Lama, began to search for an avatar.

In response to what came to be called Gandhi's "Last Will"—instructions that his followers renounce politics in favor of work for the poor—his associates met the following March and gave themselves a new name, *Lok Sevaks* (Servants of the People), and called their movement *Sarvodaya* (Welfare of All). A year later they formed another organization with an even more pompous name, the *Akhil Bharat Sarva Seva Sangh* (All-India Association for the Welfare and Service of All).

One of the Lok Sevaks—in English they called themselves "constructive workers"—was Vinoba Bhave. In 1916, at the age of twenty-one, Bhave had joined Gandhi at his Sabarmati Ashram in Gujarat. Five years later he was sent to open a new Gandhi ashram at Wardha in Maharashtra and spent the next twenty-six years there in meditation and dabbling in village industries and basic education. He emerged briefly from obscurity in 1940 when Gandhi named him to start the Quit India campaign by becoming the first resister to get himself arrested.

A Dialogue with God

In 1951 the Sarva Seva Sangh held its third session in the former princely state of Hyderabad. When the conference ended, Vinoba, in the *sadhu* (wandering holy men) tradition, walked to the Telengana region where in 1948 the army of newly independent India had brutally suppressed a Communist insurrection. At the village of Pochampalli some Dalits requested land, and at the usual Gandhian evening prayer meeting Vinoba asked if anyone could help. A farmer offered one hundred acres, and Vinoba talked with God: "I slept little on that fateful night of April 18, 1951, when all of a sudden God appeared before me and [we had] a dialogue between us. I wanted to go to the landlords the next morning and ask for more land but I was hesitating when God intervened and said, 'Keep faith in me and go, ask for more land.'"

To his followers Vinoba was obviously the sought-for avatar. Vinoba continued his Telengana padyatra, and in the following fifty-one days he was promised more than twelve thousand acres. From then on he traveled throughout India in a routine that seldom varied. He began his day with prayers and hymns at half past three in the morning and set out an hour later, trailing an entourage of a few dozen close supporters and local followers and others who simply wanted to partake of the holy experience. A few hours after sunrise Vinoba would reach a village where his arrival was anticipated and have his first meal of milk, yogurt, fruit juice, and raw vegetables and then rest for an hour. The rest of the day was devoted to meetings with local leaders or visitors from the outside world, another meal, the evening prayer meeting and sermon, and a final private session of hymns with his fellow marchers.

If a mark of divine inspiration is feckless optimism, Vinoba was undoubtedly touched by God. In 1953 he proclaimed an astounding goal: the gift, by 1957, of fifty million acres—one-sixth of the land under cultivation. Any lingering doubts about his plausibility were assuaged in 1954 when Bhoodan received an impeccable imprimatur: Jayaprakash Narayan—once a Marxist and sometimes mentioned as a successor to Nehru—announced he had abandoned politics to join Bhoodan. This, in the argot of the movement, was hailed as *jivandan* (gift of life).

A Socialist Idol

Narayan was a figure of legend. In 1922, at the age of twenty, he sailed for the United States and spent seven years in various schools, including the University of Wisconsin, where he studied sociology. He supported himself—barely—with jobs in factories and mines and even by shining shoes. In the process he became a Communist, but he broke with Stalin's Comintern-led party after his return to India, and in 1934 he was among the founders of the Socialist wing of the Congress.

JP, as he was commonly called, did not hide his Marxist beliefs: he called Gandhi a bourgeois collaborator with the upper classes. During World War II he spurned the nonviolent Quit India movement by escaping from jail to help foment active guerrilla resistance.

JP was the undoubted idol of intellectuals and the idealistic youth, but his charisma could not save a failing movement. By Vinoba's target year of 1957 it was revealed that only 4.8 million acres had been donated. (This was later reduced to four million acres, with the explanation that some had been taken back.) Undeterred, Bhave envisioned new programs: *gramdan* (gift of a village), *zilladan* (gift of an entire district), and *rajyadan* (gift of an entire state).

At the annual Sarvodaya conference in 1959 someone figured out Vinoba had proclaimed sixty-five different programs and projects, most of which were never started. His wanderings seemed without purpose. Indians will always greet a holy man reverently. One might impulsively announce a gift of land—exactly what land he need not say; another might bow temporarily to community pressure and announce a gift with no intention of giving anything, and a third might seek religious merit while fobbing off land of doubtful title.

Even if the gift were fertile land and not barren, rocky soil, who would decide its distribution? Would Dalits benefit in a caste-ridden village structure, or would the land go to a poor relative of an upper caste person? And if, by some happenstance, it did go to a needy person, where would he get tools to farm it or credit to buy seed and fertilizer? Bhave airily dismissed criticism that he failed to create a structure to handle such matters by citing a Vedic stanza that the function of a religious text is to inform and not to incite people to action: "Ours is a moral organization which disseminates knowledge. To shower rain on the fields is the *svadharma* (duty) of clouds, to raise a good crop is the duty of the farmer. I am not a farmer; I only bring rains."

Vinoba was a scholar and flavored his speech with Sanskrit terms with a wealth of meanings. For instance, he used the phrase *Bhoodan yajna* (the sacrifice of a gift of land). In the Vedas *dana* (gift) is a means of restoring equilibrium: if a person has injured someone and gives him a gift, and it is accepted, the parties return to the status quo. Similarly, yajna, or sacrifice, validates the moral right of a person to enjoy the balance. Thus, when a man or woman visits a temple and gives a coconut or a small packet of candy as yajna, they receive almost all of it back: they have a right to enjoy the remainder and are simultaneously blessed for their offering.

Indian enthusiasts termed Bhoodan and Sarvodaya "revolutionary," and Western sympathizers saw Vinoba as a "saint on the march," and perhaps a counter to the Communist danger. He was neither. He called the Gandhian tactics of fasts, strikes, picketing, marches, and filling jails with willing prisoners "negative" satyagraha and said they would rarely be needed in independent, democratic India.

For a man like Jayaprakash Narayan to join an impractical, wandering holy man is one of the many enigmas of modern India.

In 1969 Vinoba retired to his ashram at Paunar near Wardha and busied himself with experiments in *stri shakti* (female power), including a community entirely of women and a campaign to end cow slaughter. In 1982 in the tradition of Indian holy men who accept suicide as a form of renunciation, he starved himself to death at the age of eighty-seven.

When Vinoba retreated to Paunar, JP became the de facto leader of the Bhoodan movement. In 1970, spurred by the Naxalite uprising, he moved to one of the centers of terrorism—the Musahari area of Bihar—to see if gramdan could be a nonviolent alternative.

With this, the curtain rose on the final, tragic act in the life of India's most appealing antihero. In Musahari, JP finally came face to face with rural realities—and he blinked. He once wrote:

> There is a tendency among those of us who have received some education to distrust the ability and intelligence of the common people. . . . No one can learn to discharge responsibility unless responsibility is really given to one. Withholding of responsibility, either on account of lack of confidence in the people or of reluctance to surrender power, would lead naturally, as it has already done to a considerable extent, to an attitude of irresponsibility in the people, who will forever be on the lookout for heros and miracle makers to solve their problems.

This could well serve as the credo of social movement activists, but JP lacked the convictions of his rhetoric. After only eighteen months he concluded it would be impossible to rebuild India person-by-person and village-by-village. He then set out to foster *lok shakti* (people's power) through the election of *lok umeedvars* (people's candidates) to the state assemblies in Bihar and Gujarat. He claimed he was not giving up his original promise to build from below but was "building from all directions," with a goal of "Total Revolution."

To JP this apparently meant the Gandhian holistic vision of an "ever-widening, never-ascending" circle of villages where all men were equal. To others it might mean an economic struggle of the poor against the rich and to still others simply replacing the ins with the outs.

A People's Movement Without People

Hailed as *Lok Nayak* (Leader of the People), JP in early 1974 encouraged or led a series of increasingly large and turbulent student demonstrations in Gujarat and Bihar. A massive strike in Bihar in October convinced him a revolutionary situation was in the making. In March 1975 he called for a march by tens of thousands of protesters to New Delhi to present Parliament with a "People's Charter."

In June, after a High Court justice in Allahabad ruled her election to Parliament was invalid because she had used government facilities in her campaigns for the seat, Indira Gandhi declared a State of Emergency, banning political parties, muzzling the press, and arresting thousands of men and women, including JP, under the 1971 Maintenance of Internal Security Act (MISA), which provided for detention without trial.

During the twenty-one months of the Emergency talk of revolution was forgotten: the opposition's goal, as well as JP's, was simply to restore the status quo of democracy, however imperfect. JP had once written: "The politics of Sarvodaya can have no party and no concern with power. Rather, its aim will be to see all centers of power abolished. . . . A real withering away of the state."

Yet, when Mrs Gandhi allowed free elections, JP became the father of the *Janata* (People's) Party. "I helped them to come to power, because I had hoped they would yet write a new chapter of India's history," he later wrote, as if to absolve himself of the debacle that followed. The Janata Party, swept into office in March 1977, paid no attention to JP's Sarvodaya ideals. Dissension and the incapacity of its leaders brought the government to quick collapse, and when new elections were called in 1980, Mrs Gandhi won the most parliamentary seats since the early days of her long career.

JP, who suffered kidney failure and spent his last years on dialysis, died in 1979. Mrs Gandhi's victory the following year was a mocking testament to his failure. He had written of the need to trust the illiterate common people and had warned that if they did not have responsibility they would "be on the lookout for heros and miracle makers." Yet he allowed himself to be seen as a charismatic miracle maker. He was hailed as the Leader of the People, and his movement was proclaimed the people's struggle for people's self government, representing the people's will, the people's awakening, and the people's upsurge for a real people's democracy to be led by the People's Party.

The people were only instruments: it was the movement of a charismatic leader. Total Revolution was neither total nor a revolution. It did energize a number of young people—Ravindra and his wife in Bombay are obvious examples—but it was still upper castes looking for a shortcut to utopia. Indian activists have learned from JP's failure: to make democracy work the people must be empowered materially and psychologically.

In violence-prone rural India any encouragement to the poor to demand a better way of life can lead to tragedy, as evidenced in a Gujarat village called Golana.

17 ✸ The Golana Massacre

Golana is a village in a corner of
Gujarat near the Gulf of Cambay and the Arabian Sea. There, on
January 25, 1986, four Dalits were murdered by Durbars, a Kshatriya
caste linked to the courts (Durbars) of the former Rajput rulers of
Saurashtra. I went to Golana almost two years to the day after the event.
My guide was Martin Macwan, a serious man with a round face, black
hair, and a thick mustache, who was then a teacher at the Behavioral
Science Center of St. Xavier's College, an elite Jesuit institution in
Ahmedabad.

"Our group started when some professors wondered if their theories of motivation and achievement would apply to farmers in the villages," Macwan explained as we drove south over a two-lane blacktop
road. "We brought village people to motivation camps in Ahmedabad
and took them to demonstration farms to show improved methods. Here,
they seemed receptive, but there was no change in their lives when
they returned home. Our teachers stayed overnight in some villages and
saw that the lowest caste villagers had to go to the Durbars for jobs or to
borrow money to buy seeds or whatever else they needed. They were
afraid to oppose the Durbars. They asked: 'How do we survive if we go
against these people?'

"Our teachers realized the caste system was still alive away from
Ahmedabad. Here, I can work with a man and not be aware of his caste:
even if I knew he was a member of a scheduled caste, it would make no
difference."

Macwan said there were three scheduled castes in Golana: *Vankars*,
who are the highest whose traditional occupation is weaving, then
Chamars who skin dead buffalos and work in leather, and finally, at the
bottom, those who cleaned toilets and swept the streets. He called

them *Bhangis,* a caste designation out of fashion among urban English-speakers who prefer the term "sweepers."

Caste Christians

Some of the villagers are Christians, but their status was unchanged with conversion, and the Christians and Vankars consider themselves members of the same community. They were joined in tragedy too: two of the four men killed were Christian and two were Vankar. Although Macwan did not volunteer the information, I knew he was a Vankar Christian.

When the Vankar cottage industries were destroyed by spinning and weaving mills, most became landless laborers, but the more enterprising accumulated a few acres and scratched a living from the saline soil by raising wheat. After independence other Vankars acquired lands through the Gujarat Agricultural Land Ceiling Act. Then a canal was put through the region, and farmers, including Vankars, switched to the profitable cultivation of rice.

Over generations the Vankar caste, which at one time had no standing in society, became important. Some Vankar children got jobs as primary school teachers or in the lower grades of the state government or local agencies, and their examples raised the expectations of all Vankars.

"We started working in ten villages with such things as cooperatives to market farm products and distribute improved seed," Macwan said. "We also had dairy cooperatives, including one in Golana, and two forestry cooperatives. To help the landless Vankars enter the world of economic production, we persuaded the government to give us 183 acres of highly saline wasteland. People told us the only thing that would grow there was a tree called *Prosopis Juliflora;* that's sometimes used to reclaim the desert. We formed a forestry cooperative to produce charcoal and firewood. Not all the land could be salvaged, and it took a lot of money and work to build *bunds* (embankments) to keep out the sea water, but we ended up with a plantation of 125 acres."

The Importance of Local Leaders

"We owed a great deal of our success to one man: Pochabhai Punjabhai." (Actually, Pocha Punja: Gujaratis attach a suffix—*bhai* (brother) or *ben* (sister)—to the names of respected or familiar persons.) "Pochabhai wasn't educated," Macwan continued, "but illiteracy isn't a barrier: leadership is more important. Never have I met a man with such understanding and dedication. He could see the injustice and exploitation around him. Others had the attitude, 'This is the fate God has written for us: we must be the slaves of the Durbars.' They believed a man could do nothing: only God can act, so they depended on God and not themselves. Pochabhai saw this was false, and when a local man does this, expressing thoughts in his own language, it's more powerful than anything an outsider can do.

"The cooperative was the heart of the project. We saw to it there would be equality and that every household participated in the discussions: What projects will be taken up? Who will share in the profits? Will they be distributed equally? We also saw to it that knowledge would belong to all. It's not sound development if one person knows and the rest don't know. Knowledge is power: we wanted to make sure a few people could not take control.

"Before the cooperative started, the landless could get work only during the six months of the planting and harvesting season; after that they had to migrate for the rest of the year in search of low paying jobs. The cooperative provided year-round labor: improving the land, trimming the trees, and making the charcoal. It also paid wages according to the government's minimum rate of ten rupees for eight or nine hours work. The Durbars were used to paying two or three rupees a day and made people work from early in the morning to late at night. Villagers couldn't complain because plenty of labor was available, and the Durbars would get someone else. But as more and more villagers came into the cooperative, the Durbars couldn't get people to work in their fields, and so they had to pay the full ten rupees.

"Things started changing, and as Pochabhai became more popular, tension between Vankars and Durbars became greater. The final issue leading to the killings involved land for housing. The Vankar population was growing: two or three brothers lived in a single house with no privacy. Some nearby land, which had been declared surplus under the land ceiling act, was lying waste, but the Durbars still regarded it as their property. They're tough and powerful. Some are moneylenders and own rice mills in nearby cities. One had served time in jail. No one had the guts to oppose them. But Pochabhai took the lead and demanded the land for housing. The Durbars had a feudal mentality. They thought: 'We're kings of the country. These untouchables, how dare they take this land? The village is our property.' They tried to divide the Vankars by offering them other land far away, but people had learned from the cooperative. They said, 'The Durbars could rule because they could divide us, but now we're united, and they can't do anything.'

"The district collector was considerate and awarded the land to the Vankars, who built small huts there just to show ownership. The Durbars decided to act. They thought: 'If we kill their leaders, their unity will be in shambles.'"

The Crime and the Punishment

It wasn't necessary for Macwan to explain what happened next; I had already read several detailed reports. The Durbars instigated a few sweepers to put up huts on the same land and then defended them when Vankars demolished the huts. In the scuffle one Vankar had his fingers cut off. The Vankars decided to complain to the police in Cambay, twenty-five kilometers away. About twenty of the most active members of the cooperative, including Pocha Punja, gathered to wait for a truck to give them a lift. Just as they were leaving, a gang of Durbars ran up, pulled them from the truck, and beat them with sticks and iron rods.

When the Vankars retreated to their part of the village, other Durbars arrived and began a house-to-house search for the most important men. Some of them were armed. They found Pocha Punja and shot him dead at point-blank range. They couldn't find another leader, Pocha Kala, so they shot dead his twenty-two-year-old son, Prabhudas, who worked as an accountant for the cooperative.

Two brothers, Khoda and Mohan Mitha, were clubbed to death. They were a special target. Same time earlier Khoda Mitha had accidentally brushed against a Durbar's *hookah* (water pipe). The Durbar said he had been defiled and beat Mitha. But the spirit of fighting back was in the air: Khoda Mitha filed a case against the Durbar under a rarely enforced law that prohibits the practice of untouchability.

In addition to the four killed, eighteen were hospitalized with broken bones or other serious injuries, and three houses were burned. At first the press paid little attention to the event, dismissing it as another of the frequent caste clashes, but when social activists filed suit demanding the assailants be punished, headlines called it "The Golana Massacre." It was a year of growing unrest throughout Gujarat, and Congress Party politicians were anxious to make a show of maintaining social peace. One of India's draconian antiterrorist laws was invoked, and fourteen men were found guilty and sentenced to life in prison.

"The case was fought well," Macwan continued. "All the witnesses came forward without fear of the Durbars. People said: 'If we lose this case, we better not live.' I wonder sometimes about the sentence: in some families there are no men to take the bullocks to the fields: a woman must do that. But the Durbars have learned a lesson. Old people tell their children: 'Come on, son, times have changed, adjust yourself.'"

The Dead As Symbols of Victory

When we reached Golana, villagers took us to four mounds, about three feet high, where the bodies were buried. Cremation is an upper caste funeral practice: Christians and Muslims bury their dead. When untouchability was enforced, Dalits were compelled to bury their dead in unmarked graves. Nowadays, Dalit families generally follow the Brahminic practice of cremation, but in this case, because of the close relationship of Christians and Vankars and the desire to create a monument, all four were buried.

"After they were killed, their bodies were taken to Cambay," one man said. "Ten thousand scheduled castes then marched all the way from Cambay for their funeral. [Newspaper reports at the time put the number at four thousand.] We want to preserve this unity. We light a torch here and take it to all Vankar villages in the state. Thousands of people came last year on February 27 to worship and remember their sacrifice. We'll do it again this year."

A short distance away the Vankars were building a township of 113 small brick houses on the once-disputed land. We walked down the straight, paved streets and looked into some of the small unfinished brick houses. Macwan said the materials had been supplied free, and the Vankars were being paid for their work under the Rural Landless Labor Employment Guarantee Scheme.

Each of the houses had a small building in the rear for a dry latrine, that is, without piped water. I remarked on this apparent improvement over the usual practice of using vacant fields as toilets and was surprised at Macwan's reaction:

"My people didn't want these latrines. They're hard working: they get up at four-thirty or five in the morning and go to the fields and don't return until nine at night. It's difficult for women to fetch water from the well. They have to walk about a thousand feet from here, and in the monsoon you can't walk in the mud. If you have latrines and can't keep them clean, they'll stink. That's why people go out to the fields. Latrines are our city culture. Nothing should be imposed on people. We're from the outside and must respect their wishes and consider what they can afford. When they see the need, they'll build the latrines themselves."

We walked to the Vankar settlement to call on the man whose son was killed, passing slogans written in English on some walls: "Speak loudly but speak the truth" and "Morality is the real foundation of religion." I asked Macwan about them. "People are religious and one of their customs is to write good slogans on the walls," he replied.

We came to a mud-walled house and were greeted by Pocha Kala and seated on string beds in a covered area outside the house while women got out their best cups for the inevitable heavily sugared tea. Just as inevitably, we were surrounded by neighbors eager to look at a stranger, even if they did not understand what was being said.

Memories of Untouchability

Although the family was Christian, only a cross above the door distinguished the house from any other in the area: for all practical purposes they remained Dalits. In reply to my questions Pocha Kala described how they once were treated, and Macwan translated what he said:

"Ten years ago we could not ride a bicycle across a Durbar's land: we had to carry it. When we stood before the Durbars, we had to cover our heads and take off our shoes, like in a temple. We had to address them as *bapu* (father) and *dada* (grandfather), and if their ladies passed, we had to call them *ba* (mother). If we didn't, the Durbar would think 'This fellow is too proud.' He would try to get revenge.

"When we were boys, a school was built in this village, but we had to sit outside. If they had a ceremony to honor Mahatma Gandhi, or if there was a patriotic occasion, we were allowed inside, but on the next day we were put out again. That ended about ten years back, and now there are more government schools and many scheduled caste teachers. But scheduled caste teachers still can't drink water from the same pot as the upper castes."

We visited the home of Pocha Punja and were again seated outside and offered tea. There was a framed picture of him above the door with the legend:

The Golana Massacre
The First Martyr
Feb. 23. 1951

The date was his birthday. Macwan said the picture was carried at his funeral procession. There was also a slogan on a wall: "As long as the land and sky remain/The name of Paul will also remain."

Paul was his Christian name. I asked Macwan if there was any special relationship between the Jesuits of St. Xavier's College and the Christians of Golana.

"We're entirely secular," he replied. "Christianity had nothing to do with what happened here. Pochabhai was not active in his church. He was killed because he was active in the cooperative."

I asked Pocha Punja's father what he thought. "We're not divided by religion," he replied. "When Christian priests come, people will call them to their houses and offer tea. If Hindu preachers come, they will also be called for tea. *Diwali* [a Hindu festival] is celebrated by each and every household and so is Christmas."

I had seen a church not far away and asked to be shown inside. Macwan, as if to emphasize his separation from religious affairs, remained behind and a young man named Gabriel acted as a guide. It was a large oblong room with plain windows and no pews: villagers are comfortable sitting on the floor. Except for a small altar with a statue of the Virgin Mary and the Stations of the Cross on the side walls, there were no decorations.

It was the highest structure in the village, and Gabriel showed me the view from the roof. All around were flat paddy fields except for a small hill to the west where the white, stone houses of the Durbars were a physical reminder of the dominance they no longer enjoyed.

I returned to Pocha Punja's house. As we said goodbye, his father had some final thoughts: "My son's death was a great loss, but it was not in vain. It has given us awareness. We know we're not lower human beings, and we don't have to bow to the Durbars like gods."

Macwan's strong statement on the subject of toilets is evidence of the sincerity of actors in social movements in taking their lead from the people and respecting their wishes. The incident also indicates why toilets are such a problem in India. My next visit was to a man who knows the subject best, so much so he has been called Mr Toilet and the Guru of Latrines.

18 ❀ Temples and Toilets

Ishwarbhai Patel, who has dedicated his life to toilets, once wrote of the first hint of his avocation:

> When I was ten years old I entered a school cleanliness competition and took a broom from my father's house and began to sweep the street. Near the temple I spotted a much better broom and basket and decided to use them. Immediately, the local people started yelling at me. They complained it was an untouchables' broom and a caste person should not be doing a cleaning job. I realized then something was wrong with our society.

When Gandhi returned from South Africa in 1915, he established an ashram beside the Sabarmati River on the outskirts of Ahmedabad. The Sabarmati Ashram is now a cult museum. Next to it, and bustling with life, is Ishwarbhai Patel's *Safai Vidyalaya* (Sanitation Institute). Ishwarbhai—in his middle fifties, stocky, about five feet four—talks like a machine gun, spewing statistics on how many latrines he has built, how many students he has taught, and everything else concerning sanitation. All the while he smiles and laughs; for him toilets are a serious, but not somber, subject.

"Look at Harappa; you see bathrooms but no toilets," he said as we sat in his office. He referred to the extensive Harappan culture, dating to about 2500 B.C., in what is now Pakistan. Excavations show Harappan cities had paved streets, lined water channels, and waterproofed areas that appear to have been used for bathing.

"In the *Manusmriti* [the codes of Manu, from about 200 B.C.] you find exact rules for relieving yourself: one hundred yards from the village site; not on cultivated land; not seeing a cow or a temple; sitting and not standing. So, you see, the toilet was not developed in houses: sanitation was not something the community took care of."

"Everybody Is a Sweeper"

A twice-born will not dispose of his own excrement, let alone that of someone else. In his youth Ishwarbhai Patel became a disciple of one of Gandhi's ardent followers, Appa Patawardha, whose slogan was: "Everybody is a sweeper" and who went from village to village encouraging people to improve sanitary conditions. At that time sweepers collected excrement in woven wicker baskets that they carried on their heads. In some municipalities there were public latrines that also had to be cleaned. Ishwarbhai remembers an example set by Patawardha:

> The public latrines were the nearest thing to hell on earth. Appa went to a filthy latrine and picked up a basket with broken handles and put it on his head. It's disgusting: the night soil drips on their faces and soils their hands. Appa pointed to another latrine where pigs were eating the night soil and shouted: "We're treating scavengers like pigs."

Ishwarbhai has followed his guru's example, traveling through India to exhort people to better sanitation practices. In 1963 the *Harijan Sevak Sangh* (Children of God Service Society), an organization established by Gandhi to improve the life of untouchables, financed Ishwarbhai to establish his institute next to the Sabarmati Ashram.

A visitor to his office passes through a display of scores of white porcelain water-seal toilets. Instead of sit-down toilets, Indians use a squat-down design, with a ridged area at the sides where you put your feet. From a Western point of view this has the advantage of avoiding infection from contact with a toilet seat. However, health is not the reason: the squat toilet is derived from the custom of defecating in the fields. Since Indians do not use toilet paper, it is also more convenient to squat while cleaning oneself. Indians wash themselves with their left hands. (For which reason, the left hand is considered polluting. Indians, who also do not use knives and forks, eat with their right hands and give or receive something only with their right hands.)

"We worship our rivers," Ishwarbhai said, "but they're all polluted. Out of the 8,949 towns and cities, only 250 have a partial sewage system. In urban areas only 27.4 percent of homes have sanitary latrines: in rural areas only 1 percent. The problem is that local bodies don't have the money to build proper sanitation, and there's a shortage of water and of power for pumps. Besides, people don't want a latrine in their houses."

Nevertheless, Ishwarbhai said he had installed 186,000 latrines throughout Gujarat. His institute, funded by UNICEF, WHO, and the state and central governments, trains policy makers, engineers, sanitary inspectors, and masons from all parts of India. It holds training camps in other states and has sent teachers to Nepal and some countries in Africa. The walls and corridors are decorated with brightly colored posters of toilet bowls and latrines designed and produced by the institute.

"I'm doing so much," Ishwarbhai said, "a government official said, 'Why don't we clone you.' The engineers and others we've trained are taking my message from village to village and town to town. They're doing something more important than constructing latrines: they're making people aware of proper health measures. Demonstration, motivation, and orientation, that's what we teach."

A Tour with the Blessings of the Gods

Later I joined Ishwarbhai for a bus tour with a group of government employees in training from Madhya Pradesh. There was a large plastic head of Siva on a shelf in front of the driver and, pasted to the front window, a lithograph of Laxmi, the goddess of good fortune: a comforting sight in view of the carelessness of most drivers. As we stopped to visit one of Ahmedabad's tourist sights, the modern, marble Jain temple of Hutheesing, Ishwarbhai explained the halt: "Toilets, toilets, toilets: too many toilets. The students want to see something else."

The next stop was at a temple of Hanuman, the monkey god. All the trainees held their hands together and bowed their heads in brief, silent prayers. One bought a coconut, which a priest cracked as *prasad* (gift) for the god. The milk spilled out and the priest returned the coconut to the donor. Another bought a packet of white candy, which the priest opened, keeping a few bits for the god and returning the rest. The prasad was sanctified, and when we returned to the bus, bits of coconut and candy were distributed so we all could share the blessings.

"Temples and toilets," Ishwarbhai said, grinning broadly, as we started off. We were soon in the country. A large, gray langur monkey, with a black face and tail high in the air, scampered across a two-lane asphalt road. Later, shepherds with blue or red turbans tied loosely on their heads, the two ends hanging over their ears, and wearing indigo or red T-shirts and white dhotis, shooed flocks of sheep from the road so we could pass. We stopped at a village twenty-five kilometers north of Ahmedabad, with open drains, excrement in the alleys, and a large dead rat by the side of a path.

"I once made a seven-day camp here for college students to motivate people to use toilets," Ishwarbhai said. He showed us latrines next to houses. There seldom is piped water in a village, making flush toilets impossible. The proper method for the user is to bring a small pot of water with him, wet the surface of the bowl, relieve and wash himself, and pour the remaining water into the bowl to flush it. There is usually another source of water close by for washing hands.

If the waste does not wash away, no one will clean up after himself, and soon the toilet will stink. Those that Ishwarbhai showed us in this village, being next to a house and for private use, were clean. However, that was not the point of the demonstration. He was showing these to the trainees as examples of latrines with only one underground tank for holding the waste. He called this "single system." He would later show us an improved double pit system.

Wood or cow dung for cooking is expensive. We walked to another part of the village where Ishwarbhai showed a system—managed by a cooperative organized by the village *panchayat* (council)—for making methane, or biogas, from dung. Since we were relatively close to Ahmedabad, the villagers kept buffalos for milk to be sold in the city. The cooperative bought their dung to be fermented in a large tank. Twice a day, morning and night, methane gas was piped to twenty-two families at a cost of nine rupees (sixty-three cents) a month per adult: children were free. In addition, slurry from the tank was sold as fertilizer.

Ishwarbhai said everyone was happy: the buffalo owners sold their dung, families got cheap fuel for cooking, and the village cooperative earned 2,500 rupees ($175) a year from the sale of the gas and slurry. Since it was working so well, I asked Ishwarbhai if toilets could not be connected to the system to increase the methane output. He said that was tried once, but three families immediately had themselves disconnected from the system: apparently, even methane gas from human waste was polluting.

A School Without Caste

Our next stop was a Gandhian basic school named after Mahatma Gandhi's wife, Kasturba, with six hundred students, including 150 girls, in classes up to the twelfth standard. Surrounding it were 189 acres planted in wheat, potatoes, castor oil, mustard, dill, and mangoes. Students paid no fees and, instead, worked in the fields and fed themselves from the produce. In addition, the school met all its expenses from the sale of harvests in the local markets.

"Most students are accepted because they're from the lower castes and are needy," Ishwarbhai said. "There are no sweepers or servants here. Everyone is self-supporting." He said the school was started in 1958, and he installed the first toilet in 1960. But he was most proud of an ingenious system where water from a bathing area drained into the underground tanks used to ferment dung from the school's dairy, with the methane piped to the kitchen.

Although I had already guessed that since this was a Gandhian school the usual prejudices would not apply, I asked if night soil was mixed with the dung. Ishwarbhai said it was sometimes used, but it was stronger than dung, and the operator had to be careful to maintain the proper balance of fuel and water.

Our next stop was the new state capital at Gandhinagar, with ugly, barracks-style houses and office blocks and wide, empty avenues and streets. After a guided tour of the modern, circular legislative chamber, Iswarbhai took us to what would be a rival attraction: a huge temple of the Swaminaryan sect, the richest and most powerful Hindu group in Gujarat. Still under construction, it was more like a cathedral than a Hindu temple; with a high, spacious central hall lit by natural light through stone windows carved in intricate patterns of trees and leaves. Instead of saints at the entrance and portico, there were the voluptuous bare-breasted devis of Hindu iconography.

Wasting Cow Dung for Fuel

After lunch we drove to another village to inspect a methane system. "A family can install a biogas tank and save a thousand rupees a year in fuel costs," Ishwarbhai said. "In five years they can recover the cost of the system and get good manure for their fields at the same time. Look at this, what a waste!" He picked up a cake of dried cow dung, used as fuel:

"One cake is worth one rupee. Gandhiji said to burn a cow dung cake is like burning a one rupee note. In India 9.6 million tons of cow dung are burned every year. If used properly in biogas tanks, we could recover one percent of the national income. We have installed 40,000 biogas tanks. Just in this village we installed one tank, and others saw it, and now there are thirty-five tanks."

Next, he picked up a piece of black, sun-dried slurry from the side of the tank. "People said, 'It's too smelly, we can't use that thing.' But there's no smell, try it." He held it to his nose and passed it around. Some of his students looked at it but refused to touch it. Others took it, sniffed, and agreed there was nothing objectionable.

We went on to another Gandhian school where Ishwarbhai had been a hostel superintendent in the 1950s. He said that education extended from the primary level through college and that graduates were in demand as agricultural development and extension officers. Others were teachers, and some had become school principals. Since almost all the institutions Gandhi founded have decayed, basic schools like these are among the few of his remaining living testaments.

"This is a school for untouchables, shepherds, and weavers," Ishwarbhai said. "That's our work. Nowadays, parents from the higher castes want to send their children here for education because their children are not used to working. The lower castes had the skills but never had a chance. Here they do: hands and hearts are combined in a willingness to do hard labor. Everybody works in the fields, even the principal and teachers. Every day there's one-and-a-half hours of labor on the farm.

"There were only two trees when we started. We launched a campaign to grow trees and create an ecological balance. Every person must plant one tree a year, and later he can come back to the school and point, 'Look I planted this tree.' We've nearly 8,000 trees."

We went on to a large village with a major project to install six hundred latrines with attached rooms for bathing. Ishwarbhai said three hundred were completed:

"We have trained masons and have established a storehouse with all the fittings: the trap, pipe, and underground tank. If a family applies for a latrine, the whole unit costs 2,050 rupees ($144), of which the beneficiary will get a subsidy of 1,700 rupees, so the owner only has to pay 350 rupees (about $25)."

Unlike the earlier latrines, these had two tanks buried off to one side. Ishwarbhai said one would last seven years, after which the other would be used for another seven years. Then the first tank could be emptied and used again, with its now-dried and decomposed contents used as manure.

"Will they do that?" I asked.

"We hope so," he replied.

The latrine and outhouse were located at the front entrance to the house. I asked why they were not put somewhere in the back.

"Community latrines never work in India: people don't keep them clean," he replied. "So there was a suggestion, 'Why not put the latrine in the house?' The World Bank came forward with 600 million rupees ($42 million) to construct 30,000 units, half of them in Gujarat."

An old woman sitting by the path said something. When I asked, Ishwarbhai said she had made her application and wanted to know when she would get her latrine.

"You see," he said, "education and motivation works. Now a woman gets privacy. Going to the fields, there was no privacy except at night, so she has to prevent the natural call, and she had constipation and headache and everything." He demonstrated, holding his hand to his stomach and head and grimacing—and then grinned at his playfulness.

"There was a lame man," he continued. "He said, 'In the rainy season I had to go out in the mud. That was difficult with one leg, but now I can go here.'" Ishwarbhai was in his element. When we came to a man constructing an extension on his house, with no toilet in front, Ishwarbhai spoke to him and translated his reply:

"He says he is planning to add a toilet. He's a rich man and should set an example." Another man passed carrying a *lota* (small brass pot used to carry water when using empty ground as a toilet). Ishwarbhai chastened him, and the man said he could not afford his share of the cost of the installation.

Classes Under the Flamboyant Trees

It was almost dusk when we reached the last place on our schedule, a girls' school where the faculty was patiently waiting for us at an outdoor reception area. While tea was served, the principal explained admission was restricted to girls from families so poor they could not afford fees for any other school. She said a benefit music and theatrical performance was staged once a year in Bombay and that a year earlier half a million rupees ($35,000) was raised.

For me the school itself, not the biogas system Ishwarbhai showed us, was the most interesting part of the school. Classes were held outdoors in separate enclosures of clean sand surrounded by low walls and with overhead trellises of flowering purple, pink, and red vines. Students sat on the sand, facing a blackboard and a small stone platform for the teacher's desk. The principal said the girls studied indoors when it rained, but the monsoon lasted only twenty-five days.

Some of the class areas were under wide-spreading *Gul Mohr* (Flamboyant) trees, with hundreds of blossoms shading from pale orange to a deep red. It was a delightful, sylvan setting. When I asked whose idea it was, the principal replied simply: "We started under the trees, when there were no buildings, and we have remained that way."

It was dark when we returned to Ahmedabad along a wide, divided highway. Traditional India was there: the headlights picked out a temple elephant plodding by the side of the road. And so was India bruised by modernity: the body of a langur monkey, too unsophisticated to cross the highway fast enough, was tossed onto the divider.

We had driven about 150 miles, mostly in rural farming areas. Ishwarbhai said it was the government's policy to extend paved roads wherever there was a population of five hundred or more. He also said 40,000 villages had electricity, and all villages had primary schools with free midday meals. Some of the huts we saw on the tour had TV antennae sprouting from thatch roofs.

It used to be thought that the isolation of its villages was what made India "eternal" and that traditional India would melt before the hot breath of Western modernism. This is cultural arrogance. Western scholars are impatient with the popular religion of India. Like fishermen, they cast their nets for transcendental mysticism and throw back, as worthless, astrology, palmistry, charms, fatalism, idol worship, and other ritualistic practices.

But ritualism and fatalism are some of the many keys to understanding Indian society. Not a single temple in all of India, not even a small shrine at the base of a banyan tree, goes unpatronized, and everywhere more temples and shrines are being built. Every home, every office—sometimes, every desk in every office, public or private—has pictures of gods and goddesses.

A horoscope, keyed to the exact time and place of birth, is drawn for every Indian, and throughout their lives Indians will consult astrologers and palmists in the belief their future is predetermined. They also believe there is no dividing line between the seen and unseen, flocking to temples in the sure knowledge a deity will protect them if they make the proper prayers and offerings, if only a coconut or a bit of candy.

Change, in sanitation and all else, does not come easily: past and present are coterminous.

19 ☀ A Museum of Living Fossils

In 1872 the British viceroy and anthropologist Sir William Wilson Hunter compared India to an "ethnological museum in which mankind could be studied successively from the lowest to the highest cultural group."

What do you do if your country is a museum of living fossils? Do you uproot them in the name of what is perceived as progress? For example, a huge irrigation and power complex is planned for the Narmada River valley in parts of Gujarat, Maharashtra, and Madhya Pradesh. Environmentalists say the project will displace tribal families, waste scarce resources, and damage the environment. But millions of people in Gujarat insist they cannot survive without the Narmada water.

Thus the choice is not between absolute good and absolute evil: either way somebody or something will suffer.

Another example, on a much smaller scale, is a choice between a nearly extinct species of Asian lions and a caste of cattle herders who, by modern standards, should have been equally extinct generations ago.

Compared to the African species, Asian lions have a slightly different skull, bigger tail tassels, bushier elbow tufts, and a full mane on their abdomens. They once ranged from the Narmada Valley in the east to Babylon and Iran in the west. They are pictured in Assyrian hunting scenes and atop a column dating from the Asokan Empire of 250 B.C.

The last Asian lions in the Middle East were killed in Iran before the turn of the century, and the species survived at only one place in India: the hunting preserve of the *Nawab* (the equivalent of a raja) of Junagadh. In 1900, when there were fewer than one hundred Asian lions left on earth, the Nawab was persuaded to ban further destruction.

The home of the lion is now the 259 square kilometer Sasan Gir national park. I wanted to see them and sought the help of Lavkumar

Kacher, the director of the Ahmedabad Zoo and also a local officer of
the World Wildlife Fund. He arranged for me to meet his son, Captain
Nuprendra Singh, who was helping to supervise a holiday camp for several hundred city schoolchildren at the park.

Nuprendra Singh (no one called him captain) wore civilian clothes
but was still the epitome of an Indian Army officer: trim, alert, maintaining direct eye contact, and speaking in crisp, assured sentences.
When we went to the park office to arrange for a tour, Nuprendra Singh
was told no transportation was available, and, even if there were, it was
unlikely the lions could be seen from the road.

"This is a tourist attraction, but they're not interested in visitors,"
he said as we left. Like many Indian military men, he also had a poor
opinion of civilians. We strolled into the edge of the park and sat by the
bank of a stream where the children had their camp. All but a few were
away on nature study walks in the forest. At that time Gujarat was
suffering from four successive years of drought. I asked him about the
survival of the lions:

"They're doing well. The latest estimate is about 260 lions. There's
plenty of deer and other game for them to feed on, but their environment is being destroyed. A cyclone in 1983 destroyed many trees. Then
there was a long strike of forest guards, and thousands of people went in
to steal trees. A tree can be sold for three or four thousand rupees
($210–$280): a small fortune to people around here. But the worst thing
is the drought: cattle are dying for lack of water and feed. For religious
reasons people won't kill cows. Instead, thousands of cattle have been
driven into the forest. Their owners know the animals will die, but at
least they won't see it happen. The cattle are eating the low vegetation
and trampling everything into the ground. They're just more food for
the lions and other animals and birds that live on carcasses, like vultures, hyenas, and wild marsh crocodiles. But if the forest cover is
stripped away, no animals will survive.

"The Gir lion isn't like those in Africa that live on open savannah.
It's a shy animal: used to hiding in the trees and underbrush and won't
attack a human unless someone accidentally brushes against one. Sometimes a poacher might kill one, but that's rare. The skin is hard to sell,
but the claws bring good money: there are eighteen, eight in the rear
and ten in front. People wear them as charms. A single claw can sell for
as much as a thousand rupees, but there's a lot of risk. If a few Gir lions
get killed, there would be international pressure, and the forest officials
would come down hard. Poachers don't want to lose their poaching

rights, so to speak: they go for less important animals like *chitals* [spotted deer]. There are about ten thousand chitals in the sanctuary. We know you can get a meal of venison in restaurants in Bombay. Where does the meat come from? I'm no authority, but I'm told it goes from here to the coast and then is hidden on the trucks that carry fish to Bombay."

He suggested we stretch our legs with a walk to another camp for the children. We passed four women carrying bundles of branches and twigs on their heads.

"The staff is too small for the size of the sanctuary," he said. "A lot of illegal logging is being done, and people come from everywhere to get headloads of wood. They even take an axe and climb the trees to cut down green branches. In the few years I've been here I've seen the trees and undergrowth disappearing. When you ask a man why he's cutting the trees, he says to feed his buffalo. And then he says, 'What business is it of yours? It's *sarkar's* [the ruler or government] tree, not yours.' People have no sense of public pride or public ownership. It's everyone for himself. No one cares about the nation."

As we passed the cooking tents at the other camp, Nuprendra Singh pointed to a man carrying a large polished steel container for milk. He was small, with a wrinkled face, bad teeth, a thin handlebar mustache, and a stubble of beard, and was dressed in a dirty white shirt and trousers with a white, woven cloth hat pulled down to his ears.

The Maldaris

"There's one of the people who do a lot of damage to the forest," Nuprendra Singh said. "He's a *Maldari*. They're wandering cattle herders and know nothing of agriculture: if you gave them land, they wouldn't know what to do with it.

"Once Maldari families were allowed to live in the sanctuary. They're vegetarians and never poached for meat and were never destructive of trees: they built their cooking fires from dead branches. But they kept too many cows and buffalo and were ordered out of the forest in 1973. They were given some land but never used it. Maybe the officials cheated them; maybe the land was too rocky or there was no water. In any case, they never settled down as farmers."

Nuprendra Singh questioned the man and translated what he said: "His name is Samat. He says he wasn't one of the Maldaris who lived in the forest, but he did have permission to graze animals there. He has lost this permission, and now with the drought he says he's lost twelve buffalo out of thirty-five because of lack of fodder."

Buffaloes are kept for their milk, which has a high fat content and is favored for tea. I wanted to see his village, which was not far away. He went ahead and we followed, walking along the high bank of the stream.

"Everyone is in a bad way," Nuprendra Singh said. "There's a farmer near here who said to me, 'Let me work for you for a month. I don't want money, just give me food.'"

Below, near the river, vultures were tearing at a buffalo corpse. When we stopped to watch, Nuprendra Singh, the son of a naturalist family, pointed to the different birds feeding in the water: stork, cormorant, white ibis, black ibis with a red head, cattle egret, black winged stilt, and lapwing. Barely discernible among the white rocks were the skeletons of other dead cattle.

A buffalo was lying at the entrance to Samat's village, with its legs folded under and its head resting on the ground: its large eyes glazed. It was dying from hunger. Another buffalo lay in a pen next to Samat's mud and bamboo hut. It could still hold its head up, but it too was dying.

We sat on the customary string cot in a covered area outside a mud and bamboo hut and were served small cups of tea. Samat said there were eighteen people in his family, including seven brothers and a small, wizened grandfather, whom I could see sitting in the distance wrapped in a thin blanket like a mummy, never moving. Samat produced a plastic-wrapped bundle of yellowed records and gave them to Nuprendra Singh to read. They showed the family once had permission to graze seven cattle in the forest.

"We've always preserved the forest," Samat said. "We always had a close life with the animals and the trees. Now we're kept out. If we go there, the forest officers catch us and tie us to a tree and beat us. Nobody wants us. Where do we belong? If we belong to Pakistan, give us money and let us go there." He showed us empty houses, saying six out of ten families had left with their animals in search of food. He said he might go too.

"It's a distressing story," Nuprendra Singh commented, and we left.

"But think of the implications of what he told us," I said. "Those papers showed he had only seven animals in 1973. His herd grew to thirty-five before the drought started killing them off. And he said there were seven brothers in his family: eighteen people in all. With the increasing pressure of people and animals, something has to change."

As it turned out, my observations were fed back to me when Nuprendra Singh took me to meet Jamal Khan, a young scientist from the National Forest Institute who was studying the effects of the drought on the park.

"What's the use of cattle that are barely productive?" he said. "The problem is the survival of the Gir lions. The Maldaris tell a hard luck story, but they're responsible for destroying the grasses and other undergrowth. When they had permission to live inside the forest, they abused it by keeping too many animals. And those who were allowed to bring in animals from the outside cheated by taking money and bringing in animals that didn't belong to them."

The Siddis: Waifs of Africa

That night, as I was standing in line with a metal plate to receive dinner at the children's camp, I noticed a young man who was spooning out rice and curried vegetables: he looked like an African. When I remarked on this, Nuprendra Singh said he was a *Siddi*.

One of the women organizers, a college teacher from Ahmedabad, said the Siddis were brought from Africa to serve as special troops or bodyguards for Muslim rulers or princes. She said they were Muslims and spoke perfect Gujarati but retained African-style dances.

Nuprendra Singh said the Nawabs used Siddis as keepers for their large dog kennels and that others lived inside their hunting preserve as guards. After Junagadh was absorbed into Gujarat, the Siddis lost their jobs and settled in the villages surrounding the sanctuary.

"Some now work as rickshaw men or have small jobs as servants," he said. "But most are totally dependent on the forest and do a great deal of damage: they poach animals to eat and cut wood for sale."

We visited them in their dilapidated shacks in an isolated part of Sasan village, near the main entrance to the park. The men and women were dressed in rags: their children were emaciated and dirty. They offered tea, but I quickly said we just had some: I couldn't bear taking anything from people in such wretched conditions. The college teacher was with us. She talked with the women, who said they were often hungry. Their men were away most of the time but still could not earn enough for them to live.

Nuprendra Singh said Jamal Khan had a copy of the local district gazetteer in his makeshift office and we went there and read it. The description of Siddis was pure racism:

Before independence the Siddis used to harass and plunder local people stealthily and reap their harvests at night. After independence most of them left their predatory activities for peaceful avocations. . . . Local people maintain that if a Siddi has enough money for a meal he will not bother to earn more than providing for the next day and idle away that day. So primitive are their habits if they have nothing else to eat all the members of the family will climb a tree and satisfy their hunger with berries and nuts. After drinking water from the river they will retire to their huts for a quiet siesta. Whenever any animal disappears people do not hesitate to believe that it might have been caught and slaughtered by a Siddi.

A Journey Through Desolation

I left the next morning for sightseeing. The temple of Somnath, less than two hours away by bus, is famous in Indian history for its sack by the Muslim invader Mahmud of Ghazni in the year 1025 and the immense store of gold and jewels that he carried back to his kingdom in what is now Afghanistan. I took another bus west to the temple of Dwarka: once a great sea emporium known as the Mother City of the West and the legendary final home of the god Krishna.

The view along the coast unfolded mile after mile of desolation. For years farmers pumped so much water from the ground that salt water had infiltrated into the land, poisoning the ground. Rain water might have washed out the soil, but the monsoons failed, and pale brown fields plowed years ago were deserted.

I then returned east, traveling by train halfway across the state, through long stretches of deserted farms with thick dust on the stone boundaries between fields: even the cactus drooped from lack of water. There were wells and pump houses but no people: sun glinting from brass water pots carried on the heads of women was only a memory.

My destination was Jasdan, once the capital of a pocket-sized Rajput state of the same name, where the former raja is the head of the World Wildlife Fund in Gujarat. I met him in his office above the old city wall, with a window looking out on a clock tower where four peacocks perched themselves for a view of the crowd in the market below.

"If you look around, you'll see the hedges are cut down and the bushes all gone," the raja said. He was a small man, with a round face, receding hairline, small mustache, and light brown skin. He fondled a small, sleek dachshund, which he said was a prize animal. "Everyone is cutting down trees and hoarding the wood for fuel. We're losing the lovely avenues of trees we used to have along our roads. Even on trees with a religious significance, like the Banyan, you'll find the leaves gone and the branches lopped off.

"We have too many people, too many animals, and too much agriculture and are running out of groundwater. Where there were a hundred wells, there are now a thousand. Where formerly the use of water was limited because farmers used animals to draw water slowly from the wells, now they use pumps. It's much easier to start an engine and water your crops. You can increase the planted area too. To recover from all this will take many years of concentrated rain and a great deal of human labor to dig small ponds to hold the water so it will sink into the ground."

I said I had been in large cities where people had piped water in their homes for only an hour a day and seen villages where a motor was turned on to pump water for only an hour in the morning and an hour at night. I said in other countries such a lack of water would touch off riots.

"That's their nature," he said. "They're used to obeying authority. Before this government were the British and before them the Muslims and before them the rajas. They were all strong rulers, so there's a long history of being patient in the face of power. But there are limits. People are not going to put up with everything.

"That's why we need the Narmada Project. The talk of ecological damage is true: it will submerge large areas of forest. But without the Narmada Project Gujarat will be permanently drought-stricken. Our population has increased; there's absolutely no other way out. We have to learn from past errors to make sure the water is used judiciously. To prevent waterlogging, the irrigation canals will have to be lined, and we'll have to dig drainage channels to remove the saturated water. We know the government's record in building and operating large dams and canal networks isn't very good, but all problems can be solved. We must also take care of the displaced tribal people. They had their own culture and art: a special way of life. It's very sad to lose this, but with the increase in population it's not possible to hold onto the past."

I returned to Ahmedabad for a final talk with Lavkumar at the zoo. I mentioned the difficulties of the Maldaris.

"You can't have a few nomads amid a settled population," he said. "There were Maldaris all over Saurashtra, but they've been wiped out:

only this pocket is left. If it were only a matter of a few hundred lions, we could put them in a safari park. The question is: can the environment sustain more and more free-ranging cattle? For his own sake the Maldari must not move around as in the past.

"As for the Narmada Project, people are concerned about the tribals, and I agree with them. If tribal land is being submerged, we have to fight for social justice. But the people who are fighting the dams really seem to be worried about other things. They don't like a big government, so they're against all big projects, and they use the tribals to attract sympathy. They're city people. They're against the project, but they want the electricity that will come from it to light their homes and power their air conditioners."

So it comes down to a choice between two necessary evils and also a question of which side has the most power. For social activists the answer cannot be simply what is right or wrong but, pragmatically, what is best for those without power.

20 ❂ Temples or Tombs?

Jawaharlal Nehru once described the dams and irrigation works constructed after independence as "the new temples and places of pilgrimages."

Indian environmentalists say tombs would be a more appropriate simile: burial places for the homes, farms, and forests of an estimated million tribals and Dalits throughout India displaced by the colonialists of an expanding middle class eager for the profits of irrigation-fed commercial agriculture and for urban comforts made possible by hydro-electric power.

The Narmada Project, India's biggest river basin plan, is the most controversial of all. Supporters say it will transform central India; detractors call it the world's greatest planned ecological disaster.

The Narmada River originates in a holy tank amid a cluster of temples on the Amarkantak plateau in Shahdol District in Madhya Pradesh and meanders for 800 miles, draining 24.5 million acres between the Vindhya and Satpura ranges, before emptying into the Arabian Sea west of Broach in Gujarat.

When Nehru laid the foundation stone in 1961, plans envisioned the construction of thirty major dams, 135 medium dams, and over 3,000 minor dams on the Narmada and its tributaries in Gujarat, Madhya Pradesh, and Maharashtra.

The two biggest dams, the Sardar Sarovar in Gujarat and Narmada Sagar in Madhya Pradesh, would irrigate almost 4 million acres and generate around 2,500 megawatts of power. The Narmada Sagar reservoir would be the world's largest artificial lake, submerging almost 100,000 acres of forest and another 110,000 acres of cultivable land. The Sardar Sarovar in Gujarat would submerge another 100,000 acres. Together, the dams would displace 200,000 people in 500 villages.

Rising Prices and Second Thoughts

However, it is doubtful that all but a small part of the sky's-the-limit philosophies of the 1960s will be carried out. Costs have soared out of reach. In the 1970s the price tag for the entire project was 40 billion rupees ($2.8 billion). Now Sardar Sarovar alone will cost 130 billion rupees ($9.1 billion).

Moreover, Madhya Pradesh is reluctant to go ahead with its Narmada Sagar and associated smaller dams, saying they will generate power the state does not need, destroy forests, and provide little irrigation for its own farmers, with most of the benefits going to farmers and electricity consumers in Gujarat.

Environmentalists say the whole project should be junked. In addition to objections to the displacement of thousands of tribals and the destruction of some of the few large stands of timber remaining in India, they raise purely technical objections. They say without the dam at Narmada Sagar as a backup, Sardar Sarovar in Gujarat will not have a regulated supply of water. They also say the Narmada, unlike the snow-fed rivers that fill the dams in the Himalayan foothills, depends entirely on rainfall, and since the Indian monsoon is notoriously fickle, water storage in the Narmada dams may fall so low farmers who plant crops in the expectation of irrigation will be wiped out.

They say canal irrigated lands have become a curse for many farmers with 17.3 million acres already lost to production through waterlogging and salinization. Instead, they say, the government should concentrate on small catchment dams, which will replenish groundwater supplies without displacing anyone or destroying trees and which can be locally maintained at low cost.

Others advance purely economic arguments. They see the Narmada Project as a developmental monster, consuming resources better used for schools, housing, and health projects of direct benefit to the poor.

There is reason on the other side: the most cogent is to ensure there is enough to eat. Even in India, where output lags far behind the bounty of the irrigated lands of the American west, canal-fed lands produce an average of about 1,500 pounds of food grains per acre—almost twice the output from rain-fed lands. It seems axiomatic the only way India can hope to feed its rapidly expanding population is by building more dams and canals.

As for waterlogging and salinization, the amount of production lost is only a small percentage of the production gained by canal irrigation. In fact, in many areas seepage is beneficial. While water tables have sunk by as much as seventy-five feet in a single decade, water seepage from canals is an effective way to replenish groundwater in regions of light rainfall. In many parts of the south farmers not connected to feeder canals have water in their tube wells while those in more distant areas are dry.

By this reasoning, instead of damning dams, a reasonable response would be to spend the extra money to line canals in those areas where there is a heavy rainfall and an underlayer that does not allow for drainage.

Narmada As a Symptom

Much of what passes for debate concerning the Narmada Project is actually a symptom of a larger feeling that all development is oppressive. As India has gone from one five-year plan to another, the ecological and human disruptions have become more apparent, not only in big things like the dams that displace people and the factories that pollute the rivers and air, but also in the little things that make only local headlines —for instance, the damage to India's ancient, artisanal fishermen.

On the east coast thousands of fishermen were evicted from the beaches of Orissa to provide housing sites for students at the new Sanskrit University near the ancient temples of Konarak and Jaggannatha.

In Tamil Nadu in 1985 "Operation Beautification" cleared the Madras marina of a thousand fishermen and their *catamarums* (two flattened logs lashed together as a boat; the construction ensures the boat will not be swamped or overturned by heavy surf). Generations of Madras families had picnicked amid the fishermen with their nets and drying fish until the equivalent of Indian Yuppies decided they were an eyesore and moved them farther down the coast.

On the west coast high-rise tourist hotels have displaced fishermen from the beaches of Goa and the major trickle-down effect for the unemployed is tourist-generated drugs, sex shows, and cultural degeneration.

Above all, there were the tens of thousands of Kerala fishermen displaced by mechanized boats that began to overfish the coastal seas after Norwegian foreign aid introduced the technology of trawlers, deep nets, and refrigeration plants. Land-based merchants and moneylenders quickly saw the profits that could be harvested from prawns for overseas markets, so they bought the boats and established the infrastructure, and the fishermen were left to starve.

Is it possible to keep saying no to economic change? What about the Gujarati farmers and townsmen who have seen their crops die and have witnessed street fights for drinking water?

In Gujarat, where support is virtually unanimous, officials describe the Narmada Project as a lifeline that will irrigate 4.5 million acres and provide water to 131 towns and 4,720 villages in twelve of the state's nineteen districts. Come what may, Gujaratis will not be denied the Narmada water.

A characteristic of the social movement actors is that they are not windmill tilters. They are ready to compromise for immediately realizable gains in the expectation this will help enrich and unify their community, and if all goes well, help its men and women to achieve greater empowerment. Two such pragmatists are Dr Anil Patel and his wife Daxa.

21 ✺ Pragmatic Activists

Sardar Sarovar is only twenty kilo-
meters upstream from Mongrol in Southern Gujarat, where the Patels
have their home and clinic. Anil earned his medical degree in 1967 and
married Daxa in 1972. They then went to England where Anil entered
the Royal College of Physicians while Daxa worked as a doctor to support them and pay for Anil's schooling. Their plans were for Anil, after
graduation, to work while Daxa also got a higher degree, but then she
became pregnant and they returned to India.

Anil was determined to put his knowledge to social use, and so,
instead of settling in Ahmedabad or Baroda, they went to a remote area
with no other doctors and established a clinic and research organization they called Arch—from Tennyson's "Ulysses":

Yet all experience is an arch wherethro'
Gleams that untravell'd world whose margin fades
For ever and for ever when I move.

To reach Mongrol I had to take a train from Ahmedabad to Baroda,
a bus south to the former princely state of Rajpipla, and change to a
worn and rattling bus for the final twenty kilometers. It's a peaceful
village on the left bank of the Narmada, with low, brown, thatched-
roofed, mud-and-wattle houses that blend with the earth and the wide
muddy waters of the river. It's built on a slight hill with a curving dirt
path as the main street, so there are no harsh straight lines—and also
no cars: the road for the bus is out of sight down the hill.

When I remarked on his choice of a place to practice, Anil conceded his renunciation of the comforts that normally go with one of the
world's most esteemed medical degrees was unusual:

"To strike out on your own is not an Indian trait. It's not an important question in the West: if you want to do something, you're an individual and can do what you please. But individuality is not a normal part of Indian society. Here, if you refer to society as a whole, and not your own caste and family, that poses a difficulty: you must have special reasons for this.

"But no one can deny social responsibility. When I grew up in the 1950s, Gandhi's influence was pretty strong: we learned in school about the mass movements where people threw away their careers and education and joined the freedom struggle. It's true, some people cashed in on the freedom movement and some went in for political power, but the euphoria was there. Today, people wonder who you are if you say you feel for all of society."

Eviction Horror Stories

In 1980, a year after he arrived at Mongrol, Anil became aware of the threat of the Narmada Project to destroy tribal villages with virtually no rehabilitation. One group of families was evicted from five villages with compensation of only sixty rupees ($4.20) an acre for their land. Anil's early attempts to gain justice for the tribals attracted the attention of others, and his home became headquarters for what developed into an eight-year struggle.

Horror stories abound. One group of families, uprooted in the early 1970s to make way for a dike, were given forty-two plots of land. Later, it was discovered the rehabilitation office had not investigated title deeds: fifteen of the plots were encumbered by debt that should have been deducted from the price paid to the previous owner but, accidentally or through connivance, the debt was passed on to the poor tribals.

Still later, the tribals were informed a major feeder canal would run through the new settlement: one side of the administration did not know what another side was doing. When the fifteen tribal families applied for new compensation, it was denied them because their lands were encumbered by debt.

Anil agreed with the many objections to the Narmada Project raised by environmentalists:

"We've never been allowed to see detailed maps of where the canals and roads will be: we've seen only large-scale maps that show the command area of about 8 million acres to be covered by water. It's a huge project. It may bankrupt the Gujarat government, which will have to pay a major share of the costs. And one wonders whether the benefits they talk about are there.

"I, for one, also don't believe government claims they'll be able to grow forests in the catchment area to minimize erosion and siltation of the dams. Others criticize the plans for compensatory forests to replace the trees submerged by the huge reservoirs: they say reforestation is not the same thing as a natural forest of mixed wood.

"There may also be hidden ecological threats: you can't take a lot of water from one place and transfer it somewhere else without a major change in the environment. It's impossible to foresee the consequences. It would be better to build many small dams, and many small water channels.

"Some even suspect the basic plan is not water for Saurashtra, as they claim, but for electrical power. If they didn't want so much electricity, they could reduce the height of the Sardar Sarovar dam by thirty-five feet. That would reduce the area of submergence by 65 percent but would reduce the irrigation potential by only 15 or 20 percent."

A Victory for the Tribals

And yet Anil and his coworkers have devoted themselves not to opposing the dam, per se, but to trying to obtain the best possible rehabilitation for those who will be displaced. They fought for a goal they capitalized as Rehabilitation and Resettlement—and they won.

About a month before I visited Mongrol, the government of Gujarat signed an agreement under which every male eighteen years of age or older, including landowners, sharecroppers, and those who depended on grazing, will get five acres of their choice. Since little surplus land is available, the displaced persons will have to buy from private owners. If the price is higher than the official compensation, the government will make up the difference. If a man loses income during the shift from one place to another, he will get one year's income as compensation. There are other provisions for roads and wells and land for primary schools, religious buildings, and crematorial or burial places.

I asked Anil how such a small group as his could persuade the state and central governments to be considerate of the fate of poor tribals.

"We were not alone," he replied. "Others throughout India helped us: they knew events in the Narmada Valley would set a pattern for the entire country. We were also able to bring pressure on the World Bank.

Our health project is funded by several foreign groups, including Oxfam in England. Oxfam helped us a lot with lobbying with the World Bank in the rehabilitation scheme. A small group like ours could not have made viable contact on our own."

The Wicked Witch of the West

For Third World social activists the World Bank is the Wicked Witch of the West. A large percentage of its loans—perhaps as much as half—are directed to environmentally sensitive areas, such as agriculture, forestry, dams, and irrigation. In addition, the loans require borrowing governments to demonstrate commitment to projects by pledging so-called counterpart funds and making complementary investments of their own. Thus the loans divert funds from projects like rural schools and health clinics that would benefit a majority of the population.

Third World social activists also charge the World Bank uses its loans to prop up elitist oligarchies and to direct economic development toward consumerism and dependence on Western technology and capital—creating a condition of continuous dependence.

The World Bank has become increasingly sensitive to such criticism, especially charges its loans speed the destruction of those forests and water resources the poor depend on for their meager existence.

This sensitivity was demonstrated in the case of Narmada, which will be partially funded with a $450 million World Bank loan. Pressure from the Bank forced Gujarat to accede to the demands for adequate compensation. However, because Gujarat acted only under pressure, Anil and his coworkers have lingering doubts.

"Neither the government in Delhi nor the government in Gandhi-nagar took the concerns of environmentalists seriously," Anil said. "The top brass of the irrigation department and the builders and others have a vested interest in big dams. Corruption is rampant, so the bigger the project, the bigger the kickbacks. Also there's employment for the bureaucrats: filling out of forms, attending meetings, shifting papers. We know that even with a signed agreement to give the tribals full rehabilitation and resettlement, the nature of the bureaucrats and politicians has not changed. We'll have to watch them carefully every day to see they don't cheat.

"In Gujarat nineteen villages with three thousand families will be affected. We've been fully involved with them and have good rapport. But less work has been done in Madhya Pradesh, where more than two hundred tribal villages must be resettled, and in Maharashtra, where another twenty-six tribal villages are affected."

Tribals Ready for Integration

"Is the concern for tribals some sort of romanticism?" I asked.

"Up to a point," Anil replied. "They have their own music and dance and some still have bows and arrows, but their dress and appearance is the same as others. With few exceptions they've all been exposed to modern civilization, with buses going to remote areas. They listen to the radio and get all sorts of information. Except for perhaps one or two interior villages, we know the tribals are ready to leave their mountain homes for the plains—providing they get good tillable land.

"There are disadvantages, of course, but there are also the tremendous benefits of education, health care, and mobility. We've already found the desire for education is spreading: the first thing they request is schools.

"However, the tribals and scheduled castes are up against very heavy odds. The caste people are deeply entrenched in positions of privilege and power. They'll not allow these people to come up. They'll use all tactics and strategies to stall them where they are. So at the moment it looks like they'll only be able to come up to the lowest level of jobs. Higher up is very difficult."

When I set out that morning, I hadn't realized how long it would take me to reach Mongrol. I had another appointment the next day and had to rush away to catch a late bus. During our talk Anil had also talked briefly about his medical work, outlining one of the most innovative community health programs in all of India. It was not until six months later that I was free to return to Mongrol for a demonstration of how two of India's most pressing problems—rural health and population growth—are intertwined.

22 ✸ Population and Sterilization

Anil Patel was not at Mongrol when I returned: some villagers had complained that the government planned to take away their lands, and Anil had rushed to Ahmedabad to see what could be done. But Daxa Patel was there, and I asked how she felt when her husband suggested they take up rural work.

"When we returned to India, I was only sure I would work as an honest doctor," she replied. "I didn't want to make lots of money. Anil didn't press a decision on me; I realized the need for women doctors in rural areas is immense. We decided to work in community health; we didn't want to do everything by ourselves so people would become dependent on us."

Community health is part of the complexities within complexities that bedevil India. With a baby born in India every 1.2 seconds, the population is growing by 2.13 percent a year. If unchecked, that will give India a population of 1.5 billion by 2020, perhaps surpassing China as the world's most populated nation.

Indian families want two living sons to insure at least one will survive, but since a couple cannot have two sons without the probability of producing two daughters, Indians have, in effect, set a goal of at least four children. It's a form of social security: children, including girls, start adding to the family income at the age of five or six. Then adult males care for elderly parents.

In the West the rate of population growth went down as standards of living went up and democracy took hold, making people masters of their own lives. But in a grossly unequal society it is supremely difficult to duplicate this experience because politics and population are intertwined.

If an entrenched elite wants a disenfranchised majority voluntarily to limit the number of their children, it will have to follow the Western example of first improving health conditions, raising literacy rates, especially those of women, and sharing the nation's wealth more evenly. But then people would simultaneously demand a share of political power. To avoid power sharing the elite's impulse is to look for shortcuts, such as limitations of marriage and forced abortions, as in China, or by attempting to persuade or pressure the poor, especially mothers, to accept sterilization.

Daxa Patel, after working almost ten years in community health, was well aware of the nexus of politics and health:

"The mass poverty and degradation one sees in the rural areas is a direct response of exploitation by urban areas. The government disregards the needs, feelings, and perceptions of the poor: even blaming them for their poverty and underdevelopment. It's not enough to tinker with petty derivative issues: there has to be a radical social transformation. Even a modicum of improvement in the health of mothers and children will require the mobilization of skills and social forces whose size, dimensions, and nature elude those who see the problem of child and maternal health as marginal.

"There's a big advertising campaign telling people they should have only two children. But unless you give security to a family so that children not only will survive but will also be healthy, the poor will not limit themselves to two children. Conceptually the government realizes building big hospitals in the cities won't solve the country's health problems, and so it has accepted the concept of primary health centers and training health workers. But there's too much concentration on family planning, particularly sterilization. Almost all the staff, even sanitation inspectors, have to find cases for sterilization. They're hysterical about these things. All the other work, like the fight against malaria and TB, definitely suffers."

Counting Beads

When India became independent, its population was 361 million with a birthrate of forty-one per thousand and a deathrate of twenty-four. Its new leaders recognized the problem of population growth: India became the first nation in the world to accept family planning as the government's responsibility. It started by trying to teach the rhythm method to illiterate women and experimented with such things as colored beads for counting safe and unsafe days. When that failed, four thousand family planning clinics were set up to dispense condoms and intrauterine devices (IUDs), but still the population grew. Significantly the planners saw people as an impediment.

"The greatest obstacle in the path of overall economic development is the alarming rate of population growth," Family Planning Minister Sripati Chandrasekhar warned in 1967. More family planning clinics were opened and new factories churned out condoms for sale at the highly subsidized price of three for the equivalent of two American cents. For women the diaphragm proved too complex, and foam tablets and jellies were considered too unreliable. Instead, government clinics and hospitals recommended IUDs, although about 10 percent of the users suffered excessive bleeding.

For both sexes sterilization was preferred as the most effective method. Seven million vasectomies for men and tubectomies for women were performed by the end of 1970 as billboards in cities and towns displayed the smiling faces of a couple and two children with the message, "Happiness Is a Two-Child Family."

Even so, the 1971 census disclosed a population of more than 548 million. The birthrate had been reduced to thirty-five per thousand, but the deathrate had also been reduced to sixteen, and life expectancy at birth had increased from forty-five years in 1961 to fifty-one a decade later. In January 1976, seven months after assuming dictatorial powers, Prime Minister Indira Gandhi warned: "We must now act decisively and bring down the birthrate speedily to prevent the doubling of our population in a mere twenty-eight years. We shall not hesitate to take steps which might be described as drastic."

Mass Sterilization

Mrs Gandhi's younger son Sanjay (about whom his mother once said, "He isn't a thinker, he's a doer. When he wants something done, he gets it done") took family planning as his fief. He set a national target of 4.3 million sterilizations in only nine months from April 1976 through March 1977, double the number recorded in the previous twelve-month period.

The sycophancy that marks the master-client relationship of government and business in India was soon apparent: the official target was set aside and politicians competed to demonstrate loyalty. The chief minister of Uttar Pradesh raised his state's quota from 400,000 to 1.5 million; Rajasthan decreed compulsory sterilization for men with two or three children, and the states of Haryana and Punjab told employees with at least two children they would lose their government housing and be denied loans, and women workers would be denied maternity leave, if they did not get themselves sterilized.

But the number of government employees was limited: sterilization had to be inflicted on the masses. With orders to find "volunteers," and with the promise of rewards ranging up to a new automobile, police and other officials descended on villages and urban slums where they rounded up every man they could catch, including those with no teeth and barely able to walk. Almost 8 million people were sterilized in only nine months. Soon thereafter, Indira Gandhi took the risk of allowing new elections. She misjudged, or perhaps never realized, the political repercussions of forced sterilizations. Her Congress Party was swept from office. Those defeated included both Indira and Sanjay Gandhi, who was later killed while piloting a private plane.

In June 1977 the Janata Party government that succeeded Mrs Gandhi appeared to have gotten the message. It announced an integrated program to reduce the birthrate:

> It must embrace all aspects of family welfare, particularly those which are designed to protect and promote the health of mothers and children. It must become a part of the total concept of positive health. At the same time, it must find meaningful integration with other welfare programs, viz., nutrition, food, clothing, shelter, availability of safe drinking water, education, employment and women's welfare.

The Janata government, beset by internal quarrels, lasted fewer than two years. Mrs Gandhi returned to power, and the sterilization program was revived, despite overwhelming evidence that it has no demographic impact. Since 1977 the crude birthrate has stagnated at thirty-three babies born for every thousand people.

"Something Is Amiss"

A study in Uttar Pradesh of the forced sterilizations carried out during the Emergency showed almost 62 percent of vasectomies were performed on men who were widowed, separated, or never married.

Ten years later a 1987 study of vasectomies in a rural Punjab community produced the same finding. In this case the sterilizations were all voluntary, with men and women receiving a reward for agreeing to the operation. The analysis found more than 40 percent of the women acceptors were over thirty years of age, and more than half already had four or more children, with 3.72 as the mean number of children in acceptor families. It concluded:

> One has to infer that something is amiss in the implementation of the program. There are far too many sterilization operations, 51.4 percent in the study, which fail to serve the objectives of the program. [The participants] accept sterilization because they cannot bear the burden of a further increase in their families and are unable to use other methods. Indiscriminate payment of incentive money at a uniform rate to all acceptors, irrespective of the number of children, after which they opt for operations, is the prime factor that generates infructuous sterilization.

In Uttar Pradesh an eighty-year-old man and his forty-year-old son had simultaneous vasectomies, both for the second time. They said they did if for the 180 rupee ($12.60) fee the government pays to acceptors. At a clinic in Maharashtra a thirty-five-year-old woman had a tubectomy three weeks after bearing her fifth child.

Among the many social distortions of a nation ruled by Five-Year plans is that bureaucrats become target oriented. An April 1988 report of the Indian Planned Parenthood Association called it a numbers game:

> The doctor may be completely convinced about the uselessness of the requested operation from a national or even the family point of view, but he cannot withhold it. . . . The pressure for fulfilling his allotted target, and the possible loss of reward and recognition for over-shooting the target is so great he cannot afford to pay heed to biological or ethical considerations, all he is concerned with is the game of numbers.

What Daxa Patel called the "hysterical" government policy of sterilization has distorted both family planning and community health programs. A random survey of rural men, conducted by the Planning Commission in 1986, showed 70 percent thought contraception was synonymous with vasectomy. In the southern state of Tamil Nadu, where traditional birth attendants (TBAS) are trained in hygienic practices, officials also used them as motivators for sterilizing women. Sundari Ravindran, founder of the Rural Women's Social Education Center of Tamil Nadu, warned of the danger:

Because of the money incentives attached to recruiting candidates for birth control, the poorly paid TBAS are in many cases forced by economic circumstances to become active recruiters, unwilling promoters of a centrally planned population control program. Their role and how they are viewed in the community may be totally altered, undermining confidence in them generally.

Ms Ravindran found other deficiencies. The syllabus for training the birth attendants, she wrote, was designed by the urban elite with little knowledge of rural customs and beliefs; the trainers talked down to the TBAS and refused to recognize the experience of the midwives in delivering children in village homes. And caste and ritual pollution reared its head: when patients were village women, regular nurses and midwives rarely conducted a gynecological examination or inserted an IUD.

Blending sterilization with women's health programs is doubly defeating: the sterilization program is demographically meaningless, and village women are frightened away from community health services. Instead, the emphasis should be on attracting women to clinics, since there can be no effective family planning program without their full participation.

Indian males think fertility control is the function of women, believing if a man is sterilized the plants will not grow in his fields or he will lose his ability to perform at his job: they even feel using condoms diminishes their maleness. This is a huge handicap: 70 percent of Indian women aged ten years or more are illiterate, and the evidence from the West is that a decline in the birthrate is in inverse proportion to the advance in literacy.

In addition to educating women family planners must also have specific programs to attract them to community health centers, not scare them away. I asked Daxa if the government ever came to the clinic at Mongrol to learn and perhaps adopt some of the ideas.

"They want nothing to do with us," she replied. "We oppose them on Narmada, and they see us as their enemy."

And yet the Patels have a project the whole country should emulate: a community health program at the grass-roots level using local people to do most of the work.

23 ✸ A Model for Community Health

Any system of modern medicine for rural India has to be humane, effective, cheap, and self-sustaining," Daxa said. "A full-time doctor to head community health services is an impossible objective in the foreseeable future. At best some elements of primary health care can be put together with a minimum of supervision."

We were at her dispensary in a small, nondescript building a few minutes walk from her house, with a porch and benches for waiting patients, a large general room where records were kept and drugs dispensed, and an inner room for Daxa's examinations. The dispensary was administered and operated by four health workers trained on the spot.

Suresh coordinated all tests. His father was a carpenter, and he had studied only up to the fifth standard. The other three were educated to the eleventh standard. Sombhai was in charge of dispensing medicines and training part-time village health workers. He also took care of accounting and record keeping. Bachubhai was learning how to dispense medicines and also managed the TB program. If a patient failed to show up for a regular visit, Bachubhai would send a postcard reminding him or her of the appointment. Rashmi, a young woman, interviewed patients on their arrival, taking their personal and medical histories, updating previous records, and taking their blood pressure before they went to the inner room to be examined by Daxa.

Working from Dedication, Not for Wages

"Our health workers clean wounds, give penicillin injections for serious infections and vaccinations for tetanus and typhoid," Daxa said. "They handle therapeutic feeding and can examine and treat patients under our supervision. They're local people, and patients frequently consult them about social situations. I'm confident if Anil or I am not here, they can deal with 90 percent of the problems of the dispensary.

"We pay six hundred rupees ($42) a month: a good salary for a rural area, but they work hard because they're dedicated, not because of the wages. No one is here for money or position. Anil and I take only what we need.

"For the first few years our dispensary was unpopular. For one thing we don't give useless injections. In India doctors with syringes are believed to have miraculous healing powers, and people who travel long distances if only for diarrhea and scabies want injections. The drug companies have flooded the market with expensive B complex injections. They also sell expensive tonics, but we buy drugs at a subsidized price and dispense them at a low charge. They thought cheapness meant low quality."

Arch, the community health group founded by the Patels, helped develop an organization known as LOCOST, which buys essential drugs in bulk from local manufacturers, has them tested by independent laboratories to ensure high quality, and then supplies them at a low cost to community health projects working for the rural and urban poor.

"Upper caste Hindus had objections," Daxa continued. "They charged we were assigning responsibility to semiliterate persons. This reflects their deep-seated animus against the lower castes. But in the last three years our health workers have given hundreds of injections, including mass vaccination programs, and there has not been a single case of infection-induced abscesses. On the other hand we've had to incise and drain huge abscesses caused by the injections of other medical practitioners.

"The Indian tendency is to mystify everything. One of the sheet anchors of primary health care is demystification: to open medical care to the people and make it part of their daily lives. For instance, TB is one of the greatest public health problems in India: upward of 50 percent of untreated cases result in death. For more than twenty years the government has had a nationwide free diagnosis and treatment program, yet TB is as entrenched as ever. X rays are still the mainstay for examinations, while sputum examination under microscope, which is easy and provides a better quality of diagnosis, is almost totally neglected.

"The ruling medical elite and voluntary health groups have joined hands to discard this treatment without thought or consideration. The experts believed sputum microscopy would be far too complicated for village health workers to handle, but it's tailor-made for primary health care. Suresh, with education only up to the fifth standard, mastered the techniques in a few weeks. Using our locally adapted record system, our workers can easily handle a complete TB program.

"The usual treatment of TB is daily streptomycin injections over a period of eighteen months. That's very difficult under Indian conditions, but modern research has shown TB can be cured with a combination of drugs in tablet form. The drugs are expensive, but the treatment is reduced to six months. Unless TB can be handled in this way, by locally trained persons who can perform sputum analysis and can penetrate into interior villages to dispense drugs under proper supervision, the disease can't be controlled."

About a half dozen women, dressed in their best saris, were at the dispensary for monthly pregnancy checkups. Daxa disappeared into the inner room, and I returned to the house and chatted with other workers about Arch's experiments with other community work. Hunger is never distant in rural India: most children soon drop out of school to add to their family's income. In the Mongrol area their most common job is to take care of other peoples' cattle. Village parents were persuaded to send thirty-five boys and girls to a nonformal school to gain some literacy and learn some practical skills. But after three years most of the children had gone back to full-time work, and the experiment was abandoned. However, it was not a complete failure: five of the children were sent for advanced training at other centers in Gujarat and were doing well. There was another experiment to see if village women could add to their income, in Gandhian fashion, by spinning and weaving cotton, but that failed in six months and was abandoned.

The Many Ways of Community Health

Since then the Patels and their coworkers at Mongrol devoted themselves almost entirely to their two main interests: obtaining justice for the tribal families affected by the Narmada Project and running the community health program. That, in itself, is a major task: the dispensary caters to between thirty-five and forty villages and treats about six thousand patients a year. Another three thousand are treated by part-time village health workers.

Daxa returned for lunch, and we continued our talk. "There's no one way of community health," she said. "Much of the suffering of rural people results from relatively easily treated ailments: diarrhea, dysentery, boils, scabies, infected wounds, fevers like malaria, night blindness, gross anemia, chronic arthritis, and recurring acute headaches. Villagers have a strong need to get relief from these ailments, so immediate medical relief must be one part of a community health program.

"Another essential element is health education, like personal hygiene, kitchen gardening to fight Vitamin A deficiency, and child-feeding practices. We must try to change long-standing habits and beliefs, such as convincing villagers measles is caused by a virus and not by the ill will of a goddess. And there must be a drastic improvement in sanitation, water supply, housing, and the surrounding environment. To deal only with epidemics is like fighting fires and not the cause.

"To do all this village health workers are critical, and women must be involved on a much larger scale. In addition to our four full-time workers, we have six part-time workers: women living in their own villages who carry on with their normal activities and come to the dispensary once a week for training and consultation. We've made a list of minimum diseases for which they can dispense medicines. They also collect vital statistics, such as birth weights. Five or ten people may call on her at any time, morning or night. It's not necessary for a woman with anemia to come to the dispensary: a health worker can give her iron supplements and folic acid. Part-time village workers can treat about half of all ailments: skin diseases, like scabies, conjunctivitis, diarrhea, and respiratory ailments. We don't give them antibiotics to dispense, only simple medicines, and they keep an exact record of everything dispensed, like aspirins for headaches. They also keep vital statistics of newborn children and dispense supplementary food for the seriously malnourished. This helps to prevent its diversion to others in the family or outsiders. It's a slow process with a slow future, but there's no other way."

The Importance of Maternal and Child Care

"The pivot of community health has to be maternal and child health as opposed to holistic, all inclusive approaches," Daxa continued. "Thirty percent of infections occur in children below five years of age, and the effects are much more serious than for adults. The under-five population is around 10 percent and not 20 percent as should be expected. Each episode of infection, even a minor one, puts a break on the physical growth of rapidly growing children.

"Women's problems are neglected, whether it's health or anything else. A woman who is malnourished and anemic goes from pregnancy to lactation and another pregnancy and has to do all the household work too. Her status in the house is low: even when she eats, it's only what is left over by males. According to our statistics, 78 percent of our women patients weigh less than forty-five kilos [ninety-nine pounds]. Their growth is stunted, and they're lean and thin; they give birth to children with a low weight, and if these children survive, their growth will also be stunted and their productivity will be low.

"Children should weigh at least 2.5 kilos (5.5 pounds) at birth. But our statistics show 70 percent are below 2.5 kilos. Of these, 20 to 30 percent are below two kilos (4.4 lbs), meaning they'll have a low survival rate. If you want to improve birth weights and reduce infant mortality, you must focus on maternal nutrition. If the mother is healthy, the child's resistance to illness will be good and its chances of survival will be good.

"And you can't care for rural women and children unless you're aware of local customs and habits. We discovered there's a custom not to breast-feed a baby for the first three days after birth. This is awful: that's just when a mother's milk is the most rich in antibodies to prevent infections. When we persuaded young mothers to start breast-feeding immediately, we could see the sharp increase in steep growth in a matter of a few months.

"We also monitor children every month by taking their weight. We found low birth weight children grew for about six months and then stopped growing for three or four months. After that they either grew very slowly or stayed about the same, or if they got an infection, they lost weight. We discovered it's the custom to breast-feed a child for eighteen months or two years. But mother's milk is only sufficient nourishment for the first six months. After that a child needs supplementary food to grow. When mothers come for symptomatic ailments, we ask: 'Your child is getting bronchial ailments frequently and also dysentery: Why is that?' We say the child is malnourished. She replies, 'You're mad, the child is smiling and playing games.'

"So we try to educate the mothers about the need for supplementary feeding. Our experience is mixed: some women will understand and others will say: 'Give me an injection.' They only want immediate relief for the ailment that brought them to the dispensary and nothing more."

Teaching Women About Their Bodies

"We now know village women have no knowledge of their bodies," Daxa said. "When I asked a woman about food in pregnancy she said: 'I should eat less because I have a limited space in my belly. If I eat more, I'll have less space for my child to grow, and if I have a big child, it will be difficult to give birth.' We hear this from many women. They say a small child will be easy to deliver, and then the child will grow.

"They also say that after childbirth the placenta should be immediately removed or it will go up to the mother's chest and be stuck there. They don't know what the uterus is or what the stomach is: they have absolutely no idea what ovulation is or what menstruation is or how it comes. We started showing them slides of the anatomy and how a child grows in the womb. It was so well accepted many women asked for the slides again so others might see them. You see, they might not know, but they have curiosity and are willing to learn.

"Recently we began building a new structure to train and house eight additional full-time women workers who will concentrate on the care of women during pregnancy and delivery. They'll show the pictures of the womb and how a child is born. They'll also teach better eating habits. Sometimes village women live on only one vegetable: rice, lentils, fruits, milk, and eggs are not available. Even if other foods are available, they have the old medical belief that certain foods are hot or cold by nature and should be avoided in pregnancy.

"Our health workers don't push them and tell them you must do this or that. They teach them with slides and pictures. For example, village women believe milk shouldn't be taken in pregnancy because the child will be stuck in the womb. Our workers show them pictures of the child bathed in amniotic fluid to demonstrate it can't be stuck.

"You can find out all these things if you have health workers who understand local customs and beliefs. They'll see a thread around a woman's waist or a charm around her neck and recognize the work of a witch doctor who tells mothers evil spirits cause sickness. Our worker says, 'That's no good. Your child is sick because of a disease: she needs extra food.'"

Working for women has a long history in Gujarat. Among other things it is the birthplace of SEWA, the world's first labor union for women in such low status trades as vegetable vendors and rag and paper pickers.

24 ✹ Working for Women

"**W**e're not feminists in the usual sense," Meena Patel said. "We don't want to confront society. We want women to be an integral part of a larger movement."

Meena's unaccented English and confident voice reflected an elite school education. A small, young woman, with long dark hair, soft hands, and stylish, pastel-colored kameez salwar, she seemed out of place amid village women in garish saris with calloused hands and tattoos. But we were in one of the rare places in India where the barriers of caste and class have disappeared: Meena spoke of the village women with love and respect. We were in a dingy basement office of the Self-Employed Women's Association, known throughout India by the acronym SEWA, which means "service" in several Indian languages.

"SEWA is a registered trade union," Meena explained. "We have questioned the whole meaning of what trade unionism means. The unorganized sector, including farm labor, constitutes almost 90 percent of the labor force, and, of these, women are more than half."

The women who crowded SEWA's headquarters in an old three-story building near the banks of the Sabarmati told of the small tragedies and little victories of India's poor.

There was Saroj, a vegetable vendor allotted a prize place in one of the city's residential colonies; chased away by an aggressive male, she had to move to a filthy spot next to a garbage dump.

And there was Jivi. For fifteen years she sold old clothes at a place well away from the road within the walled city. She refused a policeman's demand for "gratification"—a bribe—and he gave her a ticket for obstructing traffic. Jivi's meager capital, needed to keep herself in stock, was used up in several trips to court and a fine.

"The elite thinks hawkers and vendors are creating dirt and obstructing traffic," Meena said. "They go to the West and see skyscrapers and clean streets and feel we should have clean pavements too, along with skyscrapers and shopping centers. But vendors are an essential part of our urban economy. They provide distribution cheaply, and their things are easily available. Where will the poor people shop if they're not there?"

The main battle centered on Manek *Chowk* (any open space or wide junction of streets), a bazaar area in the walled city. *Toplawalis* (sidewalk vendors) who sold vegetables in front of an enclosed market cheaper than stall owners inside were an easy prey: if they refused to pay bribes, their fruit and vegetables would be crushed under a policeman's boot. SEWA asked the municipal corporation to give rights to the toplawalis. What happened next is a textbook example of the role of counterelite activists. They are a bridge between one section of society and another and an instrument of empowerment, enabling a low-status group to struggle on equal terms with the elite.

The Mother of Women's Activism

The municipal council refused SEWA's request: worse yet, it ordered the vendors to leave the places where they had carried on their little trades for so many years. But the council reckoned without Ela Bhatt, SEWA's founder and militant leader. She led a brigade of toplawalis to Manek Chowk and told them to spread their wares in defiance of the police and the city fathers. For a few days the police did nothing, but then they broke up the demonstration.

Elaben, as she is known throughout Gujarat, got the help of Indira Jaisingh, a Bombay lawyer famous for her civil rights battles, who filed a writ petition in the Supreme Court challenging the ban. In early 1985 the court directed the municipal corporation and police to draw up a scheme, in consultation with the women vendors, that would meet the needs of both sides.

If anyone can be called the mother of women's activism in India, it is Ela Bhatt. In 1977 she received the Magsaysay prize from the Philippines and in 1984 the Right to Livelihood prize from Sweden. She has also been awarded one of India's highest honors, the *Padma Shri*, and has served as an appointed member of the *Rajya Sabha* (the upper house of India's Parliament). Once, when we talked at her small, sparsely furnished official apartment in New Delhi, she discussed her life:

"I graduated from the university in 1964 and wanted to do something for the country. I met my husband in college. We were in the same class and I was under his influence. He was a Gandhian and student leader and later followed a career in journalism. I joined the Textile Labor Association [TLA: a union formed in the 1920s after Gandhi led a strike against textile mill owners in Ahmedabad] and worked in women's activities. Slowly, slowly, I came to realize the importance of the unorganized sector, especially women. They were economically very active, but where were the laws to protect them? I was not a feminist as such, but I realized 80 percent of our women are rural, poor, and illiterate. It's these women who should play a leading role in the women's movement.

"In 1970 I went to Israel for training at the Afro-Asian Labor and Cooperatives Institute in Tel Aviv. In the Histradut I saw women in the organized, unorganized, and informal sectors joined into one organization: how they formed cooperatives and how, by joint action of labor and cooperatives, helped relieve poverty. When I came back and talked to my union leaders, they thought it seemed to be a Gandhian idea and SEWA was born in 1972.

"In 1975, when the United Nations Women's Decade was inaugurated, I went to Mexico City, and my ideas were strengthened. I realized two things. First, women are ignored and are the missing link: they don't exist in economic life. Secondly, women have no good perception of themselves: they hardly recognize themselves as workers. If they don't recognize themselves, how can the planners take them into account?"

In the same year India's Parliament passed the Equal Remuneration Act, under which women must be paid the same as men for similar work, and the government published a report on the status of women, entitled "Towards Equality," which inspired the formation of a number of women's groups.

The First Women's Cooperative Bank

Even earlier, SEWA began its most significant empowerment activity. As Prema Purao of Annapurna in Bombay and so many others have emphasized, to be free the poor must get out of the clutches of moneylenders and middlemen. A toplawali who borrows fifty rupees from a moneylender in the morning to buy her vegetables has to return fifty-five rupees at night: 10 percent interest for only one day.

The SEWA *Mahila* (Women's) Cooperative Bank was organized in 1977, the first of its kind, when four thousand women contributed ten rupees apiece as share capital and another two thousand opened accounts with their tiny savings. SEWA insists women members must control their own organizations. This posed a problem: the banking law required that members of the board of directors sign all documents. But some women were illiterate: they had to take an overnight course in signing their names before the papers could be filed. Now all bank customers, including those who attest to their name with a thumb print, are issued identity cards with their pictures.

One of the bank organizers was Ranjan Desai, a small, smiling, round-faced woman who is also head of SEWA's paper pickers cooperative.

"I come from a Brahmin family, but I tell my family my caste is paper picker," she said. "When I started with SEWA, many Harijans came to my house; drinking the same water, cooking in my own kitchen, washing in my own water buckets, but no one in my family objected. My mother and father worked in the Gandhian movement in 1931. My mother worked with Harijans. She put these ideas in my mind. All the blood in my body flows like that.

"When I joined SEWA in 1974, Indira Gandhi had nationalized the banks and told them to go to the small people. But what did the bank people know about poor women? They didn't allow them to enter their offices. Besides, the women had no clear idea of time. The banks were only open between eleven o'clock and two in the afternoon. When the women went, they found the time was over, and no one would allow them in. They were afraid, too. We went from house to house among the Harijans and any other lower castes and got them to join our bank. We learned how much money they wanted and for what reason. We came to know each and every thing from them: about their in-laws, their husbands, and their children's education.

"In the early morning the paper pickers came out from their homes to pick up the paper from the roads. We found their children dropped out of school to help their mothers. So we organized this union. Then Elaben told me to go to government offices and talk about these women. We said, 'On this day these women will come at two o'clock and collect the waste paper.' They had confidence in us, and now we have contracts with the government and textile industry, and three hundred women have got steady employment collecting paper from these offices, and their children are attending school."

In addition to providing credit the bank maintains savings accounts where women can put their earnings out of reach of husbands or male relatives—a decided advantage in a society where men are notorious for using family income to get drunk. There is also the problem of self-esteem. The bank is located on the ground floor of the SEWA headquarters building, where men are seldom seen. I asked Meena Patel if a female environment was more comfortable for women in India than it might be in the West.

"That's true to a large extent," she replied. "Not in terms of people like us, but in terms of our members. Poor women find it comforting to be among women: to see there are women who can run a bank, who can write accounts, who can go and talk to government officers. It gives them confidence."

Meena arranged an interview with one of the early SEWA members. Her name was Chandrabella, about fifty years old, with high cheek bones and short hair, slightly gray at the temples, with a wristwatch tattooed on her right wrist. She made her living bartering old clothes for utensils, which she sold at a Sunday market. Chandrabella was one of the organizers of the bank and served as a director.

"We went to every street and lane to let people know about SEWA and took money from them to start the bank," she said, with Meena translating. "Some women borrowed one hundred rupees and paid ten or twelve rupees a day interest. Others, who were more trusted, paid eight or ten rupees interest a month. Our bank charges only 1 percent a month. Our self-respect has increased; even traders give us respect. And our family life has improved now that we're making more money. I used to go out all day and hardly get anything in return. There was always tension. Now I'm more easy with myself.

"Every month we have a meeting to consider who will get loans. We get to know all the women. We talk to them about themselves, and they're happy to find somebody who'll listen to them: someone who is their own. This is a place to talk without men around."

"Chandrabella is known in all the slums and working-class areas," Meena added. "She's a born leader. Oh, you should hear her when she makes speeches. She can talk to anyone, poor people and government officials too."

"We Have to Shout to Be Heard"

SEWA has grown to more than 21,000 members, divided into six sections: vendors, tobacco and food workers, agricultural and allied workers, textile workers, and service and other home-based workers. The largest single group is made up of women who roll the cheap cigarettes called bidis.

Meena arranged an interview with Kamala Dadage, thirty-one, a senior organizer of the Bidi Union. Small, with wide eyes and a ring in her nose and uneven teeth, she said she had been making bidis since she was thirteen and that her mother had also been a bidi roller.

"Our members have learned courage," Kamala said. "Once they only came into contact with the bidi owner. Now they're not afraid of him and aren't afraid of officials either. Self-employed women are not going to be docile any more. We have to shout to be heard. And we are being heard.

"When we first organized in 1980, women were paid only six rupees for a thousand bidis. Now they're paid thirteen rupees. We're recognized as an organized labor union. Out of 10,000 bidi workers in Gujarat, more than five thousand have identity cards. This gives them the right to cheap or free medicines and puts them on a waiting list for homes. Already 250 women have been promised homes. Workers with identity cards can also get scholarships for their children. All of this was supposed to be available under existing laws, but before our union was organized they got nothing."

Kamala said she had two sons and one daughter and that in her community girls were taken out of school after the second or third standard, but she said her daughter was staying in school and so were the daughters of other bidi workers. I had been told that Kamala was once known as a battered wife and asked her about that:

"That's true. Men don't like it when their wives talk to other men. They're also jealous when a wife earns money. But I have to talk with owners: I can't avoid other men. But now my husband treats me better: he sees other people respect me. Once women have something they can call their own, and money of their own, their situation will always change."

When Kamala left, Meena said the story had a happy ending. SEWA had nominated Kamala for a training course in the Philippines, and she had been accepted. That was really the test: she would be in a foreign country surrounded by other men. Instead of objecting her husband was supportive. As a boy, he had attended an English medium school and was teaching Kamala a little English so she could make herself understood in the Philippines.

Meena had other work to do, and I was given several other guides whose English was not as good. One showed me several nurseries and preprimary schools for the children of working mothers. One crèche, open from 11:30 in the morning to 3:30 in the afternoon, had thirty children who needed little persuasion to demonstrate their talents: a boy sang a song about a trip to Delhi, another sang about swimming in a lake, and a girl sang about a mango tree.

Another crèche was for the children of bidi rollers: their mothers could increase their production with no small children to care for. All

SEWA crèches and schools serve lunch and arrange for a doctor to give children regular checkups. Mothers are also asked to attend health talks, and for future school attendance and employment their children are issued birth certificates, which few of the urban and rural poor are able to produce.

On another day I visited a block-printing cooperative, producing saris and bed and cushion covers and another cooperative for making baskets, lamp shades, tables, and chairs from cane and bamboo. Women in both groups found their markets were stagnant or declining. SEWA, as part of its function as a bridge, arranged for teachers from such organizations as the central government's All-India Handicrafts Board to teach new skills and products.

Two New Lives

I also visited a cooperative of Muslim women who made *chindis* (cheap, cotton-stuffed quilts). They are among the most exploited of the city's self-employed women. In the usual way that craft and social groups are divided by sect and caste, the chindi workers live in the Muslim Dariapur area. Merchants supplied scrap cloth, obtained from the city's textile mills, and the women, working in the seclusion of their homes, sewed together as many as sixty pieces to make a single quilt cover, for which they were paid half a rupee (less than four American cents). They could neither complain nor search for other work: as Muslims, most were seldom allowed outside their homes, and then only when hidden in a *burqa* (a garment, generally black, that goes over a woman's head and extends to her feet, with a latticework at the face to see out).

When SEWA organized them and demanded a higher piece rate, forty women were told they would be given no further work. Then, when SEWA tried to obtain direct orders for quilts from the villages surrounding Ahmedabad, the merchants harassed the SEWA workers to drive them from the streets and stopped all supplies of scrap cloth to the chindi workers.

SEWA fought the merchants on their home grounds. It opened a shop in the middle of a row of Dariapur quilt shops and got a single fifty kilo (110 pound) bag of scrap cloth for the women to start their own work. They did not know how to sort the scrap or market the finished product—but they learned, and now their cooperative sells finished quilts from the shop in Dariapur and also markets directly to the poor in surrounding villages.

Bilquish Bano, once a lowly scrap sorter, is the assistant manager of the quilt shop. "SEWA helped me get a new life," she said.

SEWA also helped another woman get a new life. She is Renana Jabvala, whose mother is the novelist and short story writer Ruth Jabvala. Mrs Jabvala, of Polish birth and married to an Indian, is the third member of the Merchant-Ivory film production group. With most of the world open to her, Renana chose to become a part of SEWA. I met her in a small crowded office on the second floor of SEWA headquarters. As is customary among social activists, hierarchy was blurred. Renana as listed was one of the two secretaries of SEWA, ranking seventh of a list of Executive Committee members, but in reality she ran SEWA when Ela Bhatt was in New Delhi for sessions of Parliament.

"I got a B.Sc. at Delhi University," she said. "Then I went to Harvard and got a B.A. and went to Yale and took an M.A. in economics. I started work on a Ph.D. but gave it up: I felt it was selfish to go on developing myself. I wanted to contribute to society not just learn and work for myself. When I returned to India in 1977, I wanted to work in a women's organization and thought SEWA was the best because it was more participatory. Women's movements are difficult. There's a stereotype of women burning bras and being antiman. The women's movement here is not antiman: it's concerned with such things as employment and police harassment."

SEWA is India's foremost women's organization. I asked Renana what it plans to do next. For instance, would it enter politics and put up candidates for election?

"If you get into the political system with one party, you invite the opposition of the rest of the parties and economic and social opposition," she replied. "In addition, political parties are linked to vested interests. We don't want to get into that."

"Will you at least branch out and try to become an all-Indian organization?" I asked.

"We have resisted suggestions like that," she said. "But we also must be prepared for a very long struggle: we don't expect to get results in five or ten years. We realize many of the things we're asking for can only be changed if there's a national movement, so we have encouraged the formation of SEWA organizations in other parts of the country, but we've always been careful that they're independent."

Despite what Meena said about wanting women to be part of a larger organization, SEWA risks isolation by limiting itself to working entirely with women. In contrast, when men extended a hand asking for help from Ila Pathak, the organizer of another women's group, she grasped it without hesitation.

25 ✸ Slaves of Sabarmati

I talked with Ila Pathak at her office in a residential section of the city where she told how she formed the Ahmedabad Women's Action Group (AWAG) in 1981:

"I got my Ph.D. in 1980 with the thesis: *The Contribution of Women Novelists in Indo-English Novels.* By then I had been teaching for more than thirty years. My classes are in the morning, and the rest of the day remains for me. I wanted to do something more, but no one wanted my thinking, so with about thirty like-minded women I formed this group.

"We wanted to counter the films giving a wrong picture of women. I had done a long study on Indian women in film. For the first nine-tenths of the film she is Westernized, and the end she's suddenly changed into a sacrificing, tearful, and nondecisive person without any individuality: to be understood only as a mother, daughter, or sister. We later decided it was true of all media. In advertisements on TV the traditional role is emphasized to show women subject to men, and the Western role is emphasized to uncover as much of the body as you can. The print media describes an attempted rape in great detail because it wants to titillate.

"We were all urban, educated, and advantaged. We later decided to start work with a community of Harijan women. It happened this way: a woman sweeper looking after the colony where I lived died when she was hardly fifty, about my age then. A friend said sweepers had a high incidence of tuberculosis. I asked her daughter-in-law, and she confirmed the woman died of TB. We formed a trust to get money, and Ela Bhatt approached Oxfam on our behalf and helped us with our first programs. We started working with the women in their homes and also opened a preschool and an under-five clinic for children. Gradually these inputs increased. We opened a demonstration center for nutrition and worked with pregnant women. We asked them to get their children immunized and to monitor their health.

"Since SEWA was looking after the self-employed, we decided to work with contract labor. There are three major transshipment points in Ahmedabad, where coal is transferred from large freight wagons or to smaller wagons or to trucks. The railroads get this work done through contractors, who hire migrant tribal people from Gujarat or other migrants from Madhya Pradesh. Half the workers are women. We found all the provisions of the labor act were violated: there were no attendance registers, no wage registers, and no primary facilities like wash places, urinals, or a shed to rest in and get out of the sun or rain."

Ila had been a free-lance journalist and knew how the press and public opinion could be manipulated. She decided to go public with what her group had discovered. In October 1983 she persuaded Ramesh Menon, the Gujarat correspondent of the nationally circulated news magazine *India Today*, to write a story about the coal workers. It was headlined "Slaves of Sabarmati" and began:

> Eleven-year-old Manu Bokhar should have been at school or out enjoying the sunshine with her little friends. Instead, for eight long hours a day, she picks load after load of coal at Sabarmati in Ahmedabad. Draped precariously around her blackened body is a torn piece of cloth improvised as a sari. After dark, she trudges back home. . . . Next morning, early, she is back at work again. Manu has missed her childhood and already attained a practical, grown-up wisdom. 'If I go to school,' she asks, 'what will we eat?'

Menon told of low pay and "nagging insecurity," with jobs distributed on a daily basis. "We do not dare ask for a raise or a regular job as we will lose what little we have," he quoted one woman as saying. Another showed him her foot, injured when a large chunk of coal dropped on it, and said there was no provision for medical care. Many workers complained of respiratory ailments from breathing the coal dust. Even babies, slung over their mother's backs, inhaled the dust. "Our children are born in the midst of coal, breathe it all along, and grow to become coal pickers. We are destined to live and die like this," Menon was told.

When the article appeared a human rights group filed a case in the High Court of Gujarat asking that the labor laws be enforced, but the suit was soon mired in technicalities. Then in June 1984 the AWAG began working in a second slum area, where there were families of workers from Asarwa, another transshipment yard. These workers could see some benefits of the stalled legal action—the contractors had put in a few taps for drinking water and some urinals and a small shed—but when AWAG activists went to the yard to tell workers of their rights, the *Mukadams* (subcontractors) threatened they would be fired and evicted from their huts if they were seen talking to outsiders.

A Death Releases Hidden Springs

In September 1984 there was an accident at the Asarwa yard in which Hirumal Ranta, twenty, was struck on the head and fell bleeding to the ground. His body lay on the ground for two hours while the Mukadams shouted at the workers to resume shoveling the coal. They refused, even after an ambulance came to take Hirumal's body away.

They had never before challenged authority, but the death of Hirumal the next day seemed to release hidden springs. The men went to their huts and found Usha, an AWAG preschool teacher. "Take us to your *benji*," they said. (Ji is an honorific: they meant Ila Pathak or, in Gujarati fashion, Ilaben.)

"The teacher brought them to our office," Ila said. "They wanted to form a union. I said, 'This is a women's organization; women will have to be in front. Do you accept that?' They said 'yes.' I asked them what they knew about unions, and they said they heard about the Textile Labor Association. We drew up a protest petition and asked them to sign or give their thumb impressions. Some never before had put their thumb print on a protest, but all 160 men and women in the room agreed. We assumed their enthusiasm would die down overnight and only a few would show up for a march to the commissioner's office. But even more showed up the next morning: one hundred women led the way, and about five hundred men followed behind. Usha walked beside them to count the marchers and help keep order. But the workers surprised us again: they shouted their own slogans, and leaders emerged from the crowd to boost morale and take charge of discipline.

"They sat down a hundred yards from the gate of the commissioner's compound, and a deputation of four women, six men, and three AWAG workers went up to the office. We had sent word we were coming, but the labor commissioner and his assistant both went away, leaving a deputy who said he was responsible for distant areas. He refused to come down to see the workers but did agree to accept the protest. With that the marchers dispersed: they had gone without food or water since early morning."

"Will the Sisters Support Us?"

"The strike ended the next day," Ila said. "A few days later 450 workers gathered at the yard to form the union: never before had there been such a gathering. When a male activist from another group addressed them, they listened respectfully and then asked, 'Will the sisters continue their support too?'

"So that's how the unionizing took off. We brought workers from the Sabarmati yard to meet those from Asarwa for a training session on the importance of forming a union. For a while nothing happened, but then there was agitation about a bonus, and they also asked us to help them form a union. They called a strike, and it was successful.

"We won other strikes as long as they remained united, but then disunity set in, and ever since it's up and down. Sometimes I feel the union is growing; sometimes I feel it's dead and gone. Some were bribed to split the union; some were victimized by being refused work, and others were threatened and even beaten by the railway police. Unity is fragile among the poor. An offer of cash can't be resisted for long. In some cases a bottle of liquor is enough to make a laborer join with the employer and desert the union."

Ila said the workers had to hire from the Mukadams the shovels they used in moving coal: just one more means of exploitation. She also said the president of one of the unions was a woman named Kanam. I asked her to arrange a tour the next day so I could see the yards and meet Kanam. There was the usual problem of a translator, but Ila said one of her staff, Aruna Parmar, could speak English fairly well.

When we met, Aruna seemed too frail a flower for the thickets of union activity. She was thin, with high cheek bones and a long pointed nose, almost like a figure from a Mayan carving. She wore a red, heart-shaped plastic *bindi* (an ornament worn as a beauty mark) on her forehead, a small diamond in her right nostril, and two diamond earrings. She was dressed in a white kameez with delicate flower stitching, a pale purple salwar, and had a paisley print shawl over her shoulders.

Aruna was no shrinking violet. We traveled in one of the three-wheeled motor scooters that serve as cheap taxis and whose drivers often take the long way around to increase fares. When one tried this on Aruna, she gave him a sharp rebuke and from then on told him which way to go and which way to turn. Neither did she show any sign of feeling out of place when we stopped at a Dalit colony of three hundred families and walked through muddy lanes, past women cooking on smoky open fires, and children everywhere. Our destination was an AWAG crèche in a small room with toys on the floor and a lithograph on the wall telling the Aesop (plagiarized by the Greeks from more ancient Indian sources) fable of the fox and the crow.

After that we went to a newer colony of sixty-five families where the AWAG had established a preschool for twenty-two children. Aruna said the children got monthly health checkups and mothers were given postnatal care.

No visitors were allowed at the Sabarmati coal yard and the Asarwa yard was almost deserted: no coal trains had arrived. Most of the laborers at Asarwa are tribals from eastern Gujarat: small and thin but very strong. First we met Manti, one of the officers of the union: barefoot, with heavy silver anklets, and wearing a yellow sari with splashes of red. Two of her daughters were with her; a son was in school. Then we met Kanam, who was also barefoot, with a tight silver anklet and wearing a similar yellow and red sari. She was rather stern-faced but every now and then showed a wide, pleasant smile.

Shovels As Symbols

On the way out I asked Aruna to stop at the gate where I had seen a stack of coal shovels. They probably cost about 150 rupees ($10.50) and were nothing much to look at, but they were powerful symbols of exploitation.

At the Asarwa yard, after several strikes for higher wages, a crew of eight men and women received fifty rupees for a three-hour shift, or 6.25 rupees per person. Most crews managed to get taken on for at least two shifts, bringing daily earnings per person to 12.50 rupees. But then 2.50 was deducted for the shovel, leaving only ten rupees (about 70 American cents) for a day's hard and dirty work. Even worse, a worker who got only one shift would have waited at the yard all day and would return to his or her family with a pittance of four rupees (about 28 cents).

"How did Kanam become president?" I asked Ila when Aruna brought me back to the office.

"She has strong opinions," she replied. "She can influence others. In addition, she's a first wife. She had no children, so Misra, her husband, married her younger sister as a co-wife. Kanam doesn't have to look after the house, so she's more mobile. But she's victimized. They don't give her work unless they're very busy."

I asked if something could not be done about paying for the shovels.

"It shouldn't be paid," she replied. "The labor commissioner, who worked out a compromise settlement for the first strike, ruled the 2.50 should not be cut, but the strike was fruitless: they're still cutting the 2.50. There's a labor surplus and lots of poverty. You can't go without work for five days together, so you say, "All right, cut the 2.50 but give me work.' No one has a magic wand to alter things overnight: everything has to be pursued with iron-willed determination."

That is what Ila Pathak has in abundance. Much of her time and resources are devoted to women's issues, including bride burning. In a six-month study, AWAG found a syndrome of causes and effects: social values, family values, deafness to a woman's cry for help, and the attitudes of doctors, the courts, and the police.

"The largest single factor is the woman's own submissiveness," Ila said. "She totally accepts her environment and believes submissiveness is the ideal life of women. If she is married and the head of the family is not strong, she will suffer. Her sense of dignity and self-worth is broken, and she has no place to go. If she returns to her parents, they say her rightful place is with her husband. We have a counseling center for women in trouble. We had a woman who went back to her parents fourteen times. The fifteenth time they sent her back; she committed suicide.

"We have three-day consciousness meetings where the women talk about anything that comes to their minds. Once, a woman came for two days and did not say a word. Finally, on the third day she said, 'I've done it.' We asked what she meant. She said, 'I won't cover my face with my sari when I leave the house. I will only wear it to here.' She pointed to her forehead. For her, that was revolutionary."

Ila's experience in dealing with the press and fighting for justice were put to use when she was named to a commission to investigate the failure to punish policemen who gang-raped a tribal woman named Guntaben.

26 ❀ The Rape of Guntaben

Indica's leading magazine of social and political comment, *Economic and Political Weekly*, once wrote: "The police in India consider the right of raping women as one of the perks of an underpaid job."

On the night of January 4, 1985, Gunta Ramji, a twenty-two-year-old tribal woman of Devidao village, was taken from her home by police from nearby Sagbara, ostensibly to investigate a kidnapping. Guntaben was stripped naked before a crowd, her husband, Hanabhai, was beaten, and they were then put in a police truck. It stopped on the way to the Sagbara station, the driver got down, and four policemen raped Guntaben in the driver's cabin. At four o'clock the next morning, the same policemen took her to an upper veranda of an adjacent building and raped her again. The last man finished by inserting a lathi into her vagina, after which she began to bleed profusely. Guntaben and Hanabhai were freed the next day after relatives paid a bribe of three thousand rupees.

Normally, for poor tribals, that would have been the end of the matter, but Guntaben and Hanabhai had someone to whom they could reach out for help: Father Joseph, a Jesuit priest who sometimes came to Sagbara as a legal advocate. What happened next was an illustration of the progress of the social movement in Gujarat: separate individuals with their own agenda had become a network serving the poor.

Father Joseph's Mission

Father Joseph's main office is in Rajpipla, where I had changed buses on my first visit to Anil Patel in Mongrol. After my second visit, to interview Daxa Patel, I talked with him in the enclosed porch of an old, thick-walled, colonial-style building that serves as his home and office. Father Joseph is about five-feet-four, with a round face and the dark skin of his native state of Kerala. He wore a white shirt and trousers with no cross or religious images in sight.

"When I was a small boy, I made up my mind to give myself to the poor," he said. "I got this from the gospel itself. I joined the Jesuits because they have a discipline and a history of work in different parts of the country. Normally, Jesuits in India took up education, but I wanted to go into this work. I had a lot of opposition and was close to being thrown out of the church for a while. It was not only the Jesuits: the local authority in the church is the bishop and normally bishops are more conservative than the superiors of religious orders. No one will give you what you want on a platter. You must have ideology, commitment, and a clear vision of your goal. We have an exploitative political system: to fight against this is hard. You must fight and start your work at the same time to show what you mean to do."

"What do you mean by exploitation?" I asked.

"Government is not the chief minister or the prime minister or other elected leaders: it's an institution," he replied. "Our whole system is bad. Top executives are hardly ever from the lower castes. To come down and help never strikes them. Bureaucrats trained in the old system have lots of prejudices and have never experienced denial of basic human rights. And there's the caste system: people want to help their kin and then extend it to their caste. Only after that, they may do something for others. Even if lower caste people have positions of power, it's difficult for them to work for their own castes.

"The exploiters always try to keep on good relations with the ruling party: today it's the Congress, tomorrow the Janata, and the day after it may be the Communists. I have not seen a single politician who hasn't made money after he has been elected: whether he was a Harijan or tribal or from any other community. When we try to expose the wrongs of the system, the politicians get exposed and make charges: they say, 'Father is a Communist and has been externed from Kerala.' At the same time they say, 'Father is trying to convert the poor.' They don't know Communists and conversions don't go together, but they'll say the same thing in the same speech. The top people hear this and don't even try to find out the truth."

Father Joseph calls his organization the Rajpipla Legal Aid Committee. "I came in 1974 when there was a drought situation," he said. "Then in 1977 I started legal work with the help of lawyers who donated their services: My only degree is as Jesuit priest. In the courts everyone joins hands against the poor. Our system is adversary, and unless you can hire the best lawyer, you have no chance.

"Another Jesuit, Father Matthew, joined me in 1977. He had a doctorate in sociology, and when he saw the situation here, he returned to Kerala and got a law degree. We take up all kinds of cases, from police cases to alienation of tribal lands. We have cases before the Supreme Court involving nearly a thousand farmers.

I asked about the rape of Guntaben:

"We had clinics in Sagbara, so they knew of our work. Several days had passed since the incident, since Guntaben and her husband had no money to come earlier: it's seventy kilometers and costs fifteen rupees ($1.05) by bus. My first reaction was to make sure a rape had taken place. I know the tribal mentality: they'll not say an outright lie, but they might have some grievances against the police and charge rape to strengthen their case. We had a second reason: If it was true, I was pretty sure the police would try to cover it up. We wanted to be on the safe side."

Father Joseph has a jeep, and Mongrol is a bit more than a half hour away. After Daxa Patel examined Guntaben and verified her condition and injuries, he went straight to New Delhi to file a complaint with the Supreme Court.

The court ordered the Central Bureau of Investigation (CBI) to look into the matter and, in March, the Gujarat unit of the CBI found there was a prima facie case that Guntaben had been illegally detained and raped. Six policemen were arrested on rape or other charges but were immediately released on bail on a technicality that they had not been charged within the prescribed time limit.

After waiting a full year for something further to happen, the Supreme Court appointed a two-member inquiry commission. One, who would represent the official side, was E. V. Joseph, a high-ranking police officer from Kerala. Ila Pathak was chosen to represent the public's side.

"When the rape took place, they asked me to go to see the woman, but I was busy with something else," she said during our talk. "Then this came up, and they looked for a woman who was independent of all political parties and had no direct connection with the case. A lawyer in the proceedings suggested me."

A Conspiracy to Avoid Justice

The commission began hearings in February 1987. Statements from 584 witnesses were recorded, and the report was submitted the following October. Pathak and Joseph looked beyond the guilt of the four policeman—that was virtually proved by the CBI report—and produced a 110 page indictment of the police and civil administration.

They named eight persons as party to a conspiracy "to save the four guilty policemen from being prosecuted in the court of law." They said Subinspector B. C. Joshi, who was in charge of the Sagbara police station, and Head Constable Kanti Mangu, started the affair by sending the four policemen to, in effect, kidnap Guntaben and her husband. Joshi was also cited for demanding the three thousand rupee bribe to set them free and for slapping Guntaben's face to keep her quiet when she returned to the station to file a complaint.

Two other accused conspirators were Deputy Superintendent J. V. Puwar and Circle Inspector B. J. Parmar. In violation of a regulation that a woman should not be brought to a station house at night, they had Guntaben picked up a second time and taken to the Sagbara station. They then, the report said, got one of her relatives, the principal of a nearby high school, to warn she would be raped again, thereby coercing her into putting her thumb print on an affidavit retracting the rape charge. The principal (one witness testified to having once seen him drunk in his school office) was included among the conspirators, along with a village official who recorded the affidavit.

A doctor at the Rajpipla hospital was also named as a conspirator. It was charged that, under pressure from Joshi and Parmar, he issued a false medical certificate that, although it confirmed her rape, did not record details of her injuries and failed to mention the accusation against the four policemen.

A second doctor was cited, although not included as a conspirator, for flatly refusing to examine Guntaben without written permission from the police.

The eighth accused conspirator was Police Superintendent Sukhdev Singh, who was said to have masterminded the cover-up.

The man at the top of the district ladder, Collector G. R. Rao, was not implicated in the cover-up but was blamed for failing to see that justice was done.

The report is sprinkled with adjectives of outrage: "inexcusable," "reprehensible," and "sordid." It accused Deputy Superintendent Puwar of the "nefarious falsehood" of telling one person Guntaben was of "loose morals" and someone else she was of "unsound mind." As an aside, noting who really was immoral, the commission called attention to a report in a local newspaper that Superintendent Sukhdev Singh and Subinspector Joshi had grown rich on bribes and had built "palatial bungalows," using teak stolen from a Sagbara forest reserve.

It was a damning report, and yet not a single policeman or other conspirator was tried or punished.

An Appeal to Stop Torture

In March 1988 Amnesty International used the Pathak-Joseph report as the basis for another in a series of appeals to India to stop "the use of torture and other forms of cruel and degrading treatment in police stations."

Just two months earlier, Prime Minister Rajiv Gandhi, in an interview with the British Broadcasting Corporation, had denied torture occurred in India: "We don't torture anybody, and you can check on that. Whenever we have had complaints of torture, we have had it checked, and we have not found it to be true."

But it happens so often there is a generic phrase—like "bride burning" for the murder of wives—for the rape of women in a police station, hospital, or other public institution: it's called "custodial rape." According to a report to the Rajya Sabha, 4,400 rape complaints were registered nationwide by scheduled caste and tribe women between March 1982 and October 1986, or an average of 2.6 complaints a day. Although there were no further details, it was understood most of the rapes were perpetrated by the locally dominant castes or other authorities, with policemen a significant element. These were only officially noticed cases: far more rapes go unreported in India because of the feeling that an entire family is dishonored.

A March 1986 editorial in the *Times of India* commented on the difficulty of dealing with rape in police custody:

> Custodial rape seems to be occurring so frequently that "cop molests woman" has become an almost daily fare for newspaper readers. Considering that as many as 97 percent of rape cases are either canceled or sent back as "untraced" by the police according to its [sic] own admission, the difficulties in dealing with custodial rape cannot be underestimated. . . . Not only do the police not cooperate

in such an investigation, they have been known to harass even those who take up the cases of custodial rape.

This conclusion was supported by a November 1983 report of the Central Reserve Police Force on custodial rapes in the state of Haryana: "A total of 828 women were raped in police custody between 1966 and 1980. Of these, 210 were from the Harijan community. Only one constable was sentenced to five years of imprisonment while others were simply dismissed or let off for want of sufficient evidence."

The Campaign to Punish Custodial Rape

What traditional Indian culture demands of women is, as Ila Pathak mentioned, meekness and submissiveness. Until as late as the 1970s this attitude was reflected in the legal attitude toward rape. If a rape charge was brought to court, it was assumed the woman had invited sexual intercourse, as if to say her gender was sufficient invitation. The burden of proof of rape was on the woman.

Efforts to revise the law began after the rape, in March 1972, of Mathura, fifteen years old, by constables Ganpat and Tukaram in the police station in Chandrapur in Maharashtra. The Sessions Court (the lowest judicial court) acquitted the policemen for lack of evidence, saying Mathura had consented to sexual intercourse. Maharashtra is one of the advanced states of India, and women were just finding their voice. The sentence was appealed, and the Bombay High Court reversed the judgment, saying it was highly unlikely a girl in police custody would "make any overtures or invite the accused to satisfy her sexual desires." The High Court recommended one year's imprisonment for Ganpat and two years for Tukaram.

On appeal the Supreme Court upheld the original finding, terming it "a peaceful affair," since there was no evidence Mathura had put up a strong resistance. In September 1979 four law teachers—Lotika Sarkar, Upendra Baxi, Vasudha Dhagamwar, and Raghunath Kelkar—wrote an open letter to the Chief Justice: "Your Lordship, does the Indian Supreme Court expect a young girl . . . when trapped by two policemen inside a police station, to successfully raise alarm for help? Does it seriously expect the girl, a laborer, to put up such stiff resistance against well-built policemen so as to have substantial marks of injury?"

Such protests nudged Parliament into reforming the rape law. After three years of deliberation it increased the punishment for rape to a minimum of ten years and shifted the onus of proof from the victim to the accused. In addition, police officers, or others in charge of a jail, hospital, or women's or children's home who had sexual intercourse with any woman or girl would be punished, even if there was no charge of rape.

The Ordeal of Maya Tyagi

It was an exercise in futility. The difficulty of obtaining a conviction for judicial rape—even after passage of the reform law—was epitomized by the ordeal of Maya Tyagi. It began in June 1980, when Maya Tyagi and her husband, Ishwar Singh, and two friends, Surendra and Rajendra Gaur, left their village in Uttar Pradesh to attend a wedding. When their car developed a flat tire, they replaced it and drove to the town of Baghpat to have the original tire repaired. For a while Maya was left alone in the car. A subinspector of police, in civilian dress, saw her and tried to make her come with him.

Ishwar happened to return, saw someone molesting his wife, and beat him, not knowing he was a policeman. Ishwar's two friends returned as the subinspector went to the Baghpat station and came back with reinforcements. They shot dead all three, Ishwar, Surendra, and Rajendra.

Then they beat Maya Tyagi, six months pregnant, with shoes and lathis, stripped her naked, and paraded her through the Baghpat bazaar. When she tried, in shame, to sit down, she was beaten and prodded with lathis to get up. She was taken to the station and gang-raped. Once again, the police added their brutal signature: a lathi was pushed into her vagina. When she was released and taken to a hospital, doctors recorded twenty-five injuries, including one to her vagina that required four stitches. (Fortunately, she later gave birth to a healthy son.)

The incident drew wide press attention, but the Baghpat police denied the whole affair, claiming the three men were killed in an encounter with a gang of *dacoits* (robbers) and that Maya was injured when she was attacked by local people incensed by the presence of the dacoits. The local courts did nothing until the case was transferred to another jurisdiction where a judge in January 1988, almost eight years after the incident, sentenced six policemen to death and four others to life imprisonment. The death sentences were later reduced to life imprisonment.

The futility of trying to outlaw custodial rape in India was also demonstrated in 1989 by the case of Suman Rani, a village girl in

Haryana. In 1984, when she was fourteen, her boyfriend enticed Suman Rani into eloping. They were picked up late at night by two constables who raped Suman Rani in the local station and then released both of them. The girl's family reported their daughter missing, and after a search she was returned to her home. A case of custodial rape was filed against the constables, and the Sessions Court awarded the mandatory minimum sentence of ten years' imprisonment, dismissing the defense argument that Suman Rani had, in effect, invited rape by her conduct: "All said and done, even a girl of easy virtue is entitled to all the protection of the law and cannot be compelled to sexual intercourse against her will and without her consent. Offenses of rape . . . were created for the protection of fallible, earthly mortals and not for goddesses."

The High Court upheld the sentence, but on further appeal the Supreme Court reduced it to five years, ruling that conduct "of easy virtue" was "adequate and special reason" for ignoring the law's mandatory sentence. It thus upheld previous findings that where there is no injury on the back, hips, or private parts of the victim, it is presumed that whatever happened was with her consent. The legal correspondent of the *Times of India* commented that unless Parliament amended the law to bar the victim's conduct from serving as a defense "protection of rape laws will be . . . confined to goddesses."

Goddesses and heroines are the concern of Mrinalini Sarabhai, for whom social awareness is a form of art.

27 ✹ The Mystic Dancer

Mrinalini Sarabhai is enchanting: a choreographer, dancer, writer, and mystic who can blend the abstractions of the *Atman* (the universal soul) with the realities of pollution, violence, and the mistreatment of women. As an Indian, she does not separate mind from body.

I called on her at her school, the Darpana Academy of Performing Arts, to ask about one of her recent poems, *Where Are We Going?*, which ended:

> Therefore I pray for humanity's sake
> That man realize
> Or study
> Or think
> That pollution of areas of existence
> Be they outward or withinwards
> Debases the quality called Man
> And we today commit ourselves
> To confront and be aware
> Make meaning
> In ecosystemic thought
> A way to serve the earth
> And save ourselves
> From total extinction
> Under a pile of dung.

Mrinalini has none of the fragile beauty associated with dancers in the West: her forehead, nose, and mouth are full and strong; her eyes —fish-shaped, in the canons of Indian beauty—are hypnotizing. Hers is the beauty of a woman, not of a fairy.

Now in her middle sixties, poised and serene, Mrinalini was born in Kerala and studied dancing with the classical masters of Tamil Nadu. She first appeared on stage in the 1940s and danced with enormous success in India and abroad. She married a physicist, Vikram Sarabhai, whose forefathers were among the pioneers of the textile industry in Gujarat.

Vikram's aunt, Anasuya Sarabhai, was an early follower of Mahatma Gandhi and was instrumental in the formation of the Textile Labor Association. Mrinalini too has lived a life of affirmation. One of her dances, *Ganga*, is ostensibly a cry of pain at the pollution of the Ganges, but the meaning is deeper.

"It's a reference to spiritual destruction," she said. "From our Vedic times we demonstrated a tremendous respect for nature and the earth. The *Rig Vedas* are pure nature hymns: 'Let the winds bless us. Let the planets bless us. Let us be one with all.' We called her Mother Earth. Now our Indian ideas are being drowned by television. Children are being taught what is foreign to us: they don't have a connection with Mother India as we thought of her.

"What I was trying to say in *Ganga* is that it's not just water for the thirsty, it's water for the entire world. It's the Atman, the spirit within us. Unless we have the attitude of the inner being; unless we have respect within us for every human being, every tree that God has given us, we're lost. We must realize: It's my mind and my hands that are destroying life and nature.

"My life is less than that of a tree. It can live a hundred years or more; by then I will be long gone. Why don't we value life in the short time we're here? We kill and pillage and rape, destroying all our ethical values. There's such a feeling of wanting power; a willingness to step over and on every person and everything just for power."

"Is it a problem of too many people?" I asked.

"That's part of it," she replied. "But it's also that people are becoming more material-minded: they feel if they don't have better things, they're not really living. But extra food and sweets are not necessary for living."

Women: Loneliness and Suicide

Mrinalini reworked the end of the fifth-century Kalidasa play *Shakuntala* to comment on the problems of modern Indian women. In the original, Shakuntala, an innocent forest girl, is seduced by a king, Dusyanta, who promises to make her his chief queen. When she bears a son and goes to the king to claim his heritage, she is disowned because she lost a ring given to her by Dusyanta. The ring was cursed: without it he cannot recognize her. She returns home to spend seven years in loneliness, uncertainty, and depression. Finally, the missing ring is returned to Dusyanta: he searches for her, comes upon a child playing with a lion, recognizes his son, and takes mother and child back to his kingdom.

In Mrinalini's version, Shakuntala challenges her fate, asking why no one protected her and why communications broke down so that no one told her of the terrible curse. At the end she cries: "I am alone, so, so, alone."

Another dance, *Memory Is a Ragged Fragment of Eternity*, is about the trauma of an Indian girl's marriage. It begins with a girl playing ball and flying kites; she is taken from her games to be married; she is excited with her new husband, but he leaves to work in the fields; her in-laws crowd around: on their side hatred and greed, on hers desperation and sorrow. The girl is an outsider, suspect whatever she does; she tries to run away, but they draw her back into a tight circle. She can bear it no longer; she kills herself and her tiny child by jumping into a well; the crowd shrugs and leaves. Mrinalini said the dance was inspired by an actual incident.

"There was a case of suicide in Saurashtra. I'm from Kerala, where we had a matriarchal society and didn't have the problem of women with a poor estimate of themselves. When I came here, I saw this problem: I was one of the first to speak out through dance in the 1960s. But I also did a dance that brought out the power of the women. In our literature women are important. That became a little dim over the years, but now women are speaking out again for themselves."

The dance, *Parashakti* (the Supreme Goddess; the embodiment of universal energy), is one of Mrinalini's more mystical works. It begins by recalling the sickness of an affluent world contrasted with the poverty of the masses and thousands of maimed and starving children, and leads to the concept of universal awareness and the perfection of the Mother, through which we can realize our true selves and return to righteousness.

The Atman and Meditative Silence

Mrinalini said she was becoming more spiritual. "I feel the deeper I go into myself the more I can create. I have always had a feeling of universality, but I feel it much more now. The Atman, the inner being, is one with everybody. When you touch the Atman in a person, you go straight through the barrier of culture and creed or country. I always see a person now as a person."

Although I had intended to discuss contemporary social problems, somehow we got to talking about silence.

"I love silence, especially meditative silence," she said. "It's so full of sound and music. You force the audience to make their own music. I did a piece once, from the *Rig Vedas*—"The Song of Creation"—with no words or music; just the sound of a piece of wood beating or tapping. That's how we rehearse our dances, hitting a wooden block with a stick. The audience was shocked for a while; then they began to like it a lot, especially when I did it in colleges. The young people liked it because I asked them to put their meaning into it. When I asked them what meaning they put into it, they had some marvelous things to tell me."

Finally, I came back to the subject. I said her *Ganga*, *Shakuntala*, and *Memory* seemed pessimistic, leaving only a mystical hope for the future.

"When one writes or dances, one does not always want to show the optimistic side," she said. "I'm making people aware of a problem by enlarging it in dance. That doesn't mean I feel the problem can't be solved or isn't being solved. If you dance or write, you must show the reality and not necessarily give a solution. The audience must find the solution: truth can touch the audience, nothing else.

"We're all desperate about what we're going to do. But I have faith in the human being. We have many groups in Ahmedabad talking about the pollution and social troubles, and the poor have a voice, which they never had before."

In many parts of India, it is difficult to sustain such optimism. For instance, there is Bihar, where civil society has all but collapsed.

28 ❋ Bihar: Blindings and Massacres

Bihar, India's second most populous state, is the land of Buddha, who taught *ahimsa* (peace), and of Ashoka, who in about 250 B.C., renounced war as an instrument of state policy to promulgate the Buddhist message of universal brotherhood throughout Asia. In this century it was at Champaran in Bihar that Mahatma Gandhi launched the first nonviolent civil disobedience campaign on Indian soil.

But Bihar's past is mocked by Bihar's present. On the night of July 5, 1980, police in Bhagalpur in central Bihar learned that Anil Yadav, wanted for murder and robbery, would attend a wedding at a nearby village. He was arrested and brought to the Sabour police station where, according to police, he confessed his crimes and agreed to go with police to a place where hidden guns were recovered.

He was brought back to the Sabour station on July 7. There, Mohammed Wasimuddin, who was in charge, ordered his men to take Yadav into the yard and tie his arms and legs. Then Wasimuddin blinded Yadav by stabbing his eyes with an iron file and pouring acid into them. Binda Prasad, a subinspector, and Mankeshwar Singh, an inspector from the Bhagalpur Sadar police station, watched the blinding.

On the night of July 24, 1980, nine men were brought to the Sabour station on charges of planning to commit a robbery. Two days later one of the men, Lakhi Mahto, was taken to a separate room and beaten with lathis. The next morning he was made to lie in the courtyard, his hands and legs were tied, and Mohammed Wasimuddin stabbed one of his eyes with an iron file. Mankeshwar Singh stabbed the other eye with a second file, after which Binda Prasad poured acid into both eyes to complete the blinding.

Two other accused, Shankar Tanti and Anirudh Tanti, were taken to Shankar's house where, after nothing was discovered during a search, Shankar was told if he did not pay a bribe of five hundred rupees he would be blinded. He did not have that much money, but Anirudh Tanti's wife managed to find 150 rupees to pay the police.

The two men were returned to the Sabour station where Shankar Tanti was blinded by Wasimuddin, who stabbed both his eyes with a file, after which Binda Prasad poured acid into the eyes. The next morning the two blinded men, along with the others arrested for planning the robbery, were sent to the Bhagalpur central jail.

When news of the blindings leaked to the press, it was discovered the Bhagalpur police had blinded as many as thirty persons. The cry for police punishment was universal, but, as the Maya Tyagi and similar cases had long since proved, the police are rarely brought to book.

Out of fifteen officers originally suspended for complicity in the numerous blindings, twelve were exonerated and reinstated. For seven years the magistrate in whose jurisdiction the incidents occurred stalled action against the remaining three relatively junior officers, Mankeshwar Singh, Mohammed Wasimuddin, and Binda Prasad. Finally, the evidence was transferred to B. P. Yadav, a special judicial magistrate in Patna, the state capital, and in September 1987 Yadav sentenced the three to life in prison. The other cases were forgotten, as was the connivance of officers much higher in the chain of command, some of whom were promoted.

The Roots of Violence

The "Bhagalpur Blindings," as they came to be called, and an endless series of intercaste massacres in Bihar, are manifestations of the weakness of civil society in India and the concomitant lack of authority of the state. The disorder is a result of two linked processes that have been reshaping India since the arrival of the British.

The first concerns land ownership and landless labor. Under the British, former tax collectors, known as Zamindars, were given ownership of vast tracts of land, making them superloyal instruments of the Raj. As such, they were obvious targets for the Indian National Congress, and their titles were abolished soon after independence.

Zamindari abolition was hailed as a land reform measure, with surplus acreage under land ceiling laws to go to the landless. Instead, the surplus was grabbed by rising rural middle castes who took advantage of laws giving them title to lands where previously they were ten-

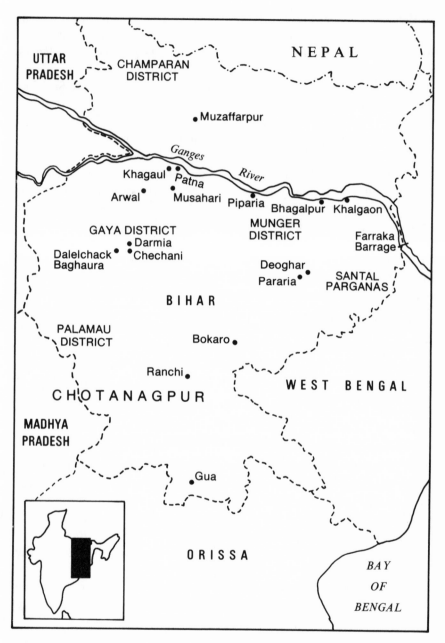

Bihar

ants. Simultaneously these large middle castes evicted poorer families to prevent them from claiming similar title as assured tenants.

The landless pool swelled with destruction of the handicraft base of village society, followed by the arrival of labor-saving machines and other high-cost inputs such as fertilizers and pesticides. These made it difficult for a farmer with no capital or access to loans to succeed even if he managed to obtain a few acres.

As a result, on a nationwide basis 45 percent of rural households own zero to less than one acre of farmland, including their homesite. In some states, notably Gujarat, Punjab and Haryana, many of the landless have found work in the expanding dairy and food-processing industries, but little of this has occurred in Bihar. In every statistical category, whether it is land ownership, per capita income, health care, or literacy, Bihar ranks at or near the bottom when compared to other states. Four percent of households operate over 25 percent of the total cultivated area, while 67 percent of rural families operate only 18 percent of the land. Impoverishment in Bihar has been a fact of life for so long that large numbers of the poor are known by the caste name of *Musahars* (Rat Eaters). They subsist on field mice, gleanings, and agricultural waste.

An estimated 600,000 Biharis migrate every year, searching for little more than subsistence wages and are so favored by labor contractors they depress rural wages throughout north India.

The Competition of Castes

The second process reshaping India is the rise of locally dominant castes.

One of the many ways in which twice-born landowners distinguish themselves is their refusal to do manual labor. They will not, as it is often phrased, "touch the handle of the plow." This meant there were always large castes who knew how to farm but simply lacked access to land. When the British introduced new commercial opportunities, these castes were able to accumulate capital to gain control of increasing amounts of land.

Indian politics is marked by the rise of one or two such castes in almost every state: the Patidars in Gujarat, the Mahars in Maharashtra, the Jats in Rajasthan and Punjab, the Lingayats in Karnataka, the Kammas and Reddis in Andhra Pradesh, the Ezhavas in Kerala, and the Nadars in Tamil Nadu.

Several ruthless land owning castes emerged in Bihar. They monopolized the benefits of Zamindari abolition and got most of the land vacated by thousands of Muslims who fled from Patna District after the partition riots.

This led, roughly, to a three-way division of Bihari society. At the top, and forming about 13 percent of the population, are the upper castes: Brahmin, Rajput, Bhoomihar, and Kayastha. The Bhoomihars emerged in the last century as a caste specific to Bihar and eastern Uttar Pradesh. Although not priests, they claimed to be Brahmins. They are "cultivators" in the sense of being close to the land and actually doing much of the work, with the exception of tabooed plowing. In the last century a British account described them as "military Brahmins and they are still prone to violence." The Kayasthas arose as "writers" or administrators for Muslim rulers and spread with the Muslims throughout India, particularly to the princely state of Hyderabad in the south.

With the rise of the militant and often violent middle castes, these upper castes have migrated in large numbers to urban areas to become civil servants, police officials, merchants, bankers, contractors, and college and university teachers and administrators: using caste solidarity virtually to monopolize new avenues of jobs and education. In 1988 when a Brahmin, Bhagwat Jha Azad, was chief minister, the collectors (highest-ranking officials) of thirty-one of Bihar's thirty-nine districts were Brahmins or Kayasthas, including five who had been promoted to the position despite accusations of corruption.

The upper castes have not abandoned their large landholdings: one or two males of the extended families, often the youngest, remain behind to manage the properties.

In the countryside their political dominance (and to a lesser extent their economic dominance) is challenged primarily by two middle castes that began to emerge after World War I: the Yadavas and Kurmis, who form about 20 percent of the population. The Yadavas and Kurmis often employ as sharecroppers lower-ranking (although not untouchable) castes who form about 22 percent of the population—taking extreme care to deny them the rights of permanent tenants.

Dalits, including tribals, form the bottom 25 percent of Bihar society. They are given only temporary employment at the lowest possible wage: generally about five or six rupees a day, or less than half the statutory minimum wage. Women are paid even less.

The Yadavas and Kurmis thus have a two-front war: against the upper castes who deny them access to the power concentrated in urban centers and against the Dalits and tribals who demand steady work and a minimum wage.

Atrocity After Atrocity

The intercaste struggle and the desperate efforts of Dalits and tribals to achieve mere subsistence has led to atrocity after atrocity. Daily killings are so common only mass murders gain media attention.

In February 1980, at Parasbigha in Gaya District, eleven Yadavas were killed by Bhoomihars. Later in the same month Kurmi landlords descended on the village of Piparia and massacred fourteen Dalits.

In August 1983 four men of the Dhanuk caste were killed by Yadavas in Munger District on the south bank of the Ganges. The Dhanuks got revenge the following January. They kidnapped fourteen children from Piparia village, some as young as eight and nine, who had crossed the river to gather fodder. All except three were murdered and their bodies chopped into pieces and thrown into the river so their remains would never be found.

In December 1985, in another part of Munger, Yadavas on horses and on foot swooped down on the village where tribal Bhinds were living. There was a dispute between Rajputs and Yadavas over ownership of the land, and the Rajputs had brought in the Bhinds to cultivate it. The raiders killed nine persons and burned and plundered more than four hundred houses. Among those killed was an infant girl snatched from her mother's lap and thrown into a burning house.

In April 1986 seven Yadavas were killed by a Rajput raiding party in Chotaki Chechani village. The following October Yadavas killed eleven Rajputs in Darmia village.

The most gruesome massacre occurred in May 1987 when the Yadavas struck again for revenge of the Chotaki Chechani killings: they slaughtered forty-two Rajput men, women, and children, ranging in age from two to eighty, in Dalelchak and Baghaura villages in Aurangabad District. After the men were killed, a pit was scooped out in front of the door of one house. Women from the house were forced to place their necks on the rim of the pit and then were beheaded with crude, locally made axes. A Dalit who unluckily happened to be in Baghaura as a tractor driver was also killed: tied to the steering wheel and burned alive.

Arvind Das, a sociologist who has long studied Bihar, wrote that the raid represented a traditional response to a perceived threat, called *gohar*:

a term representing a phenomenon so indigenous it is not easy to find an equivalent in another language and culture. It has been roughly translated as attack but that is only a small aspect of the actual process. It includes summoning friends, relations, armed retainers and dependent clients to help avenge a real or perceived attack on the social, economic or cultural position of the affected party. . . . Having gathered the solidarity group, it is supplied with food and drink and "honor" and "tradition" is invoked. . . . When sufficient intensity of emotion is built up, the group . . . proceeds generally in broad daylight to perform the gohar on the perceived enemy. . . . A gohar is the response of a divided society unmediated by the rule of the state.

All the major castes maintain their own armies, often in the guise of social welfare organizations. The Brahmins have their Azad *Sena* (Army) named after Chandra Shekhar Azad, active in the freedom movement against the British. (*Azad* also means freedom, so the name can also be translated Freedom Army.) The Azad Sena indoctrinates young people through a college named after Sanjay Gandhi.

The Rajput private army is called the Kuer Sena, named after Veer Kuer Singh, a local hero of the 1857 uprising against the British. The Rajputs also operate a college for recruiting purposes. The Bhoomihars have their *Bramharshi* Sena (literally, the Army of the Sage). The Yadavas have their Lorik Sena, named after Lorik Chand, an early Yadava hero. Kurmis call their group the Bhoomi Sena—Land Army. The Bhoomi Sena is the most vicious in attacks on Dalits.

The Bhoomi Sena supports itself though a tax known as *rangdaari* (one who can exercise dominance). It means if a person is strong enough to collect a tax or some other extortion that is what he will do. The Bhoomi Sena sets up posts along roads to collect rangdaari from all who pass.

The Bhoomi Sena can get away with this because, as a landlord group, it has the support of the police. A notorious incident occurred in February 1984 when police staged a predawn raid on the village of Anatpur and arrested fourteen Dalits who had refused to pay a Bhoomi Sena rangdaari. They were taken to a nearby village, hanged upside down, and beaten in the presence of Bhoomi Sena thugs.

Lawless Lawmen

India's police codes, taken over intact from the British, are based on the need to protect property and maintain order, with or without the formal support of law. More than a third of the operative sections of the Indian Penal Code relate to offenses against property rights. A separate chapter, titled "Maintenance of Public Order and Tranquility," gives the district administration absolute power to prevent a breach of peace and public order and to disperse any unlawful assembly by use of force.

The decision of what constitutes an unlawful assembly is left to these same local authorities. The lowest-ranking officer at a rural police post can easily take into custody a farm laborer or sharecropper who might assert his right to a minimum wage, security of tenure, or any other of the nominal provisions of the land reform and labor laws. By the logic of the Penal Code the poor who fight for their rights are enemies of law and order.

The most notorious instance in Indian colonial history of this principle occurred on April 13, 1919, when Brigadier General Reginald Dyer decided to teach a lesson to Indian nationalists, mainly Sikhs, who had gathered at a public garden known as Jallianwalla Bagh in Amritsar in Punjab in defiance of an order banning such demonstrations. Dyer's troops blocked the only exit from the garden, opened fire, and kept shooting until they had exhausted their ammunition, killing at least 379 persons and wounding over 1,200.

Sixty-seven years later, almost to the day, a miniature Jallianwalla Bagh massacre was enacted at Arwal in Bihar. On April 19, 1986, the police blocked the exit of an enclosed area in front of the Gandhi Library and opened fire on seven hundred landless laborers who had gathered in defiance of an order, issued under section 144 of the Criminal Procedure Code, prohibiting meetings of more than five persons. Twenty-one men and women were killed in an escalation of what should have been a minor police matter.

A landlord had built a wall blocking the drainage of water from the huts of nine landless families. They were arrested when they tore down the wall. Normally they would have been released on personal bond for a court hearing. But they were kept in jail, and when local activists called the meeting at the Gandhi Library to demand their release, the police decided to make it an issue of prestige and to "teach a lesson." That is exactly what Brigadier General Dyer said he had done at Jallianwalla Bagh.

The Rape of Pararia

In February 1988 forty police inspectors, subinspectors and constables, home guards, and *chowkidars* (watchmen) descended on the Yadava village of Pararia in Deoghar District and raped fourteen women between the ages of thirteen and fifty. Nose rings and earrings were bloodily torn off, and every house in the village was robbed of gold and silver, stainless steel and copper utensils, and anything else of value. A seventy-six-year-old man who tried to protect his daughter-in-law was beaten with lathis, and a lathi was inserted into his anus. The attackers wanted to avenge the assault, a week earlier, on a constable and a chowkidar.

In March 1989 all eight policemen and six chowkidars accused of the mass rape were acquitted. The judge quoted the defense counsel who argued the raped women were engaged in "menial" work and could not be equated with "such ladies who hail from decent and respectable society." The judge found: "It cannot be ruled out that these ladies might speak falsehood to get a sum of one thousand rupees which was a huge sum for them." He referred to compensation granted the victims after the mass rape was first disclosed and leading politicians proclaimed justice must be done.

One woman had described what appeared to be a common sexual position for rape, but the judge did not agree: "Radhia Devi has stated in her deposition that she was thrown on the ground on her back. Two chowkidars had caught her legs and hands and three policemen committed rape with her. It was argued by the learned defense counsel . . . that such a posture at the time of rape was inconceivable. . . . I also find much weight in the argument."

He found another victim was not the person she claimed to be because a doctor who examined her said she had a mole on her neck when it was really above her breast and "she did not answer questions properly. Sometimes she began crying. Sometimes she stated that she would not speak at all."

The doctor found sperm in the vaginal smear of another victim. The judge ruled that she was separated from her husband and was a "freelancer" and not a reliable witness. But an *India Today* reporter who visited the village after the accused were freed found the woman's husband divided his time between his own house and the nearby home of his parents and had never abandoned his wife. He said he still stood by her: "We have a four-year-old child, and it was not her fault that she was raped. Why should I leave her?"

One of the rape victims told the reporter: "The policemen pushed me inside and kicked my one-year-old child to the courtyard. When I cried for my child, they said that I could have another child."

The River of Sorrows

Bihar is crisscrossed by twenty-three large and small rivers, and there are floods every year. In 1987 floods affected thirty of the state's thirty-nine districts, killing at least 1,100 people, making 2 million homeless, destroying property worth $840 million, and burying 10,000 acres of farmland under sand.

The shifting courses of the rivers is known as the *Diara*, fertile regions with no fixed landmarks. As some land disappears, new land is constantly created. Or a village is cut in half by a change in the course of a river: does the land on the other bank still belong to the original village or is it new land?

This disappearance and appearance of land is the cause of much of the bloody caste battles. Whoever is the nearest, whoever has lost land, and whoever is the strongest will try to occupy it, and ownership will remain controversial for ten or twenty years.

The Ganges is called the "River of Sorrows," and everything in it or near it is a source of wealth, either for use or to extract rangdaari: sudden death is the retribution for claiming what another says is his.

In November 1987 eleven fishermen from Bengal set out in two boats to cast a large net, known as a *mahajal*, in the Ganges about fifty kilometers south of Bhagalpur. They had been hired by a contractor to do the work and took some lunch, thinking they would return at the end of the day with their catch. Somewhere near a sandbank called Rani Diara, they were attacked and killed. Their legs were hacked off, and their stomachs were slit so they would sink beneath the waters and never be found. Nine days later someone told a relative of one of the men what had happened, and divers were sent, and their bodies were recovered.

But even Bihar, which so reeks of blood, has its activists and its hopes. For instance, Anil Prakash, who leads the fishermen of the Ganges in a struggle called the *Ganga Mukti Andolan* (Ganges Liberation Movement).

29 ❀ The Role of Activists

Educated activists who sense a new world eager to be born are a spark for the vast majority of people who cling to established ways and beliefs. For Gramsci, their originality is that they shape the present into the future:

> Creating a new culture does not only mean one's individual "original" discoveries. It also, and most particularly, means the diffusion in a critical form of truths already discovered, their "socialization" as it were, and even making them the basis of vital action, an element of coordination and intellectual and moral order. The leading of a mass of men to think coherently and in a unitary way about present-day reality is a "philosophical" fact of much greater importance and "originality" than the discovery by a philosophical "genius" of a new truth which remains the inheritance of small groups of intellectuals.

Anil Prakash is a small, average-looking man who speaks hesitantly in even tones and who could easily be lost in a crowd. He is also modest and does not seek personal publicity. When I explained I was doing research on grass-roots social activism, Anil said I should go to Uttar Pradesh where there was a farmers' leader who held meetings of tens of thousands of people. I thanked him for his suggestion but said it was the fishermen who interested me. He said he did not have time to talk because he was leaving for a remote village on the Ganges. When I asked to go along, he said there would be no place for me to stay: it was only a fishermen's village, and, besides, we would have to travel by a country bus. When I showed I had reduced my belongings to a small canvas bag and a light blanket for sleeping on the ground, his doubts were mollified. We got into a jeep station wagon, and fifteen people squeezed into space for nine passengers, and bounced and lurched to Kahalgaon, thirty-five kilometers to the north.

The fishermen, being untouchables, were segregated at the far end of the village. We walked through several streets of the bazaar, past two-story brick houses, and finally reached narrow, winding lanes leading to the Ganges. To my eyes this was the prettiest part of the village. The lanes were dry and clean, and the mud-walled houses were smoothly plastered with the lower portions painted a cobalt blue. Our host gave me his string bed, and he and Anil slept on the floor wrapped in a single cotton quilt. The next morning he told me about himself.

"My father was a government official in Muzaffarpur in north Bihar," he said. "When I was fifteen, I read a story by Rabindranath Tagore about a student who came to a village and started education for men and women, not only literary but social education too. He also treated someone who was sick. He was not a hero; he was a simple student, and I tried to imitate him. I went to huts to see the people and coach some poor boys. I saved money from my clothing by buying cheaper clothes, and when my father and mother gave me money to go to the cinema, I bought books. I also asked people to give me books and started a library of about two hundred books. In college I studied physics and got such good marks one of my uncles wanted me to go to America to study atomic physics.

"Then, when the Naxalites began to chant, "Blood, Blood, Blood of Capitalists," and "A candle can burn a whole forest," I started reading about Marxism and Socialism. When Jayaprakash Narayan settled in Musahari in Muzaffarpur District to prove Sarvodaya could provide a nonviolent alternative to the Naxalites, he gave the slogan: 'Don't oppress anyone and don't allow anyone to oppress you.' In 1974, when I was twenty-three, I answered his call."

The Mahant and the Musahars

In 1975 JP formed the *Chhatra Yuva Sangharsh Vahini* (United Youth Organization for Change). Anil and others now prominent in social movements in Bihar and elsewhere in India got their training with the Vahini. During the 1977–78 Emergency, Anil was jailed three times for terms of from one month to six-and-a-half months. After JP's death the Vahini concentrated on a struggle against the *Mahant* (hereditary head) of the Hindu Bodh Gaya *Mutt* (monastery; also spelled Math). The Mahant controlled ten thousand acres that he claimed was temple land but most of which was registered as his personal property.

For the next few years Gaya District was the center of a struggle to redistribute the land under the Zamindari Abolition Act. There were a series of clashes with the police as activists encouraged the landless to seize parts of the Mahant's holdings. Many of the landless involved in the struggle were "rat eaters" of the Musahar caste, and when Anil and his colleagues urged them to boycott the land and leave it fallow, they obeyed with great suffering. Finally, the active phase petered out, and the battle was transferred to the courts, where a decision has yet to be reached.

The Bodh Gaya campaign had recruited and trained new activists, and its decline left many looking for new opportunities to challenge society. Some found it in another struggle against feudal rule in Kahalgaon.

Under the British, collectors of land revenues were known as Zamindars (*zamin* means land). On this analogy those who collected fees from fishermen and boatmen are called Panidars (*pani* means water). The best known is Mahashay Mahesh Ghosh, who lives in his family's ancestral home on the outskirts of Bhagalpur and claims to have been granted his rights by the Mogul Emperor Jehangir. The Ghoshes contract out their rights on long leases, and these contractors hire armed gangs to enforce their edicts.

In 1961 the Bihar government attempted to rescind Panidar rights under the Zamindari Abolition Act, but the Ghoshes filed a legal challenge. In 1964 the Patna High Court ruled in their favor. The court's reasoning was curious. It said zamin applied to land, that is, immovable property, and since the water moved, Panidars were exempt.

The Bihar government appealed to the Supreme Court in New Delhi, but the issue is politically sensitive—as are all issues that may harm the interests of property owners—and the case of the Panidars of the Ganges, like the Mahant of Bodh Gaya, has simply been left to gather dust.

A Talk by the River

Anil had been away from Kahalgaon for several months, and there was an urgent problem the fishermen wanted him to deal with. He was busy with talks and meetings for the rest of the morning, and then we took a bus a short distance down river for other meetings. After lunch we went to the river where Anil washed his clothes.

Men generally travel with a *lungi* (an ankle length circle of cloth worn loosely tied at the waist). It can also be used for undressing in public: you slip the lungi over your head and suspend it from a shoulder, removing trousers and briefs underneath. Anil undressed and stood knee deep in the mud and water of the river's edge, bending over to pound his clothes on a flat stone, chatting all the while with fishermen who came to meet him. While waiting for his clothes to dry, he told how the Ganga Mukti Andolan was formed:

"There are twenty-six castes of fishermen in Kahalgaon and its neighboring villages, but they all come under the general caste heading of *Nishad* (fishermen). Somehow, a Nishad named Ram Raj Singh managed to get a college education. He became a policeman and was appointed a subinspector at Kahalgaon. The community was in a bad state, full of prostitution and illegal alcohol. In 1969 Ram Raj Singh persuaded the Nishads to fight these twin evils. He organized a group called the Guardians to patrol the village and attend its weekly meetings. Gradually, outsiders were barred, illegal distillation and prostitution were ended, and quarrels among the villagers diminished. Ram Raj Singh has since died, but he had made a good beginning.

"It was limited, however. They organized to improve their community but had no tradition of fighting back against their oppressors. They only knew how to file petitions, which were useless. In April 1982 some of us were nearby, and they invited us to attend one of their meetings. I came for just a week. I didn't go to the bazaar. I went straight to the river and visited all the houses and went to the river every day. I thought many things could be learned, and we could start many kinds of experiments here. I came to love the people living on the banks of the Ganga, and I came to love all of nature. A few weeks later I returned and stayed for four years."

With that, I asked my usual question about how he supported himself. He said many villagers invited him to their houses to live and eat, and he wore whatever clothes they gave him. He is married and has a son. For a year his family lived with him in Kahalgaon, under the same conditions, but they now lived with his parents in Muzaffarpur. He continued his account of how he got started:

"Some of our friends thought we should not campaign on the issue of the Panidar because it was such a tough situation. Across the river there's a caste called Gangota. The contractors use them as criminals to collect their money. The whole area is a criminal area. If someone gives a gang 10,000 rupees ($700), they'll capture you and start cutting from here and here and here." He signaled with his hand an axe chopping off his leg bit by bit.

"At a conference in July 1983 I moved a resolution that the fishermen should join hands with the Gangotas and fight against the Zamindars of the land and water. At that time no one supported my resolution, but slowly, slowly the fishermen understood this was good action, and we built a bridge between the Gangotas and the fishermen. We then were in a position to fight. We organized a small procession of boats, and our movement spread to dozens of villages for thirty kilometers along both banks of the Ganga. Every exploiter sees the Ganga Mutki Andolan [GMA] is against them. We face a lot of danger, especially from guns, but we will always be a movement without arms: we're stronger than guns."

The Andolan also faced the customary police harassment of activists. When the eleven Bengali fishermen were killed at Rani Diara, two GMA men were arrested. Neither had criminal records, but the police said the Andolan had a reason because fishermen opposed outsiders coming into the area. However the press unanimously supported the activists, and they were released with no charges filed.

Reshaping a Myth

"What's your goal?" I asked. "Are you fighting for fishermen or to change society?"

"We must have a holistic approach," Anil replied. "If the poor want to change society, they must know how injustice is taking place: the mechanism, the people in front, the groups behind them, and the day-to-day consequences. The people are often fragmented and divided. The presence of a person with a real concern for them makes them come together and get organized. This is the job of an animator: not to do things for the poor or to offer monetary help but to sustain one's presence of concern.

"The Nishads suffer from an inferiority complex due to the myth of their origin. According to this, a king was cursed by a saint, and when he died, the first Nishad was born from his thigh. So they're descended from the thigh of a dead body and are supposed to do dirty things. People tell that story time and again. I felt I had to use some traditional method of mobilization and found my answer in the story of Ekalavia in the *Mahabharata*."

The *Mahabharata* is a massive collection of myths, dating from between A.D. 200 and 400 but based on song cycles from as early as 400 B.C. In bare outline it deals with a war between the Kauravas and Pandavas.

The Ekalavia story is an exegesis on the punishment for violating caste. Ekalavia, a Nishad archer who is described as "a black . . . Chandala" (outcaste), practiced so diligently he could shoot seven arrows almost simultaneously, putting the Pandava champion, Arjuna, to shame. Ekalavia falsely claimed to have been taught by Drona, the Pandava's teacher of martial arts. Drona sought him out and asked for the fee a student must give to a teacher. Ekalavia replied, "There is nothing I shall withhold from my guru." Drona then asked, "Give me your right thumb." Ekalavia kept his promise, and since he had to shoot only with his fingers, he lost his amazing speed. Nishad is a general name for the earlier, tribal society of India, but Anil took it in its modern meaning of fisherman.

"The myth says it's outrageous for a person of a low caste like a Nishad to learn to handle a bow. Well, we organized an Ekalavia *Mela* [fair]. We discussed modern things, like the pollution of the Ganga, but we had a second objective: to achieve a sense of dignity. We conveyed a message that a Nishad, Ekalavia, was a great man, and we could copy him, but we're not going to commit the same mistake of giving up our thumbs. We're not going to be exploited again by these upper caste people or the government."

The Boat Procession to Patna

"For six months about fifty men and women organized hundreds of meetings, day and night, on both sides of the river all the way to Patna," Anil continued. "We also staged cultural programs from village to village. We were obstructed by politicians, the vested interests, and the musclemen, but a new awakening was created. Then in 1987 we had a boat procession from Kahalgaon to Patna. We started with two boats and ended with more than two hundred. It took us fourteen days—the winds were against us and the current was against us—but we pulled the boats by ropes if necessary. The people came and garlanded us and gave us money." He referred to the Indian custom of greeting an honored guest by putting a long chain of flowers, generally marigolds, around his or her neck.

"All along the way we spread our message. First, there should be no Zamindari or Panidari system. Every boatman and fisherman should be free to catch fish without paying any tax. The contractors claim everything belongs to them. In the rainy season, when the rivers flood, the fish spread out and are left behind in ponds when the water recedes.

The contractors say even the fish in a farmer's yard belongs to them. They say, 'If fish from the Ganga goes into your house, even into a room where a couple is sleeping, we are entitled to enter and fish.'

"Our second demand was that small spawn should not be caught. Contractors hire men to collect fish spawn and to seed their ponds at fourteen places where the females lay eggs and males fertilize them. Ninety percent of the spawn is destroyed in the catching and half of what is caught is lost in the transmission. They're destroying the fish of the Ganga and major rivers this way.

"Third, there should be a fish ladder on the Farraka Barrage. The barrage prevents the migration of *hilsa* (a species of fish, once the major food fish of the Ganges), and fishermen have lost one of their major sources of income." He referred to the barrage (dam) built to channel water into the Hooghly River to flush out pollution at Calcutta.

"Fourth," Anil continued, "they should close a fertilizer plant that's polluting the river and they should not build a thermal power station that has been planned and which will also harm the fishing.

"Fifth, no chemical fertilizers or pesticides should be used on any of the fields on both sides of the Ganga: only organic matter to promote natural nitrogen fixing.

"Sixth, no cutting of trees in the Himalayas and an intensive afforestation program to control floods.

"And seventh and last, the landlords of the Diara should throw away their guns and come with us and start a nonviolent movement."

"Aren't you using the fishermen?" I asked. "It seems to me you're putting ideas into people's heads for purposes beyond their immediate concern."

"No, everything I tell you I learned from these people," Anil replied. "The thought to oppose the Farraka Barrage came from the fishermen's wives because fish and lobster disappeared, and their income was threatened. They were also being sexually exploited because the fishermen had to go to other places to fish or find jobs. People from the upper castes, the contractors and their musclemen, started exploiting the women in the absence of their husbands.

"The fishermen also said the effluent from the fertilizer plant was flowing into the Ganga and killing thousands of tons of fish. But it's true a high scientist advised us to include the demand to ban fertilizers and pesticides. He said it not only harms the ecosystem of the Ganga but also kills the soil.

"After the boat march the fishermen were so excited they demanded that we start a no-tax campaign against Zamindars and Panidars. But I stopped it. Instead, myself and others went all through the Diara and met people in different villages. We even met criminals. Then, when we were sure we had full support, we launched it.

"The fishermen and women were tremendous. They surrounded the boats and stopped the spawn collection, and they made sure no one paid anything to the contractors. The women were in front, and people were beaten, but no one was afraid. Police went into the villages and demanded the people come out. 'Who are the ones not paying taxes?' the police asked. Everyone replied, 'I'm the one. I have obstructed the Zamindar's men.' And they asked questions back: 'What right do the police have to interfere in a private action? This is a civil dispute between the fishermen and the contractors.'

"Still the contractors bribed the police, and between thirty and fifty men and women were arrested. But they were later freed, and to this day, after almost two years, no one has paid anything to the contractors and Zamindars."

Anil was not among those arrested. He was ill at the time, living with his family in Muzaffarpur. The fact that he was absent at such a critical time is evidence leadership had been devolved to the local people.

When Anil's clothes were dry, we returned to Kahalgaon, and Anil went off for more talks. Late in the afternoon he arranged a meeting with three men and a woman who were leaders of the village Fishermen's Cooperative Society, which he described as the most recent success story. It was also an act of village courtesy. We met at an outdoor tea stall, where all could see us, and someone produced a brass tray of puffed rice and spiced nuts and grains for snacks.

The chairman was Kailash Prasad Sahni, a short, thin, serious man. He said he had studied through the first year of college and that his father was a high school graduate who had taken part in the freedom movement. In the process the family had raised itself from being simple fishermen to owners of a fish store in Calcutta. When the fishermen decided to fight to gain control of the cooperative, they persuaded Kailash to agree to spend part of his time in the village to handle things.

With Anil translating they questioned me: why had I come to their village; was I married; how many children did I have; how old was I? Their curiosity satisfied, I was free to ask Anil about the cooperative.

A Second Victory

"There are 409 fishermen's cooperatives in Bihar," he said. "The government gets revenues by selling fishing and other rights. It gives the contract to some big person, some goonda, some monied man, who pretends he has a cooperative society. That fellow then rents out the right to fishermen. He charges according to the size of the pond or boat, which fish will be caught, or which nets of what size. According to law, the rights are supposed to go to cooperatives controlled by the people, but they go to middlemen.

"The law also says there has to be an election of cooperative officers every three years and that all fishermen and their wives, who are also fishing workers, must be enrolled, but the big men and their goondas frighten people away. Then, last December, the fishermen of Kahalgaon and neighboring villages got organized. They enrolled members for a fee of one rupee a year and elected Kailash as cooperative chairman by a vote of 139 to 103. Now they'll enroll hundreds of new members to make sure they keep control.

"The cooperative will give them a lot of money. It controls a small stream near here that produces a revenue of 200,000 rupees ($14,000) a year. Of this, 45,000 to 50,000 ($3,150–$3,500) will go in taxes to the government. Another 100,000 ($7,000) will have to be paid to the fishermen who do the work. That will leave 50,000 to 55,000 ($3,500–$3,850) for the cooperative. We'll use some of that money to build a community center with a library and a women's emancipation center. We'll also have some money every year to help spread the movement to other areas.

"The Ganga Mukti Andolan has activated fisher folk of all directions and all the rivers. People are calling us eager to displace their old leaders. Honest new leaders will emerge from working fishermen and women. There are seven million fishermen in Bihar: about 10 percent of the total population. If we bring this 10 percent of the population together, it will be a huge political force."

I asked my usual question: were they thinking of forming a political party?

"No, political parties are corrupt," he replied. "None of us will be candidates. There are not only fishermen. There are weavers, farmers, tribals, coal workers, and landless workers. A day will come when we will form a workers' council in our area of influence. We have already started a weavers' movement, and some of them have come to our meetings. We urge people to boycott polyester cloth, and we say the Bata shoe factory should be closed and small shoemakers should be supported."

Bata Shoes, an international chain that makes and sells cheap shoes, originated in India. However, they are still expensive compared to sandals made by village cobblers.

"Do villagers buy Bata shoes?" I asked.

"Generally not," he replied. "But such products are signs of wealth. People want to wear Bata shoes for important occasions, like marriages. This is a dangerous trend. We have a Youth Forum for students. We plan to campaign all over Bihar against this consumer culture."

Anil and the others went off to a meeting, and I was taken to Kailash's house for a special fish dinner. I returned to the home of our original host and was asleep when Anil returned. The next morning I wanted to ask him about that long meeting, but we left early to return to Bhagalpur, where Anil was arranging a protest demonstration.

The Role of an Animator

After 1986 Anil spent more time with his family in Muzaffarpur and with statewide activities: he is Bihar chairman of the *Sampurna Kranti Manch* (Society for Total Revolution), a national alliance of fourteen organizations that was created during the latter days of Jayaprakash Narayan. Although he shuns party politics, he is a political activist. About two weeks earlier the Bhagalpur leader of the National Students Union of India and some of his musclemen had barged into the house of a doctor, kidnapped his eighteen-year-old daughter, and forced her at gunpoint to go through a marriage ceremony.

The misnamed Students Union is widely regarded as the criminal arm of the ruling Congress Party. Several of its members, including one of its general secretaries, were implicated in bank robberies in Patna and two other cities. Anil had come to Bhagalpur for a demonstration against the entire political establishment. He needed people to march and shout slogans, and when I met him, he was enroute to Kahalgaon to recruit fishermen and their wives for this purpose.

When we arrived back in Bhagalpur, he began work on his demonstration, planned for the next day, and it was not until evening that he had time to tell me about the long meeting the night before.

"Four or five months ago," he said, "a gang leader of the Gangotas from across the river came and said his men were unemployed: the fishermen were not paying taxes, and so they had been dismissed by the contractors. He wanted the fishermen to hire his gang as guards. There was a reason for this: every month somebody shoots at our boats to steal the catch or nets. A few of our leaders agreed to give four hundred rupees to the gang leader without taking the issue to the entire membership. When the rest of the group found out, they stopped all contributions to the organization. They felt the leaders should not have acted on their own.

"Last night all this was discussed. People said it was a bad thing: no money should be given to criminals. It was decided if we want to recruit anyone to protect us, he must not guard with an unlicensed gun and must act under terms of our organization. They said, 'If anyone wants to join us, let him, but he should first throw his guns into the Ganga.'

"It was also decided the people who had approved paying the four hundred rupees would have to give the money out of their own pockets and would also have to pay a fine of eight hundred rupees."

"What did you have to say on this?" I asked.

"Nothing. The whole night I spoke only four or five sentences."

"Then why all those consultations for two days and why were they so anxious to have you attend the meeting?"

"Because I had been there only a few days in the past four months. There was a communications gap and internal tension. The people think I'm their son and brother and nephew: they love me as a family member and as a good man. They don't need any decisions or suggestions from above. In my absence the movement can go on. But when there's an intragroup crisis, I am called to bridge the gap."

"Then," I said, "I'll repeat my earlier question: What is your role? Are you the leader of the Ganga Mukti Andolan?"

"I'm not against leadership. When I thought they were planning to start the no-tax campaign without adequate preparation, I asked them to postpone it, and they did. But I'm against all hierarchy, against all misuse of position, against all types of artistocracy: intellectual, social, or bureaucratic. The people are the source of all my ideas: I only articulate them in a larger perspective. I'm a kind of computer, taking information from different sources and organizing it to do everyone the most good. This is not the same as leadership; it's people working together."

The next morning I watched as the men and women from Kahalgaon sat at a crossroads in Bhagalpur to protest the kidnapping of the young woman. I waved goodbye to Anil (he barely looked up as he sat on the street, hunched over with friends writing a placard denouncing the kidnapping) and took a train to Patna to meet a man who is using plays, songs, and dances to challenge an oppressive society.

30 ☀ Nonviolent Melodrama

I arrived, as usual without notice, at the combination office and home of a man I knew only as a name: Raghupati. I was told he was devoted to nonviolence and had dropped his second name because it denoted caste. His center, appropriately, was near a circle called Buddha *Murti* (statue: in this instance a large, seated image of the Buddha) not far from one of the main streets of Patna.

I had a letter of introduction from a friend in Delhi asking that I be put up for a few days, but I came at an inopportune time. His organization, *Samta Gram Seva Sansthan* (roughly, Service Organization for Rural Equality), was preparing for its annual *Rang Mela* (Cultural Fair), and several other guests had arrived before me. I could have stayed at any of several nearby small hotels, but I can only learn about people by living with them.

Raghupati—about five-feet-five, heavily built, with a trim, black beard—arrived after dark. He read the letter and noted things were crowded, but it is the height of impropriety for an Indian to turn away a guest, and he said I was welcome to what they had. Three of us, and sometimes four, would share a medium-sized room used for sleeping, eating, working, and lounging. The only bed was reserved for the guest of honor, Kamleshwar Prasad Singh.

Raghupati had to go out again. I had told him I was interested in the link between culture and social protest. He said Kamleshwar, a small, neat man in his middle sixties who was one of Bihar's leading poets and the founder of an academy of dance and drama in Samastipur District near the Nepali border, could answer my questions.

"I began to write poetry of nationalism and patriotism in 1948," Kamleshwar said. "Then I wrote plays and songs and traveled with sixty-five artists and two trucks that could be converted into a stage. We put on seven and as many as fifteen different performances: social dramas against dowry, prostitution, and alcohol and national dramas, for instance, about the Jallianwalla Bagh massacre. You must speak in the language of the people and use their images. Social development does not depend on the talk of politicians."

The next morning I went in a cycle rickshaw with Raghupati to a school with a large assembly room, surrounded by smaller rooms, where the performers had settled in. A gathering of a hundred or so people is surprisingly easy in India. Everyone travels with his or her own bedding, and no one minds sleeping on the floor (with, of course, no mingling of the sexes). And everyone is satisfied with simple meals of chapatis, a curried vegetable, and *dal* (a gram, such as split peas or lentils).

Raghupati spent the day overseeing arrangements and going over with Kamleshwar the songs and scripts some of the groups had prepared. In the afternoon, when there was a lunch break, I was able to ask Raghupati about himself.

In and Out of Jail

"My family was Rajput, but we were poor, and my father could not afford a good school or warm clothes. In 1962, when I was fifteen, I joined the Socialist Youth Front, and in 1969 I was elected joint secretary for Bihar. The same year I was arrested for the first time for leading a peaceful demonstration and was sent to jail for one month. I was arrested again for leading peaceful demonstrations in 1971, 1972, and 1973 and served three or four months each time.

"In 1974 I joined JP's movement in Bihar. Just before the Emergency I was arrested while making a speech at Gandhi *Maidan* (an open space or park) and was beaten unconscious. The police then took me to the *kotwali* (police station) for interrogation, and when I didn't reply to their questions, they beat me with sticks on the soles of my feet and with their hands. I was later sent to jail for six months. Just one day after I was released I was arrested again under the Defense of India Act, which allows the government to hold someone for six months without explaining why. When that six months was up, they put me in a camp jail for three months.

"I thought everything would be fine in 1977 when the Janata Party was elected, and the chief minister was Kapoori Thakur, a Socialist. But the newspapers revealed the story of a Rajput boy who married a scheduled caste girl. The people caught them and cut their hair. They rode the boy backward on a donkey and put the girl in a dark house for six months. The man who instigated the torture was a member of the state legislature. We *gheraoed* [to detain a person by surrounding him, sometimes for several days] Kapoori Thakur, and he put me in jail for five months.

"Politics was not serving the people, and in 1979 I organized my own movement for social work in villages. About four years ago we started this organization. It's an alliance of many groups, but each is independent."

I asked him about funding.

"The other groups contribute one rupee a year per member. We also have about a hundred members who give 1 percent of their salary or 1 percent of their income or 1 percent of their expenditures, however they want to figure it. We're very active in emergencies: we distributed food and blankets during the floods a few years ago and after the big earthquake in Bihar earlier this year."

"And are things peaceful with you now?"

"No, I still make protests. I once went to Muzaffarpur for a small meeting on some disputed paddy fields. The police came in the night and beat me like anything and then caught me by the legs and pulled me for about a kilometer through the paddy. People went to the jail to protest and got my release. I was arrested again and was sent to a jail in the town of Arora. The next time I went to a jail in Rupar. I've been charged with everything from robbery to arson. There's no jail in Bihar I haven't seen.

"The most recent arrest was in 1987, when I went to Gaya to protest corruption. Nearby, there was a protest about the land of the Mahant of Bodh Gaya. I had nothing to do with it: I was making a peaceful protest about another matter, but they came and arrested me in the middle of the night. They put me in a camp with just a slit trench for a latrine. I protested against unsanitary conditions, and they grabbed me and beat me on my feet. Then I went on a fast, and after I stopped eating for three days, things got better. Altogether, I've been in jail more than five years."

"Save Me, Save Me"

The cultural fair started the next day at a nearby community center with a large auditorium. After an entire morning of speeches, the melodramas with messages began.

In one a crippled man teeters about the stage crying "Save Me, Save Me." Dressed in rags, he has a sign around his neck with the word "Democracy." He makes a speech, exits, and then a man in a leather jacket and large red turban and wearing huge red earrings, swaggers on stage carrying a rifle and a whip, with a big knife in his belt. His label says "Terrorism." Next comes "Corruption," wearing a suit and jacket. "Politics" enters next, wearing the white hand-spun clothes and cap of the Congress Party; and finally "Immorality," dressed in white with the caste marks of a Brahmin on his forehead. Each of them, in turn, struts and declaims long speeches like in a medieval morality play. "Terrorism," who seems about eighteen, has a loud, mad laugh that he demonstrates at every pause. Now and then, "Democracy" limps back across the stage repeating, "Save Me, Save Me."

Finally, they all turn on him with shouts and threats. He drops to his knees, shaking with terror and begging with folded hands for mercy. They knock him to the ground and beat him. One of them goes into the wings and returns with a bamboo bier. They put "Democracy" on it and carry him off with shouts of triumph and the mad laughter of "Terrorism."

Since I depended on the inadequate translation of a man sitting beside me, I could not follow what happened next. Somehow or other, "Democracy" comes back on stage without his crutches and makes a speech saying unless people are careful he will really be killed.

The succession of plays went on all day with almost no space in between. It was all rank amateurism. The actors had to be cued for their lines with loud whispers from behind a curtain, or they forgot which way they were to exit and had to be called in the right direction. The two hundred people in the audience, mostly women and young people, came and went, opening the side doors to allow in great glares of mid-day sun or just sat talking through the dull moments, while children wandered in the aisles. It was a friendly, family affair.

But the message was getting across. There were explosions of laughter at funny lines and strong applause for effective speeches denouncing injustice in all its guises. And when sections of the plot were unfolding, there was fixed attention on the stage.

A Dowry Tragedy

One of the plays was about dowry, beginning once again with a speech by a man with a crude bamboo crutch, dressed in rags and with his face blacked with soot. Apparently this was the stock image of anyone in distress. My interpreter said he represented someone who had been ruined by giving dowry to marry off his daughters.

The only props are two groups of chairs, stage right and stage left, to indicate two different homes. First, we are at the home of a family with a grown daughter. A middleman comes and talks with the father, arranging a marriage. He leaves and the father of the other family then arrives with his son for the customary inspection of the girl. During this the girl sits with her face and head covered by her sari while the potential groom reads a newspaper with studied indifference. They leave and the middleman comes in, saying there is a disagreement on the dowry and suggests a mediator be summoned. The mediator talks with the proposed groom's father and mother. She disagrees strongly and wants much more.

Back to the girl's family: She is sitting with her father and mother talking when someone comes with a letter. The girl reads it, screams, and falls to the ground in a faint. Her father reads the letter and reveals the girl's younger sister has killed herself, so there would be more money for the elder sister's marriage.

This is a cue for the dowry victim with his crutch to stagger back on stage to declaim the evils of the system. Now the marriage takes place: the bride with her head and face covered and the groom nonchalant. The groom's mother is in the background calling for more money. The mediator appears and produces a paper on which the bride's father puts his thumb print. The agreement is for him to give his last bit of property.

After another entr'acte from the dowry victim, we are in the bride's new home. She is on her knees, grinding spices, and her mother-in-law stands nearby, berating her, while her husband says nothing. The in-laws go off stage right, and the girl leaves stage left and then returns with her parents. She has left her husband's family and begs her father to take her back. There are tears and wailing and long speeches directed at the audience. But she has to return to her husband.

Back at her new home her mother-in-law shouts at her while the father-in-law says nothing and the husband reads a newspaper. The girl drops to her knees and tries to touch her mother-in-law's feet as a sign of surrender, begging for mercy. The mother-in-law kicks her to the ground.

The girl gets up and answers back. The audience cheers, especially the women and girls who have been looking intently, whispering among themselves about plot points. But this is India: there are no happy endings for women.

The husband comes in with a can labeled kerosene. His father and mother stand nearby, hiding the action from the audience. The girl falls, and there is a burst of flame and black smoke from the ground. The bride has been burned in a "dowry death." Despite the tragedy, the audience applauds the stage effect of the burst of flame, but then, as the girl's parents reappear and stand over their daughter's body, there is a silence, and that is the end of the play.

The plays ended at about eight that night, and the performers and audience, who apparently were affiliated with Raghupati's organizations, walked to a nearby community hall for dinner. I knew the drill. Long strips of cloth were spread on the floor of a large room. We removed our shoes, tucked them behind us, and sat cross-legged in rows with a clear space left as an aisle in the center. The rows of people were arranged back to back, so the servers could walk down an aisle, giving food to those on either side and then turn and go down the next aisle, serving both sides.

First came men and women, boys and girls — all volunteers — who distributed plates made of wide leaves stitched together with bits of wood. They also put in front of each person similar leaves shaped as bowls and a metal tumbler for water. Next two persons dragged a huge pot of rice down the aisle, from which one of them scooped large globs onto the leaf plates. Someone else came with dal, pouring it on the rice, and another brought a curried vegetable that was put in the leaf bowl. Others filled the tumblers with water or distributed bits of hot pickles for flavoring. We ate quickly, using our right hands and, when finished, folded our used plates and bowls, dropped them in a pile of trash, and gave the tumblers to someone who was busy washing them as fast as they were returned. Finally, we washed our hands under a line of running taps.

The space occupied by those who arrived first, and were finished first, was quickly swept and swabbed with wet cloths, and latecomers seated themselves, and the process started over again. It was a continuous flow, so a person could eat and leave in about half an hour. More was involved than eating: it was community-bonding and an acting-out of equality, with no distinction of caste, age, or sex.

Making Fun of Brahmin Greed

Among the next day's plays was a lampoon of Brahmins. It opens with a common sight in India, a group of people following a corpse on a bamboo bier and shouting *"Ram Satyaha"* (God's Name is True). Behind the bier, dressed in silk with his head realistically shaven, is a young man, whose father has died. The mourners exit, and the stock character of the victim arrives on his crutches, lamenting he has been ruined by the exactions of Brahmins.

He leaves and three Brahmins—bare chested, with exaggerated caste signs streaked on their arms and faces—enter and discuss the varieties of money and offerings they can squeeze from the son. One is a Brahmin clown, prancing about the stage, making funny faces, and shouting one greedy invention after the other as the audience shouts, laughs, and applauds: encouraging him to be even more outrageous.

A beggar, apparently a Dalit, enters and sits with his hand stretched out, intoning the names of God and asking for help. The Brahmins look at him in disgust, raising their hands as shields from his untouchability, and continue their plotting. The son, with his shaven head, enters, and they circle him like the familiar scavenger hawks, known as kites, that pick at the remains of dead animals in the fields. The Brahmin clown shouts more suggestions for exacting tribute, and the audience is in tears with laughter.

Now another stock character, who had appeared in earlier plays, enters: the wise activist, neatly dressed in shirt and trousers. He lectures the Brahmins on the need for reform, and they quickly absorb the message. Someone comes and puts leaf plates on the ground, and the Brahmins, beggar, socialist, and mourner sit down to eat together.

There were so many plays and acts that a lunch of fried wheat cakes and cold curried potatoes was served in little plastic bags so the audience could eat and watch at the same time. When I went outside for water and to wash my hands, I found Raghupati and asked him about the play.

"I'm not anti-Brahmin, but a society where someone is born to be a priest is not a good society. Why does someone say 'I'm Brahmin, he's a Chamar?' We're against the entire system: there should be no Brahmin, Sudra, or Chamar. We're against the *purohit* (Brahmin priest). We say the priest should be selected by the community, not born. When someone dies, after the twelfth day there is a *shraddha* (a periodic rite) ceremony. The purohit comes and says, 'I have given your father in heaven some milk so you give me a cow.' [He laughed at the absurdity of what he had said.] We teach by drama and song that the milk cannot reach there. [He laughed again.]

"In the Hindu marriage ceremony the Brahmin lectures that the daughter is a thing given to a man. He attaches the hand of a woman to the hand of a man. We have a new system: men and women are equal and take an oath in a public meeting. Sometimes, six couples get married at the same time, and there's no dowry. When the newspaper publicized this, people came and said, 'Organize for us too.'"

The Stepdaughter's Victory

That afternoon Santali women staged a drama about marriage, playing the roles of both sexes. The Santals are one of India's largest tribes, numbering about four million. Their homeland is the hilly Chotanagpur area of southern Bihar and the Santal *Parganas* (the tribal designation for a grouping of ten or twelve panchayats, or councils) District of southeastern Bihar, as well as the bordering Twenty-Four Parganas District of West Bengal. They are divided into eleven exogamous, totemic clans so that their women, who are sisters to one clan and wives to another, link the community through kinship and affinity.

One woman, in male clothes, wore dark glasses and had a small, painted moustache. They performed entirely in the Santali language, and yet the audience sat politely, paying them the respect of listening and looking. But the plot was a stock situation and not hard to follow.

A widower with a daughter marries a woman who is also a widow with a daughter. (The Brahminic injunctions against widow remarriage, of course, do not apply to the tribes, Dalits, and the lower castes in general.) The stepmother treats her new daughter as a servant while her own daughter sits at leisure, wearing a fine sari. There are several incidents of the stepdaughter being criticized for not cooking the food right or not keeping the house clean.

A middleman arranges a marriage, and a group comes from a neighboring village to inspect the prospective bride. The proposed groom is seated on a chair (others sit on the ground) and is fed tea and sweets. While the girl with the pretty sari is walked before him, the visitors notice the girl who makes and serves the food. They leave and come back again, and after permutations of one girl doing all the work while the other sits and primps, they announce their choice: they want the girl who knows how to cook and keep the house.

The final scene is a Santali marriage ceremony. The bride, her head covered by a cloth, is put into a basket and lifted into the air and carried about. The audience cheers, reacting both to the happy ending and the strength of the women in lifting the basket so high.

No Santali event is complete without the *Sohrae* (Harvest) dance of the women. The actor with the dark glasses and moustache produced a drum to keep time as the women linked arms and grasped hands; then, with a slightly bobbing step forward and back and a side shuffle, they undulated in a rhythmic circle while chanting a simple, haunting melody.

I wandered in and out, as plays of social significance varied with songs and variety acts. One man imitated a train and another made sounds with his mouth and nose of a violin, trumpet, flute, and drum. On the third and final day Raghupati said there would be a play about nonviolence that would interest me: about a man who had a beloved son.

A Bereaved Father Forgives

The play opens with the father playing with the boy and hugging him. At the front of the stage there is a cardboard circle painted like bricks to represent a well and next to it is a bucket attached to a rope tied to a crossbar. To drive home the point someone comes, takes the rope, lowers the bucket into the well, draws it out, and carries it away as if it were full of water.

The man leaves the stage with his son but soon returns, searching frantically: the child has disappeared. Finally, after much shouting and turmoil, the father peers into the well and sees the body of his son. He screams and declaims his misery. Relatives come, lower the bucket, and lift it out. In it is a large doll, representing the body. (The audience cheers the effect.)

The father carries the child, wrapped as a corpse in white cloth, to a nearby field for burial. (Obviously, a Dalit family.) Time passes and a landlord wants to seize the field and plant it. But first he must get rid of the body. He bribes the father's brother to dig it up and throw it into a stream.

When the father comes by and sees the empty hole, he shouts in grief and anger. The neighbors come and ask each other what could have happened. The brother confesses, and the entire village is incensed at the indecency of the landlord in bribing someone to disinter and throw away a body so that it will be food for fishes. They rush off and bring the landlord, ready to kill him.

But the father intercedes. The landlord falls at his feet, asking forgiveness, and the father raises him up, and everyone shouts praises for peace.

Later, I was outside having a cup of tea and Raghupati brought over Ram Uchit Prasad, who wrote the play and acted the role of the father. He said he was a clerk in a bank and had produced the play throughout Bihar.

"We face many problems in the struggle for justice," he said, "but still we never want to shed the blood of society. We want to change the human view. Suppose I'm attacked and shed blood. My people will see it and want to shed the blood of the man who attacked me. Then they'll want to shed more blood. We lose so many people this way."

Since the fair was coming to a close, Raghupati had time to chat. "You were once in politics. Do you still believe there is a political solution?" I asked.

"At one time we boycotted elections, but now we support candidates who are nearest to us. But we believe village people should select their representatives in the state assembly and the national Parliament. Real village candidates don't need funds or propaganda machinery: the people will publicize them. We tried to put up our own candidates in 1984, but we failed because some parties bribed the villagers and grabbed the voting booths. There are three or four parties in Delhi who select people to represent this constituency. Of the four one is godless, one is a dacoit, one is a drunkard, and the other believes in the caste system or violence."

"You've been put in jail so many times, why don't you call for violence against the system that mistreats you?"

"In a violent system there's secrecy, and that's the path of dictatorship. Some people decide who shall be killed but not the people or a general meeting. Also, people have no heart for violence, and they have no money to feed themselves or clothe themselves or blankets to keep them warm. How can they buy a rifle that might cost 10,000 rupees ($700)? The *maliks* [rulers] have the money. They're the decision makers: the ones who make the violence. The rich people are violent and are showing the way to dictatorship."

"The government claims there are many Naxalite pockets in the state: Is this true?"

"Who is giving strength to the Naxalites? The nonviolent people work to educate the people, but the government doesn't want to be voted out of power, so it cooperates with those who are violent so they can blame violence on the nonviolent people and torture them. They encourage the Yadavas to fight the Rajputs and Bhoomihars."

"And what is the role of culture, like this fair?"

"Culture is not individual; it's the community: the community dances and sings. The people don't just watch culture; they act in it. Now, what has this rich society done? It has centralized the economy and also culture by way of radio and television. For people their own dancing, singing, and drama is finished, and they enjoy only radio and television. Culture and economics, culture and development: they go together. To get back control of our village economy, we also must get back control of our village culture. We must use culture as a means of social transformation—to teach people by songs, drama, and dancing. Culture is a tool to refashion society."

Another way to justify protest, making it part of the air people breath, is through newspapers. And with growing literacy advocacy journalism is beginning to reach beyond the limited English-language press to newspapers in the regional languages. During dry spells of the Rang Mela I met a young woman who writes for the leading paper in Hindi, the most widely spoken language. Like Raghupati, she used only one name: Manimala.

31 ✺ Journalism and Its Perils

Manimala became a journalist because she wanted justice, not a job. As a student in Patna University, she joined Anil Prakash and others in the struggle of the United Youth Organization for Change to redistribute the lands of the Bodh Gaya Mahant and began to write free-lance articles in Hindi and English on women's and other social issues. Several Bihar newspapers printed her pieces but would not give her a staff position.

One of India's oldest English-language newspapers is the *Times of India*, with a Hindi edition called *Navbharat Times* (New India Times). Their main offices are in Delhi. Although the growth of literacy has been slow, the expansion of regional language newspapers and magazines has been enormous: with a population of more than 800 million, even an additional 5 percent growth in literacy means a growth of 40 million in potential readers.

The *Navbharat Times* started a regional edition in the huge Hindi-speaking state of Uttar Pradesh in 1984 and in 1985 added a Rajasthan edition. The editor, hunting for Hindi reporters who could attract readers, learned Manimala had an article reproduced in a book published in England, and on that recommendation Manimala got her first staff job on a national paper.

Outwardly, Manimala does not suggest heroics. She is small, round-faced, with an engaging, slightly gap-toothed smile. But her writings are like artillery salvos. One of her stories in Rajasthan forced a state cabinet minister to resign. It ran under a headline:

I Want to Live

Right from the day she expressed the desire to live her own life, death has been staring her in the eyes. She has bled, she has passed out, and she has had her bones broken. She has lived for more than fourteen months under the shadow of death. She has pleaded with the deputy superintendent of police for her right to live. Time and again she has pinned her hopes on the women members of the state legislation. Time and again she tried to write to the chief minister, Harideo Joshi, and the prime minister, Mr Rajiv Gandhi. But she was helpless, forcibly confined under heavy guards.

The name of this twenty-year-old girl is Indra. She lives in Bilara, Jodhpur District. Her father, Ram Singh Vishnoee, is the minister for animal husbandry in the Rajasthan government. Ram Singh is enraged at Indra just because she does not want to bear the burden of her father's crime. Ram Singh Vishnoee committed the first crime against his daughter thirteen years ago. In 1973, when she was only seven years old, she was married to a child who was younger than her by three years. This was in blatant disregard of the Sharda Act of 1929, which makes child-marriage a crime, with a provision of three months imprisonment and fine. But Ram Singh Vishnoee was crowned with a ministry instead of punishment.

Ram Singh Vishnoee committed the second crime fifteen months ago. When Indra flatly refused to accept Mohanlal Vishnoee as her husband and to go with him, Ram Singh confined her to a cell for almost one month in October 1985. He beat her himself and also got others to beat her so brutally her whole body was blue and black. She bled profusely, and her arm was broken, and she was in plaster.

The state minister of Rajasthan Government, Mr Vishnoee, committed the third crime by snatching away her liberty with the influence of his political status. None could dare to help her, not even the police. She had gone to Deputy Superintendent of Police Ram Vallabh Mukul to seek protection and to say she did not want to go with Mohanlal. The reply she got was: "If I help you, your father will get me transferred."

Ram Singh Vishnoee committed the fourth crime against Indra on November 24, 1984. That day he forcibly sent Indra at gunpoint to Mohanlal for the *gauna* [a second marriage, when a child bride is sent to her in-law's house] ceremony. Mohanlal is not her legal husband for the reason that child-marriages are illegal and also because adult Indra refused point-blank to accept him as her husband.

Ram Singh Vishnoee committed the fifth crime, a shameless one, by saying to his daughter: "First go with that boy and then become a prostitute if you like to." Who gave Ram Singh the right to say this to his grown-up daughter? If anyone pressures a girl to become a prostitute, does he not render himself liable to conviction under the Immoral Traffic Act?

Ram Singh Vishnoee committed the sixth crime by trying to seek medical help to make her insane. When wounded, Indra went to a doctor for treatment; her father told him: "Make her insane by giving electric shocks." As it is, he had done his utmost to create conditions that were cruel and severe enough to blight her mental balance. Is it not a crime to try to turn a healthy person insane by deliberate and dubious efforts?

And Ram Singh committed the seventh and most atrocious crime by trying to kill her himself or get her killed. Ram Singh has threatened his daughter time and again: "We will kill you in such a manner people will take it as a case of suicide, or we will ask your in-laws to get your ears and nose chopped off or to kill you straight away. We won't go to court."

This is not the end: They even tried to strangle and poison her and, having failed in this, they once tried to make her hang herself. Ram Singh has now stated: "I will bury her and declare she has fled away."

The animal husbandry minister of Rajasthan is treating his daughter worse than an animal. Through physical torture and mental agony he wants her to bear the burden of the crime he committed against her thirteen years ago.

The marriage of a child, the gauna marriage at gunpoint, beating her, fracturing her bones, abetment to suicide, relentless efforts to kill her, confinement for months together: what a barbarous attitude toward human life! Is Ram Singh not a criminal under sections 306 (provocation to suicide) and 307 (attempt to murder) of the Indian Penal Code? Why are the people of Bilara, the state assembly, and the whole society mute spectators of his crimes? Is such blatant usurpation of human and legal rights excusable if committed by a minister?

The Piparia Massacre Revisited

In 1986 the *Navbharat Times* began a Bihar edition, and Manimala returned to her home state. "I'm the first woman reporter in Bihar," she said. "In fact, I'm the only woman reporter in all of Hindi journalism in Bihar. There are two other women working for Hindi newspapers and sixteen who work for English-language papers in Bihar, but they all have desk jobs. Management thinks women can't go in the field at night."

"In 1987 I did a report on the eleven children who were killed in Piparia village in January 1984. That's a totally criminal region, and no one would go with me: not even a photographer. I'm no good at it, but I brought a camera and took my own pictures. No bus or car went there. For the final distance I had to walk for ten hours by myself and stay the night with some women who gave me protection."

What set Manimala in motion was a report that leaders of three of the all-India parties in Bihar, the Congress, the *Lok Dal* (People's Party), and the Communist Party of India had sent letters asking the chief minister to withdraw charges against eleven men being tried for the murders. The verdict was about to be handed down, and the politicians said caste feelings ran so high it would be best if local people settled their own affairs. They also said the leaders of the three main caste gangs in the region had pledged to maintain the peace if the accused were freed.

"I was incensed," Manimala said. "By what right did they ask that the criminals not be punished? I got my editor's permission to go back to reconstruct the events."

The Piparia murders were committed by about fifty men of the Dhanuk caste who kidnapped the children after they had crossed the Ganges to gather fodder. Three, who managed to hide, saw the eleven others killed, dismembered, and thrown into the river. Manimala's story ran in three parts. The first two concentrated on the events and the treatment of Dalits in the Diara. She interviewed about a dozen young people and adults, among them a Dalit student who stood first in a high school examination and then was forced to lick the spit of high caste students. The final article ended with a carpet bombing of those who asked for amnesty:

> Can they tell the reason for their demand? Did they consult the mothers whose eleven lovely children were cut to pieces and thrown into the Ganges? Did they consult those innocent children who have no future now since their fathers were massacred? Did they consult those whose husbands were killed? And above all, were those three horrified children consulted who had seen eleven of their playmates being butchered like animals and who were not able to utter a word for seven days due to the shock received? . . .

In Bihar there are quite a few areas where a joint front of administrators, politicians, and criminals is playing havoc with the lives of common people. The goondas among different castes keep their tribes under perfect control. . . . The common person is sandwiched between the warring groups. These tribal gang dictators cash in on the needs of the politicians.

The police . . . not only help the criminals but very often connive with them. . . . The officers need politicians who in turn need both officers and criminal gangs at the time of elections. At places the officers help them get votes and even collect money for them. Corrupt officers need political assistance in order to settle their transfer and posting matters. . . . The situation is such it makes many queer combinations. Criminals, police, and politicians who belong to the same caste make a viable triangle. Then, there are combinations of gang leaders of all castes, officials of all castes, and politicians of all castes; each forming a powerful triangle in its own place. . . . Bihar . . . is groaning under these triangles.

With that all talk of an amnesty was forgotten: ten of the accused were sentenced to life in prison.

Manimala's contribution was recognized when a panel of four of the country's most respected journalists and two jurists honored her with the Human Rights Award for Journalism of the Peoples Union for Civil Liberties, one of India's two national civil rights organizations. The award came with a check for 20,000 rupees ($1,400).

"I kept some of it to meet incidental expenses and am contributing three hundred rupees [$21] a month toward the maintenance of a woman activist. Quite a few landlords have offered me money or a house if I would do something for them, but I refused. Even if the government offered me an award, I would refuse it. This government is antipeople. How could I accept anything from it?"

Superstition and Persecution

In November 1987 a single column story in the *Navbharat Times* told of a woman being paraded through the streets of Ranchi, Bihar's second largest city. She was followed by a crowd of men and boys shouting for her death as a witch. A photographer who happened to be passing took the picture and then went to the police and asked them to save the woman's life, which they did.

"When I saw that picture," Manimala said, "I asked myself, 'How is this possible?' That procession took place in broad daylight in front of the police *thana* (station). I told my editor, 'This is news. We must notice it.' "

He agreed, and Manimala spent a week gathering her facts and came back to write a series of five articles for her paper. Then the *Illustrated Weekly of India*, which is also part of the *Times of India* group, asked her for an English-language version of the story, and she set out again on a fifteen-day tour, bringing the total of her interviews to more than fifty.

"They all told terrible stories of mistreatment: some were made to eat human excrement. One woman said if I went to a place called Mirza Chowki in Chotanagpur I could find a woman whose hand had been chopped off. I went there, and it was all mountains and rivers. I contacted the police and got the name of the village where the woman lived, but they said there was no bus: in fact no road; I couldn't even go by cycle. I said I would walk. They said, 'You can't. It will take you at least five hours.' I went anyway and met her."

Manimala brought out a copy of the story and pointed to a picture of a woman named Badaki Handsa with her right hand cut off just above the wrist. In the article Manimala quoted Badaki on how she lost her hand:

Phagun Marandi came with eight others and told me I must cure my nephew Mahal Marandi, who had been ill for two months. I told them I was his aunt and I was making arrangements for his treatment, but they threatened to kill me if Mahal died. Next morning, Mahal died. He could not have been saved: we tried everything.

Shortly after his death, they came to see me again. I was feeding my six-year-old daughter. They snatched away my baby and threw her on the ground. I broke into tears. I touched their feet, bowed with folded hands, and begged them to give me back my daughter. They told me they were going to cut off my hand. Seven of them caught me and then Phagun Marandi cut off my hand. I am now handicapped. All I can do is beg. I was hard-working, but now I am helpless.

In her search Manimala found forty-eight-year-old Basanti, whose picture had inspired her to search for the story behind the witch hunt. Basanti's life had been saved, but she was shunned by everyone in her village.

Manimala also heard the story of four women who were tortured to death in March 1984. A young man in their village died and an *ojha* (male diviner) from a neighboring village was asked to identify the "witches" who were responsible. He came and said every woman must appear before him and eat an ash he would give them. Those who refused or became sick would be branded as witches.

Either because there was something poisonous in the ash or out of hysteria, four women, ranging in age from twenty-six to sixty, began to scream in terror. They were surrounded by men, stripped naked, their bodies painted white, their faces blackened, and their heads shaved, and then they were forced to run around the village while men beat them with burning sticks and other weapons. This went on, in broad daylight, for seven hours until the women died.

Not Superstition but Male Chauvinism

Manimala estimated at least two hundred women were killed every year as witches in Singhbhum District of south Bihar alone. The men claimed it was simply a matter of good and evil, but Manimala concluded it was not superstition that perpetuated the crimes; it was male chauvinism and greed:

> The assumption that evil forces act through women and good forces act through men . . . is beyond doubt the product of a male-dominated social structure. . . . Superstitious beliefs are merely used as a cover to capture the lands of widows, deserted women, or single women by their own male relatives. . . . The Chotanagpur Tenancy Act does not provide land rights to Ho tribal women, for instance, but gives them only usufructuary rights. For the nearest male agnate, it is only necessary to get the female out of the way so that he can be the sole owner of the land.

In another district Manimala found five women of the Pahadia tribe ranging in age from thirty to sixty-five, who were branded as witches and were living together beside a road, begging for food. Even there they suffered. She wrote:

> Many social activists . . . told this reporter about the endless harassment these women face. . . . The village chief wants to capture land, and for this he seeks the support of the police. The policemen and labor contractors demand women to satisfy their lust. . . .
> Little can be expected from the guardians of law and order by way of protection when they are often the perpetrators themselves. At midnight on August 13, 1987, the house of Tuna Devi in village Madangang of Jehanabad District was forced open by *sipahi* (constable) Brahmdeo Tiwari and his police force. She was told that Tiwari's son was ill and was asked to cure him. Tiwari then accused

her of being a witch. Tuna Devi started weeping . . . but the police-men beat her up severely, looted the house, and left.

In March 1988, after the witches story was published, Manimala heard about a girl who had been sold ten times and, with her usual thoroughness, set out to find the details.

"I visited all ten buyers and interviewed them," she said. "They buy a wife, keep her for four, five, or six months, and then sell her to some other man, and he keeps her for four or five months, and finally she is sold to a prostitute center. This woman escaped, and someone heard about it. I went and interviewed the girl and took photographs of all the places she had been.

"While she was being bought and sold, five persons were murdered. They had sympathy for the girl and said it was not good to buy and sell women. This set off a quarrel between two groups and the stronger group murdered the weaker group. I collected pictures of the five men who had been killed and also interviewed their families. It was a front-page story in the *Navbharat Times*, but no English-language newspaper picked it up."

Press Bashing

After she received the Human Rights Award for her stories on Piparia, Manimala was asked if she was afraid. "Journalism has its occupational hazards," she replied, "and we have to face them. Once, when I was coming out of my office, some goondas tried to kidnap me, and I only escaped with difficulties. It was a terrible experience."

These "occupational hazards" have a generic label: press bashing. S. Nihal Singh, one of India's most respected journalists and editors, called it "The Unseen Battle":

The real struggle for press freedom is being waged by the brave jour-nalists who work outside the major centers—away from interna-tional gaze. They are the journalists in Punjab and in Bihar, where the law of the jungle rather than the rule of law, operates all too often. In Punjab, terrorism has introduced its own compulsions. While in parts of Bihar the venality of politicians, often in league with underworld dons, coupled with the arbitrariness of the police and administrative apparatus, is a formidable combination to take on.

In 1988 alone, four reporters were killed amid Punjab's Sikh terrorism. In May 1989 terrorists demanded the *Hind Samachar* group shut down its three widely circulated newspapers. Its founding editor and his son had already been killed. When the owners refused to stop publication, three distribution agents were murdered. Yet the newspaper continued to publish.

In Bihar in July 1989 a police superintendent resented criticism from Brahmadeo Singh Sharma, the eighty-four-year-old editor of the Hindi newspaper *Awaaz*. Seven policemen broke into the hut of Malati Majhiyan, a sixteen-year-old tribal girl in the coal-mining city of Dhanbad, and attempted to gang-rape her. Malati fought back and was brutally beaten with lathis. Sharma criticized the police superintendent for justifying the assault by describing Malati as "characterless." The superintendent had Sharma dragged off to the lock-up in handcuffs. An *Awaaz* photographer and five local journalists who went to see him were also detained, and the photographer's camera was smashed. Sharma was released early the next morning when, on the intervention of the state's chief minister, a local magistrate granted bail. After protests in the state legislature the police superintendent was transferred and a lower-ranking officer was suspended.

In February 1988 Umesh Dobhal, a reporter for the Hindi journal *Amar Ujala* in Garwal, Uttar Pradesh, disappeared and is presumed dead after reporting on links between the police and bootleggers.

For several years politicians and criminals have tried to silence *Samaj*, the largest circulating Oriya daily in Orissa. Radhanand Rath, its eighty-five-year-old editor, narrowly escaped injury when his car was ambushed and bombed. In another attack Rath was waylaid and beaten up. Both incidents were ascribed to Congress Party goondas. In 1986 the wife of a *Samaj* reporter in a rural district was kidnapped from her home, gang-raped, and killed after her husband wrote a series of stories on links between criminals and the police. And in 1987 another *Samaj* reporter was arrested by the police, handcuffed, and forced to drink his own urine.

Not only Congress governments indulge in press bashing: all parties do it.

Andhra Pradesh is ruled by the opposition *Telugu Desam* (Telugu is the word for both the language and people of Andhra; Desam means country). Pingali Dasaratharam, a twenty-nine-year-old editor, began publishing a weekly called *Encounter* out of the coastal city of Vijayawada. He quickly attracted readers among ordinary people by writing in slangy, streetwise speech. For instance, he described a politician as a "eunuch who had pimped for the Nehru family" and now wanted to "get into the brothel at Hyderabad (the state capital) by licking the behind" of the leader of the Telugu Desam. Dasaratharam was stabbed to death in October 1985.

The best-known journalist in Andhra is K. Balagopal, a regular correspondent for the *Economic and Political Weekly*. He has often been threatened because of his frequent articles on police brutality and lives an underground life, moving from city to city, staying only with friends. One of his stories told what happened to a young journalist with the single name of Sivaramkumar, who edits and publishes *Gowthami Times*, a small newspaper in Rajahmundry in the coastal East Godavari District.

Sivaramkumar had written several stories on police brutality. In an attempt to silence him, the police arrested him four times in March 1988, on charges of abduction, blackmail, theft, and arson and told him he would die in an "encounter" if he did not stop. Uncowed, he filed charges of illegal detention, harassment, and implication in false criminal cases.

In December the police sensed an opportunity to take revenge during the suppression of widespread riots in Vijayawada following the murder of a popular politician. A curfew was declared, putting the police in total authority. Sivaramkumar asked for a curfew pass as a journalist, and when his name was struck off a list prepared by the city's Press Club, he went around without one and for three days filed stories for his paper.

On December 29 the police stopped a group of reporters, including Sivaramkumar. They used their lathis to drive away those with curfew passes and took Sivaramkumar to a local station where he was beaten and put into a cell. Later he was told to undress to his underwear, and two eunuchs were put in the cell with him. He described what happened next in a complaint filed with the Andhra Pradesh Press Council:

> The assistant superintendent of police of Rajahmundry, Mr Rajiv Trivedi . . . dragged me out of the lockup, made me remove even my underwear, and thrashed me unremittingly for one full hour on my naked skin. Then I was photographed in that condition. The ASP then directed the fifty-five policemen who were in the station compound to come inside and hit me on my head one by one with their boots. Then he himself put his feet on my head and declared that *Gowthami Times* was now under his feet.
>
> Then the two eunuchs in the lockup were asked to come out. They were also forced to undress. Then myself and the eunuchs

were forced to adopt indecent postures, and we were photographed forty times in different postures. When I asked for some water to drink out of exhaustion, the ASP tried in vain to make the eunuchs urinate in my mouth. . . .

The ASP beat me so badly that I lost consciousness. After I regained consciousness, I was brought out of the police sation, and at about 2:45 P.M. . . . I was forced to run stark naked up and down the street. Later, the ASP again put me in lockup and thrashed me. . . . A tape recorder was brought, and I was forced to make all kinds of allegations into it against other journalists and important persons of Rajahmundry town. I was beaten continuously throughout this process, and I finally lost consciousness again.

On the evening of January 2, after he was moved around to different police stations, made to sign some papers, and beaten again by the ASP, who used three lathis in the process, he was taken to another station and booked under the Terrorist and Disruptive Activities (Prevention) Act in connection with the burning of a bus during the riots. Three weeks later he managed to gain his freedom on bail, upon which he returned to Rajahmundry to start his paper again.

Greedy Wives and Vengeful Husbands

Owners spend so little on news gathering that most rural reporters are stringers with other full-time occupations. Any attempt by a stringer to report what really happens in a village is at the risk of his other interests and safety. For instance, there is the series of events that began in April 1988 in the town of Orai in Jalaun District of Uttar Pradesh. Stringers for two Hindi dailies published from Kanpur, the major industrial city of central Uttar Pradesh, reported merchants in Orai had called for a *bandh* (a strike; in this case businessmen closing their shutters) to protest the conduct of the wives of the district magistrate and police chief. The women had strolled in the bazaar and bought sixty-six saris for only 1,700 rupees ($119). When the stories were played back to Orai, the district magistrate complained to the editors in Kanpur, and the two stringers were promptly fired.

Radhey Shyam Dantre, the Orai stringer for the Patna edition of the *Navbharat Times*, filed a story about the dismissal of the reporters. Reprisals were swift. The district magistrate had notice served on Dantre, who owned a shop and other properties, that his assessments had been raised 800 percent retroactive to 1982. Immediate payment was demanded. When Dantre made light of the notice, he was arrested and put in a filthy jail, where he suffered a heart attack ten hours later. Jail officials released him without any further action.

The district magistrate, still seeking reprisal, wrote a letter to the state information department, which controls journalistic activities, asking that Dantre's credentials be withdrawn and also wrote to the *Navbharat Times* asking that he be dismissed.

This led to a series of investigations in which Dantre was found to have been abused. The only punishment inflicted on the district magistrate and the police chief was their transfer to other posts. As for the two stringers who filed the original stories, they never got their jobs back.

While in Patna, I heard of a Jesuit priest, Philip Manthara, who was using dialogue as a method to justify resistance to oppression and went to find him.

32 ☀ We Have a Dream

The Reverend Philip Manthara shared the dream of social activists throughout the world of a new society of peace and equality. It was Mahatma Gandhi's dream. He used the circle, the symbol of wholeness, as a metaphor for a community of heroes pledged to nonviolence yet willing to risk their lives. His dream was paraphrased by Jayaprakash Narayan:

> In this structure, composed of innumerable villages, there will be ever-widening, ever-ascending circles. Life will not be a pyramid with the apex sustained by the base. But it will be an oceanic circle whose center will be the individual, always ready to perish for the circle of villages, till at last the whole becomes one life composed of individuals, never aggressive in their arrogance, but ever humble, sharing the majesty of the oceanic circle of which they are integral units.

The vision is still alluring: glowing beyond the horizon. Getting there involves long and patient work.

Father Philip was in Khagaul, about ten kilometers west of Patna. The town grew up around what the British called a "Railway Colony" —orderly rows of red brick houses built for the running staff and administrators of the railways. Rail lines were originally built to facilitate the fast deployment of troops, and, to keep them out of the hands of potential subversives, the British cultivated Anglo-Indians—the children of British fathers and Indian mothers—as a sort of caste to operate the railroads, providing them with separate housing colonies.

As Christians the Anglo-Indians needed churches and that was where I found Father Philip: in the rectory of an ugly brick church, built in 1904, surrounded by a moldering garden and rusted gates. The rectory had been converted into a sort of barracks with a large central common room and two side rooms, each with six iron beds draped with mosquito netting. He said he was from Kottayam District in Kerala and was fifty-six years old, although he looked younger, with an unlined face and black hair showing just a touch of gray and wearing heavy-rimmed glasses. He spoke with a resonant voice in almost unaccented English.

"I was first attracted to the church by the personality of Jesus," he said when I asked him how he became a social activist. "But my ideas have changed a great deal since I was twenty. I now realize Jesus was against the structures of his time: of the temple and the priests, the law and the sabbath. When Jesus worked miracles, it was to bring whole-someness to people: I see Him as standing for empowering the people."

How the Villagers Got a Water Pump

After we talked for a while, Father Philip told a long story that illustrated his dialogical approach:

"Once in 1979 I was in a village on a very hot day. I was thirsty and asked for some water, but after I waited twenty minutes and there was no water, I asked, 'What's the matter? Isn't there any water in this village?' They said there was none. When the water finally came, I asked if there was any water in other villages, and they said yes. 'Then why is it you have no water?' I asked. They said, 'We had a hand pump, sir, but for the last one year it hasn't worked.' They said they went to a landlord's place far away and were often abused and scolded and chased away.

"I then asked different sectors how they were affected by the lack of water. Now our people are very concrete in their descriptions of reality. An old man said, 'One night I woke up and asked for water to drink. They said, "You're asking for water at this time of night? You're mad." Somehow I managed.'

"I asked women and they said they needed water for cooking and washing. I asked youngsters and they gave me their own reasons. So I said all groups are suffering: it is our common problem, and from there we started a movement of the whole village to think of getting water. They asked, 'Where can we go for water?' and they found they would have to go to the block development officer." For centralized planning India is divided into units known as development blocks, each with two hundred to three hundred villages. The BDO, as he is called, allocates funds for projects the authorities want to encourage, such as the supply of safe drinking water.

"Then they asked," Manthara continued, "What will we tell him, or should we go with something in writing so if he is not there he will read it?' They decided they would need something in writing.

"At the next stage they asked what they should write. Someone said, 'We'll write there's no water here.' But then I asked, 'Is that enough? Don't we also have to write about the difficulty we're facing because there's no water?' They said, 'Oh yes.' And so, like that, they agreed we would put all the reasons on the paper: the reasons of the old people, the men and women, and the children.

"Then I asked, 'Who shall write this?' They said, 'You'll do it.' I said, 'I'm not suffering for lack of water. I have plenty. This is your problem so you write it.' I wanted to drive home the point the fact they could not write was related to their not having water. They agreed, but said again they didn't know how to write.

"I said, 'Fine, I'll find someone to write, but where is the paper?' They had none. I said, 'OK, you bring the paper.' It took them two or three days to find a piece of paper. They had never thought how paper is obtained, and someone has to take trouble to get it. Finally, when they brought the paper, and the whole assembly discussed it, we wrote an application to the BDO.

"So then I asked, 'Who'll deliver this?' There was silence for a while, and finally one person said, 'I'll do it.' They're all daily wage earners, so if someone had to go to the BDO, he would suffer a loss for that day, and there might not be anything to eat at home. It's a definite problem they have. The man said he needed a companion, and after much discussion two more people agreed. The three of them left the next day, but when they saw the office far away, they were frightened and came back.

"We have methodology of action and reflection, so we brought the whole group together and asked what happened: why didn't the application reach the BDO? We decided we would have to go again. They could not go the next day because the loss of two consecutive days would be too much, so it took another week, maybe. Another person was willing, and there were two companions, but when they reached up to the block office and talked to someone at the entrance, they got frightened and came back.

"Again we had the process of reflection, but now the trend was toward action. Another group went and handed the paper to someone who looked at it and said, 'You have written on this paper that five people have died in your village for lack of water. Can you prove this? You're in trouble if this is not true: You'll go to jail.' So they ran away and came frightened back to the village.

We had a meeting, and they explained they were in trouble because of the mention that five people had died. I said there was no such mention in the application. We reflected on this, and they decided because they could not read they had to believe whatever they were told. From there we came to the conclusion: 'Unless we can read and write other people will cheat or mislead us.' At that point they agreed to hold adult education classes.

"Fortunately, the subdivisional officer [sDO], above the block level, had standing instructions that any application must be kept and a copy sent to him. He read the petition and came to the village, saw what the conditions were, and said he wanted a hand pump installed.

"In two days the workers came with the equipment, but they said, 'You have to give the labor.' The people came to me and explained what happened, so we had a meeting to discuss it, and they decided they would give nothing free because the sDO had agreed the pump would be installed at no cost. The work continued for a while, and then the workers explained there was a five-foot-long wire mesh at the end to serve as a strainer. They said, 'You have to give this.' The people had another meeting, and decided if the pump was provided by the government, they didn't see why they had to provide the mesh, and they told the workers they would not give. Again the work proceeded, but now the workers said, 'At least give us two chickens.' Once again we had a meeting and discussion, and they said they would not give them chickens. Finally the workers said, 'You must give ten rupees for the washer on the pump.' Again they had a meeting, and said they would not give ten rupees. Finally, the pump was installed and the cover put on, but it did not work.

"They went to the sDO and told him in spite of his order there was no water. He sent a magistrate for an inquiry, and the people told him the stories about having been asked for money and gifts. The magistrate also had the pump inspected and discovered the workmen had installed the washer backward. The magistrate said he would punish the workers, but they came to the village and asked pardon and said, 'From now on if there's any problem with the pump, we'll fix it.'

"So after waiting months and months they got water through their efforts, without bribing. This was their first experience of the whole village getting together for what we call animation work among themselves."

The Initiative Takes Root

"Was it worth spending all your time on a single village for a single pump?" I asked.

"That's true. For two months I was totally in that village. But I was learning too: discovering the potential of uneducated village folk. A solution brought from above can't reach them because an educated person from the outside either over- or underestimates their capacities. The long-range effect has been remarkable. They used to make country li- quor, but most of the profit was lost since they consumed it themselves. At any time, day or night, if you went to that village you would find outsiders in various states of consciousness, and they too were in a totally dissipated condition. We took up the issue and had many meetings: they stopped and started and stopped and started, but finally after four years they decided to stop making liquor. I'm not saying people have stopped drinking: they do drink. But now no outsiders disturb them, and they have much fewer quarrels and fights. They have a lot more enthusiasm for life, and they can manage on what they get from their wages.

"There is also social integration: this is my pet idea. There are about ten caste groups in the village, no upper castes but middle and lower castes. Even a little higher status was very important. Some felt they were better than someone else and would have no social interaction, like eating, being together, and marriages.

"Now, with our help and the consensus of the people, they're developing new economic opportunities that also provide new ways for social interaction. For the past seven or eight years a milk cooperative society has been functioning. It has given them confidence and a feeling of togetherness: they say they belong to the *samiti* [society].

"Once a month they walk from the village and hold a meeting in this room. It's full of people, with very low caste people sitting with the others. It was not that way in the beginning: the very low caste people would sit just outside the door. But now, if a little higher caste tries to assert himself in the village, the lower caste man will say, 'You can't feel more superior than me. You're only as good a member as I am: You paid eleven rupees and I paid eleven rupees.' That's the primary membership fee.

"So this economic articulation is growing. Economically we've not improved too much, but socially there's a major change. They also come together to celebrate things like Independence Day and Republic Day and for children's programs and drama competitions."

Networking and Empowerment

"What else has happened? It's more than ten years since you asked for a glass of water."

"Of course, we haven't only been sitting there. We believe we must change our present oppressive and exploitive social and economic structure. We need a radical change in the landownership pattern. We also need a change from an employer-employee structure to something more cooperative. In one village it may be a milk cooperative, in another a pig growers cooperative. In a third village it may be a workers union demanding better wages. In another it may be a cultural group.

"Our first village has become a focal point. In the cooperative society there's a place for visitors. And now we have an outlet for rationed food. Bihar has a system to distribute essential commodities at subsidized prices to the poor: things like wheat, cooking oil, and sugar. Before, a truck went from village to village distributing the foods. They were supposed to go only to ration card holders, but there was a lot of cheating. Now our village has established a permanent office, and the village leaders see everything is distributed properly.

"The situation in ten or fifteen surrounding villages is encouraging. I went first to one village and then to the next, conducting night meetings and taking up problems like wages and bonded labor. We had role-playing and dramas as a focus of discussion for the entire village. We asked questions: what about this and that and we put special questions to women, starting dialogues.

"This is empowerment: the villagers experience their power as a group. I used to conduct these meetings, but now the villagers don't need me: they call a meeting themselves and conduct it, or a meeting for two or three villages together might be called.

"We also do networking and empowerment through children. We brought together five government primary schools. Each had its own drama or cultural program, but now they came together. We had some programs performed by all five schools at the same time. Without practice they sang the same songs together. We also asked them questions like the names of local officials and the statutory daily wage.

"We had a youth cultural program with about ten villages involved. This is not TV culture or the controlled monoculture of some societies. It's a culture you can create; a song you can sing. If you enjoy and struggle in life, that will be your song. It's a drama from your own reality which, when presented, gives you and others something to think about."

"Has there been an acceptance of education?" I asked.

"It's an uphill task. When we began, there was not one boy, girl, man, or woman who was literate. They saw no profit in it. But now, through our efforts, there's a government school in the village. If the older boys and girls are going, the little ones see this and also want to go. Going to school is becoming an expected part of life.

"We have a few sisters [nuns] in the village. They don't teach; they just try to help the children get started, collecting them for extra attention, like games and songs. Along with playing together the sisters add a little education, and now 50 percent of the children are enrolled in the school. We also have a young man in class nine. Child marriages are common: he's sixteen or seventeen and is married and has a child, but he still goes to school. He's one of our best animators: anytime he's ready to work for the society and to be in the forefront."

Developing Animators

I prompted him to say more about animators.

"We try to identify individuals and groups, or even potential groups, who can be trained or animated to enter into their own community and be a force for social change: doing something in their own way, without special training. Perhaps the police have arrested some people in the village, maybe for interrogation; maybe they want to create a fear complex in the village. Among the people there may be a traditional leader or a new force. He would go to the police station to find out what had happened and try to get those people off. This would be a starting point. They have gained some experience from this, and others have also been activated. This gives them added confidence, and the next time they'll take stronger action.

"All they need is further encouragement. My goal is to call them out: dialogue with them and say I'm also with you. The animators meet in their own village, or we bring them here for three or five days of training. Sometimes we arrange for half a dozen groups to get together.

We go into minianalysis: what's happening in the village; who owns the land; who owns the means of production; who has the government jobs; what do the people want; what do they need?

"A number of times, when the police have come to pick up somebody, the people have surrounded and challenged them. For a group of people who had to take an application three times before it was delivered, this is a remarkable change. One woman is extremely good. She can lecture, pester, and argue with anybody. Once the police came to ask if there was an illegal making of liquor. They were not interested in stopping it, they only wanted bribes. This woman told them, 'You get away from this village. We don't do any of these illegal things. You have no right to come into the village.'"

I remarked much of what he said echoed Gandhi's call for a society of concentric circles, but if Gandhi with all his power could not realize his dream, why did he and other activists think they could succeed?

"Why not?" Father Philip asked. "Gandhi did not live long enough to see his dream come true, nor will this generation, because our dream is of a totally different society, with no aggression and with a more equitable distribution of wealth, not only in the monetary sense but also as land and opportunity. When people everywhere are dreaming like this and several dreams are coalescing and life is coming together, I don't see why this dream can't grow even more."

As I said good-bye, he added a final note: "In any case we're looking for something meaningful here and now that has a chance of spreading."

His casual sentence was suggestive of the entire process of the social movement. Melucci calls the actors of the social movement "nomads who dwell within the present":

In complex systems, signs become interchangeable: power lies increasingly in the codes that regulate the flow of information. . . . Apart from selecting new elites, these forms of action modernize institutions and at the same time, call into question the implementation of goals which have been decided by an anonymous and impersonal power. . . . In complex societies, collective action creates new spaces which function as a genuine sub-system. . . . The problems raised by collective actors could easily become contentious issues for other social groups, representing different actors and demands. . . . Whether this plurality of actors and problems can be effective depends on society's capacity to transform the questions raised by collective action into negotiated decisions and institutional changes of a political type.

This is what the social movement is about: changing codes and signs, creating spaces, and challenging the capacity of a society to transform itself. Social movement actors deal with ethnicity, identity, myths, and symbols.

33 ❂ Myths and Identity

In India myths are reality. The nineteenth-century Bengali novelist and critic Bankimchandra Chattopadhyay (Anglicized as Chatterji) wrote:

> If the English go out to shoot birds, a history is written of the expedition. . . . There is a specific reason why Indians have no history. Partly because of the environment, partly the fear of invaders, Indians are greatly devoted to their gods. . . . They do not think themselves the subjects of their own actions: it is always the gods who act through them. . . . Proud nations have an abundance of historical writing: we have none.

During the independence movement there was the myth of a nation that had existed, as Nehru phrased it, "since the dawn of civilization." Nehru saw this unity as secular and political and spoke of unification as the ideal of Buddhist, Brahminic, and Muslim rulers.

Hindu chauvinists, rejecting the possibility that Muslims could have contributed to Indian culture and history, traced unity to another myth: the Aryan conquest. This new myth developed from the search for a reply to missionaries who condemned Hinduism as fit only for a garbage heap.

The Aryan myth was first given form by European scholars. In 1783 Sir William Jones arrived in Calcutta as a judge of the High Court, and since scholarship was then the mark of a gentleman, he began to search for missing Indian history. He started with Indian languages and demonstrated Sanskrit was related to all major European languages.

It was Sir William who introduced the word *Arya* into European literature. In the original it meant noble and was applied especially to gods. Jones used it to differentiate the languages of India. It then came to denote speakers of a branch of the Indo-European family of languages. Later when Indian languages and philosophy became the rage for the German Romantic school of literature, the Prussian minister to Britain, Baron Christian Karl Josias Bunsen, brought this enthusiasm to Oxford where, in 1847, he read a paper to show the whole of mankind could be classified according to language.

Bunsen helped a young German scholar, Max Müller, to settle in Oxford in 1845, where he remained the rest of his life, letting his romantic enthusiasm get the better of his scholarship. He theorized the Indo-Persian group of languages, which he called Aryan, were the oldest of all and could be traced to a cradle, known as Ariana, in the mountains of central Asia.

His greatest error was to speak not only of a definite Aryan language but also of its descendants as an Aryan race. The virus spread by way of writers and thinkers like Thomas Carlyle and Charles Kingsley in England, Count Gobineau in France, and Friedrich Nietzsche in Germany, culminating in the epidemic of Adolf Hitler. Long before, in 1888, Müller tried to correct the implications of his errors: "I have declared again and again that if I say Aryas, I mean neither blood nor bones nor hair nor skull. I mean simply those who speak an Aryan language. . . . An ethnologist who speaks of Aryan race, Aryan blood, Aryan eyes and hair is as great a sinner as a linguist who speaks of a dolichocephalic dictionary or a brachycephalic grammar."

About the time Müller was correcting his errors, Hindu revivalists were embracing them. Revivalists proclaimed a Golden Age beyond the Hindu Kush, from which the Aryans arrived bringing truth, virtue, and justice, followed, unfortunately, by a decline to the degeneration of contemporary life. The Master Race–Golden Age theory put Aryan Hindus on an equal footing with their British detractors. Now Hindus could advocate a ban on the burning of widows, education for women, and other reforms without admitting Western moral superiority.

This solved one problem but created many others. Whom did these Aryans conquer? Were the many tribal societies, in the phrase Kipling used to describe colonized nonwhites, a "lesser breed without the law"? What was the mainstream of the Indian nation?

The Polluted Mainstream

Anciently much of the hill regions of what is now south Bihar was roadless forest called *Jharkhand* (from the Sanskrit *jhar*/jungle and *khand*/place). It was never a state or nation, but social movement activists say its time has come. I went to Ranchi, at the heart of Jharkhand, to meet Bishop Nirmal Minz, who has devoted his life to the cause.

"How can the dominant community expect us to join a filthy stream that's becoming dirtier with no hope of change?" asked Bishop Minz. "The dominant part of Indian society is full of corruption and hiding of evils. In our tribal society we would rather be simple, honest, straightforward, and do justice wherever we can rather than connive and maneuver. People go to court and are instructed to tell lies. But our people will stand before the magistrate and say the truth. The mainstream is polluted, but all through the history of our country there has been a small pure stream, and this has been preserved by our people. The dominant society should accept it and make use of it for the greatness of our country."

It was identity building: separating the Jharkhandis from the *Dikkus* (outsiders). We were sitting in the living room of his home on the sprawling grounds of Ranchi's Gossner Evangelical Lutheran Church, one of three Christian organizations in the Chotanagpur tribal region of south Bihar. Bishop Minz, of medium height, with a round face, graying hair, and a soft voice, is an Oraon, one of the major tribes of the region.

He said his parents were farmers with little education, and he walked twenty-five miles in six hours to go to high school. After college in Patna he studied in Calcutta to become a Lutheran minister, and then, aided by a scholarship, he obtained two master's degrees—in theology and anthropology—at the Luther Theological Seminary and the University of Minnesota in St. Paul. He returned to India to work and went a second time to the United States where, in 1968, he received a doctorate from the University of Chicago with a thesis on systematic theology. Along the way he married and is now the father of four daughters.

Bihar's First Tribal College

"The day after I got my degree from Chicago we left to return home," he continued. "In 1971 I founded Gossner College with fifty-three rupees, ten part-time teachers, and twenty-six students in three rooms. I thought language would be an instrument for the awakening of tribal people, so we began teaching in five tribal languages: Santali, Kharia, Munda, Ho, and Oraon plus English as the link language. The first four are easily understood by the different speakers, like the Scandinavian languages.

Oraon, however, is different: it's derived from the Dravidian languages of south India.

"There was no literature, only bits and pieces of what some missionary or scholar had done. We had to write our own grammars and textbooks. Now others are teaching in the tribal languages, but we were alone for five or six years.

"We make the tribal languages interesting. We'll hold a debate on the same subject in all five languages and see how we express similar ideas in the different languages. Or we stage a small drama of a problem, and each language group will present its own version.

"This became the second best college in the Bihar university system. In one year there was a competitive examination for entrance into a medical school in Bihar. The first six candidates were from Gossner College, and they had only second and third divisions from us: candidates from other colleges had firsts. A second division Gossner College student competed for entrance into the All-India Institute for Medical Science in Delhi and was the only one selected from Bihar.

"I retired from the college in 1981. Now, there are 4,500 students of whom 75 to 80 percent are tribal with 55 percent boys and 45 percent girls. This shows there's not only an increasing desire for education, but also an increasing search for identity. Students come from all over Bihar and West Bengal and from as far away as Manipur and Nepal."

Obstacles to Jharkhand

The proposed state of Jharkhand would be formed out of the southern half of Bihar, with about a quarter of its population, along with adjacent tribal areas in West Bengal, Orissa, and Madhya Pradesh: twenty-one districts in all. The region is homeland for about a dozen tribes, including the major ones mentioned by Bishop Minz. However, tribals comprise only 28 percent of the region's population. The largest single group —about half the population—is known as *Sadans*: a catch-all designation for many Hindu artisan and service castes who live in a symbiotic relationship with tribes people, although there is no intermarriage. Conversely, the Sadans have little contact with similar castes outside the region.

The Chotanagpur plateau and the Santal Parganas districts of Bihar are the Ruhr of India, with a quarter of the country's mines and steel mills. Nearly 20 percent of the money invested by the central government since independence to create an industrial base has been spent in these two districts alone. But while Jharkhand's forests have been stripped and its water polluted, only a small fraction of the revenues generated by industrialization have been returned to the region for social projects, and with rare exceptions all except menial, low-paid work has gone to the upper caste elite who monopolize technical and administrative positions.

"How do you reply to those who say Jharkhand is so vital to the nation, it can't slip from the control of Delhi or Patna?" I asked Bishop Minz.

"We never eat alone: we share," he replied. "The wealth here doesn't belong to us only but to the whole nation. We don't want to eat it up ourselves, so our keeping it is not the question. The question is: What has development done for the sons of the soil in various parts of the country? The major products have benefited the dominant society, not the tribal people. We are victims of progress."

"But still, how can there be Jharkhand without a tribal majority?" I asked.

"No, that's not correct. The Kurmis were changed from a tribal to a scheduled caste only in 1931 because of some mistakes. Only the day before yesterday they gave me all the documents proving they are tribals. If these are included, at least two-thirds will be tribal."

"What right do you have to include the Sadans?"

"The whole tribal attitude toward other people is not excluding but including. If someone comes to our courtyard, we don't say, 'You don't belong to us.' We accept him as a member of the family. The Sadans have been within Jharkhand for many generations, and their leaders have now realized their future is dark unless they have a place to live together with the tribals. They're Hindus, but we don't mind if a person is a Hindu or Christian or tribal. They never practiced untouchability or other forms of discrimination—we use the same wells and water —it's just there are no intermarriages.

"All doubts can be resolved. The customary laws of tribal society are the basic instruments of human living but are being eroded. There are many identical or similar customary laws in all the tribes. These can be shaped into a common ground for all. We need a space to have our identity. We're standing on one leg and must stand on both legs. In my school and college days I outdid Brahmin and Rajput students, but they wouldn't admit even equality. At a birthday party six or seven years ago a lawyer who was the principal of the law college in Ranchi argued with me. I forget the subject. I outdid him, but he wouldn't accept that.

Finally I had to say to him, 'The day you'll accept me as an intellectual equal, if not superior, will be a great day for our country.'

"When the Aryans came they defeated the people already in India, so naturally they had a superiority complex. And now the Aryans are trying to extend their power. No one is born a priest. We believe a community should select its own priests. But now many small temples are being constructed, and these are looked after by Brahmin priests. Thirty years ago there was hardly one or two temples in the entire city. Now you see them all along the main road and throughout other streets. The dominant community never cared for our people before the missionaries came: Never! Never!

"Missionaries came about 140 years ago and started to care for tribal people, and naturally, if you care for someone, they'll accept you. The Aryans had the chance for thousands of years, but they rejected us. Now they're doing all sorts of things to claim our people, but we never belonged to them throughout history. This is a political movement to include our people and make the dominant community stronger.

"About a year or two ago a small image was found in a village seventy miles west of here. They said this was the mother of Hanuman, and this meant Hanuman was born there. A fair was created, and even the government supported it. Now all kinds of melas are being held in that area. This is a kind of myth creation. People from outside are creating tension that was never present before.

"The low self-image of our people is because they've been told by the dominant community, 'You're no good; your language is no good; your society is no good.' We should know we're the original occupants of this country. Our history is related to Mohenjo-Daro and Harappa and the Indus Valley civilization of five thousand years ago. The dominant community was not here then."

Missionary Emasculation

When I asked about missionaries, his criticism was equally unsparing:

"There are three basic missions: the Gossner Mission Society from Berlin; the Society for the Propagation of the Gospel from England; and the Jesuit Roman Catholic Mission from Belgium. They all can be found in the same community, even in the same village. We should form one Christian community with our own identity as Christians and not as the outgrowth of mission activity.

"Christian educational agencies have domesticated tribals more than it has liberated them. Though the church and missionary institutions brought literacy, real education did not take place. Our people were never taught to do things for themselves: it's hard to find a responsible person as a leader of the community.

"A year ago I was at a small meeting with a Catholic father from Belgium. We were trying to find a good person to do a specific task. He said, 'It's distressing we can't find a responsible Christian layman among us.' I replied, 'Who's responsible for that? You and me. We've given a mentality to them of being completely domesticated.'

"There's another tragedy. Many of us have gone into education and have done well and been appointed to government services, but we forget the society from which we came, and we behave like others. We're so alienated by this type of education we become a party to exploitation. This is a painful experience with very few exceptions."

I said even well-read Indians were only vaguely aware of the Jharkhand movement, and most newspaper reports stressed the obstacles, making it appear a hopeless cause.

"They may say so," Bishop Minz replied, "but the Jharkhand movement began in the 1930s, and any movement that has continued for fifty years must have some political validity. In the beginning, however, it was weak because it spoke only in the name of the scheduled tribes and not the Sadans and the Kurmis. Now it has a different form: it has a cultural and social base for political achievement. Before it was just political and didn't take into account music, dance, drama, and language. And now tribal young people—college and university graduates —are taking a keen interest. The hope of the movement is young people. They must be encouraged and organized."

Nonviolent Noncooperation

I had been trying for several days to meet Prabakar Tirkey, one of the leaders of the All-Jharkhand Students Union, formed in 1986. I finally cornered him at his home early one morning. Tirkey, an Oraon like Bishop Minz, had been a student at Ranchi Agricultural College: now twenty-five, unmarried, and living at his parent's home, he was totally involved with the AJSU.

"Our identity is being crushed," he said. "There's a provision in the constitution for the development of all the citizens of the country, especially for tribals who are downtrodden, but the government does nothing.

"We presented a written memorandum to Delhi listing our problems and grievances. They have not responded, and now we will start a noncooperation movement. We'll ask students not to go to schools and colleges. What's the good of getting higher degrees if we don't get jobs? And we'll ask for a boycott of the administration and courts. Our farmers go to the block development office for seeds and fertilizer, but they don't get anything on time and have to pay a bribe even if the government has sent it to be distributed free. We'll say, 'Don't go to the BDO to get seed and fertilizer: we'll arrange it.'

"If there's any mishappening, people go to the courts and police. If two villagers fight, the police officer will take money from both sides, and no decision is handed down. A court case may last five to ten years. We'll decide problems in our own villages. We'll also stop resources from going out of this area. Coal and iron comes out of our soil, and the government gets huge revenues, but only a small amount is spent here. We'll not let any minerals go out of Jharkhand."

"But the government will bring in police and paramilitary forces and the army if necessary," I said. "How can you expect to win?"

"The people are with us: hundreds of thousands of people. They'll lay down on the roads. We will win. We have a long history behind this. Our ancestors fought for the same rights before independence. In 1855 Sidhu Kanu led the Santals in blocking the British advance and thousands of Santals were killed. In 1874 Baba Tilka Majoo was hanged for shooting a British official, Colonel Cleveland, with an arrow, and in 1895 Birsa Munda fought the administration."

The Threat of Repression

The incidents Tirkey cited as assertions of tribal identity are also examples of ruthless suppression. The change from a British to an Indian government has not brought change in the government's attitude.

As India rushed to create a modern industrial state, tribals complained their lands were seized by nationalized coal-mining companies with the protection of Congress Party politicians in Patna. In the early 1970s a group calling itself the Jharkhand *Mukti Morcha* (Liberation Struggle; JMM) began demonstrations to reclaim a forest area clearly indicated as tribal land by *sarangs* (memorial stones) marking ancestral burial grounds. A contingent of the Bihar Military Police (BMP) was assigned to the region and harassed tribals by stealing their chickens and vegetables, arresting those who dared to complain. The JMM scheduled a protest meeting in the mining town of Gua.

On the appointed day a large contingent of the BMP, accompanied by two magistrates, was dispatched to Gua, where three thousand tribals had assembled in the market square. As the first speaker began addressing the crowd, the police dragged him away. With that fighting broke out. An official statement claimed the tribals fired first, shooting volleys of arrows that killed four policemen. The police, according to this account, responded by firing thirty-seven rounds that killed three tribals. The tribals say it was the police who began the shooting and fired many more than thirty-seven rounds, killing scores of tribals and wounding many others.

The tribals carried nine of their most critically injured men to the Gua Mines Hospital half a kilometer away. There they were told to deposit their bows and arrows at the gate and lay the wounded under a tree in the compound and that doctors would come out to treat them. Instead, the nine wounded were shot dead by the BMP.

When newspapers in Patna investigated, it was discovered the incident did not happen by chance. At a meeting on August 30 government officials had decided on "deterrent action" against the JMM movement in the Gua area. The state forest minister was reported to have said, "We have to stop this at all costs."

The ready resort to punitive action is part of the conditioning of Indian history. When a handful of Bengali Communists thought they could replicate Mao Zedong's peasant-based revolution, they caused such a fright that all guarantees of justice and legal rights were discarded.

34 ✸ The Front Paw of the Revolution

O n June 28, 1967, Radio Beijing took note of events in a distant corner of northern India: "A phase of peasants' armed struggle, led by the revolutionaries of the Indian Communist Party, has been set up in the countryside in the Darjeeling District of West Bengal state of India. This is the front paw of the revolutionary armed struggle launched by the Indian people under the guidance of Mao Zedong's teachings."

Charu Mazumdar, the son of a landlord, saw the small town of Naxalbari as the place to repeat Mao's victorious march from remote Yenan through all of China. Mazumdar, as a member of the Communist *Kisan Sabha* (Farmers or, to Marxists, Peasants Assembly) in north Bengal, had been in and out of prison since 1945. While in jail in 1965, he wrote nine essays calling the Cultural Revolution "an exploding moral atom bomb" and explicating the failures and future of Communism in India. He believed city-bred cadres could instigate a mass uprising in rural areas that would eventually escalate into a "Peoples War."

He thought he could find his first mass base among land-hungry Santals evicted from their hill homelands by settlers and moneylenders from the plains and transported as bonded laborers to work sites and tea plantations throughout West Bengal and neighboring states. Yet they retained their language and customs, particularly the *Lo Bir* (Hunt Council), at whose call quarrels and links with non-Santals are forgotten and clan members rushed to one another's aid. This solidarity lay behind the ease with which the Naxalites mustered thousands of dedicated workers.

While the Santals were among the most naive, the Communist cadres were drawn from the most urban and sophisticated: the Bengali *bhadralok*. The word is difficult to translate. It is the equivalent of the

Western middle class, but it is more a status than a class designation. It denotes "polite" people or gentlemanly society as distinguished from the *chotolok* (little people) or *garib lok* (poor people). The bhadralok who dominate the "workers" Communist Party are almost entirely professionals or otherwise skilled employees: the menial work of Bengal is done by emigrants from Bihar and Orissa, who generally vote Congress.

There is no clearly defined Bengali upper class. In colonial times the British occupied this position. Now Bengalis feel the *Marwaris* (businessmen originally from Marwar in Rajasthan) have all the money while political control is in the hands of power brokers from Delhi. This feeling of being exiles in their own land contributes to a bhadralok sense of resentment and an urge to revolt. Almost a century ago they formed terrorist cells, and daring tales of raiding banks and armories and assassinating the British and their collaborators are part of Bengali schoolboy lore.

The Communists Divide into Three Parts

The Communist Party of India (CPI), a handful of underground fugitives during the 1920s and 1930s, was allowed to flourish during World War II, when it supported the British war effort as part of the Stalinist line of a united front against Fascism. After independence, due to bhadralok resentment of rule by the Congress Party from Delhi, the Communists became strong in Bengal.

In 1964 a faction split off to form the Communist Party of India (Marxist) (CPI-M). The split is usually ascribed to the conflict within world Communism, with the CPI seen as pro-Moscow and the CPI-M as pro-Beijing. But there was a deeper cause: the CPI clung to the old line of supporting the Congress as the ally of the Soviet Union, while the CPI-M represented power-hungry activists who wanted greater freedom to challenge the Congress in local and national elections.

In March 1967 two decades of Congress Party rule in West Bengal ended with the swearing in of a United Front (UF) coalition made up of leftist political parties, including the CPI and CPI-M, and ten smaller parties.

For Charu Mazumdar parliamentary democracy was a sham. He organized squads to act independently, with no direct connections with the leaders at the top, with communications to be arranged through a convoluted system of couriers. He believed people, not arms, were the source of victory and "peasants" should fight with bows and arrows and

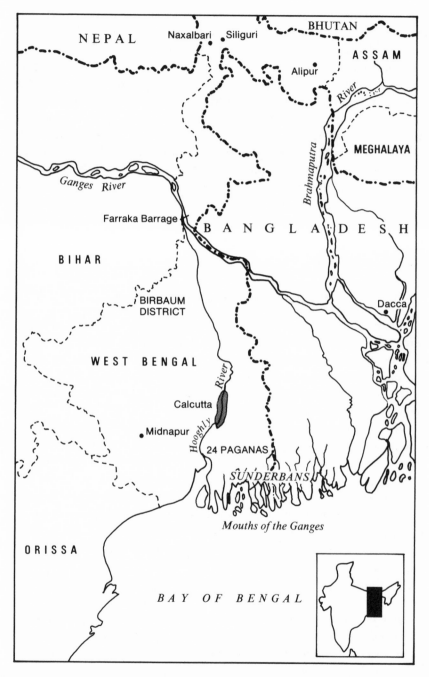

West Bengal

farm implements and thus gain confidence to struggle even with their bare hands. He made one concession: they could make their own guns. This was the origin of his most famous weapon: the pipegun, generally made from the steering column of a truck altered to fire a single bullet with, of course, no accuracy. He wrote that while Mao's Peoples Liberation Army had begun a revolution with two hundred rifles, the Liberation Army of India could be formed with two hundred pipeguns and as few as sixty rifles.

In the Naxalbari area it was estimated 65,000 acres of surplus land were owned by tea estates with another 19,000 acres controlled by the government. The United Front government had no clear policy for the distribution of this land to the poor, but it did promise not to deploy police in the settlement of land disputes. That was practically an invitation to Charu Mazumdar and other CPI-M activists to take matters into their own hands.

Between March and May 1967 there were almost one hundred incidents in the Naxalbari area of Santals armed with bows and arrows occupying land and then symbolically establishing their ownership by plowing small parcels. It started peacefully, but on May 24 a police party was ambushed and shot with arrows, leading to the death of a subinspector. The next day police sent to "investigate" got revenge by firing on a gathering of six hundred Santals, killing one adult male, six women, and two children.

A short while later, the headless corpse of a *jotedar* (a medium-size landholder; "kulak" in Marxist terminology) was discovered. When the cases of looting, arson, intimidation, and murder rose to almost 150, with warrants issued for the arrest of seven hundred others, the United Front government revoked the policy of not using police. Police and paramilitary forces combed rural villages to arrest fugitives and reclaim seized grains, denying the Santals the food they needed to continue. By August the uprising was crushed.

For the next two years there was relative calm while politics were sorted out. Most Naxalite cadres came from the CPI-M rather than the CPI or other leftist groups. To hold the United Front coalition together, the CPI-M expelled the dissidents and supported the police. In reaction, on April 22, 1969 (Lenin's birthday), Mazumdar and his followers founded the Communist Party of India (Marxist-Leninist) (CPI-ML) and announced the birth of the party on the following May Day.

The uprising resumed in July 1969. Mazumdar tried to convert the Midnapur area, on the West Bengal-Bihar-Orissa border, into a liberated zone, and students from Calcutta responded to his call to integrate with poor and landless peasants. But again, after the seizure of land and harvesting the paddy by as many as five thousand landless, mostly Santals armed with bows and arrows, and the killing of "lackeys of landlords" and "class enemies," police and paramilitary units broke the back of the resistance, and by November the second Naxalite offensive had collapsed.

Mazumdar's Murder Manual

In February 1970 Mazumdar unveiled a campaign of "annihilation" with an article published under the title, "A Few Words About Guerrilla Actions." Others called it a "murder manual." He said the cadres should move into an area and conduct propaganda about the class enemy and the need to seize land and crops. They should try to find the most likely persons and whisper in their ears, "How would it be if we killed such and such?" They should then form a squad of those who hated the class enemy the most and advise them to kill the enemy secretly. This accomplished, the cadres would return to their secret bases. The killer squad should also disappear and return only after things cooled down.

Mazumdar said this would generate further enthusiasm among the poor and terrorize the privileged. He also said it would separate the wheat from the chaff as the belief spread "he who has not dipped his hand in the blood of class enemies can hardly be called a Communist."

Students in Calcutta were relatively quiescent during the initial two uprisings: remarkable considering their tendency to paralyze the city with mass strikes at the least provocation. Then, in March 1970, Naxalite youth tested the waters with a simultaneous attack on seven cinemas showing a film called *Prem Pujari* (Priest of Love), which they found objectionable because it allegedly depicted China in a bad light. April and May brought large-scale clashes between police and Naxalites who used the universities as sanctuaries. They also, in the spirit of the Cultural Revolution, attacked and defaced statues of Bengali heroes. In addition Mahatma Gandhi's statue in fashionable Park Street was so often a target a permanent guard had to be put around it.

Earlier, starting in March, other students streamed into Birbhum in northwestern Bengal to join what proved to be the last battle for a liberated rural base. In May, amid annihilation murders and peoples courts to try and sentence landholders to death, Mazumdar proclaimed he had finally established a secure base for his Peoples Army. But in

June the central government used its constitutional powers to oust the United Front government and assumed direct rule through an appointed governor. A leading member of the Congress Party, Siddhartha Shankar Ray, was named as his "adviser." In reality he was the wielder of power.

Ray deployed three entire army divisions in Calcutta and in every police station in rural districts. In addition to the army, units of state armed police and several thousand men of the Central Reserve Police Force moved into Birbhum with permission to shoot in "self-defense," which was interpreted to mean indiscriminately. The Santals and other landless supporters, who had joined the fight only for land, returned to their villages when the pressure became too strong: they had no interest in Mazumdar's revolution. By November 1971 the fight was over: without a mass base the surviving cadres and students surrendered or returned to Calcutta to fight on more familiar ground.

The Calcutta Cleansing

By then their gruesome posturing—some students in Calcutta actually dipped their hands in the blood of a dead "class enemy" to prove their zeal—had clearly separated Naxalites from other leftists. The last thread of support for the Maoist Naxalites was snapped in December 1971 when China opposed the Indian invasion of East Pakistan to support the independence of what came to be called Bangladesh. Bengal, even that part under Muslim rule, was sacred ground, and its "liberation" from West Pakistani rule was greeted with joy by all Bengalis. The disenchantment of Bengalis with all leftists was demonstrated in March 1972 when the Congress Party won control of the state assembly and Siddhartha Shankar Ray was sworn in as chief minister.

Bengalis, as well as all Indians, then closed their eyes as Ray set out to exterminate Maoism on Indian soil. Since it was difficult for the army and paramilitary units to fight an urban guerrilla war, Ray forged a new weapon. The Congress Party recruited criminals for "resistance groups" and turned them loose on Naxalites and their sympathizers.

The Naxalites tried to defend themselves by recruiting their own criminals, but they were overpowered. By October 300,000 criminals and other "antisocials" were organized into sixteen thousand Congress resistance groups throughout West Bengal, of which twelve thousand were in Calcutta. Murders were so common the Calcutta crematories were covered in red graffiti epitaphs to slain comrades.

The most notorious "cleansing action" occurred the following August in the Cossipore-Baranagar area of suburban Calcutta. The neighborhood, thought to be a Naxalite stronghold, was cordoned off and hundreds of alleged Naxalites or sympathizers were massacred. For days the banks of the Hooghly River were dotted with mutilated corpses washed ashore.

In addition to an estimated five thousand alleged Naxalites killed over a period of four years, thousands were arrested on the slightest pretext and tortured to reveal the hiding places of others. One arrest led to the most wanted man of all: Charu Mazumdar. In July, acting on information from an arrested courier, Mazumdar was plucked from a flat in East Calcutta. He had long been ill and was sent to a hospital under armed guard. His death, of "heart failure," was announced eleven days later.

Among others whose deaths were announced were those said to have been killed in "encounters" with the police, that is, while resisting arrest or trying to escape. Over a two hundred day period in 1971 the police reported 202 persons had died in such "encounters."

One victim lived to tell the tale. Shambunath Shah was tortured to discover the hiding places of his accomplices, and when he said he did not know any such persons, he was handcuffed and taken to the Salt Lake area outside the city where he was told to get out of the car and walk away. However, the police sent to kill him did not have much will or expertise. They fired three shots, only one of which wounded Shah. They then took him to the bank of a river and fired another three shots, two of which wounded him. He fell unconscious, but when it was discovered he was still alive, he was taken to a third place and shot once more, after which he was taken to a hospital to die. When police came the next morning to dispose of Shah's body, they discovered his life had been saved by an operation. Their report said he had been wounded in an encounter.

The Octopus Snares the Elite

Although the mistreatment of prisoners was as bad as in Argentina or elsewhere, it was not until years later that the full story began to be revealed. When Mrs Gandhi's State of Emergency was ended in 1977, it was realized the disease of Bengal had spread. *India Today*, which began publication following the Emergency, commented:

> Planned torture and bestiality as an instrument of state policy became apparent from late 1967 and soon developed into an integral

part of the system. . . . When [during the Emergency] the elites found themselves in handcuffs and solitary confinement, they suddenly realized that the octopus which had till now only strangled the Naxalites who were considered outside the system, had now spread its tentacles to include them too.

The magazine described the tortures and the names given to them. In paraphrase they were:

The Submarine: A prisoner is immersed in water, or sometimes urine, until he feels he is about to drown.

The Parrot's Perch: A prisoner, his hands and ankles tied together, is hung by his knees from a horizontal bar.

The Telephone: Sharp, simultaneous blows to the ears, causing great pain and rupturing the prisoner's eardrums.

The Aeroplane: A prisoner's hands are tied behind his back with a rope, which is then looped over a pulley on the ceiling. The prisoner is pulled above the ground and dangles in midair, suspended with his arms stretched upward behind his back. The pain is intense. In another variation the prisoner is tied with iron chains to a ceiling fan and struck with a lathi at every rotation.

The Horseman: A prisoner is stripped naked and made to straddle a wood beam for hours and even days with his hands and feet tied.

The Roller: One of the most dreaded. A prisoner is made to lie on his back on a bench with his head dangling at one end and his undergarments stuffed in his mouth to silence his screams. A long heavy wooden roller is placed on his legs and two policemen sit on either end and roll it up and down the thighs. The pain is excruciating: often ligaments are torn and bones crack.

Other tortures included: pins or other sharp instruments inserted under a prisoner's nails or into his genitals; ripping off nails; electric shocks; a chili-coated rod or live electrical wire inserted into the anus and/or vagina; beatings on the soles of feet; and bare bodies stamped with heeled boots.

By 1973 about 25,000 persons had been detained under provisions of the Maintenance of Internal Security Act (MISA) or the Defense of India Act. This allowed a person to be locked up without specifying the charges and held for six months, extendable for another six months. Even after release the alleged Naxalite would be rearrested on spurious charges and held indefinitely as an "under trial" waiting for court proceedings.

Eighty to a hundred prisoners were locked at night in dark, airless rooms for twelve hours and let out for two hours in the morning to have a meal, wash, and use the lavatories. In Calcutta's Presidency Jail one water tap was available for as many as two hundred persons. At Alipore Special Jail there was one water tap for seven hundred prisoners. In other jails prisoners had to drink from ponds that were also used for bathing and washing clothes.

Prisoners regarded as security risks were kept in fetters day and night "to avoid further trouble." The fetters were an iron ring on each ankle, attached to an iron bar about twenty inches long. These bars were attached to another bar attached to the waist.

The horrors finally eased and most of the prisoners were released when the Emergency ended in 1977, and a new Left Front government, dominated by the CPI-M, regained control of West Bengal.

The CPI-ML still exists, not as a single party but as a number of Naxalite sects, principally in Bihar and Andhra Pradesh. Most former Naxalites have retreated to obscurity, trying to erase the horrors from their minds. One, whose name is Tapas Banerjee, has gained from his experience and is attempting renewal not through revolution but through nonviolent social action.

35 ✸ From Revolt to Renewal

While Tapas Banerjee was in jail as a Naxalite, he realized the error of using people as instruments to achieve a prefigured ideology and that someone hoping to change society must work together with people for renewal rather than revolution. Upon his release he decided to confront the greatest of all evils—aside from poverty itself—afflicting the urban poor: drugs and alcohol.

Little media or other attention is given to social activists in India, and I had to ask several persons if they knew of anyone working for nonviolent change in Bengal. Someone mentioned Tapas Banerjee and arranged a meeting with him.

"We are the first organization to start a movement against alcohol and drugs," he said. "These are very dangerous for working people. If they make twenty rupees, after their work they spend more than half on alcohol and drugs. There is no other recreation besides drugs and alcohol, and men return to their houses and torture their wives. If one stops, others will stop, and they will have a community spirit. In our areas drugs and alcohol have completely stopped."

It seemed a large claim. I said I would like to see the work in action, and he arranged for me to go with a slim, eager young man named Anowar Hossain to a Muslim slum in the Tollygunge area of south Calcutta. Neither Anowar nor the half dozen other youths who crowded around when I arrived at their clubhouse spoke much English, but they produced a stream of documents and pictures to supplement their words.

Their club was a few rooms in a run-down, single-story building with a bamboo structure in front. They said it had been a drug hangout, and when they went to the owner to ask to rent it, he said they could have it rent free: but if he came and saw anything wrong, he would throw them out.

They said the club was five years old and had thirty-five members, mostly teenagers, but some up to twenty-one years old. Most of the space was used for supplementary education for children from kindergarten to eighth grade. They studied from six-thirty to nine-thirty in the evening with club members as teachers, as evidence of which they showed books with the names of fifty-one students with boxes to be checked off to indicate attendance. They said two of their students had taken first place in their regular schools. Previously derelict rooms had been cleaned and painted for classrooms, and a new tile roof had been put on the shed: they said they did it all themselves. Their main club room had a small library and a television set: they said they had saved their money to buy it and that the children were allowed to watch on weekends or during school holidays.

There was a clear area outside. Once a marsh, they had filled and leveled it as a sports field, with posts for a volleyball net on either side. At the end, where the ground was lower and still wet, they had planted a garden of roses and other flowers. They said a club member had won a hundred-meter race against competitors from forty-eight schools. They were also proud of their "sit-and-draw" competitions and brought out winning pictures from a recent contest involving eighty-eight children from three schools.

It was like taking rabbits out of a hat: the more they showed, the more interested I became. They showed pictures of themselves walking through the streets, stretching out a large cloth for people to toss in donations for flood relief, and said they sent medicines and clothing to flood victims in 1987 and 1988. They showed other pictures of blood collection camps in 1986, 1987, and 1988, with records of from forty to fifty-five donations each year. Donors were given certificates, and when a relative or someone else was sick and required blood, they donated what was needed. They showed one certificate from a hospital of two bottles of blood issued to a patient with severe anemia.

They also lent money, to be repaid at the rate of ten rupees a month over five years, to meet individual needs: two persons got loans for a daughter's marriage and two others borrowed money to pay fees for railroad hawker's licenses. Finally, they showed pictures of their annual meetings, with speakers including a judge, a deputy commissioner, and a police official. Their financial report for 1988 showed they received and spent a bit more than five thousand rupees ($350), including a donation of five hundred rupees ($35) from a nearby iron merchant.

There was so much I had not expected; it was not until I was leaving that I asked about their campaign against drugs and alcohol. Yes, they said, that was their main purpose. All members, and anyone who joined in their activities, took a pledge not to drink or use drugs, and they had brought pressure on residents and shop owners to drive out liquor shops from a one kilometer radius.

With customary Indian politeness, showing a guest to the door or the property line, they walked with me back to the main road, through narrow lanes of low, brick huts. Not once did we have to step over garbage or excrement: all was cleanly swept and dry, and yet this was regarded by outsiders as one of the worst slums of Calcutta.

A "Dying City" Revived

It had been an impressive few hours. Calcutta is the cliché for Third World evils: a "dying city" where visitors only talk of people sleeping and living on the streets. Yet here were teenagers getting joy out of helping younger children with their studies and being role models for them. They were also reaching out to the surrounding world with blood collection drives and by raising money for flood relief and through sports and drawing contests.

The landlord gave them a place to stay; the iron merchant gave them a donation equaling 10 percent of their expenditures, and they said a neighboring doctor gave free treatment for club members and others they recommended. Together the club members, the business and professional people, and all their neighbors had created an environment free of garbage, drugs, and alcohol.

When I said I wanted to see more, my contact arranged for another guide to show me a club in a section of Tollygunge with small manufacturing shops. Club members were small businessmen organized to fight crime as well as drugs and alcohol. A dozen of us squeezed into a room barely six feet wide: two Muslims, identified by their white skull caps, a burly, bearded, and turbaned Sikh, and others whom I assumed were Hindus or Christians. An elderly man, who spoke halting English, was their chairman:

"None of the political parties did anything to help us. And the police did nothing to stop the goondas. In every street, on every corner there were antisocial elements who took money from the factories and merchants. The situation became miserable. All the parties, and certainly this Left Front government, are involved with the goondas and so are the police. There were bombings and stabbings, and the antisocial elements harassed the people, so we made this self-defense organization."

I said I was surprised he made such a broad statement. The Communists, I said, were a workers' party, and the Congress was the party of Mahatma Gandhi. He conceded he had perhaps gone too far:

"Not everyone is bad: there are some good men in every political party and some police help us and other groups like us, but there are not many like that."

I asked several questions, trying to find out what they did, but they never got beyond generalized statements. I gathered the mere fact of having an organization and a way, through Tapas Banerjee, of reaching out to others for assistance made it possible to resist demands for bribes and protection money and to curb the sale and distribution of drugs and liquor.

The Torture of Tapas Banerjee

The next morning I called on Tapas Banerjee at his apartment (he is not married) in a housing development in Tollygunge. An even earlier visitor left just as I arrived, and Banerjee had not yet changed from his night clothes: a cotton undershirt and lungi. He is a soft spoken man: stocky, about five feet eight, with a round face, neatly clipped moustache, and black, wavy hair tinged with gray. Unperturbed at this new intrusion, he kicked off his sandals and sat cross-legged on one end of his bed while I sat on the other.

"My father was a Communist and I was a Communist," he said. "We were very poor, but I was able to go to Calcutta University. In 1967, when the Naxalite movement began, I helped it, mainly in rural areas. I was captured in 1972 and was released in Bihar in 1977 and returned to Calcutta."

"Were you tortured?" I asked.

"They beat me with lathis and rifle butts when they arrested me," he replied. "My sight is bad in my left eye, and I can't hear in my left ear. Both my knees are weak, and there's a lot of pain in my legs." He also pointed to scars on his arms and legs.

"When I was in prison, it was mental torture. They put me in a small cell and let me out only half an hour to go to the toilet. It was complete isolation for four and a half years: no mail, no relatives. At night four or six police came in and said, 'Tapas Banerjee we must search you.' What could I hide? I had only a shirt and lungi, but they made me take my clothes off, and they shouted questions at me.

"When I was freed, I wanted to work for basic people in the rural and urban areas. In India there is no peoples-based organization: no good political party that feels for the people. I started work with education. When people are educated, the political parties will not cheat and exploit them. The Communists and all parties are corrupt and polluted."

I asked him about the club for businessmen. I said I could easily understand his work with young people and students, but it seemed unusual for someone who had once been associated with the Naxalites, who preached annihilation of class enemies, to be working with businessmen.

"We work with anyone who needs our help. A man came to see me this morning and left just as you arrived. He's an engineer. His younger brother was murdered, and the police did nothing. He wants us to help him find who did it, so he can be punished, and we will help him get action.

"The goondas and political parties are against small businessmen, but we protect them. The police are upset about me: they support the goondas and try to stop my work. I was attacked by the goondas three times. Once they threw a bomb over a wall to try to kill me. But then people in Tollygunge got upset. A thousand people sat and blocked the main road to show the police and politicians we had support."

"You've been political for most of your life. Are you giving up all politics?" I asked.

"No, we will put up our own candidates for the municipal corporation and other local offices. We want to fight corruption. But our candidates will be men like Anowar Hossain, basic people. They will be Hindus, Muslims, and Sikhs. We will give them our support."

I later went back to the contact who had steered me toward Tapas Banerjee and asked if he could suggest someone else in Calcutta involved in nonviolent social action. He had just the man: Pannalal Dasgupta, a former Communist who was now a Gandhian. I got his address and went to see him.

36 ☀ A Civilization That Doesn't Work

Pannalal Dasgupta was eighty-four, although he hardly appeared so: small and thin, he walked with strong, fast steps and climbed flights of stairs with no shortage of breath. Of his eighty-four years he spent twenty in prison and twelve years underground: more than one-third of his long life was given to violence. And now he shared the Gandhian dream of a self-sufficient, egalitarian society.

I called on him at the office of the Tagore Society, on the second floor of an old building on a back street in north Calcutta. Pannalal founded the society in 1969 to foster voluntary rural development. It has since grown into an umbrella group for ninety organizations in West Bengal, Orissa, and the northeastern states. When he is in Calcutta (more often he is away, visiting the many projects), Pannalal lives and works in a tiny, crowded room, sitting on his bed to read and answer his mail.

"Gandhi said our strength depends on the amount of our sacrifice," he said. "But modern activity is how to get more out of things, not less. Some people have said this city needs a new airport and our Communist Party government has said 'Fine.' What do the people have to do with an airport? In Delhi too they're throwing people off their farms to build a bigger and bigger airport. At the same time we send a begging bowl to Europe and America. Why don't we reduce our needs, so we can do things for ourselves?"

Pannalal invited me to join him on a visit to an extensive project at Rangebelia in the Sunderbans, a maze of islands formed by the thousands of tons of silt poured into the Bay of Bengal by the many mouths of the Ganges.

I arrived at 8:30 A.M. for a departure scheduled at nine. A driver had been told to bring a car at 7:30 and at 9:30, when he still had not appeared, someone began dialing a phone, over and over, trying to get a connection that was not a wrong number. Finally, he got through to the right person only to be told they had not heard of the arrangement but would send someone to find the driver.

"It's a civilization that doesn't work," Pannalal said. "We have phones but can't keep them repaired, and we have people with no sense of responsibility or time."

At 10:30, after dozens of attempts, we learned the driver had been found but could not start the car. He arrived at 11:30, and we set out fifteen minutes later. Caught in traffic jams, we inhaled the black exhausts of faulty engines, and when we broke clear of the city, we drove through garbage heaped twenty feet high on both sides of the road and breathed through handkerchiefs.

Then we paralleled a sewer canal that spilled the untreated wastes of Bengalis into the sea. The smell was almost as bad until we crossed a bridge and turned into the open countryside. After miles of pounding over potholes the driver began stretching his neck to look backward out the window at the right rear tire: it was going flat. When he stopped to change it, and took out the spare, that too appeared soft. He made the replacement, and we started again, easing gently over deep holes in the asphalt pavement.

It was an anxious time. Except for trucks and buses, there are few motor vehicles on rural roads in India: local transport is by cart and cycle. We passed long files of cycle rickshaws loaded with cabbages and other vegetables for the Calcutta market: with such heavy loads it took a man six or seven hours of hard peddling to reach the city.

The paucity of motor traffic meant few places where a tire could be repaired. We drove for almost an hour until we found a large market town with a tire shop equipped with a gasoline engine to create air pressure.

While waiting, I wandered around and noticed a solar panel high on a lamp post. I asked Pannalal to translate so I could ask about this intrusion of late twentieth-century technology into a region where human muscles were a principal source of energy. A shopkeeper said the solar panel and storage batteries were installed two years earlier to provide light from six at night until six in the morning.

"Does it give you enough light at night?" I asked.

"It doesn't give us any light," he replied. "It doesn't work."

"How long did it last?" I asked.

"Nine nights. We've been trying to get them to fix it ever since, but no one comes," he said.

Pannalal grinned: "You see, it's a civilization that doesn't work. No matter what machines or other things we get, we can't repair them. It's all a waste."

The Life of a Rebel

The wait also gave me time to ask Pannalal about his earlier life. As a student in Calcutta University in the 1920s, he was part of the shifting, secret world of Bengali terrorists. In 1929 he was arrested and tried, with about two hundred others, in a bomb conspiracy case. He was jailed for eight years and, on his release, was supposed to remain "interned" in a rural village. But when World War II started, he went underground, and in 1940 he joined the army under an assumed name to get weapons training. A year later, when his true identity was discovered, he was discharged and handed over to police to be returned to Calcutta. En route, he jumped off the train, returned to the underground, and was in Bombay during the 1946 Royal Indian Navy mutiny.

Two years after that aborted uprising, Pannalal and about thirty others tried to seize power in Calcutta. Through their labor union activities they had the support of workers at the large British-owned Jessup Company factory. In February 1948 they seized the Jessup factory, capturing several British civilians, intending to launch a further assault on Calcutta's Dum Dum airport.

That was only five months after independence, and Nehru and the Congress Party were determined not to appear weak before the world. The revolt was crushed, with dead and wounded on both sides, and the civilians rescued. Pannalal escaped, but he was arrested in 1950, and after two years in prison waiting for trial, he and several others were sentenced to life in prison.

In 1962 Pannalal was freed as part of a general amnesty and came out of prison a Communist hero. In the following years he was on the state planning board for agriculture and was a director of a state bank. In 1967, when the Left Front government captured the state legislature, he was elected as an independent but found politics uncongenial and resigned after a year to edit and publish what became a leading Bengali news and literary magazine called the *Compass*. Finally, he ended all other activities to devote himself to voluntary rural development.

We got back into the car and, without further mishap, arrived at the bank of a river and clambered down a slippery mud slope to a small launch for the final leg of the trip to Rangebelia. Until the turn of the century the Sunderbans was a mangrove forest inhabited mainly by fishermen and wild animals, including tigers. But with the insatiable hunger for land almost all the trees were cut down and the tigers confined to a small, wooded sanctuary.

Our destination was one of hundreds of isolated islands inadequately protected by high banks of mud. The region had been struck by a cyclone a few weeks earlier, and when we climbed the bank, we found uprooted trees and buildings with their roofs blown off and some completely destroyed.

We were taken to a room with iron beds and mosquito nets on the upper floor of a partly destroyed high school. It was late, and I went to the balcony to look at the sun setting in a dust haze over the flat countryside. Pannalal joined me and pointed out a field of green chilies.

"You see, instead of growing food for themselves, they are growing a commercial crop," he said. "With the increase in the standard of living and numbers of people, they have greater expenses, and to meet these expenses they have to do more and more intensive agriculture. That means greater cropping intensity by two or three times. And so we have a need for irrigation, tractors, fertilizers, insecticides, and other Western technology. All this is making the people more dependent and destroying the microorganisms in the soil."

"One Straw Revolution"

Pannalal had become a believer in the farming technique developed by the Japanese farmer-researcher Masanobu Fukuoka, who calls it the "One Straw Revolution." Under this method crops are raised with no tilling, no use of chemical fertilizers or natural compost, no weeding, and no chemicals or pesticides of any kind. The land is simply leveled and leaves removed to allow a mixture of seeds, that are broadcast and not drilled into the ground. The plot is covered with a layer of straw to inhibit evaporation and left to nature.

The idea is that over time a farmer will learn which seeds are best suited to his soil and the most resistant to local diseases and insects. He will also be able to work out a timetable of growth, reaping a continual harvest as the different plants reach maturity while the ground builds a layer rich in insects and other organisms needed to create a new and natural soil chemistry.

Pannalal had persuaded several farmers to use bits of their lands for experimental plots, which he inspected the next morning, although there wasn't much to see: shoots were just breaking through the cover of straw. Once he stopped to talk with a young woman. When we left her, he said she was another illustration of a civilization that doesn't work:

"She has an M.A., so a lot of money was spent for her education, but there's no employment for her here. The money spent to educate her came from agriculture. To get that money they had to develop more productivity, which meant more land was needed and more artificial inputs. Even the education itself is a commercial product. So it comes to this: commercial agriculture is developed to educate children to make them saleable in the commercial market as a result of which they are good for nothing in agriculture. Can you explain the logic of that?"

Planning for People

As much as Pannalal disagreed with the push for productivity and higher technology, he made no attempt to force his objections on others. Rangebelia believes in modern productivity and technology and has become one of the most successful voluntary development programs in all of India. It was started in 1975 by Tushar Kanjilal, the headmaster of the local high school. It was subsequently sponsored by the Tagore Society and now covers seventy-five villages with more than twenty thousand inhabitants.

It is a complicated structure that starts with a single family as a unit. The family, using a master list as a guide, prepares a yearly statement detailing how much land it has, what crops will be grown, how much money must be borrowed for such things as seeds or to dig irrigation or fish ponds, what clothing will be needed, what schooling and adult education, what training for a wife to get extra income, what animals may need inoculation: on and on, fitting all contingencies.

Ten or twelve families are formed into the next highest unit, which helps an individual family—in case of illiteracy—fill out its annual plan. The family plans are consolidated into a group plan, and this is sent up to be consolidated with other plans until finally a master plan for the entire region is drawn up.

With this as a guide inputs are marshaled and distributed: tractors and power tillers, seeds to diversify crops, a unit for animal husbandry, technicians to demonstrate poultry rearing and backyard gardening, group savings plans, mutual service societies—just about everything ever devised for rural uplift.

An English-speaking schoolteacher was assigned to show me how it worked. We visited a women's cooperative that made garments and handloom products and a fishermen's cooperative where aid was given for boats, nets, and marketing and even a honey collectors' cooperative.

At the health care unit I met the doctor, radiologist, and pathologist and was told of antenatal and postnatal care and immunization and nutritional training. I was shown samples of health status cards maintained by almost all families, listing what treatment they had received and when inoculation or other care was next required. I was also told of forty village-level health workers who visited people in their homes.

I was inundated with statistics. At a small office for nonformal education I was told there were 504 centers in 292 villages, each with one teacher and a total enrollment of fourteen thousand boys and girls for two hours a day, six days a week. Elsewhere I was told of the number of canals excavated, the number of diesel pump sets used for irrigation, the acreage under second crop, and the amount of additional income earned per family from pig or duck rearing or using nets to catch prawns.

One evening I attended a meeting of a group of ten families and listened as they discussed the repayment of debts. The cyclone had destroyed an entire season's crops. It was decided existing debts would be extended, and more money could be borrowed to plant a second crop. A veterinarian spoke of the need to bring animals to the inoculation center because dead animals were infecting village ponds.

The following afternoon I attended a women's meeting for a discussion which again centered on measures to deal with the cyclone damage.

In a harsh environment, at the edge of survival, Rangebelia was an impressive example of what could be accomplished by people involved in planning for themselves. The cyclone, more than anything else, proved the value of united, voluntary community development. On neighboring islands tens of thousands of people were homeless and the government and voluntary agencies were rushing to their aid with food, clothing, and drinking water. But the people of Rangebelia were saving themselves, largely because of two developments that Tushar Kanjilal had stressed over all else: a second crop and safe drinking water.

With loans to meet their immediate needs and the fast delivery of technical services, the farmers could expect a new crop within a few months. Early in the project a deep well had been dug to tap a sweet-water aquifer. Underground pipes, safe from the elements, distributed the water to large metal storage tanks spaced every hundred yards or so. People drew their water from taps in the tanks.

An Island of Self-Sufficiency

When I asked my guide what the individual benefits were, statistics were produced showing a family might have increased its annual farm income by five hundred to a thousand rupees ($35–$70) per person and that subsidiary income for women, from things like tailoring or catching prawns with improved nets, might add another five hundred rupees. Thus, no one was getting rich, but neither was anyone starving. And the supplementary benefits were enormous: more children and adults were getting educated, and everyone was more healthy. And they had become a united community: giving them strength to recover from the effects of the cyclone and also to resist the caste and class social structure that oppresses the poor throughout India.

I told Pannalal I had not seen anything on this scale anywhere in India. He did not disagree but saw it as part of the pull toward a civilization that doesn't work.

"I've told them they should try to achieve *swaraj* [self-rule] on this island. They've tied themselves to Calcutta and, as a result, need diesel-operated boats. If they run out of fuel, or can't repair a boat, they're lost. I said, 'You can make a benefit of this difficulty. You can achieve swaraj here. You can have your own farms, your own food, and your own clothing.' I tried to introduce the bamboo *charkha* (spinning wheel). They could make it themselves from local material and grow their own cotton: everything is here for them to make their own clothes. In the past they could have done it, but no longer. They can't accept it ideologically."

The next day we returned to Calcutta and had a final talk. I said I had been told the Left Front considered him an agent of the central government. He said that was true:

"The left overthrows all democratic and liberal ideas. They can't stand anyone who is independent of them. If we gave loyalty to them, they would be very glad to help us. They're envious because they can't do any service to the people. They've given some benefits here and there, but mostly it's merely distributing what they get from New Delhi. They would like to crush us, but they can't: our workers are daily with the masses, so they can't separate us from the people.

"But the Congress is equally corrupt. Had it been a little less corrupt, the Communists would have disappeared. They have survived not because of their Marxist ideology but because of the feeling they can defend Bengalis against Marwaris and others. Bengalis were the first to suffer from the British imperialists, and they feel India got independence at the cost of Bengal: by splitting away Bangladesh. They also feel Calcutta is no longer their city: that Marwaris, Gujaratis, and others rule it while Bengalis have to leave their land to earn a living. But the Communists can't admit their main attraction for Bengalis is because of this feeling of general disorganization: they have to say it is the result of their Marxist ideology."

"Have you given up entirely on politics?" I asked.

"Not entirely, but we have so many things to do at the grass roots we must concentrate on this for at least five or ten years. We must be continuously with the people and work to stop the madness of industrialization and commercialization. If we continue on this road, we're heading for disaster. Most of the material resources are being exhausted. Our forests are going, our water is polluted, our air vitiated. This is why I say, 'Be simple.' The simple life is the richest life, the only practical life. Each of us must do what we can. Gandhi said you can't plan for others, you can only plan for yourself."

We had arrived late, and I spent the night sleeping on blankets stretched on a large table. The next morning I said goodbye and took a train south to Andhra Pradesh where there were still vestiges of Naxalite violence.

37 ❀ Death by Encounter

For twenty years police and paramilitary units have waged a war of siege and attrition against Naxalite terrorists in the hilly tribal areas of northern and eastern Andhra Pradesh. Police superintendents of the four most affected districts—Karimnagar, Adilabad, Warangal, and Khammam—carry Sten guns as personal weapons and travel in jeeps with five bodyguards, and police posts are guarded by lookouts in concrete bunkers in the front and rear. In June 1988 the government formed an elite corps of a thousand men to be known as "Greyhounds" and to be equipped with the most modern of weapons and communications devices and bullet-proof vests.

Villages have been regrouped to facilitate police control, and homes of persons suspected of aiding the Naxalites have been burned. Others have been held for a year or more without charges filed against them or have been killed in police "encounters"—the equivalent of Latin American death squads.

With rare exceptions the defense of human rights in India is left to a handful of dedicated activists. One of them is K. G. Kannabiran. His initials refer to his ancestral village, and for simplicity he is generally referred to by his last name. Kannabiran, fifty-nine, is an attorney and president of the Andhra Pradesh Civil Liberties Committee (APCLC). I called on him at his home in Secunderabad, the twin city of the Andhra Pradesh capital of Hyderabad.

"When people in the rural areas are not able to get employment or food and the government can't solve problems, conditions deteriorate and there's a crisis," he said. "One may not agree with the policies of Naxalites, but this type of radical situation gives rise to radical politics. The more you use force, the greater the mobilization of these people, since a group fighting for some political issue must respond with force.

When you use force, you are absolutely mindless. You drive people to the state where they actually think the Naxalites are better."

From Nonviolence to Terrorism

In the late 1950s Vempatapu Satyanarayana, a schoolteacher from the plains who had married two tribal women, formed a tribal organization to reclaim traditional lands and extinguish debts. Although he later became a member of the CPI and then the CPI-M, he limited himself to the Gandhian nonviolent tactics of demonstrations and the symbolic seizure of land.

As the police began to kill and beat his followers, Satyanarayana became steadily more militant, and when the Naxalite movement began, he gave it his support, thus providing the cadres from the plains with a mass base. Then when the government poured paramilitary units into the region and the annihilation of "class enemies" became frequent, the tribals began to lose interest. They were particularly repelled by the Naxalite maiming or killing of tribals declared to be police spies. Satyanarayana himself was killed by police in June 1970 after a tip from two tribals whose brother had been killed by Naxalites.

The revolt was crushed by the end of 1970. Now tribal support is often more coerced than freely given, and the Naxalites draw recruits entirely from urban areas. There are about a dozen factions divided into *dalams* (squads). They carry guns seized from the police and country-made bombs, grenades, and *tarpanchas* (pipe guns) twelve to eighteen inches long with two triggers, one to open the barrel and the second for firing. They can kill at fifteen to twenty yards and are small enough to be hidden under the user's clothes. The Naxalites support themselves with "money actions"—robberies of banks or merchants—and exactions from contractors and businessmen.

The Naxalites have long followed the practice of amputating the hands or feet of alleged police spies. In Karimnagar District alone there are about fifty people whose legs and hands have been cut off. They also use amputations as a method of murder, thereby conserving scarce bullets. In November 1985 fifteen members of the most notorious faction, the People's War Group (PWG), ambushed a jeep carrying two CPI-M workers. They cut off the hands and legs of one of them, leaving him to bleed to death, and then began chopping off the arm of the other with an axe. The axe handle broke, and they shot their victim and disappeared. He later died in a Hyderabad hospital.

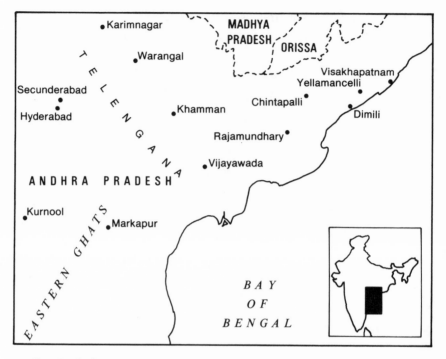

Andhra Pradesh

The PWG is led by Kondapalli Seetharamiah; in his late sixties, he has been a Communist for almost fifty years. He joined the Naxalites in 1969 and built a base in the Kondapalli area and quickly gained a reputation for both murder and money actions. In April 1977 he was arrested for murder in Nagpur, in the neighboring state of Maharashtra, but was released on bail two years later and promptly disappeared. He was arrested again in January 1981 and put in a Hyderabad jail.

When Seetharamiah complained of chest pains, he was taken to the government-run Osmania General Hospital where he was chained to his bed and two policemen were stationed nearby in around-the-clock shifts. Despite the guards Seetharamiah was able to exchange information with confederates on the outside. In early January 1984 he received a telegram saying his father had died. That was a signal he would soon be freed.

Four men dressed as doctors and policemen entered the hospital and hid in toilet cubicles adjoining Seetharamiah's ward. At four in the morning he said he had to go to the toilet and was unchained and escorted by one of the guards. The four men bungled an attempt to chloroform the guard and, instead, shot and killed him and walked out the front door, telling a sleepy watchman they were taking Seetharamiah back to jail.

Police incompetence was compounded a week later when, despite proclamations of an intensive search, Seetharamiah and one other left Hyderabad by car. When the car hit a tree, they simply got on a public bus to complete their trip to Bangalore, in Karnataka, where Seetharamiah, as did many criminals, had safe links with businessmen.

Police Death Squads

The main Naxalite uprising was crushed by police and paramilitary units using the same torture and encounter killings employed in West Bengal. And just as in West Bengal the media and the elite of the cities looked away as the police "protected" society. But when similar brutality was used against the elite during the Emergency of 1975–1977, it became possible to appeal to the public conscience. The central government in New Delhi appointed an official inquiry commission headed by retired Supreme Court Justice Vashisht Bhargava to look into all encounter deaths from 1968 to 1977. One witness told how he and four others, in July 1975, were driven into a forest:

> We were made to get down from the van and taken about a mile to walk. . . . Then the subinspector addressed me, "at least even now divulge the truth." . . . I was kept there. The remaining four people were taken to a distance of fifty feet and tied to trees by ropes from foot to chest, with the handcuffs on. A black cloth was tied over my eyes. The other four were also blindfolded. I heard the s.p. directing to fire. I heard one of them refusing to fire. Thereupon the s.p. abused him in English. The people who were tied were raising slogans: "Long live Mao, Long live the Revolution." I heard the firing of guns six times. . . . Then the s.p. approached me and said, "You bastard you are lucky you are still alive." . . . After I was put into the van my blindfold was removed and I happened to look and I found those four people with their heads hanging. Then I saw their ropes being removed and the four dead bodies were taken away in a jeep. . . . I was warned not to disclose this incident to anybody otherwise I will be shot dead like the other four."

The evidence was so damning that the state government demanded the hearings be held in secret. With this, and the intimidation of witnesses, Kannabiran and others withdrew their support, and the inquiry was dropped without issuing a report. Kannabiran said the issue in these hearings was not excusing the Naxalites but upholding justice:

"None of us are connected with the Naxalite movement, but we do say you can't take the law into your own hands and kill them. That's not the way to be followed by a civilized country that has a constitution to guide it. If you can't solve affairs politically, you should leave power and go away. There's no alternative: go away and let someone else try. If you think a man is a Naxalite, put him up for trial and see what happens. But just don't kill him. If the state does not follow democratic principles, how can they expect others to do so?"

To the police those who publicize the mistreatment of Naxalites are as much the enemy as the Naxalites themselves. This had tragic consequences when in 1985 factional infighting led to increased militancy and a change in PWG tactics. Previously, it had not targeted police for terrorist reprisals. But in September 1985 police subinspector Yadagiri Reddy was killed in a bomb attack at the Warangal railway station. His funeral procession the next day, which included a deputy inspector and superintendent of police, passed the house of Dr Auduluthila Ramanadham, a practicing pediatrician in Warangal. About twenty police, half of them in uniform, some of them drunk, broke open his front door, beat waiting patients, and chased the doctor into a back lane where one of them then shot Ramanadham in the back with his service revolver, killing him instantly. The police later denied involvement and made no arrests.

Dr Ramanadham, a former vice president of the APCLC, was fifty-one. He opened his clinic to the poor and was never involved in politics: only justice. For his outspoken opinions he had been detained without trial for the entire eighteen months of the Emergency and was later active in many investigations of torture and encounter deaths.

The Andhra police also began a drive to frighten the APCLC into silence. Mallikarjun Rao, a Karimnagar attorney who had long been an active supporter, resigned after he was arrested and tortured. Then in May 1986 police raided the house of Japa Laxma Reddy, the president of the APCLC unit in Karimnagar and told him he would meet the same fate. Japa Reddy, sixty-five, had been a senior member of the CPI and later the CPI-M. He resigned from politics and several years later joined the Karimnagar APCLC.

In November 1986 persons unknown but believed to be PWG Naxalites killed deputy police superintendent Bucci Reddy at the town of Pedapalli, fifty kilometers from Karimnagar. Early the following morning four men in civilian clothes called Japa Reddy out of his house and shot him dead. The police later claimed he had been killed by "extremists," but a local newspaper said the assassins were all policemen and even gave their names. Nevertheless, there were no investigations or arrests.

A Tale of Police Arson

Another police attempt to silence critics occurred in December 1987. The incident began with the mass arson of tribal hamlets in the Chintapalli area of the coastal Eastern Ghats, where the wooded hills range to above three thousand feet. Most of what was once extensive tribal land is now claimed by the government, and if anyone tries to cultivate it or graze his animals, he is beaten and evicted or made to pay a bribe to the police or forest officers.

Three different tribes inhabit the area: Bagatas, who are small landowners with a degree of education, Valmikis, who have lesser learning but also own some land and indulge in petty trade, and Konds, who are immigrants from Orissa, practicing slash-and-burn cultivation, which puts them in direct opposition to the forest officers. The Communist Party of India has long been active in Chintapalli, and the exactions of forest officers decreased when Naxalite dalams moved into the area. But the Konds were frequently arrested for allegedly harboring Naxalites.

In May 1987 a police party led by a subinspector set out to burn down the entire Kond community. They started at one end of a valley and moved methodically to the other end, burning forty-six hamlets with a total of 638 houses, along with livestock and thousands of chickens and bags of grain.

But they also burned down a hamlet occupied mainly by Bagatas and Gadabas (a minor tribe). When the village headman complained, the head constable of the Chintapalli police station sent a handwritten note "to the officer in charge of the combing party" telling him "villages other than those of the Konds should not be burnt down." The headman also sent a complaint to a Visakhapatnam newspaper, whereupon the paper sent a reporter to the area and printed a report about the police arson, complete with pictures.

With that the authorities said it was an understandable error attributable to police anger over the killing of a policeman in the area a few weeks earlier and that the extent of the damage was exaggerated.

The Indian People's Human Rights Tribunal, a group established by Pellisary Antony Sebastian (whom I had interviewed in Bombay in connection with the SITA antiprostitution law), decided to establish the facts. The IPHRT follows standard Indian courtroom practices. It gathers pictures and affidavits to document what it regards to be gross violations of human rights and presents this and the testimony of witnesses before a panel of retired justices.

An IPHRT team recorded 227 statements and took sixty photographs of burnt-down hamlets and arranged to bring more than sixty tribal victims to Visakhapatnam for a hearing before a tribunal consisting of retired Calcutta High Court Judge Jyotimoy Nag and retired Kerala High Court Judge Chandrashekhara Menon.

When police learned of the hearings, they visited each of the hamlets and threatened to break the legs or arms of witnesses and burn down their reconstructed huts. With that, fifteen Konds decided not to board the buses that would take them to Visakhapatnam. Those who did go were further threatened while waiting to give their testimony at a hearing in an auditorium on the campus of Andhra University.

Two hours after the hearing began and a dozen witnesses had answered questions about what had happened to them, the door of the auditorium was pushed open and a gang of men and women rushed in, shouting they were widows and relatives of policemen killed in ambushes. The remaining witnesses fled in terror and the hearing was adjourned. It was later established the intruders were police in civilian clothes.

Despite threats and the killing of men like Ramanadham and Japa Reddy, human rights activists in India refuse to be silenced. A few months later the IPHRT resumed its hearing in Visakhapatnam, although this time without tribal witnesses. The relevant documents, affidavits, and pictures were later published in booklet form.

Liberal Laws But No Enforcement

I asked Kannabiran if the government had lost control of the police.

"I don't think so," he replied. "The police serve the government well. They're almost like the army: they have a paramilitary character. If you use police and not the army, you can keep a low profile: what you're doing is law and order, nothing else. If you use the army, it becomes war. Also, the police department is without the praetorian urge that is present in the army: it's safer for politicians."

I asked if he saw any difference between the Congress Party and the Telugu Desam of former film star N. T. Ram Rao, who had ruled Andhra Pradesh as chief minister since January 1983.

"There's absolutely no difference," he replied. "Governments don't want to give up power. In the beginning they may try something new, but after a year they're doing only crisis management. Once a government feels it's losing its hold, it labels all opposition groups as extremist."

"Is there a political solution to India's problems?"

"I don't think a solution is beyond the realm of possibility. If you can't devise means to rule without force, it's because you're dishonest. But the role of all governments today is simply to keep themselves in power and for that they're bound to be dishonest and must resort to force."

"Does that mean there will be a violent revolution?" I asked.

"When you look around, the feeling you get is it can't last much longer. Every time you open the paper you see institutions being destroyed or subverted. Parliament is a farce. The only democratic feature of this country is elections. When elections are held, we seem to be a democracy. This is international opinion: India is a democracy because large numbers of people cast votes and people get elected. There's no democracy in this country at any point and yet nothing is happening. People take all sorts of atrocities without protest. This country has a wide range of liberal laws but no enforcement. There's no will to enforce social change."

Neither is there any slackening in the government's determination to crush resistance. In April 1988 the police killed a Naxalite leader and another man in Warangal, and the People's War Group retaliated by burning dozens of state-owned buses, a few railway stations, a microwave station, and a telephone exchange. The first six months of 1988 also saw fifteen encounter deaths or outright killings. One occurred in Warangal District. A young man of the Lambada tribe had been detained for more than a month, and his father had met the superintendent of police to beg for his son's safety. In January the youth died of torture, although the police listed the cause of death as suicide. As if to prove their point, the police used his own shirt to suspend the youth's body from an electric transformer in the middle of Warangal town and left it there for twelve hours. When the youth's father later met the superintendent of police, the officer replied with a gruesome pun. The youth's name was Meghyam. The superintendent told him, "We have sent your Meghyam to the clouds (*Megh*)."

Human rights activists believe the solution to violence is nonviolence and dialogue. There is a man in Hyderabad whose spine was cracked by police torture who used dialogue to return evicted Dalits to their village homes.

38 ❀ A Village Confrontation

Korivi Jagadeshwara Prasad—known simply as Prasad—wears the long orange robes of a *swami* (religious teacher).

Since Indians believe spiritual knowledge comes directly from God and not from books or seminaries, anyone can call himself a swami. While some swamis do have great knowledge and schooling, others rest their claims on the performance of ostensible miracles, while still others simply exemplify renunciation.

The orange robe is a sign of austerity and chastity but not necessarily of renunciation of the secular world: swamis can be passionately involved in what goes on around them, but, at least in theory, their ambitions are for others, not themselves. I asked Prasad how he became a swami.

"From my childhood I had aching for love and justice," he said. "I was starving for it. I remember asking the principal of my elementary school why some children beg in the streets and not others. It was a Christian school, and the principal inspired me to be a teacher. But after I completed junior college, my father wanted me to be an engineer and said if I didn't agree with him I should leave the house, and I walked out.

"I needed some way to earn a living, so I went to a typing institute and asked what was the minimum time required to learn. The owner said six months. I asked, 'Can you give me six hours?' He said if I could really sit and learn in six hours, he would not charge me at all. So I learned typing, and a month later I started working at the same institute, earning twenty rupees a day. That gave me confidence that if a person wants to do something, and his conscience and objectives are clear, God shows the way.

"Later, I learned there was a college course in community development with a degree in social work. I belong to a backward caste, the Yadavas, and was eligible for a scholarship. But I don't believe in caste and don't want it to be mentioned. Some friends contributed money for the fees for the semester and also arranged for me to earn money by tutoring at nights and on the weekends.

"At the end of the term I went to the chairman of the school board and said I had no money to continue my studies. He agreed to give me a scholarship if I stood in the top rank. I took the challenge and received a B.A. in social work in 1978. While in college, I was active in the student movement to allow separate statehood for the Telengana region of northern Andhra Pradesh. There were many clashes with the police, and scores of students were killed. But then the leader of the agitation joined the Congress Party and got himself elected chief minister. We students were shocked. Some groups I am still associated with took a vow never to take part in any political activity.

"We formed a Youth Welfare Federation, and I was elected chairman. When we started activities in slum areas, the police wanted to arrest me. Leftist youth groups also did not agree with us. They said the chief minister must be removed. I said, 'If your little finger is diseased, do you cut if off right away or do you first try some medicine and remove it if necessary as a final result? That is life: good and bad. We must accept it because we're part and parcel of it.'"

Marriage and Torture

"During the Emergency," Prasad continued, "one of our women became pregnant. We knew each other very well. The group said the only way for her was marriage, and it was decided I should marry her. But she belonged to a high caste, and her elder sister was angry at this marriage with a member of a backward caste and filed a complaint with the police that I stole ten thousand rupees ($700) worth of gold from her sister. I was arrested and tortured for four and a half hours. A rod was tied under my knees and another across my back, so I was bent double, and they crushed me. Two of the lower vertebra in my spine were cracked. The pain was terrible, so I gave a written statement saying I had robbed the gold. They then went to our home and stole all our belongings, leaving us with just the clothes on our backs. They also demanded a bribe of five thousand rupees. I said I would have to go to someone to get the money.

"I could barely walk and went with my wife to a friend who was editor of a newspaper and told him what happened. Luckily, an inspector for the Criminal Investigation Division was with him. He told me to leave the city immediately, and I went to a village and stayed underground for three months and got treatment for my spinal cord by saying I injured myself playing cricket.

"After my return I sat for the examination and got my degree. But I didn't drop the case. I knew if I intended to attack the ills of society, I needed a firm base. I fought for six years to clear my name and spent five or six thousand rupees, but I won and the subinspector responsible for my torture was removed.

"As I grew older and put on weight, the pain in my spine grew worse. In August 1987 three or four bones broke, and the nerves jammed up. I was taken to a government hospital but was refused admittance. I had only a hundred rupees in my pocket, and when I was taken to a commercial hospital, it was unbelievable: they didn't know me, yet when I said it would take me time to pay, they admitted me.

"When I left the hospital and started the process of recovery, I realized I had been given a second life. Others had shared expenses and shared emotions with me. From then on I have worn this robe of a swami."

The chastity signified by the orange robe was, by then, justified because Prasad's wife had left him, taking the child, and was living with another man. His elder brother had come to work in Hyderabad and had rented a small house. He allowed Prasad to use one room as a place to sleep and another as an office for his public work. He calls his organization SALT, an acronym for Society for Awareness through Learning and Training.

SALT: Seasoning for Slums

"We form people into small groups of ten families who elect their own family representatives. Then ten of these groups are formed into *sangams* (societies) or growth centers. They take on the responsibility of using whatever government rehabilitation programs are available to them. So far we have organized twenty-five sangams, or a total of 2,500 families. Occasionally, we give them management experience in finances and accounting and advice on how to meet government officials. But we only guide them: we're trying to develop a secondary level of leadership who can, when the occasion arises, take leadership into their own hands.

"In chemical terms I am like a catalyst: I supply the implementation for government programs. We analyze the learning points of individuals in terms of their own slums or villages. In providing a water tap, how is the decision made? In providing a park or health program, who is the person controlling the decision? In a village we ask, 'How much land is available, who occupies it and has how much? Why should the other person occupy so much while you're not able to occupy anything?'

"We have sangams in fifteen slums in Hyderabad, each with its own meeting places. For instance, we have a center where eighty or ninety construction workers gather every morning. We're trying to eliminate the contractor or middleman, so we have prepared a sheet showing standard wages and the type of work our men can do. Then, if you need a job done, you can just come to this center and hire someone without paying anything to the middleman. Both sides benefit: the worker gets an honest wage and the employer pays less than if a contractor took a profit."

I often found Indian hospitality embarrassing. They see foreigners as guests and think they should supply extra food or use taxis instead of buses or going by foot. In situations where money was obviously short —and that was in most cases—I tried to pay my own way. If that failed, I offered a contribution for which they would give a receipt: thus it would be an official transaction between me and their group and no lessening of my standing as a guest.

Prasad has no funding source. Sometimes SALT earns fees by conducting research. Among other things he took part in Sister Rita's study of nationwide prostitution. He also earns fees by conducting seminars and training programs for government agencies and private social organizations. But he depends mostly on volunteers to help in the clerical work and on gifts from friends for overhead expenses.

Prasad said he would take me to a village where sixty Dalit men had been evicted, and he had helped them to return to their homes. He walks slowly, using a cane, and has to be careful of sudden motions. Someone had given him an old car to help him get about, and I made a contribution for the driver and other expenses. We set out the next morning through rolling hills to a village Prasad said was about an hour's drive away. There was trouble with the rear wheel, and we had to stop several times to tinker with it, so it took two hours. That gave him time to tell of the eviction:

"In 1976 the land ceiling act became effective, and a Dalit man was allotted 2.2 acres, but he couldn't take possession. As soon as land reform came, the landlord dug a well and installed a diesel pump to show the land was his, but later, when the dispute became stronger, he couldn't hire labor to cultivate the land, and so it lay vacant. Then the Dalits began cutting trees on the plot for firewood. When the landlord threatened them, someone from a Dalit society stirred them up, telling them to file a complaint with the police, but they told them to go to the revenue department.

"Then higher caste people got angry. They came to the Dalits with knives and lathis and told the men of all the sixty Dalit families in the village to go away. The men came to Hyderabad, but now the Dalit society deserted them. Somebody informed them about us, and we went through the land records and filed a court petition on their behalf. They would certainly have won in the courts, but a legal case is long and expensive, so we sought compromise and conciliation.

"The high caste people now realized things had gotten out of hand, and the landlord said he was willing to compromise. I said to him, 'Don't compromise with me, compromise with the people.' The landlord said he would give the land but wanted compensation for digging the well and installing the pump. The villagers said they had been driven from their homes for a month and had the expense of living in the city. So the final compromise was the landlord removed his pump, and the Dalit got the land with no exchange of money. The landlord changed his mind because the Dalits did not use any violence, even though they were shown lathis and knives by the landlords.

"A year after the settlement there was a ceremony for presentation of gifts. The Dalits went to the surrounding villages and brought representatives to a meeting with the landlord and all the local important people. It was the first time Dalit families had crossed into the upper caste part of the village and the first time they had gone to a landlord's house to eat food."

A Gandhi Statue Without Gandhianism

When we arrived, I was surprised because we drove straight into the Dalit portion of the village. The usual pattern is for the Dalits to be segregated to the rear of a village, away from the road or bazaar. Prasad explained a road was built many years earlier and passed through the low-lying Dalit section instead of the higher ground occupied by upper castes.

There was an open area separating the two caste areas, and in the middle was a cement statue of Mahatma Gandhi. I said I thought it shocking that a statue of Gandhi, in effect, served to divide the castes.

"The landlords put it up," Prasad said. "The Dalits had never heard of him before and were amazed a big leader who started the struggle for independence was dressed like them. But they never understood exactly who he was or what he meant. No Gandhian leader has ever come here."

"Why did Gandhi fail?" I asked.

"His goal was the independence of India. Afterward the tricks and techniques of the struggle for power became the reality. A political leader only thinks, 'How can I give them a small piece of bread, so they'll keep quiet. I'm in power. When I walk the streets, this dog should not bark: give it something to eat.' He never thinks how he can stop discontent permanently."

"You sound discouraged," I said. "Are you?"

"No. I believe in human beings. The seeds we plant today may bear fruit tomorrow. The next generation may see the result, not me."

We went to a small office, built with the help of landlords, which Dalits used as a community center. As was his practice, Prasad had joined this village into a sangam of ten villages, and this office served both the village and the sangam. Prasad had not visited the village for about a year, and a dozen men surrounded us as we crowded into the room to await tea and snacks.

"Several important things happened," he said. "They developed unity and maintained this unity after they were threatened. They have also found they have real support from the outside. And they have a new dignity. Previously, when a high caste person walked on the road, Harijans were not supposed to walk in front of them: they had to remove their *chappals* (sandals), hold them on their shoulders, and stand to one side.

"They have received many benefits. We supplied hybrid seed on loan and created competition by saying the person whose crop improves the most will get the loan as a gift. Now hybrid seed is a universal practice. They have educational programs and a place where women can leave their small children while they work. Last year, after a woman died from an abortion, they realized they had to link up with a primary health center, and they have done that. Women have come up: both husband and wives can take loans. All Dalits now have courage. They have gone straight to the BDO to ask for help. For the first two years we gave them a full-time organizer, and we trained them to maintain this society and file the correspondence. He was removed last year, and they now keep their own records."

Prasad said there were five Dalit castes in the village, two of which disposed of dead animals and worked in leather. We went to look at an incomplete tannery project on land donated by one of the landlords. There was a cleared area for skinning animals, concrete basins to soak the skins, and concrete stalls to stretch and clean the leather. This much had been done with a grant from a German funding agency, but then the money was suddenly cut off.

It was an example of the danger of depending on foreign funding. The villagers had done the work themselves, but their time and efforts had been wasted: when they asked for a bank loan of three thousand rupees to complete the work, they were refused on the grounds of technical unfeasibility.

With the steady increase in population there was a need for new housing. Prasad told what happened when the villages tried to get help:

"Under the land ceiling act and wasteland regulations each village has some property. When the village must expand, the *Gram Panchayat* [Village Council] meets to allocate housing *pattas* [title deeds]. It's village land, and the people have no right to sell it, but they're allowed to construct a house. There's a government program that provides four thousand rupees as a loan and another thousand as a subsidy for a Dalit to build a home. The money is allocated by the Block Development Officer through the Gram Panchayat. Money for sixty houses was sanctioned, but after only twenty-five were constructed, the *sarpanch* [head of the panchayat] said it all was spent. Actually, he took the money. But a village sarpanch is usually tied in with the dominant castes and political party and does what he pleases.

"The Dalits went back to the BDO and asked for more money. This time they said they would build the houses and not waste money on a contractor. Once again funds were allocated through the sarpanch. No building society was created. There was not even a bank account. That's how the system works. The politicians and officials make sure they get a big cut of anything that's spent.

"After the villagers laid the foundations and built the walls and roofs, the sarpanch said the money was exhausted: there was no money for flooring or doors. This means they don't have houses but will still have to pay the four thousand rupees charged to them as a loan."

A Devadasi Retirement Community

On the way back to Hyderabad I told Prasad about the other places I had been and the people I had met. That's when I learned he had taken part in Sister Rita's survey. He said SALT had also conducted research on the Devadasi cult in Andhra:

"We have long known the cult was strong in our next-door neighbor, Karnataka. The idea came to me this practice might be in Andhra too. The government asked me to do a study, and we found a Yellamma temple in Kurnool District. There are two types of Devadasis. One group wears long, matted hair. They are handed from one man to another: it's not commercial prostitution as such. The others look like ordinary women and are usually commercial prostitutes.

"We found *joginis* [a female ascetic or yogi: a common euphemism for Devadasi] at the Kurnool temple were employed by contractors to recruit prostitutes. The government asked all district collectors to undertake a study and identified 16,500 women under this practice in Andhra Pradesh. When it realized the extent of the system in Andhra, it passed a law, similar to the one in Karnataka, banning the Devadasi cult. At the same time it set up programs to care for the joginis who could no longer practice their religion."

During his research Prasad discovered thirty aged joginis in a Dalit slum in Hyderabad known as Ambedkar Nagar, after B. R. Ambedkar, the preindependence untouchable leader. The next day we crossed the railroad tracks to a vast area of shacks made of corrugated tin and sacking to visit the community.

"In the beginning our aim was only to know them: we were not clear what else we would do," he said. "Then other women asked for help too, and we organized a meeting, and more than a hundred families came and formed a women's growth center. It's an official society, registered with the government, so members get the benefits of government programs. The land is provided free by the government, and members pay two rupees a month as a contribution. People who are helped in income-generating schemes pay another one rupee a month."

We entered a small building, trailed by a score of women, for the welcoming tea. Prasad said the structure was built with the government's help, and SALT contributed a table and some chairs. It was divided by a partition into two parts. The half we were in was an office for the joginis who, being unmarried, had no families and lived elsewhere in small rooms. The other half was occupied by a volunteer who took care of whatever paperwork was necessary. Prasad introduced her, a small, neatly dressed woman of about twenty. Her name was Annapurna. Prasad said she had completed the seventh grade and liked to do community work. In addition to her room she was paid a small salary by the women's center.

"That's always our aim: to start things and then turn it over to the people. This center has been running independently since January 1988. Many women have been helped. They can get subsidized loans of one hundred or two hundred rupees at 4 percent interest to start income generating projects and can also get help with marketing. In addition the Joginis get outright grants of from five hundred to fifteen hundred rupees.

"They have buffaloes and sell milk, and they also buy vegetables from the wholesale market and sell as retail vendors, or they go from house to house. Some of them make a supplementary food out of grain that's sold as a nutritious addition to a person's regular diet. Some of the joginis have been trained to make hand-printed cloth, and they sell their handicrafts through their own small shop."

There was a small Yellamma shrine—waist high, square, and pinnacled—in the center of a cleared space. The joginis, small, withered, and some with long matted hair, had crowded around Prasad when he arrived, bowing to touch his feet and standing before him with their hands raised and pressed together as if in prayer. Since he was a swami, and they regarded themselves as dedicated servants of god, there was a stronger relationship between him and them than with the other women of the colony.

"They say they were six or seven years old when they were dedicated to the goddess," Prasad said. I tried several times to get them to talk about how they became Devadasis, but they said that was a secret between them and Yellamma. Finally, when I asked one what she thought of her present condition, she was eager to talk, and Prasad translated:

"We don't know why we have come to this and why the goddess looks on us with disfavor. We're not even able to beg because no one believes in us. People used to think we were auspicious and would give us food and clothing. Now they say, 'If you're hungry, why don't you work. Why do you come for begging?'

"We're not able to work and not able to beg, so we're starving. We're being made a laughing stock. Yellamma is not influencing people to help us. We don't know why. We're supposed to celebrate the Yellamma's marriage every year. But it becomes more and more expensive, yet no one gives us rice or saris or ornaments. We need oil to light a lamp before the goddess, but we don't have it. All our practices and customs are disappearing. We're helpless."

Their lament at being deserted by the goddess is the dirge of traditional India, but some still have faith in their civilization. They say India's people are strong and it is possible to use this strength to build a new society. One such man in Parameshwara Rao, who got a Ph.D. in atomic science and returned home to work in village India.

39 ☀ A Man with Faith in India

At the age of thirty-one Parameshwara Rao put aside a newly earned American Ph.D. in atomic science and turned down several good job offers to fulfill his life's ambition to work among the villagers of India. Almost thirty years have passed, and he has become one of the most respected social activists in India.

We talked at his father's house in Visakhapatnam (usually shortened to Vizag), a rapidly developing naval base, port, and industrial city on the Bay of Bengal about halfway between Calcutta and Madras. As a boy, visiting his grandmother in her village of Dimili, sixty-five kilometers southwest of Vizag, Parameshwara had dreamed of becoming a schoolteacher:

"When I visited her, I saw people who were illiterate but could recite our great epics. I felt if only they could read and write, how immeasurably good it would be. The most human group on the face of the earth is a village group. Despite their poverty, they're concerned about one another and want to see that everyone gets some morsel of food. The growth of towns and cities is dehumanizing all this."

Parameshwara was waylaid by scholarships, awards, and job offers and finally the chance to study atomic science at Pennsylvania State University in the United States. But the day after he got his degree, he boarded a ship to return home and went straight to Dimili.

"I used to do two things meticulously: keep my eyes and ears open and keep my mouth shut," he said. "I wanted to un-Westernize myself. On the second day I ran into a bunch of boys who were waiting for other boys to go to school together. It was five miles away, and I learned there were a hundred boys walking five miles each way.

"I held a meeting every day with the villagers to discuss things openly, and they said they wanted a school. We could have gotten the money from somebody outside, but I said everyone should contribute so this would be their school and not someone else's. I prepared a list of the farmers and the land they owned, but after six months I had collected nothing. Then the richest man, and hence the most miserly, came and said, 'Sir, I'm supposed to give you three thousand rupees by way of my contribution. Only yesterday I came to know the boat fare to the United States is three thousand rupees. So what am I to do if you buy a ticket with my money and run away to the United States?'

"After my brothers said I had refused two positive job offers in the United States and one in India, the rich man came to the meeting with a wad of notes, which he counted out and took a receipt. For the first time in his seventy-eight years the most miserly man openly gave away money. That broke the ice. In three months the money was collected, and we built the school by *shramdan* [voluntary labor].

"I also learned it may be a fight at every step, but there's always someone in the wings ready to help you if you try. We had to get teachers and supplies. As an educated person, I was able to get an interview with the governor, although it took some time. He sent me to one man, and when that didn't work, he sent me to another and then to the chief minister. When I returned to say I did everything without success, he said, 'This is no more your problem. God has sent you to me. I feel it is now my job.'"

The school, a low rambling building with large, airy classrooms, was completed in 1968 and later turned over to the government. Some of its supplies were paid for by the American Peace Corps. A small sign in the science lab memorializes a volunteer named Richard Scarborough who, it says, used 570 rupees worth of waste material to construct equipment worth seven thousand rupees.

Finding a Way to Live

"I come from a lower-middle-class family and had to support myself," Parameshwara continued. "I came across a village where they were manufacturing salt. The technology is so low, and the potentiality is so great, I felt it was the best industry to give sustenance to really poor people in a backward area. It was a fight against nature, the government, and villagers who didn't understand what I was trying to do. I also had to fight my family. My mother asked, 'Why don't you go back to the United States and be happy?' I said, 'I have only one life. Why don't you let me live it the way I would like?'

"The salt project became my livelihood, more or less even today. We floated a company, and I styled myself managing director. At present a trust holds the shares, and the workers are wage earners. At first they had no confidence. They were brought up to believe they couldn't do things themselves. First the skills had to be imparted in preparing the land producing salt. Then to make a year-round program we had to train them in prawn cultivation. And now it will all be turned over to the workers. Two or three will handle the sales and accounts part, and the rest will be in production."

I visited the salt farm. It was hard to believe the area was once barren mud flats. More than 450 acres have been leveled and divided by small embankments into oblong units where the sea water is passed from section to section, becoming progressively more saline until the water has evaporated, leaving behind a white layer of salt. The annual production of edible and industrial salts is more than four thousand tons. About 250 workers will become owners, and another two hundred will have seasonal employment.

In 1976 a cyclone and tidal wave swept the Vijayawada area, south of Vizag, killing thousands of people and destroying villages, farms, and livestock. Parameshwara spent two years working for their rehabilitation, giving him a wider experience in social work. In addition, with the help of a West German organization called EZE (Central Protestant Agency for Rural Development Assistance), he formed the Bhagavatula Charitable Trust (BCT), named after his family. The trust is now the overall financial agency. Government funds are used for such things as education, health, wasteland development, and training schemes so that 20 percent of the trust's budget comes from the central and state governments. Seventy percent of the costs are met through the sale of produce and bank loans, and 10 percent is from foreign agencies.

The Risks of Government Funding

Dependence on government funding is a sore point among voluntary agencies. "If you invite the government in, isn't there a danger the government will seize control?" I asked.

"Yes and no," he replied. "When you take from the government, they want to set targets and do things in a particular manner so your flexibility is gone. It's also true that part of the government is full of people who will grab everything. But, believe me, there are also people who are trying to reach out to the poor. I say, let us use the government's officers, funds, and resources wherever possible and continue with our mission. I also say unless and until these creative energies are released, the government may sink billions and billions of rupees into its different schemes and nothing will happen.

"Responsible people's organizations in due course can take over. We're doing that: teaching people to take matters in their own hands. But if you approach government in a confrontation manner, you must remember government has all the means, money and machinery to keep itself in power."

BCT's headquarters is in Yellamancilli, fifty-five kilometers southwest of Vizag. But its activities are centered in a farm about twenty minutes drive away. The feeder road passes through hills that are bare and red except during the monsoon, when a low cover of green bush hides the laterite soil. Then the road approaches two hundred acres of hillside lush with cashew, banana, and silk cotton trees, date palms, garden plots of tomatoes and other vegetables, a large seed nursery, and banks of roses, jasmines, and bougainvillea. The low, white-walled, thatch-roofed buildings are hidden in a sea of green speckled with the red, pink, white, and yellow flowers.

"We have 25,000 acres of barren hill slopes in our area," Parameshwara said. "The government owns it and calls it wasteland. I call it wasted land. I don't believe this nation lacks resources or productivity. The only thing wrong is mismanagement or not proper management. Knowledge is confined to cities, laboratories, and universities. Once we got the idea of what kind of plantation we wanted, we went to a research station and got all the techniques necessary for raising trees on this kind of soil.

"We took two hundred acres on a twenty-year lease as an experimental demonstration and training program. Now, ten years later, it has proved a success. This leased land will be returned to the government, but the government has designated other land where farmers can get loans to reclaim the barren land, and eventually they'll own the land cooperatively."

I was given a jeep and a guide, and we visited several BCT projects. At one of the new farms two-year-old cashew and coconut palm plantings were spaced over a wide hillside. The trees would develop in another eight years. Meantime, flat ground at the base of the hill was planted in peanuts to provide current income. Two diesel pumps chugged water into irrigation channels, interrupted now and then by teams of thin, bare-footed women who filled large, bulbous aluminum pots and then helped one another to lift the pots onto their heads and glided away.

We also visited a farm where more than two thousand cashews and six hundred mango trees were being planted. At a veterinarian station there were the usual facilities for cross-breeding and inoculations. But there was also a project—unique for India—for training village women to be paraveterinarians. The training lasts three months, during which time they get food and lodging and a monthly seventy-five rupee stipend. They are taught artificial insemination, fodder development, deworming of animals, and general first aid. Bihar sent twenty-five village women as the first batch of a program to train three hundred. Orissa was also sending women.

Another project trained women as paramedics, emphasizing prenatal and postnatal care and better nutrition. My guide said seventy villages in the BCT area wanted their services and that so far twenty-six women had been trained or were undergoing training.

Getting the Participation of Women

Midway in his work Parameshwara realized the success of village development depended more on women than on men. A single village got him started.

"I felt I shouldn't work in the villages myself but should motivate local youth to take up the work. I was fascinated by the village of Marripalem where 60 percent of the people were starving, and almost everyone was in debt. When it rained, they would go through knee-deep mud to get a pail of water. Land for housing was given by the state government in 1958, but not even one hut was built.

"In 1978 we introduced small income-generating activities such as stitching leaf plates. The women made only one rupee a day, but that was a fantastic sum in those days. Our main effort was to develop animators, but in two years nothing was accomplished. One day an old woman from a neighboring village said to me, 'Sir, at no point do you talk about women. Do you think we women are incapable of learning and doing things?' I said, '*Amma* [mother], why don't you come to our animator training program?'

"At our next session, out of twenty-five trainees, fourteen were men and eleven were women. The men were all under twenty and educated, while the women were all illiterate and above sixty. Not one woman spoke, even the woman who said we had neglected women. On the third day, during the evaluation session, I said to her, 'Amma, for two days none of you opened your mouths. How can I be sure you have learned and want to do something?'

"The woman took me by the hand and led me outside the hall. She said, 'Look at the men you have invited. You call them men. They're all the age of my grandchildren, and they are all educated. If you're serious that we should talk, call workshops only for women.'

"We had an exclusive workshop for women, and one item they mentioned as a good possibility for income generation was raising chicks. The next time I went into Marripalem a poor woman who had participated in the workshop came to me and asked me to help her get a bank loan of five hundred rupees to start a poultry project. She said her husband didn't have land, and they were hungry.

"When I told her banks were for the rich people, she asked me, 'Then how are we poor people to survive?' I said, 'Why don't you save?' She said, 'Sir, at best I can save twenty-five or fifty paise in a week or ten days.' I then asked her why she didn't save that amount. She asked if I was serious, and I said yes. She got together with eighty women and collected money, and one of our women colleagues put it in the bank. We started the savings program in 1981, and at the end of the year, when we went to see the bank account, we were stunned to find they had pooled thirteen thousand rupees out of these twenty-five and fifty paise savings."

Leveraging Savings

"We have formed twenty-seven *mahila mandals* (women's organizations)," Parameshwara continued, "with three thousand members and have introduced new income projects based on these savings. When a woman has saved fifty rupees, the mahila mandal gives her a loan of fifty rupees. With this hundred rupees she can buy four chicks and raise them to hatch eggs and produce more chicks. She can sell eggs and chickens, and in a year she'll save about two hundred rupees. Then the mahila mandal gives a loan of two hundred rupees. With this four hundred rupees she buys two small lambs, feeds them for six months, sells them, and makes six hundred rupees profit. Then the mandal gives six hundred rupees, and with twelve hundred rupees she buys a small buffalo and raises this to give milk. In 1988 the mahila mandals had 750,000 rupees in savings, and for the first time women have gained confidence in themselves."

One day my guide took me to a village to meet members of a mahila mandal. Yedla Ademma, the group's president, a woman of about fifty, with gray hair, heavy ivory bangles, silver anklets, and two toe rings on her bare feet, said she had been with BCT for five years. She was a widow, with one son and three grown daughters. She showed small fields, planted with the advice and guidance of BCT, of tobacco, chilies, and onions and other plots of tightly spaced casuarina trees, grown for lumber or fuel. Casuarina, a fast-growing tree from Australia, is a kind of bank account: it grows fast and after the first two months requires no care or irrigation and can be harvested after five years.

The village was away from the road with no sound to break the silence except the crowing of cocks. In Andhra style the houses were circular, built around the tall, thick trunk of a palmyra palm to resist the cyclonic winds. The houses are thatched with long palmyra leaves extending almost to the ground, so it is necessary to duck low to get into the door. The outside walls, almost hidden by the low eaves, were whitewashed, and red lines and circles were added to please the eye. The path before the entrance to each house was smoothed with a weak solution of cow dung and decorated with what's called *rangoli* in Hindi and *muggu* in Telugu: sinuous lines and circles that housewives draw on their doorsteps every morning by dribbling a chalky substance through their fingers, thus demonstrating the area is freshly cleaned.

A Courageous Young Woman

Yedla called two other members, and we sat near the well to discuss the benefits of the mahila mandal.

"We help one another now," Yedla said. "We never did that before. One of our women was in charge of the nursery and got sick and couldn't work. Even her husband wouldn't care for her. But we all got together and contributed money, and now she is well and can work again. We have a thrift advisory group that meets once a week in my house. If someone misses the meeting, she must pay a half rupee fine. For every ten members there's a leader of the street. If the leader does not show up for a meeting, she pays a fine of five rupees. And now all the women are interested in education: they go to night school so they can read labels and things like that."

I asked the second woman, dressed in an old, soiled sari, about the loan program. She said she had borrowed fifty rupees about five months earlier to buy a chicken and a rooster. They hatched three chicks but a fox snatched them away, and she had since sold the male for fifty rupees to repay the loan.

The third woman was twenty years old, unmarried, and taking care of her widowed father. She was small and avoided eye contact: looking like a terrorized mite. But she had recently leased land and had taken a loan from the mahila mandal to plant tobacco and chilies and hoped to make a profit, after repaying the loan and the rent on the land, of two thousand rupees. It was a remarkable story: a young unmarried woman —the lowest of the low by Indian standards—who had gained the courage to embark on such a large project. With other women getting loans and doing well, it was an example of the power of demonstration in a society where information is verbal and visual.

BCT has trained more than a hundred teachers for nonformal night classes and at that time had more than three thousand students in classes. One night my guide took me to one of the classes, accompanied by his wife, who was a supervisor for a group of nonformal education classes. Ducking low under the thatch into a small round hut, we entered a room lighted by a kerosene lantern in the middle of the floor. The teacher was a boy of about sixteen, and there were eighteen students, boys and girls, ranging from about five to twelve. A blackboard was propped against one side of the hut. Lithographs of the Telugu alphabet and animals representing the letters were suspended at another side.

The students were asked to go to the blackboard and write their names and do two-digit sums. Then the guide's wife gave more difficult writing assignments, and three older girls wrote sentences on the blackboard. All the while there was intense solemnity, with the lantern picking out faces and the porcelain white of large Indian eyes. The three girls then sang a song asking all children to come and join nonformal education to make India strong.

In south India, girls who have not attained menses wear, instead of a sari, a half-sleeve, high-neck blouse and an ankle-length skirt. Since I was sitting on the ground, I noticed the torn and frayed hems of their skirts as they rose and began to sing. I looked closer, and there were patches on their skirts and blouses. I assumed these were the only dresses they owned.

I was deeply moved. I thought: Here were poor children who had to work from morning to night and still their eyes sparkled with the desire to learn. Who, I asked myself, has done this? Who has denied them the promise of youth?

A Grass-roots Literacy Program

I returned to Parameshwara and told him of my thoughts. He had long been equally troubled. In his mind two things converged: the need for education and the need to link the scattered voluntary agencies into a meaningful force.

"There are about two thousand voluntary agencies registered with the central government," he said, "and another seven to ten thousand agencies doing some semblance of good work in the villages. How can you bring together voluntary agencies that are so different in their ideologies, practices, and methodologies? We find a keen desire for literacy everywhere we go. I felt: Why don't we take that as our rallying point?

"As luck would have it I was inducted into the national literacy mission as a council member. I attended a few meetings in Delhi and was thoroughly disappointed because there was the same bureaucratic approach. For forty years we have failed, and now we were going to repeat the same structure of bureaucracy, budgets, and corruption. I felt we should make it a people's program.

"Adult education is bound to fail because everyone is concentrating on the age group of fifteen to thirty-five. Education is not their priority item: they have to make their living, so if we concentrate on adult education, we are bound to fail. We have to concentrate on the age group of six to fourteen, when people like to learn just by themselves. Moreover, a classroom approach will never succeed in a village. At any one point of time not all young people will find it convenient.

"We don't need large budgets or highly trained teachers. We can do this by mobilizing voluntary agencies and youth groups. Each one can teach two or three in their own homes. They already have the books and slates, or they can easily raise the funds for such things on their own.

"Four months ago I was touring Karnataka and spoke to a youth group in a remote village. I asked what is the difference between a town and a village. One boy said, 'Sir, cities have all the facilities, and we have nothing.' I said, 'You are as much an Indian as a boy in a city, then why are you discriminated against?' He said, 'Sir, there are many illiterates in the villages and few in the cities.' I asked, 'Who will change this situation?'

"We discussed this for a while and one boy said, 'Sir, no one spoke to us about this. Never did we sit and think together about our problems and the way you are asking we feel ashamed we have not done anything so far.' Another young man said, 'Believe me sir, I will do this right today.' And a girl said, 'Fifteen of us will start teaching today, sir. We will not care whether anyone is watching what we do or helps us.'

"That was the greatest living lesson I ever had from anyone. Since then I must have gone into a hundred villages to speak at schools and clubs in Karnataka, Andhra, and Tamil Nadu. I said we must root out illiteracy from our villages, and we must not depend on outsiders. For every twenty-five boys and girls who receive formal education, there are 250 boys and girls who are outside the system. We are not opposing the government but trying to complement what the government does in every possible way. The money it takes to put a graduate through college is enough to put eighty illiterates through primary school. Just imagine how much social responsibility each college graduate has.

"People have told me it is hard to get volunteers. I don't believe that. Sacrifice is the hallmark of Indian culture. We only have to give them a social cause and a direction. In spite of these days, where people only seem to talk of money alone, if you meet youngsters in colleges and schools and villages, they jump—just jump—at the chance to do something. We don't need hundreds. Just one boy or girl can turn around an entire village.

"We have to involve everyone—voluntary agencies, teachers, and students—and build a movement, and then people will listen to us. Now we have no communication channels. We hear about rapes and robberies and how the politicians are hoodwinking us but not about the good work being done by voluntary agencies. We can build a national movement on the basis of literacy.

"Somehow we have lost our moorings. British rule totally undermined our self-confidence. But look anywhere in the world and you'll find Indians as engineers and doctors. If our house is not clean, we must clean it. If we are sleeping, who else will wake us up? We must do small things that will bring us out of this stupor."

Nowadays Parameshwara constantly travels throughout India trying to persuade voluntary agencies to join the fight against illiteracy. It is a huge challenge. Indian children want to learn: the girls in that hut, studying by the light of a kerosene lamp, are proof of that, but they are kept from classrooms by the poverty of their parents and the exploitation of factory owners. Child labor in India is a Dickensian horror multiplied by hundreds of thousands.

40 ❀ Broken Promises, Broken Children

Acharacteristic of a nation with a high birthrate, widespread destitution, and poor health conditions is a high percentage of children. This is true of India, where 42 percent of the population is below the age of fourteen. The short life expectancy also means a high percentage of orphans. It is estimated that by 1991 there will be about 30 million orphans in India younger than fourteen, of whom 12 million will be classified as destitute.

India's constitution was written as a Gandhian beacon to the former colonial world. Article twenty-four says children below the age of fourteen shall not be employed in any factory or mine or be engaged in any other hazardous employment. Article forty-five directs the state to endeavor to provide free and compulsory education until children complete the age of fourteen. Article thirty-nine of the Directive Principles of State Policy provides that children should not be forced by economic necessity to enter avocations unsuited to their age or strength and that childhood and youth should be protected against moral and material abandonment. There is also the Factories Act of 1948. It prohibits children under fourteen from working in a factory and says children above that age may not work more than four and a half hours a day and that a register must be kept, available for inspection, of their employment.

Whatever the hopes, India's children remain prisoners of poverty. The British Anti-Slavery Society for the Protection of Human Rights, founded in 1898 to further the intent of the new laws against chattel slavery, has taken up the cause of modern forms of debt slavery, concentrating on child labor in south and southeast Asia. The society estimates fifty million children are working in exploitative conditions in India.

In 1986 the legal prohibition against child labor was eased when

Parliament passed the Child Labor (Prohibition and Regulation) Act. This only bans child labor in an ill-defined category called "hazardous industries." Otherwise, child labor is permitted subject to the provision of educational and recreational facilities, minimum wages, weekly rest days, hygienic working conditions, and a ban on overtime that affects the health of the child.

Members argued that child labor was the result of poverty, and since poverty could not be easily eradicated, it would be better to regulate child labor in nonhazardous industries rather than try to ban it entirely. It was a lame excuse: all studies have shown children are employed not because of the widespread poverty but because they are the cheapest and most easily managed source of labor.

Exploiting Children to Replace Adults

A study in one of the major concentrations of child labor—the gem-polishing industry of Jaipur in Rajasthan—quoted one employer: "Why engage an adult for five hundred rupees to do a job that a child is willing to do for fifty rupees?" Far from being the result of poverty, child labor adds to poverty by denying work to adults and by creating successive generations of malnourished illiterates who can do little to improve the economy.

Another major center of child exploitation is the lock industry of Aligarh in Uttar Pradesh, where seven to ten thousand children below the age of fifteen comprise 8 or 9 percent of the work force. Employers go to great length to hide the facts, and these estimates are necessarily rough approximates: some observers believe the number of children employed is much greater.

A study by a group at Aligarh Muslim University (the lock industry is a traditional Muslim occupation) showed child labor existed despite high adult unemployment and underemployment: "There are many children who are earning and many adults who are not able to find remunerative work. . . . [Artisans] who are able to get work for eight or nine months a year regard themselves as fully engaged. A lock assembly worker feels himself fortunate if he gets work for the fourth day in a week."

Children have always worked in India, as they have in all traditional societies. They work beside their parents on farms or migrate with them for seasonal employment in harvesting crops, pulling fishing nets, or as unskilled construction workers. A World Bank survey in

North Central India

1975 estimated 15 million Indian children were employed as household servants. The number since then has probably doubled. All restaurants except luxury establishments catering to tourists employ boys as young as eight to clear tables and swab floors. However, the vast majority of such labor may be considered acceptable when alternatives are kept in mind. Cleaning vegetables in a woman's kitchen for a few rupees is better than digging through garbage to find food. Clearing tables is better than picking rags and papers. And as hard as it is to cut sugar cane or carry bricks up bamboo scaffolding, there is at least the safety of being with one's family and clan.

It is the exploitation of children in factories that exposes the weakness of the government in enforcing its laws. Labor Minister P. A. Sangma, in a statement to Parliament in December 1987, estimated six million children are employed in totally banned hazardous industries.

The Lock and Gem-Polishing Industries

In the Aligarh lock industry children earn five to ten rupees for a day that extends to twelve or fourteen hours, often inhaling clouds of metal dust, emery powder, paint, and paint thinners. More than 60 percent of the workers in the polishing units, and at least half the labor force in spray-painting units are made up of children below fourteen.

A manufacturing process is legally defined as a factory if there are ten or more workers and power is used or, where no power is used, if there are twenty or more workers. Employers get around this by partitioning their premises and isolating certain areas. They say each unit is under a different owner, and thus the factory act against employing children below fourteen does not apply.

There is a clause, meant to exclude family handicrafts, that says employers may hire their own children. Lock industry operators blandly claim excess child workers are their own children, and no one questions them.

In the Jaipur gem-polishing industry (another predominantly Muslim occupation) 13,000 children below the age of fourteen comprise 20 percent of the work force. Again, because of secrecy (perhaps two-thirds of the stones are traded on the black market to evade taxes) and lack of enforcement, these may well be underestimates.

Raw stones are imported: either gemstones, like sapphires, rubies, and emeralds, or semiprecious stones like lapis lazuli, turquoise, corals, amethysts, and topaz. Most of the finished stones are exported. India is fourth in the export of emeralds and fifth in the export of rubies and sapphires, mostly to the United States.

The children, almost entirely boys, come for the poorest families of Jaipur. They are "apprenticed" by their parents in the hope they will learn a skilled trade and not, when they grow up, have to pull a rickshaw and carry back-breaking sacks of grain like their parents. Fathers know their sons will be exploited, as they themselves have been exploited, but they shrug it off: it is *duniya dari* (figuratively, "the way of the world").

Gems are ground by turning a wheel with a bow and string, gradually shaping and faceting the stone first with various grades of emery and then oxides. The purported learning process begins when a child is six or seven. He works from eight in the morning to six at night without any wages, not even a cup of tea or food. He learns to attach the unpolished gems on sticks for the first polishing; he cleans the shop and acts as a domestic servant at his master's home. After eighteen months of this he is shown how to grind one facet on a stone, besides doing the domestic work. After about two years he is paid fifty rupees a month and perhaps is given old clothes, tea, and sometimes food. At the end of three or four years he may make a hundred rupees a month.

Finally, at the age of fourteen or fifteen he has learnt most of the finer points of polishing, requiring concentration and good eyesight (no lenses are used).

In Jaipur all the final polishing, where a slip would destroy a gem worth thousands of rupees, is done by children below the age of fourteen. They are paid four hundred to five hundred rupees a month: an adult doing the same work earns about a thousand rupees a month.

At least half the children are completely illiterate, including those who had a few years of early schooling but soon forgot what they learned. Most work six days a week and get only a half day off on Friday for prayers. They all complain of arms that ache from pulling the bow, of thick callouses on their hands, of heavy coughs from inhaling the dust and poor eyesight. Because of damage to their eyes, few workers, no matter how great the skills they have mastered, are employed after the age of thirty-five.

A lengthy research paper published by the *Economic and Political Weekly* concluded the exploitation was carried out with tacit government approval:

> While . . . polished colored gem stones net the Government of India foreign exchange to the tune of 140 *crore* rupees [14 billion, the equivalent of $980 million], no labor laws apply to this industry. Informed sources in the industry say that one of the main reasons why India is able to compete in the international market in spite of not getting the best quality raw material is because of the availability of cheap labor. . . . Informed sources said the political clout of gem traders was such that attempts to bring this industry under the Factories Act had been abandoned. Some said that while the government was interested in the welfare of workers at one level, the need for earning foreign exchange was paramount and so production would therefore always have an edge over labor welfare.

The Carpet and Handloom Industry

The purported need for foreign exchange is also used to justify the employment of children as young as eight and nine in the carpet and handloom industry of Uttar Pradesh. The factories are concentrated around Mirzapur and Varanasi (the now-accepted spelling for Banaras). With the usual caveat of imprecise estimates the number of below-fifteen children employed is about 140,000.

The vast expansion of the Indian carpet industry began in 1975 when the shah of Iran severely reduced production of Persian carpets by banning the employment of children below the age of eighteen. Liberation for the children of Iran was a virtual sentence of slavery for the children of central India. The Indian government granted easy-credit loans for the expansion of the Mirzapur carpet weavers, and in ten years exports soared more than 700 percent to 2.5 billion rupees ($175 million) in 1986.

As exports also increased from China, Indian carpet manufacturers claimed that if regulations against child labor were strictly enforced the cost of carpets would rise by 60 percent and India would lose out to international competition. Said one: "The government rather than realizing the gravity of the situation is proposing to bring up measures to raise the minimum ages on the pretext of regulating the wages of bonded child workers, which shall prove suicidal to the development of the industry."

Child labor in the carpet and handloom industries duplicates the pattern of Jaipur and elsewhere. Children, some of them bought from their parents in payment for debts, begin work as "apprentices" at seven or eight years of age. They have to be fed because, unlike the Jaipur children, they are away from their homes, but they are not paid until the third year, when they may earn sixty rupees a month. But then provision of food and lodging is considered part of the wage, and their net income is reduced to almost nothing. Beatings, hunger, and sickness due to ill-heated, poorly lit rooms and exposure to fluff and dust are common complaints.

Other Centers of Child Exploitation

Another large center of hazardous child employment is the diamond-polishing industry in Surat in Gujarat where children fifteen years or younger make up 16 percent of the labor force. Other thousands of children are employed in agate polishing in Cambay, Gujarat. In neither industry are masks used, and the workers suffer from silicosis. Conditions are almost as bad for children in the slate industries in Markapur in Andhra Pradesh and Mandsaur in Madhya Pradesh. In the glass bangle industries of Ferozabad and Agra in Uttar Pradesh, children have to work at extremely high temperatures. Also in Uttar Pradesh ten thousand children work for fourteen hours a day in the Saharanpur woodcarving industry.

Half of all the cotton hosiery in India is produced in the town of Tiruppur in Coimbatore District of Tamil Nadu, where 27 percent of the estimated thirty thousand workers are below the age of fourteen. Despite the 1986 law detailing the amenities required for employing children, they earn three or four rupees a day—well below the minimum wage—and work at least ten hours a day, giving them no time for regular school or recreation.

The largest concentration of child laborers anywhere in the world is in the Sivakasi area of central Tamil Nadu where 45,000 children, or almost half the work force, is engaged in making matches. It is a high unemployment area, with tens of thousands of men and women eager for employment. But they would have to be paid as adults and, as a foreman at a factory explained, "We prefer child labor. Children work faster, work longer hours, and are more dependable."

The exploitation of children is so widespread and the complicity of government officials in protecting private profits is so extensive that there is little social activists can do. Nevertheless, Champa Devi Srivastava is trying to free the little slaves of the carpet factories.

41 ✹ The Little Carpet Makers

Apolice report once called Champa Srivastava "Queen of the Dacoits" (Robbers). The oppressed weavers and blanket makers of Mirzapur have another name for her: Champa *Devi* (a generic term for goddess).

"I was the principal of a government intermediate college in Madhya Pradesh from 1958 to 1964," she said when I called on her at her home and office. "I visited nearby coal mines and saw men and women, all dirty and in rags with straps over their shoulders, pulling carts of coal like horses or other animals. There were dirty pools of water and a bad smell coming from everywhere. Even their clothes smelled, and I had to cover my nose. Babies lay on the ground crying while their mothers worked. I felt: these are human beings; they belong to the same race as I do. That night I couldn't sleep thinking about them. I made up my mind to work for poor people. I proposed it to my husband and then resigned as principal."

Champa Devi is fifty, small, matronly, and with black wavy hair touched with gray. She wears glasses and goes about dressed in an old, white cotton sari with a green border. As their name implies, the Srivastavas are high caste Kayasthas. Champa Devi's husband is an attorney who once specialized in criminal law, but that changed when she became a social activist.

"I said I'm working in this house for his health and welfare," she said, "so he should work for the workers who are my interests. Now he is famous for labor cases."

Champa Devi calls herself a child of the freedom movement, and when she decided to work for the poor, she joined the Congress Party. Then, when the Congress split in a protest against the policies of Indira Gandhi, she sided with the old or official wing, known as the Congress

(O), as distinct from the larger section known as the Congress (I) (for Indira). In 1974 she was defeated as a Congress (O) candidate for the state assembly and gave up politics.

Like many activists, Champa Devi began intensive agitational work after the Emergency of 1975–1977, campaigning for weavers who had to pay a two rupee municipal tax when they sold a carpet.

"A weaver didn't dare sit on a carpet in the presence of the upper castes. I said, 'Don't pay the tax: it's the duty of the principal employer to pay the money.' I tell people not to be cowards. If you're dying of exploitation, at least fight so there may be change. You'll still die, if it's the will of God, but at least you'll die with hope.

"I concentrated on the village of Mewali, about ten kilometers from here, where 150 Brahmin families exploited the weavers. If they produced something nice, the Brahmins simply took it and beat the workers if they resisted. In 1979 and 1980 we started a 'No Fear' campaign. If anything was done wrong, they lodged complaints with the police station and took processions to the district magistrate and asked for protection.

"Then we started a 'Fill the Jails' campaign, and about fifty persons a day courted arrest. I was with the first batch. After seven days there were 311 people in jail and no room or meals for any more. Then the state government asked why the dispute was not settled, and all our demands were accepted and the people released.

"People told us of another village where the Brahmins sometimes stole people's crops, even maintained their own jail, and levied fines against the villagers. I went there and held a meeting and said I would fight to the death for their cause. I said, 'Even if I have to work constantly in this village for years, I will not stop until the exploiters are defeated.' The Brahmins used to implicate villagers in false charges, and the people were afraid. I told them, 'These Brahmins are implicating you in false cases. I'll implicate them in a real case under the untouchability law.' I filed cases for three Harijans, and they showed up in court and fought the battle. As a result, the exploiters had to surrender and are not giving the people any trouble.

"In 1978 I went on a hunger strike for fourteen days on behalf of the blanket makers who were not given the protection of the Factory Act and were also denied their customary bonus and medical aid. It was a successful strike: our demands were accepted."

"Don't you ever get the government's help?" I asked.

"No," she replied. "We're an agitational organization, and they call us antisocial. Workers are mistreated, and the quality of production is decreasing day by day. Only if workers are paid sufficiently and are healthy will they work efficiently. The people in power don't care for human lives. The government talks as if we live in a palatial new building, but if you see it with your own eyes, you'll see it is very, very old and decrepit."

Bonded and Child Labor

Champa Devi organized and became president of two unions, for blanket and carpet workers, and another group called the Harijan and Backward Women's Front. She is also local secretary of the *Akhil Bharatiya Seva Dal* (All-India Service Society), the service arm of the Janata Party. In 1984, at a Seva Dal conference at the Gandhi Ashram at Sevagram in central Maharashtra, she met Swami Agnivesh, the leading liberal religious reformer in north India.

Agnivesh, a former college lecturer, assumed the orange robes of a swami to combine politics, Marxism, and religious reform and organized the *Bandhua Mukti Morcha* (Bonded Labor Liberation Front) to publicize the continued presence, long after independence, of millions of bonded laborers.

"Swami Agnivesh asked us to work on bonded and child labor," Champa Devi said. "At the time I knew nothing of bonded labor, but now we believe there are 75,000 bonded laborers in Mirzapur District, including 20,000 to 25,000 children seven to fourteen years old. They work in distant villages, so they can't easily be identified and to make it impossible to check on illegal working conditions. The employers also have goondas as guards, so it's dangerous if we try to visit their workplaces. Instead, we have field-workers, mostly Harijans, who make investigations for us.

"Middlemen search for children in the Palamau District of Bihar, just across the border from Uttar Pradesh, where people are starving. A middleman gives two hundred rupees to a parent and promises the child will get a good job and good treatment. But it's all lies. Parents have come to us and said they had not seen the faces of their children for two years. When one came here looking for his son, he learned the boy was dead, and he had not been informed.

"The middlemen sell the children—almost all are boys—to master weavers. The principal employer avoids the factory act by supplying materials and patterns to master weavers who are contractors. They return the finished carpets to the principal employer, who sells them to buyers from outside markets. A contractor uses all kinds of tricks. The workers' accounts are not settled until the carpet is finished. Then the contractor will say, 'Hey, you have made a mistake at this place,' and he points to some spot. It might be corrected by a specialist for ten or a hundred rupees, but he will fine them all their wages for three or four months. Sometimes the fine is so high they have to start work on the next carpet to pay the balance.

"Even where a master is humble and kind, the wages are miserable. Say, four or five children work honestly for three or four months. What they get paid for the carpet will work out to only three rupees a day for each child. They're so poor they can't purchase even a glass of tea. If the masters are cruel, they give them no time to rest and beat them regularly. They're made to work fourteen or fifteen hours a day in badly lighted rooms and develop asthma and poor eyesight. Sometimes they try to escape, but most get used to mistreatment and remain even if they are beaten."

"Why do weavers employ children?" I asked. "Is it because their hands are small, and they can work faster?"

"No," she replied. "The children are bought and used because they can't complain about their wages and working conditions. Children are cheap and can be exploited."

A Helping Hand

Champa Devi had little success in her early years of trying to free children and bonded laborers.

"We told the labor commissioner it was his duty to do something for these adults and children not being paid an adequate wage," she said. "But Mirzapur District is large, and if a labor official goes to a village, he stays with the masters. They'll have a cup of tea and maybe some money will be exchanged, and no inquiry will ever be made into the conditions of the workers."

Then an official from a Dalit caste was appointed as Additional District Magistrate. In February 1988 he sent a raiding party, accompanied by Swami Agnivesh and Champa Devi, to a carpet factory to rescue fifteen children ranging from nine to thirteen years. They said their parents were given advances against their wages, and they were promised three hundred rupees a month, plus free lodging, food, and clothing, but they worked from dawn to dusk, with a one hour midday meal break, and were never paid or allowed to seek other employment.

The following March, Champa Devi staged a Seva Dal meeting in a distant village, complete with banners and songs. They then converged on a carpet factory and freed thirty-five bonded laborers, including seven children from eleven to fourteen years.

"We were told about that place," Champa Devi said. "If children tried to run away, they were tied to a trunk of a tree and left there for hours. The master also had a room for punishment: room number four. Anyone suspected of thinking of running away was sent to room number four and was beaten and left there all night."

At a hearing before the Additional District Magistrate the adults said they were given advances ranging from fifteen hundred to five thousand rupees and then were never paid, except for small sums at festivals. They said when they asked for wages, they were told they had not even met their interest payments and had to work twelve hours a day and were beaten if they complained. Asked why they had not sought the help of the police, they said the police were on the side of the masters and filed false charges against anyone who complained.

"The magistrate issued a summary judgment and sent the master to prison for nine months," Champa Devi said. "He was very powerful and would not have been convicted if the magistrate had not been helpful. The magistrate always gave us a force of police to go to a factory to inspect for bonded labor. Before him we couldn't make a sudden inspection. The labor officials and others delayed for three or four days while bonded laborers were moved elsewhere. But with the magistrate's support we released five hundred bonded laborers in just nine months. We just gave him the names, and he passed the orders.

"There are many difficulties after they're freed. They're in such a pitiful condition, if anyone has any emotion in his heart, he must be moved. Once my eldest son gave his shirt and pants. He did a good thing, but it's not possible for us to provide for every freed laborer.

"After they're legally released, they're supposed to get a rehabilitation grant of 6,250 rupees ($448). But it happens only if we watch things closely. The government is corrupt: officials take a thumb impression on a document to show they have bought goods worth 6,250 rupees for such and such a person, and they have opened a shop. But they only receive articles worth five hundred or a thousand rupees.

"The law also says if a bonded laborer is released, and an official certificate is issued to this effect, the master shall be prosecuted. But the factory owners are mostly criminals or associated with politicians and rich persons. So far, fourteen persons have been charged in Mirzapur District and face three years imprisonment. We'll try our level best to get them convicted, but we think there's a good possibility they'll be freed. The goondas threaten the freed laborers, and they have no courage to give evidence."

A Political Reversal

Champa Devi's string of victories was ending: the magistrate who was so helpful was being transferred.

"The politicians were anxious to get rid of him," she said. "The tradition is for a district magistrate to stay in one post for three years, but he's being transferred after only nine months because of his interest in freeing bonded labor."

She had to go to a meeting to plan a reaction to this transfer and arranged for a man from Mewali to come on his motorcycle to take me to the scene of her early triumph. My guide showed me workrooms where they made pastel-colored cotton durries on frames stretched flat on the ground. He said two men could make a six-by-nine foot durry in ten days and sell it for six hundred rupees. I asked other prices. A four-by-six durry in pale blues and pinks sold for three hundred rupees, a nine-by-ten of better quality sold for 750 rupees, and an eight-by-ten of the best quality sold for nine hundred. Then we sat for tea, and my guide told me of their debt to Champa Devi:

"Before we were tortured and were slaves, but now we are free to do our own work. Before we had to work with no wages, and if we complained, our voices had no value: the police were upper castes or in the pay of the upper castes. Now our children go to school, and we have tractors and electricity, and some families have purchased land."

They sealed their economic gains in *Gram Sabha* (village council) elections in June 1988. "The Brahmins were village chiefs for as long as anyone remembers," my guide said. "But we maintained our unity, even when the Brahmins put up a Harijan to split the vote, and one of us was elected as *pradhan* (head of the council). In the next village a Harijan woman was elected pradhan. There are now twenty pradhans in the Seva Dal, and they have taken a vow that all of the villages of Mirzapur will be the same way. But people and conditions are different, so it will take time."

As we left, they said the narrow dirt road to Mewali had been built with voluntary labor. They pointed across some fields to the white stone houses of the Brahmin part of the village and said they had offered to build a road to that section too but the Brahmins had refused.

I had planned to call at Champa Devi's house the next day to say goodbye but received a message saying she had started a twenty-four hour token hunger strike at the district offices to protest the planned transfer of the friendly magistrate. When I went there the next morning, I found her seated on the veranda with a group of men and women who had joined her in her fast.

"We want to give a push to the government," she said, "and let them know it is the sweet will of the people that should reign. The administrative officers are meant to serve the will of the nation. They should not be made to serve at the whim of politicians. This country got its independence because of Mahatma Gandhi, but the people are still not independent."

I said goodbye and went to south India, where the tender years of tens of thousands of girls are spent in the drudgery of match factories. In the face of official apathy hopes for a better life are bleak, as a young man discovered when he set out to teach them to read, write, and play.

42 ✸ The Little Match Girls

The word coolie is generally associated with China as a name for illiterate peasants who do menial labor. Actually, it is an Indian word. It spread through the world after the African slave trade was abolished, and British plantation owners recruited the landless untouchables of south India as indentured laborers, promising them decent wages and working conditions and eventual repatriation. They were slaves by another name: beaten and discarded when no longer worth what it cost to feed them.

Tirunelveli District in central Tamil Nadu, where periodic droughts brought millions to the edge of starvation, was one of the great reservoirs for coolie labor. But while generations of untouchable castes were mired in poverty, one—the Nadars—was transformed.

The Nadars were untouchable toddy tappers: climbing palm trees to extract the sweet juice for making cheap liquor known as *arrack*. In the early nineteenth century they took to trading and set up *petrais* (fortified enclosures) along travel routes. By the beginning of this century the Nadars were major landholders and were looking for new opportunities in industry.

In 1922 two Nadars from the Sivakasi area, which includes most of Tirunelveli District and some adjacent areas, went to Calcutta to learn match making and then imported machinery and set up India's first match factory. Today the Nadars control more than seven hundred small-scale and 1,300 cottage units in the match and fireworks industries of Sivakasi. The words "small scale" and "cottage units" designate sections of the economy that receive tax or other benefits as welfare measures to provide work for landless laborers. For instance, the Sivakasi match factories pay one-fifth the excise duties charged to the West India Match Company, which dominates mechanized output.

In 1953 Nadar dominance of Tamil Nadu was sealed when the previously entrenched Brahmin political elite was ousted and K. Kamraj Nadar became chief minister. The Nadars used their power to subvert the labor laws, dividing their factories into hundreds of small units hidden away from the main towns and employing children as the cheapest, least complaining source of labor.

There are 100,000 workers in the Sivakasi match industry, of whom 45 percent are children below the age of fifteen. Of these girls outnumber boys three to one. Children as young as six years old sit in low rows with piles of sticks in front of them. The sticks are placed in wooden holders that are latched together to form a frame. The tips of the sticks in the frame are then dipped into chemicals to add the head. Other children assemble boxes and paste labels, their fingers dancing at an incredible speed.

Paid by the piece, they work ten hours at a feverish pace to earn from six to fifteen rupees a day. Ventilation in the blazing hot climate is poor, and dust fills the air, mixing with the acrid fumes of the chemicals used for the match tips. The children usually ignore simple illnesses, but when questioned, they tell of headaches and skin rashes. Doctors report a higher than usual incidence of tuberculosis and respiratory ailments, with 20 percent of those examined suffering from worms or other intestinal infections and 30 percent with vitamin deficiencies.

Often children are the sole support of their families, and thus school is out of the question. Of those who do attend classes, 80 percent drop out by the end of the fourth grade by which time—such is the poor quality of public education—they have learned little and soon forget even that. They grow up stunted in mind and body and become the mothers of a generation like themselves.

Helping Children to Learn and Play

I was told of a young man named Prabhakaran who was helping match children in an out-of-the-way Tirunelveli village and took a crowded bus south from the temple city of Madurai. The south is a swarming panorama of small, often barefoot people. The men tuck the bottom of their lungis into the fold at the waist, showing bare knees as if they are wearing miniskirts. Old women, with no bodice and only the loose end of a sari tossed over a shoulder, have huge gold earrings that stretch their lobes down to their shoulders. Town streets are narrow, and there is always a loudspeaker blaring somewhere.

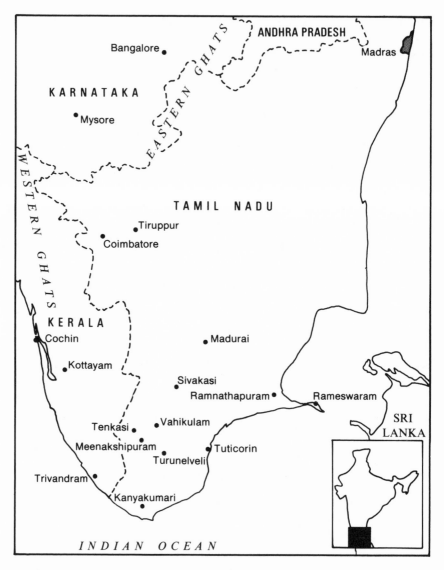

South India

Prabhakaran was about thirty years old: five-foot-five, with a trim mustache, and a smiling, direct look. He said he was a Dalit and his caste used only one name. His father was a forest guard, and this enabled him to complete high school in 1973. At first he became a forest guard but then quit.

"Our community suffers humiliation and oppression from other castes," he said. "Our girls are raped, and we can't do anything about it. You read about such things and experience some of it in your own life, and you feel you should do something for your own people. I took up social service and worked with some Indian and foreign institutions, but I found a lot of contradictions between what they preached and what they practiced. Then a British agency, Action Aid, wanted to get beyond welfare. They offered to pay me and a friend named Balakrishnan 250 rupees a month if we could develop something different.

"We went to one place and another, but they suspected we might be Naxalites or some other extremists or the secret police. Finally we came to a small village called Meenakshipuram and explained we wanted to establish a nonformal education center for children. A man said, 'Your idea is good, but I don't know if you're good men or bad men. Time will tell. If you're good men, you'll stay on forever. If you're bad, you'll be discovered.'

"It was a village of forty-three houses. We started schools in the street in the night and morning and played with the children, but they were terribly tired and fell asleep in the classroom. Besides, their parents were not motivated: they had no thirst for knowledge. We concluded we had to do something else along with education."

Balakrishnan left for other work, and in 1983 Prabhakaran moved about ten kilometers to his present village, Vahikulum, and formed the Malarchi Trust as an agency to get government grants to start health and income-generating programs. A year later a drought began and stretched for four years. He recalled the bitter years:

"There was no water or fodder for cattle, and farmers who had bought cows for three thousand rupees sold them for fifteen hundred. Later, cows were sold for only two or three hundred rupees. Thousands of people migrated to the rock quarries of Kerala; school attendance dropped by 30 percent, and the children in the match factories had to work harder than ever. People started stealing, and even the illegal arrack sellers had no business.

"People believed it was God's anger for their sins. They made a big image of a man called *Kodumbavi* [the Great Sinner] and dragged it through the streets, kicking it, spitting on it, and finally burning it to ashes. They believed once the great sinner was no more, there would be rain. But it was no use.

"We had to provide work so people could buy food. The government had some projects but not enough. Action Aid and Oxfam gave us money, and we deepened wells, cleared streams, and built new village ponds to store water when the drought ended. We generated 18,000 man-days of labor, with men paid ten rupees a day and women eight rupees."

"Everyone Wants His Own Palace"

In the process the Malarchi Trust spread to twenty-three villages with a staff of twenty. With government and foreign funding it established a nutrition supplement program for schoolchildren, a TB detection program, child and maternity care, and a small cooperative bakery. It also organized women's groups to press for such things as better drinking water or fixing village streets.

"In this area 15 to 20 percent of Dalit families do not earn even two thousand rupees ($140) a year," Prabhakaran said. "Fewer than 10 percent earn more than seven thousand rupees ($490). There are so many government programs, but they don't reach the poor."

"Why do the match factories hire so many children?" I asked. "Is it because their margin of profit is low?"

"No, they can hire adults and pay the full minimum wage and still do very well," he replied. "But they're greedy and find it easy to buy politicians with money for elections. The owners, the officials, and the politicians are allies against the poor. Greed is everywhere: a belief that only if you have wealth and power can you be respected. Everyone wants his own palace. In the process they lose their humanity and their respect for honesty and truth. People live a double life. They pretend to be honest, but they're dishonest. They pretend to care for others, but they don't."

One evening we visited a literacy class for children of the match factories. They said thirty-five girls and five boys from thirty-three houses left home at seven in the morning and did not return until eight at night. They said many years ago, when they were little girls, they had to wake up at three in the morning and run to catch a bus five kilometers away, but now a company bus picked up and dropped off children from several villages at a point about a kilometer away.

The girls did the same job, making boxes and pasting labels, for which they were paid by the gross. An eighteen year old had worked at the same task for ten years and could make forty to forty-five gross boxes a day, earning twelve to thirteen and a half rupees. A seventeen-year-old girl had worked since she was five and had achieved the same rate of production. A fifteen-year-old, who had worked since she was seven, and a thirteen-year-old, who had also started at seven, produced thirty-five to forty gross of boxes a day, earning from ten and a half to twelve rupees. One said she had two sisters, who also worked in the match factory, and four brothers, two of whom were in primary school. The three sisters were the sole support of their family.

The girls said it was the custom of the match factories for children from certain villages to specialize in one type of work so making match boxes was the only task they had learned. They said because of this specialization they could sit with friends and talk about common interests.

They had been coming to the after-hours class for several years but had learned little. They said they could write their names and the names of family members, do simple arithmetic, and read labels on packages and movie posters.

"Will you get married?" I asked.

"Who can tell what we will do," one replied.

"But if you do, will you stop working?" I asked.

"I will stop until my child is old enough to walk in the street and then return to work."

"What happens if you get sick?" I asked another.

"We have to take care of ourselves," she replied. "Some factories have doctors but not ours. Even if a factory has a doctor, the girls have to pay for the treatment."

I asked a third girl if they kept any of their wages for themselves.

"Maybe five or ten rupees for hairpins or a glass of tea," she replied. "Two or three times a year, when the factories are closed during festivals, we go to the cinema."

"Don't you want to do anything else?" I asked.

"We went to the match factory when we were small children," she replied. "Now it is our life."

"They have pocket money and a false sense of confidence in themselves," Prabhakaran said as we left. "We have tried many ways to break the cycle. We are now experimenting with alternative education centers to teach both literacy and alternative skills. Children now go to school where the teaching style is monotonous, and they learn almost nothing. The teacher calls them lazy and idiots. She doesn't realize she can do something to stir the children.

"We have applied to the education ministry in New Delhi and a foreign agency in Belgium for funding for a pilot project involving 150 children. It will be costly: they can't attend unless we pay a small stipend and provide a midday meal. They will learn literacy and vocational subjects, but we also want games and sports, and we want to put on plays they'll write and act themselves.

"I want to revive the dying art of drums. Once Tamil Nadu was famous for its many kinds of drums: drums played with one hand, drums played with sticks on two sides, big drums and small drums. Our traditional culture is lost. Our people have their own ways of expression, but this is being suppressed. They sing commercial songs from the cinema. The man who writes the lyrics or the man acting in the film is doing that for money. But our own songs were not for money but for ourselves. People see things in the cinema and think only that is good: our own expressions are not to be admired or appreciated.

"Our plan is to recognize the talents of children. Acting—helping them come out of themselves and giving them pleasure and courage —doesn't need money. And educational concepts can be introduced through games and art forms: reading, writing, and doing sums can be taught in a pleasing way that brings out the best in children."

Cooperative Flower Farming

Simultaneously, Prabhakaran is developing an idea he got from Meenakshipuram, where sixteen families had equal ownership of three acres of land divided into thirty-two pieces. The land was deeded to their grandparents in return for service at a Meenakshi temple. Men had to plow the temple land, for which they got a meal, and women (who normally did not wear a bodice) cleaned the temple and surrounding area while wearing the upper portion of their saris tied at their hips, just as Brahmins are bare chested when serving a god.

In addition one member from each family had to go once a year to the estate of the Zamindar to repair his boundary walls, and at the annual temple festival the families offered a pumpkin, a chicken, and some vegetables to the goddess. The services to the temple and the Zamindar ended many years ago, but the families retained the land.

Because of the temple, there was a large demand for floral offerings, and Prabhakaran saw the jointly held land as a chance to experiment in raising roses, jasmine, chrysanthemums, and other flowers for this market. He formed the families into a cooperative, and under a government program to aid the scheduled castes he got a 6,500 rupee grant ($455) to dig a well. The co-op members raised another three thousand rupees ($210) to buy a pump, and Action Aid and the Malarchi Trust gave loans of eleven thousand rupees ($770) to begin the work. It was a success from its first year, but only because Prabhakaran eased the jealousies that often plague Dalit society.

"They were all Pallars," Prabhakaran said, referring to the dominant untouchable caste in southern Tamil Nadu. "But when they were brought to a common platform, accumulated hatreds came out. One said, 'I'm a leader.' Another didn't like him to be in charge, so he always made quarrels. We made people reason out their problems. We asked, 'Is this the position of an individual or is it good for everyone?' We also asked, 'If the collective decides something, what should be the basis for this decision?'

"In the beginning we had weekly quarrels, but now they have experience in living in a group and see the fruits of cooperation. In the first year people earned one or two thousand rupees after paying their expenses and the cost of their loans. None of the families ever dreamed it was possible to make so much.

"And now we have asked the central government for a grant of 550,000 rupees [$35,000] to experiment in cooperative farming for women. In the past women had no money because property is owned by men. But they're not as quarrelsome as men, and they're very practical, very result-oriented. Under this scheme they'll gain confidence and won't think they're inferior to men."

Prabhakaran planned to use the grant to buy cultivable land in five different villages and dig wells for irrigation. Plots of three and a half acres would be distributed among twenty groups of landless Dalit women for collective farming: raising flowers, fruits and vegetables, and trees like neem, which yield valuable oil, seeds, and leaves.

"Every morning a woman can pluck the flowers at seven o'clock and sell them in the market by 7:30, so by 8 o'clock she can do other work," he said. "After two years the Malarchi Trust will withdraw from active participation. At the end of twelve years the debt for the purchase of the land and other improvements will be paid, and the women will own it, but they'll not be allowed to sell it to outsiders."

Prabhakaran, although aware of caste indignities, takes the reform-ist approach. In Bangalore, a day's bus ride to the north, another man rejects palliatives: he describes Brahmins as Nazis and says there must be a revolution to root them out.

43 ❋ Riddles of Hinduism

India appears to epitomize democracy and Gandhian nonviolence, yet it gave the word coolie to the world and contributed *pariah* (the name of an untouchable caste) as a synonym for a person so despised and rejected that starving dogs are called pariahs. A few generations ago castes like the Pariahs had to tie tree branches to their waists to sweep away their footprints, hang earthen pots around their necks to catch their spit, and drink water from a stagnant pool, sharing it with animals.

The humiliation continues. In April 1987 some 150 Dalit families in Gaya District of Bihar complained that excrement was forced into their mouths. In August 1987 Dalits in the Belgaum District of Karnataka were forced to eat excrement for allegedly stealing fodder from upper castes' fields. The following February, in the state's Shimoga District, a Dalit was beaten and made to bite a slipper dipped in excreta. In Kerala in February 1988 a Dalit was forced to eat excrement in the Cochin area, and three months later another Dalit was forced to eat excrement in the Trivandrum area.

In 1989, not far from the large city of Indore in Madhya Pradesh, a visitor discovered Dalit schoolchildren were not allowed to sit on the palm-leaf mats used by other students but had to sit on the floor.

Every village of India is segregated, and in towns and cities landlords ask a person's caste before renting rooms. Every candidate in every election is chosen because of his caste or religion.

Periodically, untouchables are killed in what journalists and others describe as actions "to set an example." Some incidents are remembered, like the miniature Jallianwalla Bagh massacre of twenty-one men and women at Arwal in Bihar in April 1986 and the extermination of the wounded tribal coal miners at Gua, in Bihar, in September 1980.

Others are all but forgotten, like the mass arson of untouchable huts in a Tamil Nadu village on Christmas Day 1968, in which forty-two Dalits were burned alive. All twenty-three landlords accused of the atrocity were acquitted by the Madras High Court.

Similarly, when in May 1980 a Dalit marriage party passed through an upper caste village in Almora District, Uttar Pradesh, with the groom carried in a palanquin, upper caste women objected to this breach of caste privileges. The Dalits were attacked and fled. Six who took shelter in a building were burned alive, and another eight were fatally injured with knives and lathis. Originally, ten of the accused were acquitted, but on appeal a higher court sentenced two of them to five years in prison.

Churning the Stinking Waters

India presents a benign face to the world, and if someone like Vontibetu Thimmappa Rajshekar tells a different story, he is ignored by the English-language press and scholarly journals that are the principal source of foreign knowledge of India. Rajshekar, the most outspoken and sharp-tongued defender of the untouchables and tribals of India, is the editor of *Dalit Voice*, a fortnightly magazine published from his home in Bangalore, the capital of Karnataka. He is a handsome man, with an aquiline nose, wide expressive eyes, and long, tapering fingers that he waves to punctuate his emphatic expressions.

"India has been a pond of stinking waters," he said when we met in the small living room of his house. "People are advised to drink a flowing water. So this stinking pond must be churned and the garbage at the bottom removed so the water is made drinkable. We need idol-breakers, not idol-worshippers."

In 1986 he wrote an editorial comparing the assassination of Indira Gandhi by a Sikh with the assassination of Mahatma Gandhi by a Brahmin. A police officer (Rajshekar notes he was a Brahmin) came from Punjab and took him in handcuffs to Chandigarh, the Punjab capital, for detention under an antiterrorist act. There were international protests against this threat to journalistic freedom, and Rajshekar was released after fifteen days with an apology from the government of India.

There are other cases pending against him for inciting one community against another, creating disharmony in society, indulging in antinational activities, and sedition. Although the charges have not been pressed, his passport has been impounded, he must get police permission to leave Bangalore, he is shadowed, his mail is read, and his telephone is tapped.

"They've called me a Muslim agent, a Christian agent, a Sikh agent, and an antinational. Who are the people running away to America and other places? The upper castes. So who's antinational, me or the great Brahmin so-called scientists? The Brahmins don't even belong to this country. We are the original inhabitants, and they don't have to teach us nationalism. When the Aryans came to this country, the original inhabitants, who are the creators of the Harappan civilization, were defeated and were treated as untouchables and confined outside the village limits. Those who fled to save themselves became tribals. I belong to a backward caste, but actually we're all tribals.

"I was not deprived: my father was a district collector. I was a Marxist for twenty years, but I never joined the Communist Party. I was in the newspaper racket for twenty-five years. I started with the *Deccan Herald* in Bangalore and then was a reporter for the *Indian Express* in Bombay and Delhi and returned here when the *Indian Express* started a Bangalore edition. I was chief reporter for thirteen years but was dismissed because I excelled the Brahmins in everything. I was made president of the press association, and they were jealous. Brahmins will never tolerate a low caste man coming up."

Gods to Gutters

The radicalization of Rajshekar began in 1973 following anti-Dalit riots touched off by the quixotic actions of Basappa Basavalingappa, who held the obscure position of minister for municipal administration in the state government. He came from a section of Karnataka where, in the twelfth century, the poet-saint Basava started a movement to do away with caste. Caste practices there have not disappeared, but they are not rigid, and his father and grandfather became small cloth merchants, and he became a lawyer, but his status was still that of an untouchable.

Once in the cabinet, Basavalingappa banned the practice of municipal scavengers carrying excrement in baskets on their heads, distributed house sites to the homeless, and tried to improve Bangalore's water supply. In terms of Gandhian political ethics such reforms are applauded, but he did not stop there. He denounced the Sanskritized literature of Karnataka as *boosa* (cattle feed) and said Dalits should fight for their rights, calling for a "Holiday for *Ahimsa*" (nonviolence). The ultimate act was a speech epitomized as "Gods to Gutters":

Brothers of the downtrodden communities, what benefits have you derived from worshipping pictures of Hindu gods in your homes for the last five thousand years? Have these pictures helped you to get out of your huts and dwell in decent houses? Bundle them all and throw them into places meant for keeping useless things. If you don't have the space, throw them into drains or gutters or into wells.

Upper caste college students in a half-dozen cities poured into the streets, demanding his dismissal, and turned on the small number of Dalit students, beating them with sticks and bicycle chains. Hundreds of Dalits fled to the safety of their villages. Basavalingappa was fired as a minister, but he is still a member of the legislature. I met him at his house in Bangalore.

"Brahmins have social control: they decide what the people should and should not do," he said. "All the illiterate, superstitious people follow them and don't question them. The Brahmins keep caste intact and talk of the integration of the country."

His ideas have not changed, but at sixty-five and more than fifteen years since his Gods to Gutters speech, Basavalingappa no longer attracts renewed attention.

"Who Is the Mother of Hitler?"

"The anti-Basavalingappa rioting proved to what extent nonviolent-seeming Hindus can become cruel and blood-thirsty," Rajshekar said. "Hindu society does not tolerate persons who honestly differ from its dogmatic views. On my newspaper so-called Letters to the Editor condemning Basavalingappa were manufactured in the night to be published under false names. One morning I came in and found some letters from remote areas already set in type. I asked the proofreader to show me the originals, but there were none. They tried to fire me, saying I was writing articles for other papers. But they lied. I took them to the high court and won the case, and then I resigned."

After his resignation in 1979 he visited China twice, Japan once, and finally Libya, which precipitated the lifting of his passport. He also began *Dalit Voice*, now published in English and five Indian languages and consisting mainly of editorial comments on current events affecting Dalits, newspaper accounts of anti-Dalit atrocities, and letters from like-minded readers. He also established the Dalit *Sahitya Akademy*

(Literature Academy) to publish his ideas in pamphlet form. A 1984 pamphlet, *Who is the Mother of Hitler?*, traced Hitler's Aryan ideas to Max Müller's ethnology of an Aryan race. In it he insisted India's Brahmins, whom he routinely describes as Nazis, still believe there is a master race and a slave race:

> As the parliament and the legislature have provided representation to untouchables, tribals, backward classes and other persecuted minorities, the ruling class is increasingly ignoring these elected bodies. Power has passed out from the hands of the legislature to the executive. This is a clear sign of Fascism. . . . The English-speaking ruling class . . . will assume the leadership of the Indian brand of Fascism. At the right time the Hindu Hitler with a religious garb will be thrown up. . . . Beware, the man-eater is on the rampage. Get ready with the gun.

When I said he exaggerated, and that I had met many Brahmins and other upper caste people who were working for Dalits, Rajshekar had a ready answer:

"The Brahmins controlled this country for 3,500 years, and for the last forty years they've been ruling directly. When they can't set right their own house, how can they set right our house? They have not even been treating their own women properly: they have been burning them and shaving their heads and making them sit outside during menses. They have been asking dowry and burning them for not bringing enough. So we say, 'Keep your kindness for your own women. Our liberation will be up to ourselves.'

"We have nothing against Brahmins as individuals, but we don't trust them. First they enslaved us through their religious practices. Now, they've been coming in different clothes, calling themselves Gandhians, Marxists, Socialists, and human rights people, but they're the same people."

Rajshekar divides Brahmins into sacred Brahmins and Socialist Brahmins, saying the aim in both instances is to ensure their continued dominance. He specifically accuses "Socialist Brahmins" of masking the overwhelming importance of caste in Indian society: "They maintain the economic element is the only determining factor. That's nonsense. Dalit poverty is a by-product of Dalit oppression. Half the population is below the poverty line, but attacks focus on the Dalits and tribals. Why not on the other poor? Because they are not untouchables."

Although he apparently was not aware of it, his analysis parallels

Gramsci's: that hegemony is a product of many factors, including culture. Industrialization, urbanization, and technological progress in India have not displaced the hierarchical values and institutions of caste. Rajshekar compares untouchables with American blacks: "Whites in the United States and upper caste Hindus will tolerate a black or an untouchable only as long as he remains uneducated, poor, and a slave. The moment he starts demanding a share in power because of his education and economic status, the prejudice reaches explosive proportions and ends up in violence."

Untouchables Are Not Hindus

As the source of most of his ideas, Rajshekar cites Bhimrao "Babasaheb" Ambedkar, the scholarly (doctorates in economic studies from Columbia University and London University) preindependence leader of India's untouchables.

In *The Riddles of Hinduism*, written shortly before his death in 1956, Ambedkar cited verses from the epics *Mahabharata* and *Ramayana* and described the Aryans as a race of flesh-eating drunkards and gamblers "who offered their kingdoms and wives as stakes" and as an utterly immoral people with "brother cohabiting with sister, son with mother, father with daughter, and grandfather with granddaughter." He said he wanted to awaken Hindus to the "quagmire the Brahmins have placed them in and to lead them on to the road of rational thinking." Ambedkar insisted untouchables were not Hindus, and although they might worship Hindu deities, they remained as separate as two aliens: "Is there any human tie that binds them to the rest of Hindus? . . . The whole tradition of the Hindus is to recognize the untouchable as a separate element and insist upon it as a fact. . . . Hinduism preaches separation instead of union. To be a Hindu means not to mix, to be separate in everything."

Mahatma Gandhi insisted the Varnashrama (code of four castes) was a valid method for organizing society. Although he called untouchability a sin, he said the ideal *bhangi* (scavenger) should continue to do "sanitation": "The law of Varna prescribes that his living follow the lawful occupation of his forefathers, but with the understanding that all occupations are equally honorable. A scavenger has the same status as a Brahmin."

Ambedkar called this "a cruel joke on the helpless classes":

What is the use of telling the scavenger that even a Brahmin is prepared to do scavenging when it is clear that . . . even if a Brahmin did scavenging, he would never be subject to the disabilities of one who is a born scavenger? . . . Why appeal to the scavenger's pride and vanity in order to induce him, and him only, to keep scavenging by telling him that scavenging is a noble profession and that he need not be ashamed of it.

Ambedkar argued only the complete "annihilation of caste" would end untouchability: "There have been Mahatmas in India whose sole object was to remove untouchability and to elevate and absorb the Depressed Classes, but every one of them failed in his mission. Mahatmas came and Mahatmas have gone, but the untouchables have remained untouchables."

The Limitations of Saintliness

More than anything else, Gandhi's actions and attitudes on untouchability capture the quandaries of a saint-who-would-be-a-politician. Bhikhu Parekh, a former vice-chancellor of the University of Baroda, and now professor of political theory at the University of Hull in England, believes Gandhi "cannot escape part of the responsibility for" the hardships of Dalits long after independence and the constitutional ban on the practice of untouchability.

Gandhi, Parekh writes, "insisted that untouchability was essentially and exclusively a problem for caste Hindus and not for the untouchables who were merely their helpless victims . . . waiting for their masters to get off their backs. . . . Gandhi spoke for them, but did not allow, let alone encourage, them to speak for themselves." Parekh summarizes Gandhi's failure:

Untouchability was both a moral and a political problem. . . . It had therefore to be fought at *both* levels. Gandhi's campaign was conducted only at the moral and religious level. Hence, he concentrated on caste Hindus rather than the Harijans, appealed to their sense of duty and honor, mobilized their feelings of shame and guilt, and succeeded in achieving his initial objective of discrediting untouchability and raising the level of the Hindu and, to a limited extent, Harijan consciousness. Since he did not organize and politicize the Harijans [or] stress their rights and fight for a radical reconstruction of the established social and economic order, Gandhi's campaign . . . did not put sufficient pressure on [caste Hindus] to make it in their interest to share their power and privileges.

The tensions resulting from postindependence attempts to speed empowerment through positive discrimination illustrate how little Gandhi succeeded in his appeal to the moral instincts of caste Hindus. The Indian constitution bans untouchability but also recognizes it by reserving a percentage of government jobs and admissions to colleges and universities for the scheduled castes and tribes to compensate for their social disabilities. Caste is also legitimized by the coalition-making impulses of party politics. Since no single caste has a majority, politicians must appeal to the ambitions of leaders of the castes below them. One way to curry such favor is by extending reservations.

Toward this end a new category — the Other Backward Classes — was devised. The use of the word class, instead of caste, was meant to stress economic standing rather than birth: those who worked in poorly paid, low-status manual and service trades but were not ranked among the untouchable castes. It was a distinction more honored in the breach than in practice. A commission appointed to designate such classes produced lists totaling 52 percent of the population.

The constitutionally mandated reservations for untouchables and tribals apply to both the central government and the states. The new reservations apply only at the state level, with each state free to decide when the process would begin, which groups would be included, and the percentage of jobs and school placements reserved for them.

The Agony of Gujarat

In 1978 Gujarat extended 10 percent reservations to eighty-two groups classified as the Socially and Educationally Backward Classes. Since the scheduled castes and tribes already had reservations of 21 percent (their percentage of the population), the total for all groups in Gujarat rose to 31 percent.

This extension resulted from maneuvering within the Congress Party. The Congress in Gujarat had long been controlled by the Patidars, a landowning caste that was the principal organizing force behind Mahatma Gandhi in Gujarat. Other Congress politicians formed a coalition supported by the lower and middle castes and ousted the Patidars from political power. But the Patidars remained as the dominant economic community. The pieces of a time bomb were being assembled: the lower castes were becoming assertive, demanding a share of power, and the privileged castes felt threatened. The bomb exploded in 1981.

The Dalit Panthers—a militant group that takes its name from the American Black Panthers—had formed a branch in Ahmedabad, Gujarat's largest city. Some of its members went to a village about fifteen kilometers away, where for several years Dalits had claimed grazing land from Patidar landlords. In late December 1980, "to teach the Dalits a lesson" as one account put it, a Dalit Panther worker named Sakrabhai was seized and beaten by Patidar youths. He was then taken to the office of the village chief and set on fire. When Dalits in Ahmedabad learned of this, they went to the village and took the mortally injured Sakrabhai to an Ahmedabad hospital. He died the next day, and his body was carried in a huge procession.

To calm the Dalits ten Patidars were arrested for the murder of Sakrabhai. To show their displeasure the Patidars instigated a social boycott of Dalits in Ahmedabad: merchants were asked not to sell them goods and employers not to give them jobs. The boycott was little heeded, but then in early January students at an Ahmedabad medical college began to strike against the reservation of admissions for the lower castes, claiming this reduced the quality of education. The implication was untouchables and tribals were mentally unfit to become doctors.

The medical students were joined by doctors and interns at government hospitals, and then antireservationists in government offices also went on strike. Fights spread to the street, and wide sections of Ahmedabad and several other large cities and towns were swept by atrocities, looting, and the burning of government buildings and Dalit slums. A pregnant woman was thrown into a fire and burnt alive. Two men who went to a hospital to see their ailing father-in-law were chased and thrown out of a third-floor window and then their bodies were burned.

Army units were called to help the police. Time and again the soldiers and police fired tear gas and bullets into crowds in vain attempts to restore order. As 1981 dragged on, Gujarat's major cities were paralyzed by strikes and curfews for 103 days, until finally a negotiated settlement was reached in which a larger percentage of college admissions were exempted from the reservation restrictions.

A second time bomb exploded in 1985, after a Congress Party leader, in a bid for greater lower caste support, raised the reservations for the Backward Classes from 10 percent to 28 percent. This would have brought the total of all reservations to 49 percent. Upper caste students and office workers immediately went on strike, and although the order was rescinded as soon as the politician was elected chief minister, the strikes and accompanying riots did not end.

Furthermore, rioting broke out between Hindu and Muslim neighborhoods in Ahmedabad. When the army was summoned and restored order in Ahmedabad, rioting broke out in three other cities. As soon as order was restored there, rioting broke out again in Ahmedabad. Back and forth it went with sections of Ahmedabad under continuous curfew from March to mid-August 1985, when government workers ended a seventy-three-day strike and a new agreement was negotiated further modifying reservations.

A new round of clashes between Muslims and Hindus—attributed mainly to bootleggers and other criminal gangs fighting for turf—flared in the first months of 1986. Peace was finally restored by using a draconian antiterrorist law to arrest 2,230 persons engaged in any and all protests, including farmers agitating for lower electricity charges, union members at a private factory demanding higher wages, and students protesting an increase in milk prices.

When the riot toll for 1985 and 1986 was computed, it showed Ahmedabad and fifteen other cities and towns had 334 killed, 904 injured, and 5,323 homes and other properties destroyed. The direct monetary loss was 435 million rupees ($31 million), but the cost in wages and business lost was probably six times that amount.

Who and What Is a Hindu?

Modern political and economic power is acted out as games of numbers and identity. While Nehru and other secular nationalists decried the "fissiparous" tendencies of religion, language, and caste, identity cannot be easily dismissed: it is part of the socialization that helps a group survive in a hostile world. It is also two-sided. Like narcissism, it is healthy when it gives an individual confidence to relate to others on a fairly equal basis but pathological when he is concerned only with himself.

In Europe the neurotic's delusions of grandeur and fears of inadequacy were magnified and projected into the Fascism of Hitler and Mussolini. Analogies between Fascism and Hinduism have frequently been made in India, not only by Dalit advocates such as V. T. Rajshekar but also earlier by Nehru and Indira Gandhi who called Hindu communalists Fascists.

The term Hindu does not appear anywhere in early Indian religious books. The Persian emperor Darius (522–486 B.C.) referred to Hidu, and the Greeks used the term Indoi. For the Arabs, Hindus were people living beyond the Indus River who had no common name for themselves and no sense of a religious community cutting across caste and region. The nearest notion of a common identity, *Varnashramadharma* (freely translated, the caste way of life), emphasized segmentation and exclusion rather than community.

The geographic term has a religious concept only in the Brahmin sense of hegemony, as elaborated circa A.D. 800 by Sankara, the preceptor of the monist doctrine of Brahma as a single agent that supports all existence despite infinite forms. Sankara founded four religious centers: Dwarka on the west coast in Gujarat, Puri on the east coast in Orissa, Sringeri, Sankara's own home in the Mysore region of Karnataka, and Badrinath near the snow line of the Himalayas, where to this day Brahmins from southern India officiate.

While insisting on one essence, Sankara accepted the many paths to God that are the hallmark of Hinduism, as noted by the British orientalist Monier Williams in 1877:

> It is all-tolerant, all-compliant, all-comprehensive, all-absorbing. It has its spiritual and its material aspects, its esoteric and exoteric; its subjective and its objective; its rational and its irrational; its pure and its impure. It may be compared to a huge polygon . . . [with] one side for the practical, another for the severely moral, another for the devotional and imaginative, another for the sensuous and sensual and another for the philosophical and speculative.

Someone counted 34,000 temples and shrines in the single city of Madras. Hinduism as a political label denies the heterogeneity that is the essence of Hinduism. The most sweeping claim was made in 1947 by Madhav Sadashiv Gowalkar, the leader of the *Rashtriya Swayamsevak Sangh* (RSS, National Volunteer Corps):

> The non-Hindu people of Hindustan must either adopt Hindu culture and language, must learn and respect and hold in reverence the Hindu religion, must entertain no idea but those of glorification of the Hindu race and culture, i.e., they must not only give up their attitude of intolerance and ungratefulness towards this land and its age-long traditions but must also cultivate the positive attitude of love and devotion instead. In a word, they must cease to be foreign-

ers, or may stay in the country while subordinated to the Hindu nation, claiming nothing, deserving no privileges, far less any preferential treatment—not even citizen's rights.

His statement came soon after partition. He was saying now that Muslims had their Pakistan, Indians had Hindustan. But there never was a Hindustan. Prior to British sovereignty Muslims accepted local Hindu autonomy in the form of maharajahs and rajas as long as there was nominal acceptance of an overarching political identity. In all important battles Hindus and Muslims fought on both sides depending on clan or territorial allegiances, and the same Muslim ruler who might destroy a temple in one place might grant lands to support a temple somewhere else.

The concept of a Hindu *rashtra* (nation) was born when British applied the three-age periodization—ancient, medieval, and modern—of European history to India. When the two earliest periods were given religious names, Hindu and Muslim, the Orientalist concept of an Aryan community turned the "Hindu" period into a golden age as contrasted to the Muslim period, seen as an age of decline.

In any religion, as in any political system, the dominant elite is tolerant or intolerant depending on its social situation and the challenge of opponents. The disappearance of Buddhist stupas and once-extensive Buddhist universities was accomplished by Hindu chauvinists. Hinduism is syncretic at the bottom but never at the top when real power is at stake.

Nevertheless, there is a striking difference between the Hindu form of religious politics and the Christian and Islamic form: there have been no Hindu inquisitions, jihads, or holy wars. Hindu political and cultural aggression is a process of nibbling, swallowing, and digesting, not extermination.

Even the arrival of the Aryans, contrary to earlier theories, was not a sudden invasion. The accepted modern theory is that a people who called themselves Aryan (the word means noble) were a hodgepodge of cattle-herding nomads who developed an early form of Sanskrit during centuries of slow migration to India, beginning in about 2000 B.C. via what is now Iran and Afghanistan. They had two advantages: chariots, which gave them military ascendancy, and a priesthood with secret rituals for access to the gods. They also had an excessive regard for purity, calling other people *mlechhas* (unclean), and somehow this became caste.

Brahminic society apparently spread through cultural osmosis. The caste blueprint gave rulers an ideal way to organize their societies: kings and tribal chiefs became Kshatriyas, priests became Brahmins, and merchants became Vaishyas, while those who worked with their hands were relegated to the lowly position of Sudras. Another large group who disposed of night soil or the bodies of dead humans and animals, thus offending Brahminic vegetarianism (a heritage of the defeat and absorption of Buddhism), became untouchables.

There were city-states with popularly elected councils in northern India at about the same time, and in a similar form, as Athenian democracy. And, as travelers from China attested, the Buddhist universities were models of humanistic studies. Even the strongest critic of Brahminism and casteism, Bhimrao Ambedkar, had no doubt democracy and equality were an integral part of Indian civilization, pointing to Sankara's concept of Brahma: "To recognize and to realize that you and I are parts of the same cosmic principle leaves room for no other theory of associated life except democracy. It does not merely preach democracy. It makes democracy an obligation of one and all."

Ambedkar anticipated the message of modern social activists: the solution to inequality can be found within the Hindu tradition of tolerance for all. Instead, there is growing intolerance born from the fear that Hinduism is threatened and must be protected. A small thing like a few hundred Dalits converting to Islam in an obscure village of southern India can have nationwide repercussions.

44 ✸ The Conversions at Meenakshipuram

In the eyes of its true believers Hinduism is Indian nationalism. Its most important deity is *Bharat Mata* (Mother India). Its myths are India's sacred books; its rivers and mountains are its sacred places, and its mythological heroes are its gods. In this view Hindus alone represent India's heritage and the transnational affinities of Christians and Muslims dilute an Indian's loyalty.

One of the fathers of Hindu chauvinism was Vinayak Damodar *"Veer"* (Hero) Savarkar who in the 1920s ended his speeches with the cry, "Hinduise all politics and militarize Hindudom." To Savarkar, Hindu masculinity could only be redeemed by fighting the Muslims and subjecting them to majority rule, meaning, of course, Hindu rule.

Generations of Hindus have been conditioned to a view of ruthless Muslims destroying temples and forcing converts at the point of a sword. There is no doubt temples were destroyed, just as earlier Hindus obliterated most vestiges of Buddhism. As for conversions, almost all Indian Muslims are descendants of tribes and castes who welcomed Islam as a liberation from the oppression of the twice-born. Islam thereby indigenized itself, and much of India's art, architecture, music, and poetry bears its imprint.

The two-nation theory of preindependence Muslims and Hindus had no historic validity. But as the prospects of British departure became real, attitudes changed. The Hindu elite, who dominated industry, trade, the bureaucracy, and the universities, anticipated new vistas of advancement and wealth, while the Muslim elite, who had been coddled and protected by the British, awaited the event with foreboding.

Partition solved nothing. It left residual India with what is now the world's fourth largest Muslim population and merely gave another excuse for Hindu chauvinists to picture Muslims as outsiders in the land of their birth.

The Elopement of Thangaraj

Hindu paranoia was demonstrated in 1981 by events following an intercaste elopement and the conversion to Islam of fifteen hundred Dalits in a Tamil Nadu village so remote it still has no paved approach road. Scores of politicians flocked to the village amid warnings that if such conversions were not checked Hindus would become a minority in their own land: a patent impossibility in a nation where Muslims are an 11 percent minority.

Rajshekar used the word "churning" for stirring the waters of caste. The word has a special meaning in Indian myth. When the "heaven born" devas joined the "impious" asuras, they churned the cream of life from the milky waters of the primeval ocean, bringing forth the Magic Tree that grants all wishes. Political and economic churning has progressively displaced the twice-born castes from the central and state legislatures and from rural dominance. While their virtual monopoly of bureaucracy and industry has been maintained, they have been replaced elsewhere by Sudra and even previously untouchable castes so that power is dispersed among a much larger number of castes. In the process abrasive caste frictions have been moved down the status scale to the emerging middle castes and the Dalits, such as between the Durbars and Vankars in Gujarat and the Yadavas and Dalits in Bihar.

The conversions in Tamil Nadu took place at a village called Meenakshipuram, but not the one where Prabhakaran got his start as an activist. This Meenakshipuram is also in Tirunelveli District, but it is farther south only a few hours by bus from the tip of India.

Conversions are a familiar process in south India. For more than two hundred years there had been conversions of Dalits to Christianity in Tamil Nadu. In the 1930s and again in 1944 there were also several small mass conversions of untouchables to Islam.

The two castes in conflict in Tirunelveli are the Thevars and Pallars. The Thevars exploited Pallars as tenants and agricultural workers and also felt they had sexual rights over Pallar women. It was this that Prabhakaran referred to when he spoke of the rape of "our women."

For eight or nine years, as more and more Pallars of Meenakshipuram got educated in the village elementary school and a high school less than a kilometer away and then went on to white-collar jobs, there was increasing discontent against discrimination and petty harassment. Pallars were not allowed to use the village well; they were not served at tea stalls, and barbers would not touch them, so they had to get their hair cut or a shave from a Dalit barber sitting by the roadside. The younger men urged conversion to Islam, but the elders were afraid of retaliation from the Thevars.

A young, tough, and militant Pallar named Thangaraj was one of those who argued that only by becoming Muslims could the Pallars claim equality and dignity. Gradually the elders died off, and young men like Thangaraj became influential.

When Thangaraj eloped with a Thevar girl, the villagers were still afraid of Thevar vengeance, and he was forced to take the girl to Kerala, where they became Muslims and were married. Thangaraj, who had changed his name to Yusuf, wanted to come back, but they would still not have him, so he went to a nearby village and got a job as a watchman on an agricultural estate. There was a labor dispute, and he was fired and two Thevars were hired as watchmen. When they were murdered, the local police inspector, who was a Thevar, arrested Yusuf. He insisted he was innocent, but he was secretly kept in the police lockup and beaten every day.

The Thevar inspector also ordered a number of arrests of Pallars from Meenakshipuram on what the villagers alleged were false charges. They said men and women were taken to the station and beaten repeatedly and one man was kept in a cell without charges for thirty-four days and a woman for five days.

Yusuf's mistreatment, and the arrests and beatings of the others, ended resistance to conversion to Islam. Yusuf, free on bail, persuaded two others to embrace Islam. The three learned of an organization called the South India *Isha-Athul Islam Sabai* (Islamic Missionary Society), which they were told was able to carry out mass conversions. They contacted the society, and after some hesitation and questioning they were given applications that were filled out by 220 of the 280 Pallar families in Meenakshipuram.

Some of them later changed their minds so that only 180 families were ready for the ceremony on February 19, 1981. They bathed and put on new clothes, and the men covered their heads with a cap or towel, and the women pulled the *pallu* (the long end of a sari) over their heads. They stood on a cleanly swept ground, with people from neighboring villages looking on, as a Muslim priest asked them to recite after him the *Kalima*, the words that declare someone a Muslim: "There is no God except Allah and Mohammed is his prophet."

There was no attempt at secrecy, but Meenakshipuram is tucked away in the countryside, and no newspaper reported the ceremony. Another was scheduled for May 23 to convert a second group of twenty-seven families, and this time Abul Hasan Nadvi, an influential Islamic scholar from Lucknow in Uttar Pradesh, came to bless the converts. This attracted local newspaper reporters. Their stories were picked up by the wire services and national editions, and within days Meenakshipuram was famous throughout India as a place that seemed to herald an Islamic tidal wave sweeping over India.

The Muslims Are Coming! The Muslims Are Coming!

Prime Minister Indira Gandhi was reported to be unhappy, and Home Minister Zail Singh wondered whether "a conspiracy or political motivation" was behind the conversions. Parliament appointed a thirteen-member committee to visit Meenakshipuram and also to inquire into mass conversions of Dalits in other parts of the country.

The chief minister of Tamil Nadu called for a law to ban conversions but modified this to suggest only "forcible" conversions should be outlawed. The chief minister of Maharashtra said conversions were against the interests of the nation, democracy, and secularism.

Newspaper stories played up speculation that "Arab" money was behind the conversions and a "foreign hand" was undermining India. The body at the other end of this hand was never specified. One newspaper even printed a picture of a currency note from a Gulf country, presumably part of the money that had changed hands. One of the most sensational newspaper stories told of a plan by the London-based Islamic Cultural Center to use Kuwaiti money to attract 80 million untouchables to Islam. This was taken so seriously that a question was asked in Parliament, and the home minister had to say there was no truth in the report.

The denial was ignored. *The Organizer*, the national newspaper of the RSS, called the events "shock therapy":

> The mass conversion at Meenakshipuram seems to have shaken Hindu society out of its sloganized slumber. . . . Hindu society should have taken these conversions in its stride, as in the past, had not the spokesman of Islam proclaimed publicly that mass

conversions of the weaker sections of Hindu society was a part of a political plan to win power for Islam and convert secular India into an Islamic state.

Thousands of people, from ranking politicians and saffron-clad priests to the merely curious, came to the village to stare at a temporary mosque that had been constructed for the second conversion ceremony: a mud wall with thatched roof, mats to kneel on, and a loudspeaker to call the faithful to prayer.

The visitors included Atal Bihari Vajpayee, the leader of the *Bharatiya Janata* Party (Indian Peoples Party), the foremost national Hindu political organization, along with the Tamil Nadu chief of the militant Hindu RSS. They stayed for several days in the area to contact and, if possible, reconvert the new Muslims. Seven families did change their minds and later explained they were afraid of losing their jobs or being evicted from their lands. One convert, who had an illegal shop on the road near the village, was told the police would shut him down if he did not reconvert, and he did.

Posters were pasted on walls reading "Do not make Pakistan or Padaristan (Christian priests are called Padres) in India. Let us unite and fight." With this call for action the BJP and RSS planned a huge procession to demonstrate the strength of Hinduism and told police they would enter the village and pass the mosque. The police were worried because a false report was spread that the mosque was on land owned by the village temple and that Hindu militants might try to destroy it.

The conversions in Meenakshipuram had been reported in newspapers in Kuwait and other Gulf countries, and the government of India worried about adverse international publicity. More than eight hundred policemen were mobilized to maintain order, and they prevented the shouting, chanting, banner-waving marchers from getting near the mosque.

Calm Returns

The fact that the storm that raged over Meenakshipuram was politically inspired, and had little to do with religious and social relations between Hindus and Muslims, was demonstrated by what happened when the outsiders folded their banners and their wall posters were torn down. Aside from a few incidents, such as a fight on a bus and a dispute about an untouchable who was blocked from becoming a village postmaster, Hindus and Muslims continued the coexistence that had marked their lives for centuries.

Muslims are well integrated in south Indian society. Arab traders came to the coastal cities of southern India long before the birth of Islam. Even when Muslim invaders established their kingdoms in the north, Muslims in the south lived peacefully with their neighbors as traders, businessmen, and small manufacturers. Muslim women generally wear saris, although not the bindi on their forehead as Hindu women do, and only the elderly, more religious-minded Muslim men wear skull-caps and beards.

I wanted to visit Meenakshipuram and sought the help of Ahmed Kabeer Refaye, who had arranged the conversion of the Pallars in 1981 and whose father had formed the Islamic Missionary Society in the 1940s. Refaye had been editor for twelve years of *Voice of Race*, a Tamil Muslim weekly, and served in both the Tamil Nadu legislature and the *Rajya Sabha* (the upper house of Parliament in New Delhi).

"There have been even larger conversions since then in Ramnad [Ramnathapuram] District, where there was a communal war between Thevars and Harijans in 1978 and 1979," he said. "The people there saw what happened in Meenakshipuram, and a majority of people in more than twenty villages in Ramnad have embraced Islam.

"Forty to fifty children from Meenakshipuram have been sent to Arabic-language colleges for one or two years in many places in Tamil Nadu, and some have become preachers and can lead prayers. Some boys can repeat the Koran by heart. Women study separately. They keep the sari over their heads and are very proud of their religion.

"Everyone's social outlook has improved. After embracing Islam a majority of people—I can't say 100 percent—have given up drinking. They used to be terrible drinkers. And the dowry problem is not so great. We're asking youths to be generous and marry girls even if they don't get a lot of money."

I said I had been told some of those who converted at Meenakshipuram were Christians, and he said it was true:

"Islam alone will end caste completely. If they embrace Christianity, caste is still there. Eighty percent of Indian Christians are from Harijan and poorer castes, but even though they form the majority of the church, the leadership is in the hands of the high caste Christians, like Brahmins, Mudaliars, Nadars, and others. Harijan Christians sit separately: the higher castes take the front portion and these people are relegated to the back. The high caste Christians also live separately. It's a pity this is not known to the outside world because Christians in America and Germany are giving a lot of money to these people thinking it will reach the poorest Christians, but the high caste Christians are eating it up."

Meenakshipuram is twelve kilometers from the subdistrict headquarters of Tenkasi, whose major attraction is a temple, dating from 1463, with a nine tier *Gopuram* (gateway) decorated in Tamil Nadu style with thousands of insipid, painted plaster gods.

Refaye provided a young guide who helped me to fight my way into a packed and infrequent bus, and it was a relief to walk the final half kilometer along a dirt road to the village. It was a Friday, and there would be special late afternoon prayers. I was surprised to find the mosque still looked temporary and had only a pointed tin roof. My guide said the original mosque had mysteriously burned down and money and material had been collected to build a new structure, but the caste Hindus still claimed the site was temple land and had sued to block construction. When the Muslims won in a lower court, the caste Hindus filed an appeal, and no one knew when a decision would be reached.

As we took off our sandals and washed our hands and feet in preparation for entering the mosque, my guide told the story of their well, which I had heard several times before.

"Before, the Pallars had no well in this village. Then we embraced Islam, and a merchant gave money for a well. Right away, we got good sweet water, much better than the water in the Hindu well. That showed God favored us. And we told everyone, 'Come and drink from our well. No one is excluded from Islam.'"

Other men gathered around, some with beards and skull caps, others clean shaven with any bits of cloth wrapped around their heads as turbans. Through the guide I asked one man why he was a Muslim.

"We wanted respect," he said. "And in Hinduism people worship idols. In Islam there is one God. He is Allah."

Another, with a brown scarf wrapped around his head, said he used to be a Christian.

"Muslims are all one," he said. "That was not true among Christians. There were Nadar Christians and Pallar Christians, and the Nadars looked down on us even if we went to the same church."

An Imam, dressed in pure white with a great black beard, led the opening group prayer and later gave a long sermon. Finally, a plate was passed for offerings, and after another joint prayer we left.

The next day I made a tourist trip to Kanyakumari at the tip of India and then returned north, following a fuse lit by the conversions at Meenakshipuram.

45 ✵ Manipulating Myths and Symbols

Manipulating symbols and myths and searching for scapegoats is a way to try to create solidarity and commitment in the face of deteriorating economic and political life. The Nazis and Fascists did this in Europe, but it is perilous, as the fate of Germany and Italy demonstrated.

The conversion of an insignificant number of Dalits in Meenakshipuram was perceived by upper caste Hindus as a portent, along with the rise of regional, linguistic political parties, of a weakening of Brahminic hegemony. In 1982, at a meeting attended by leaders of the Rashtriya Swayamsevak Sangh (RSS) and the Bharatiya Janata Party (BJP), it was decided there was an urgent need to stimulate Hindu unity. The instrument chosen for this effort was an RSS front group, the *Vishwa Hindu Parishad* (VHP, roughly, World Hindu Congress).

The RSS itself was formed in 1925 to assert the right of Hindus to set the policies and agenda for India after the departure of the British. It was banned in 1948 on suspicion of participation in a conspiracy to assassinate Mahatma Gandhi, but many second-ranking Congress Party leaders had a long and close association with the RSS, and the ban was lifted after a year when no direct connection was proved.

The VHP was organized in 1964 with three ostensible goals: to consolidate and strengthen Hindu society, to protect and spread Hindu ethical and spiritual values and make them relevant to contemporary society, and to establish links with Hindus in foreign countries.

Little of this was actively pursued, particularly the development of a corpus of modern doctrines. Instead, the VHP concentrated on campaigns to prevent Hindu girls from marrying non-Hindus and to reconvert Christians and Muslims to Hinduism by building temples and proselytizing tribals in the northeast and the Chotanagpur region of Bihar.

In May 1983, at a meeting attended by leaders of eighty-five of the main Hindu sects, it was agreed the RSS, acting through the VHP, would conduct an *Ekatmata Yajna* (Sacrifice for Unanimity or Rite for Integration).

It was the sort of thing the RSS did best. It is organized on military lines, although its members are armed only with lathis. Dressed in khaki shorts and white shirts and wearing saffron-colored caps, they daily gather on an open field in neat lines with their lathis at their sides, salute a saffron flag, and go through a series of drills and exercises after which they listen to a speech, generally warning of the threats to Hinduism.

The Ekatmata Yajna consisted of three main *yatras* (marches or processions). One started from the Pashupatinath Temple in Katmandu and ended at the Rameswaram Temple in Tamil Nadu at the southern tip of India. A second made the north-south journey along another route, from the pilgrimage center of Hardwar in the foothills of the Himalayas to Kanyakumari in Tamil Nadu. The third traveled from Gangasagar in West Bengal to the Somnath temple in Gujarat.

The yajna honored Bharat Mata (Mother India), deified as a goddess clad in a modest sari and seated on the back of a lion. Another symbol was the Ganga, the mother of all waters in heaven and on earth. In each yatra a truck carried an eight-foot-high bronze *kalasha* (container) of water drawn from the headwaters of the Ganga or substitute sacred sources. Along the way the devout offered pitchers of water from local sacred sources, like the tank of a temple, to be poured into the kalasha. Plastic bottles of the mingled waters were sold to raise money for the yajna.

There were also fifty-three *upayatras* (shorter marches), and in less than a month 300,000 of India's half-million villages were visited. Villagers, mostly women and girls, brought their local water and stood with folded hands before a picture of Bharat Mata as a loudspeaker blared a taped hymn to the Ganga. The few who could afford it bought bottles of the combined waters for ten rupees, but most settled for a lithograph of Bharat Mata for half a rupee.

Liberating God's Birthplace

It was so successful, the VHP decided, as a sequel, to demand the "liberation" of three legendary temples from Muslim control. They claimed a mosque in Ayodhya, Uttar Pradesh, built in 1528 by Babar, the first Mogul emperor, was on the site of a temple marking the spot where the god Rama was born. They said a second mosque, built in 1661 by the sixth Mogul emperor, Aurangzeb, at Mathura, Uttar Pradesh, replaced a temple marking the birthplace of the god Krishna. Both Rama and Krishna are avatars of Vishnu, one of the two most important Hindu deities. The third mosque is in Varanasi, Uttar Pradesh—the holiest of Hindu cities. It was built by Aurangzeb in 1669 on the site of the Vishvanath temple of Siva, the other important Hindu deity.

Uttar Pradesh, with 130 million people, is India's most populous state and the center of ancient Hindu culture. It is also the heartland of Muslim India. One-quarter of all Indian Muslims live in Uttar Pradesh, and it is the home of Urdu, the closest approximate to a national language for Indian Muslims. Jawaharlal Nehru, whose family home was in Allahabad in Uttar Pradesh, spoke fine Urdu and broken Hindi and delighted in the Islamic culture of his native soil. The high-buttoned, knee-length *achkan* jacket he made a male national costume is in Muslim style.

The VHP selected the mosque at Ayodhya as the prime target. Ayodhya is a *tirtha* on the bank of the holy river Sarayu. Literally, tirtha means the ford of a river. Metaphysically, it is a place where a person crosses a river descending from heaven and makes contact with the ancestral world. It is also home for once-peripatetic Ramanandi sadhus now settled down to a sedentary life, allowing pilgrims to acquire merit by bestowing alms on them.

In Hindu cosmology existence is a vast cycle divided into four *yugas* (periods). Rama lived in the *Treta* or second period, which lasted 1,296,000 years, at the end of which Ayodhya disappeared. According to myth, it was rediscovered in this present *Kali Yuga* of strife and toil by a king named Vikramaditya, who is said to have reigned in the first century B.C. Although there is no factual evidence of his existence, he ranked high in ancient esteem and later rulers took his name, just as in Europe Caesar's name became a term for German kings.

What may have happened is this: an upstart kingdom of the Gupta clan emerged in north central India in the fifth century A.D., when Buddhism was in decline and what we now perceive as Hinduism was taking form. As part of this churning, an early Gupta king took the name Vikramaditya and built his capital on a bank of the Sarayu and called it Ayodhya, after the kingdom of a mythical Tetra-era ruler Rama. Vikramaditya Gupta then built a temple on the exact spot where, so he claimed, Rama was born millions of years earlier, thus linking his dynasty with the gods.

It is a mythic hodgepodge. Rama is said to be a northern prince whose wife, Sita, is kidnapped by the demon king Ravana of modern Sri Lanka. Sita is rescued by Rama with the help of an army of monkeys. However, in earlier myths that migrated to Indonesia, Ravana is a wise and beneficent king. Does the Rama story signify the victory of a northern king over a southern king, perhaps in the mountains of central India and not all the way to Sri Lanka? This is the interpretation of modern Dalits who claim the legend depicts the Brahminic destruction of earlier civilizations.

With the decline of the Guptas toward the end of the fifth century, Ayodhya was abandoned and reclaimed by jungle vines but retained its religious attraction. When Babar passed through the region in 1528, he was approached by two *pirs* (Muslim saints) who, in Indian syncretic tradition, were impressed by the holiness of the place and persuaded the emperor to build a mosque on the site of one of the surviving temples. In the same syncretic tradition Hindus continued to worship by tossing flowers into a pit said to be the spot of Rama's birth.

The British Try to Keep the Peace

As centuries passed Ayodhya attracted an increasing number of ascetic, drug-addicted, and volatile Hindu and Muslim holy men, virtually identical in their ecstasies but distinguishable in doctrine and dress or, to be more precise, absence of dress, since the Ramanandi sadhus flaunted their total renunciation by wearing no clothes.

After the British annexed the then Muslim principality of Awadh (or Oudh, a corruption of Ayodhya) in 1856, they found themselves arbiters of clashes between the two groups. They first built a railing around the Babri Mosque (as it is called) to keep Hindus out, but after more clashes Hindus and Muslims were allowed to offer prayers in separate arched chambers of the building.

This harmony was shattered with the preindependence rise of aggressive Hinduism, which used the cow as a symbol of unity against the beef-eating British and Muslims. The "cow protection" movement inspired noisy processions and confrontations with Muslims in many parts of India, including Ayodhya. There was a strong Hindu attack on the Babri Mosque during the Muslim festival of Bakr-Id in 1912 and another attack in 1934, in which the mosque was heavily damaged, and several hundred Muslims were killed.

The departure of the British offered an opportunity to challenge the status quo. On the night of December 22–23, 1949, despite the presence of guards, an idol of Rama appeared in the inner chamber where Hindus were allowed to offer prayers. Although local Hindus claimed it was a miraculous appearance, it was a patent Hindu attempt to seize the mosque under cover of the partition disturbances. A magistrate avoided further trouble by confiscating the property and locking the gate to keep everyone out.

It was not a total loss for the Hindus. They were granted the right to hold continuous *kirtans* (song sessions) on a cement platform known as the Ram *Chabutra* (platform) and to take *darshan* (the viewing of a deity) of the idol through a window from a specified distance away.

In the Indian tradition of not trying to solve explosive issues, the gate remained padlocked for thirty-four years. Then the Vishwa Hindu Parishad and Rashtriya Swayamsevak Sangh decided to use the mosque to revive memories of purported past Muslim oppression. In October 1984 they formed the *Ram Janmabhoomi Mukti Yajna* (Sacrifice for the Liberation of Rama's Birthplace) Committee and announced a *Tola Kholo* (Open the Lock) campaign to raise 250 million rupees ($17.5 million) to construct a new temple on the spot.

It took a full year to work out the showmanship of *rath yatras* (temple processions in which the deity is taken through the street in a "chariot") in which villagers would be shown Rama behind a padlocked iron gate: God was in prison and had to be liberated. But the campaign was canceled two weeks after its start because of the assassination of Indira Gandhi on October 31, 1984.

A Hindu Coup d'Etat

The drive to liberate Rama's birthplace was resumed in March 1985, when sixty thousand Hindus gathered at New Delhi's Ram Lila Grounds, where every year huge bamboo and paper images of Ravana and two other "demons" are burned with fiery arrows shot by Rama and his companions. A pamphlet read:

> Three prominent places of Hindu faith . . . have yet to be liberated even after thirty-eight years of independence. The status quo remains despite hundreds of thousands of sacrifices. The original birthplaces of the gods of millions and millions of Hindus and their places of worship which were captured and decimated by the in-

vaders are still in alien hands. It is an attack on the identity of the society, a black spot on its manhood and a dark page in its glorious history. As long as these three black spots are not removed [the] Hindu mind cannot feel peace and satisfaction and would continue to writhe in pain and distress of dishonor.

The following October twenty-five rath yatras were set in motion to revive the Open the Lock agitation and collect money to "educate the masses about the struggle."

On February 1, 1986, a judge in Ayodhya, with no prior notice or hearings, ended centuries of debate by ordering the locks removed from the entrance gate to the Babri Mosque. He claimed to be acting on the application of a local lawyer who had pointed out the order locking the gates was legally invalid. Journalists dismissed the judge's excuse out-of-hand, saying nothing the lower courts do in India is without the approval of dominant castes and politicians. Muslims in Ayodhya called it a "judicial coup d'etat," noting that paramilitary forces were deployed before the order was issued. And newsmen learned Bir Bahadur Singh, the Congress Party chief minister of Uttar Pradesh, had visited Ayodhya during a Hindu fair in December and had met Vishwa Hindu Parishad leaders. He had then called for the legal file to look into the very issue the lawyer had raised: was there a specific court order regarding the padlocking of the gates?

Once the gates were flung open, Hindus flocked inside with lamps, garlands, sweets, and coconuts to worship the idol they believed marked the spot where Rama was born. Then, in effect, the central government in New Delhi added its stamp of approval. *Doordarshan* ("far-seen," the Sanskritized official name for the government-owned television network) and the government's All-India Radio broadcast the news nationwide, showing the convergence of worshippers into what was described as the Ram Janmabhoomi temple. The very name of Babri Mosque had disappeared.

The Peepul Tree of Old Delhi

Among the many trees and plants that Hindus hold sacred is the *pipal* (spelled peepul in English). It is also known as the Bo tree. It was under a Bo tree that Prince Siddhartha meditated, found enlightenment, and became the Buddha. When Hinduism absorbed Buddhism, the peepul was associated with Vishnu and Siva, and no one was allowed to harm it. There is also a belief that if a woman worships the tree and ties a thread around it, she will give birth to a son.

There is a peepul tree on *Lal Kuan* (Red Street) in the old walled city of Delhi. The area is predominantly Muslim, and few people paid much attention to it until the early 1960s, when Hindu midwives began bringing pregnant women to offer prayers and tie a thread around it. This brought the tree to the attention of Hindus in the local government, and after some resistance from Muslim leaders, who pointed out the tree stood on ground owned by a Muslim charitable trust, it was agreed Hindus could build a platform around the base of the tree and place an idol on it.

In 1984 RSS activists tried to build a wall around the tree, but a local official, a Sikh, intervened, and the wall was demolished. However, when the Sikh official was transferred, no one in authority was willing to listen to Muslim objections, and the RSS built a small temple next to the tree and installed a full-time *pujari* (priest, one who accepted offerings).

Two weeks after the Babri Mosque was turned over to Hindus, Muslims staged a show of strength at the *Juma Masjid* (Friday Mosque) opposite the Red Fort in Old Delhi. The seventeenth-century mosque, set on a high plinth with a delicate dome of white marble with reddish-brown stripes, is the largest in India, with a *sahn* (courtyard) that can easily accommodate twenty thousand of the faithful. On this Friday, January 14, it was filled to capacity.

Imam (prayer leader) Maulana Abdullah Bukhari spoke of the grievances of Muslims in India but cautioned the struggle was with the government and not with ordinary Hindus. He asked the faithful to return to their homes peacefully and not shout slogans. Volunteers at the exits repeated the injunctions to leave peacefully.

In the surrounding old city Muslim shops had downed their shutters, and some houses flew black flags as signs of protest. Hindu and Sikh businesses also closed, and people remained indoors as armed police patrols marched through the narrow, winding streets. There were a few minor clashes, rocks were thrown, and the police fired several shots to disperse crowds, but no one was injured.

But there was tension at the peepul tree of Lal Kuan. Overnight someone had stretched a banner near the tree reading "Prachin Shiv Mandir" (Ancient Siva Temple), and there was a poster congratulating Hindus on the liberation of the Ram Janmabhoomi Temple. Local people tried to get the police to remove the banner and poster, saying it was a provocation, but the police refused.

Then, about 350 Muslims, mostly young men, came shouting slogans, and a police jeep, under the command of Station House Officer Jag Parvesh Kaushal, overtook them. People in the surrounding houses later said Kaushal shouted anti-Muslim epithets, ordering the marchers to disperse. He also fired shots in the air with his pistol, and there was a stampede away from the jeep. The police followed the crowd, some firing shots in the air.

Two men, Suban Hashmi, twenty, and Mohammed Zakir, eighteen, turned into a blind alley. Kaushal, following them, turned the corner and ordered a constable to shoot them with his rifle. When the constable refused, Kaushal took the rifle and fired two shots, killing one and mortally wounding the other, who died two days later at a hospital.

The police later charged rioters had burned vehicles and looted shops. A general curfew was imposed on Old Delhi, and for the next six days police ranged through the streets and into houses and restaurants apparently picking up people at random. In all more than eight hundred persons were arrested, almost all of them Muslims.

When the curfew was lifted, investigators from the People's Union for Civil Liberties went through the area, gathering evidence of what happened. They saw no burned vehicles, and no merchants said their shops had been looted. The team also interviewed some of those who had been arrested.

Mohammed Nasir, twenty-two, said police were suspicious of those who gave Hindu names, and men were made to open their trousers to see if they had been circumcised. Another man, Zamiruddin, said he was beaten about the head and had to be taken to a hospital for stitches. He said the officers who beat him kept asking, "Why don't you people go away to Pakistan? Why should you continue to stay here?"

Police, searching a bus, saw a man named Zamiruddin and recognized him by his clothes as a visitor from Pakistan. He was taken to a station house, beaten so badly he had to be hospitalized, and five hundred Indian rupees along with twenty-five American dollars and a wristwatch were stolen from him.

Mohammed Asif, twenty-four, was beaten for an hour. When he asked for water, a police officer said he should be given urine to drink. He was taken to a hospital where his wounds were dressed and then back to the police station where he was told to clean the latrine. He refused, but when he gave the police fifty rupees, they let him go.

A Mrs Zubeida said police broke into her house and struck her twice on the chest with the metal end of a lathi, and one officer shouted, "Dogs, why don't you go to Pakistan? You are illegitimate in our country."

The PUCL team was told police later went through the streets telling shopkeepers to remove bullet marks. One man said he was taken to a police station and made to sign a statement saying he had seen four to five thousand people indulging in rioting, and the police had to intervene to quell the unruly mobs but had fired only in the air.

Why Are There Riots?

One member of the PUCL team was Inder Mohan, a man in his late sixties. After I read the report, I asked him to show me the scene and tell me something about himself.

"I joined the Communist Party in 1930 in Lahore as a student," he said. "I also took part in the freedom movement and spent three and a half years in jail. It would have been easy for me to continue in politics and get elected to a legislative seat. In those days we were members of the Congress Party as well as the Communist Party. After the war things changed, and in 1952 I was so disgusted with Communist Party politics I gave up politics forever.

"After that I worked in the slums. One day I read in the newspaper that the government had declared Old Delhi a slum. I realized the declaration was really meant to destroy the character of the city. Sanjay Gandhi, Prime Minister Gandhi's son, planned a fifty-story commercial complex near one of the old gates and a fifteen-story structure near the mosque.

"There were two motives. One, to change the land to commercial because it is valuable property. A great deal of money would be gained by the speculators, and a lot of money would be made available in kickbacks to the politicians. Sanjay needed this money. The other motive was to disperse the Muslim community and destroy the Muslim character of Old Delhi once and for all."

We took a taxi as far as we could go and walked the remaining few blocks through streets piled with garbage higher than a man's head. We saw the tree: a twisted, dust-covered patch of green in a harsh environment. Behind it was the temple with a permanent, round-the-clock guard of three policemen armed with rifles. We then walked a few hundred yards to the cul-de-sac where the two men had been killed. A store owner pointed to a sign on the wall. A year after the killings the little area had been renamed Mohammed Zakir Suban Hashmi *Chowk* (an open space).

I asked Inder why there are so many clashes in which minorities are killed.

"Riots are the last resort: the most dangerous weapon the government can use against the people. When the administration realizes police or official repression alone has not been able to break the backs of the people, they instigate communal riots. When we interviewed Hindus and Muslims here, they said the communities had always lived in peace. The administration tries to foment trouble to keep people divided, but they will not succeed. A consciousness has arisen among the rural and urban poor that they will not quarrel among themselves, and as this develops the communal riots will subside. But it will take another generation."

In the near term many India analysts believe the death throes of a weak and insecure government will lead to greater violence. As proof they point to events in the city of Meerut, just outside New Delhi, where religious violence became state violence, culminating in the cold-blooded shooting of Muslims by paramilitary police.

46 ✹ The Juggernaut Claims Its Victims

The RSS speaks of Hindu *jagaran* (revival) and says it is working for Indian unity, but it is polarizing India. The magazine *India Today*, in a jumble of images, compared jagaran to the huge temple cart of Juggernaut at Puri in Orissa, before whose wheels devotees once lay to be crushed as a sacrifice to the god:

> Frenzied in pace, frenetic in character, the religious and communal combat vehicle is freewheeling across the collective Hindu consciousness, dragging in its slip-stream a divergent following —shopkeepers, sadhus, social activists, professionals, businessmen —and threatening to trigger off transformations of unfathomable dimensions in the country's tightly stretched political and social fabric.

The RSS claims it has twenty-five thousand *shakhas* (its basic training and "brotherhood" unit) in almost nineteen thousand cities and villages. Participation in the daily drills increased from one million in 1979 to 1.8 million in 1989. The RSS operates through thirty-eight front organizations with an additional membership of 5 million. It claims to have used its network of volunteers to distribute 20 million copies of an anti-Muslim and anti-Christian leaflet titled, "Warning: India in Danger." The Delhi branch alone has sold 5 million postcards and envelopes showing India, Afghanistan, Pakistan, Nepal, Sri Lanka, and Bangladesh under a saffron flag.

Kerala, with a large Christian and Muslim population, is one of the main targets of the RSS; 962 temples were renovated to raise Hindu enthusiasm. The campaign has been a major success. At the Ganesh Temple in Trivandrum, the state's capital, sixteen thousand coconuts were broken every day in 1986 compared to nine thousand three years earlier.

In Gujarat, a year after Hindu-Muslim clashes paralyzed the state, permission was granted for the annual rath yatra of an Ahmedabad temple to pass through a Muslim area. *India Today* described what happened: "With Hindus dancing jubilantly to the tune of religious fervor, frayed tempers on both sides produced the inevitable clashes. Within minutes, seven people lay dead: victims of gunfire. The incident has re-created a surge of communalism in which Hindus who live in Muslim-dominated areas are selling their houses and moving out. Muslims are doing the same."

The Ministry for Home Affairs in New Delhi reported statistics showing an "unprecedented spurt" in the construction of religious buildings throughout the country, and an official expressed concern that the increase would mean more processions and a greater use of loudspeakers, leading to "violent situations."

When K. C. Sudarshan, the sixty-six-year-old *boudhik pramukh* (principal intellectual) of the RSS, was asked about the "bloodshed" that resulted from the Ram Janmabhoomi campaign he replied: "This is nothing. There will be more. We are not scared."

The VHP, which claims a million members in 3,500 branches throughout the country, was jubilant. Ashok Singal, its *mahamantri* (chief minister), told another reporter it was "like God himself in action. . . . You will soon see within this country a vertical divide within each political party—those who accept Hindu nationalism and those who don't."

Do Muslims Refuse to Integrate?

For militant Hindus the question of maintenance for an elderly Muslim woman was proof of what they saw as the refusal of Muslims to integrate into Indian society.

Shah Bano had been married for forty-three years to a prosperous Madhya Pradesh lawyer. When he divorced her and drove her out of the house, she asked a court to grant her a small maintenance. There were several decisions and appeals, and Shah Bano was seventy-three when her case was finally decided by the Supreme Court, which granted her maintenance of five hundred rupees a month.

Muslims, who insisted on their own code of personal law, denounced the ruling as part of a conspiracy to deny them what little protection they had under the Indian constitution. The most bitterly contested issue faced by the framers of India's constitution was a demand by Hindus for a uniform personal code for all faiths. The real question was whether India was a single secular nation or two nations, justifying partition. Ambiguous phrasing was devised to pigeonhole the issue. Article forty-four reads: "The state shall endeavor to secure for the citizens a uniform civil code throughout the territory of India."

In Islam personal law, including marriage and divorce, is part of the *Shariat* (Islamic Law). In custom, a bride receives *mehr* (dowry): just the opposite of the Hindu practice of the groom's family receiving a dowry. After divorce the Muslim woman keeps her mehr and returns to her parent's house to be supported by her father, brothers, or sons, and the former husband has no responsibility for her.

In October an estimated 200,000 Muslims in Bombay marched in protest of what was condemned as "a death warrant of Muslim identity." Surprisingly, the Muslims won a complete victory because, in the view of cynics, the government, having given the Babri Mosque to Hindus, wanted to recapture Muslim votes by overturning the court's Shah Bano ruling.

In May, in a single, thirteen-hour session of Parliament, the Congress Party rammed through the Muslim Women (Protection of Rights on Divorce) Bill. The law retains the separate Muslim personal law code while spelling out, for the first time, exactly who is legally responsible for the maintenance of a divorced Muslim woman.

The law was widely criticized. Feminists said it threw Muslim women to the religious wolves, liberals attacked it as an affront to secularism, and Hindus called it another example of the government's pampering of fundamentalists.

Then Syed Shahabuddin, a fifty-year-old Janata Party member of Parliament from Bihar and editor of *Muslim India*, a monthly magazine of comment and opinion, began a campaign to reclaim the Babri Mosque. Shahabuddin, who had resigned from the Indian Foreign Service in 1978 to enter politics, organized the Babri Mosque Coordination Committee and in December 1986 urged Muslims to show their dismay at the Hindu occupation of the mosque by boycotting the annual Republic Day celebrations scheduled for the following January 26. Republic Day, marking the anniversary of India's constitution, is the most important national holiday.

Shahabuddin later said he did not mean Muslims should not respect the anniversary but that they should not associate themselves with official functions. His mild backtracking was lost in the chorus of criticism, including that of other Muslim leaders. One said a boycott would "alienate Muslims from their common heritage of democratic India," and another called it "suicidal." But Shahabuddin refused to be silenced. "Why shouldn't we speak out?" he told some of the reporters who called at his office seeking a reaction to the criticism. "Ours is not a communal fight. It only amounts to resisting the inexorable processes of assimilation."

Some Muslim leaders accused Shahabuddin of stirring Muslim antipathies to keep himself in office. Others questioned his stress on the mosque issue, saying Muslims worship Allah, not buildings, and only three mosques have religious sanctity: those at Mecca, Medina, and Jerusalem.

Another critic was Asghar Ali Engineer, India's leading spokesman for Islamic liberalism, who said continued confrontation on the Babri Mosque issue was hurting the community and urged Muslims to forgo any interest in the structure:

> One can construct other mosques, but one cannot bring back those killed to life. The mosque is made by human beings . . . but life, once destroyed, cannot be retrieved. Will it not be a sign of weakness to surrender the mosque, some Muslims may argue? Here I would submit that what can be construed as weakness from the point of view of some Muslims can be described as a strategy of survival from another point of view.

Muslims Suffer the Most

The question of survival arises because the worst sufferers in communal clashes are the Muslim small shopkeepers, manufacturers, and laborers.

The first great communal killing after the partition riots was at Ahmedabad in 1960. According to the official report, 413 Muslims and 24 Hindus were killed, plus 75 not identified. Official figures in such cases are always vastly understated. Ahmedabad residents put the death toll at 1,500. In addition, of the houses and shops destroyed 6,071 belonged to Muslims and 671 to Hindus. Stated in monetary terms, Muslim losses came to 34.7 million rupees ($7.3 million at the prevailing exchange rate) as against Hindu losses of 7.6 million ($1.6 million).

In the extensive Bombay-Bhiwandi riots of 1984 more than 275 people were killed, 1,115 were injured, and properties worth more than five million dollars were destroyed. About 80 percent of the casualties and property losses were suffered by Muslims. This disparity explains the usual Muslim practice of avoiding confrontations. When the provocation is great, and they do strike back, they suffer accordingly.

Most of the communal violence since independence has occurred in Uttar Pradesh. Here the word communal is misleading. Fifteen out of thirty-one incidents recorded as Hindu-Muslim clashes between 1971 and 1987 in Uttar Pradesh involved Muslims and the state's Provincial Armed Constabulary (PAC), a thirty-two-thousand-man paramilitary force recruited almost entirely from the upper and middle Hindu castes. Only 2 or 3 percent are Muslims in a state with a 15 percent Muslim minority.

A notorious incident of PAC killings occurred in 1980 in Moradabad, a brass manufacturing center in central Uttar Pradesh with a population of over a million, more than half of them Muslims. On August 13, the day after the month-long *Ramadan* fast, men, women and children put on new clothes and went to the *idgah* for prayers. An idgah is an open space surrounded by a wall where a large section of the community can gather in a reaffirmation of Islamic brotherhood.

As the last prayers were intoned, someone let a pig—to Muslims the most defiling of animals—into the idgah. When people turned and saw the pig, they picked up stones and threw them at police standing at the only exit. The officer in command was struck and fell to the ground, and the men of the PAC raised their rifles and shot into the mass of people. There is a small mosque at the corner of the idgah, and many ran there, thinking it would be safe. It was not. A Muslim doctor retrieved twenty-four bodies from the compound of the mosque, thirteen of them children.

The authorities called it a Hindu-Muslim riot, but reporters who went to the scene found not a single non-Muslim house or business had been attacked. Officials also said Muslims had attacked a police station and that only after some PAC constables were lynched did the firing begin in self-defense. Reporters confirmed some police were killed and many rocks were thrown but only after the shooting of men, women, and children at the idgah.

An official report put the death toll at 144. Muslims say as many as five hundred died. There was no inquiry into the actions of the PAC, whose officers said it was not their responsibility to keep a pig out of a Muslim ceremony.

The Meerut Massacre

Meerut, sixty kilometers east of Delhi, entered Indian history as a place where Hindu and Muslim soldiers began the 1857 mutiny that patriots would later term India's First War of Independence. But now Meerut, a dreary manufacturing city of about one million people, 45 percent of whom are Muslims, is best known for the frequency and horror of communal incidents.

In 1973 Hindu-Muslim clashes touched off by an accident involving a cyclist and a cycle rickshaw driver took one hundred lives. Rioting in 1982, arising from a dispute over a peepul tree and a graveyard and then involving the PAC, left 150 dead.

Nothing that occurred earlier can compare to what happened from May 18 to 23, 1987. Thirteen thousand members of the Indian Army, the PAC, and the ordinary police were mustered to control unarmed civilians. Normally, a force that size would be expected to restore order in twenty-four hours. Instead, almost all of the killings and destruction occurred after the military, paramilitary, and civilian police had assumed control. Some who died were taken to the bank of a canal, shot, and dumped in the water.

Far from attempting to seek out and punish the guilty, the commandant of the PAC was later made deputy inspector general of police, the superintendent of police was promoted to a position in the central excise department, and the district magistrate was made managing director of the State Textile Corporation and given an award for his "contribution to communal peace and harmony in Uttar Pradesh." As for the killings on the canal bank, a police report described the perpetrators as "unknown persons wearing khaki uniforms."

Indians who ask why it happened find the answer in economics and politics. Ninety percent of the 344 shops and fourteen factories looted and destroyed were owned by Muslims. Entire rows of Muslim shops were burned, along with about fifty Muslim-owned motor mechanic shops in a one kilometer radius. As for politics, a reporter for *Sunday*, a Calcutta-based weekly magazine, quoted "one of the weary citizens of Meerut" as saying, "It suits *netas* [leaders] to whip up tension and sow the seeds of hatred so they can reap a harvest of votes during election time."

There are three localities of importance. The first is the Muslim area of Hashimpura, a weavers' colony with the Imliyan Mosque as its cultural center. The second is Moradnagar, twenty-five kilometers to the west on the Ganga canal, a major distributory for waters in north central India. The third is a collection of small villages known as Maliana, about five kilometers from Meerut.

In the week before the massacre there were scattered incidents of communal violence in various parts of Meerut, with several people killed. Then, at about nine o'clock on the night of May 18, a Muslim stall was set afire in Hashimpura, and then a Hindu stall was burned and its owner killed. The PAC was summoned and called people to come out so their houses could be searched. No one came, and when the PAC entered the area, the residents threw stones, and the PAC retreated. In so doing one *jawan* (soldier: as a paramilitary force, the PAC uses army terminology) lost his rifle: some say he dropped it, others say it was snatched away. In either case the PAC views the loss of a weapon as a mortal affront.

The PAC returned in greater force after midnight and announced over loudspeakers if the people did not come out there would be shooting. With that three thousand people, including women and children, came and sat on the road outside the Imliyan Mosque. The PAC found the missing rifle outside a house and two brothers sitting inside were killed.

When a police officer wanted to drive off in a jeep with arrested persons, some women tried to stop him, but the jeep drove on. People later said one girl was killed; others said three women were killed; a third version said no one was killed, but some women were injured.

The Muslims started stoning the PAC, and the jawans opened fire and killed several people. The crowd then attacked Hindu shops and small factories, upon which Hindus retaliated by attacking Muslim places. Perhaps as many as a dozen people died in the burning buildings.

On May 19 morning curfew was imposed, and for the next four days Hindu mobs were allowed to loot and burn Muslim establishments, and a pall of smoke hung over the city. In one neighborhood of poor Muslim rickshaw drivers, vegetable vendors, and bricklayers, all 228 houses were looted and burned to the ground. The looting spread to a mixed middle-class neighborhood known as Shashtri Nagar where 250 Muslim houses were burned, and not a single house occupied by a Hindu was touched. In two of the torched Muslim houses thirty-three persons were burned alive.

All the while the PAC conducted mass arrests. About 2,500 persons, almost all Muslims, were taken into custody and repeatedly beaten. At least five died from such beatings.

The Moradnagar executions occurred on the night of May 22 but only became known days later when people living or walking farther down the canal saw bloated bodies floating or washed up on the bank. At least forty-three were killed there.

The Maliana killings occurred on the afternoon of the next day, May 23. Although there had been no trouble and there was no curfew, the PAC suddenly appeared at one end of the village and asked people to come out. When they refused, the PAC took up positions on surrounding rooftops and began firing into the streets. Hindu Dalits in these adjacent houses then surged into the Muslim portion of Maliana and began to kill, loot, and burn.

Unofficial estimates put the total death toll in Hashimpura, Moradnagar, Maliana, and in various jails at four hundred. As is customary after such violence, the government offered to compensate victims according to lives lost and property destroyed. It is a long and complicated process, but by the middle of 1988, a year after the events, 161 payments for deaths had been made and one hundred were pending, so the death toll is at least 261.

Jamaluddin's Story

A young woman journalist, Aditi Phadnis, interviewed survivors and relatives of victims shortly after the killings and went with me to Meerut as guide and translator.

Jamaluddin, about fifty years old, who owns a small factory manufacturing scissors, has a house down an alley in Hashimpura. His living room is dominated by a large wedding picture of his son Qamauddin hanging on a wall. Jamaluddin had five sons. One was in Delhi, two managed to hide, a third was in jail, but Qamauddin was at home. He was twenty-two when he was taken to the canal bank and killed.

"Some people from this area were rounded up on the night of May eighteenth after some Hindu huts were set on fire," Jamaluddin said. "On the next night the PAC and Hindus climbed to the roofs of houses and began to throw rags soaked in petrol on our houses to set fires to drive us out. They also used their guns to shoot two people.

"The same thing happened on the night of May twentieth, but then there was a lull until after three o'clock on the afternoon of May twenty-second. The army and the PAC and women police surrounded the entire *mohalla* [area]. They made people open their doors or broke them down and ordered everyone to come out. All the males were made to stand in a line on the road outside the mohalla. My son, Qamauddin, was among them. The men were separated into two groups. Those with gray hair or who appeared sick or were children were put in one group, and younger men were put in a separate group.

"We thought they just wanted to take the younger men for special inquiries, and they would be released soon. They were paying special attention to those they selected. One of the PAC jawans said certain young men should not be taken, but the army people insisted on including them. We could hear two army majors talking with the commander of the PAC. As a result they came again and selected some of those who had been put with the other group and put them in the group who were told to enter closed vans.

"There were forty-two men, from fourteen to twenty-four, in the vans. Some were taken to the canal to be shot; others were taken to the Hindon River and shot there. We got back thirty-six bodies. The rest are still missing. Perhaps they are still under the water, or perhaps their bodies were found far away and disposed of as unidentified persons.

"The others, about 450 in all, were taken to the Meerut police station where they were beaten with lathis, iron rods, everything. Five were killed, and many others had their arms or legs broken. Two or three days later they were taken to Fatehgarh jail and were again beaten there."

One of the men listening to our conversation pulled up his shirt to show a scar on his stomach and rolled up his sleeve to show a scar on his arm, both from injuries received in these beatings. A second man raised his trousers to show several scars on his legs.

Jamaluddin showed a book he said he had begun to prepare just after the troubles. It was a register of all those who were killed from his area: with their names, ages, and pictures (where available), plus a brief description of their occupations and how they were identified after their bodies were returned.

"They are all martyrs," he said. "We hold a service every year on May twenty-third in their name. Now there is greater unity among Muslims, and this much is clear: we are not going to be taken unawares again by anyone. If the police come again, we'll fight here, and we'll die fighting here. We won't be taken to the canal to die there. We can use bricks, or we can fight with our bare hands."

Mohammed Osman's Story

When Aditi and I arrived, they said one of the survivors of the Morad-nagar canal shooting lived nearby. He was sent for and came after we finished the customary tea and sweets. His name was Mohammed Osman. He repeated a story he had told many times before:

"They rounded us up and took us to the main road. We could see the army, the police, the PAC, and the lady police. The young men were in one group and the old and infirm in another. They made another selection, and then we were herded into the PAC truck and taken away. All around us there were men with rifles, and we were frightened and had no idea where we were going and what would be done to us, though we had a general idea of the direction.

"When we reached Moradnagar, where the road crosses the canal, another car was coming toward us, so the van went a little distance ahead and then, after the car had passed, it backed up and came to a halt. It then turned to the right and went along the canal bank. The policemen got off the truck and told the driver to cut the light.

"Then they made one man get down, and they shot him. Then the second was made to get down, and he was shot. So inside, when we saw this, we felt in any case we had to die so let's try to overcome the police-man guarding us and just get off the truck. We shouted the name of Allah and struggled with the guard, but those outside saw this and shot inside the truck, and we stopped the struggle.

"Then it was my turn. They made me jump out, and two PAC men picked me up, and I started crying and pleaded with them to spare me because I had two small children and old parents. A third PAC man came toward me, pointing a rifle. I caught the barrel and pointed it away from me, and then he put the gun on my stomach and shot. The PAC men thought I was dead. They took hold of me by my arms and legs and threw me into the canal. To stop myself from drowning I caught hold of the grass that grows on the sides of the canal. I could still hear shots and knew more people were being killed. Then, after a long time, when I could hear nothing more, I climbed out to the canal bank and lay down. Two boys who were also wounded came and lay near me. They got up and said they would go for help, but they didn't return.

"At about three o'clock in the morning I saw the lights of a vehicle. It was a motorcycle with a sidecar and a police inspector. He asked me what had happened, and I told him the PAC had shot me, and he sent his driver to get a jeep. He told me: 'Son, I'm going to take you to the hospital, but don't say anything about the PAC. Don't even mention it, otherwise I'll get you injected with poison in the hospital. If anyone asks you what happened, just say you went to look for your brother and were shot by accident for violating the curfew. Don't say anything about the PAC.'

"So I did what he told me. Later, I was brought to Delhi for treatment, and my parents were informed and came to see me. Only then did I say what had actually happened."

Mohammed Osman showed an entry wound on the lower right side of his abdomen and a larger exit wound on his back.

Siddiqi's Story

One of the men who had been listening all the while and interjecting occasional comments was Naeemuddin. Aditi knew him well: he had become a local activist since the massacre. She said he was married with two children, was a nephew of Jamaluddin, and that one of his brothers was among those shot on the canal bank.

Jamaluddin insisted we stay for lunch. Since it would take time to prepare, Naeemuddin said we should go to Maliana to see what happened there. The route was along a narrow, crowded road, across railroad tracks, and finally down a turnoff to the usual segregated area for Dalits. The small stone houses, with narrow lanes and open drains, were built under some program to house the lowest Hindu castes and their economic equivalents among Muslims. One section was occupied by *bhangis* (scavengers) and *chamars* (leather workers); the other was home mainly for Muslim rickshaw men, the most arduous and poorly paid of occupations.

There was an open, marshy area before the houses into which much of the sewage from the house drains collected. On slightly higher ground, just before the houses, there were graves: some with headstones, some unmarked. Also, some of the mounds were wider than others. Naeemuddin said these were graves of persons killed on the afternoon of May 23. The wider graves were where two or three people had been put in a single pit. There were about a dozen persons buried in the area. Others were buried in a formal Muslim graveyard some distance away. A young man named Siddiqi told of the start of the killings:

"Four or five PAC trucks came, and the jawans surrounded the Muslim population from all sides. They gave no warning; they just began to fire. Then they entered houses, and the chamars came with them and began looting and setting fire to the houses. The people came out of their houses and gathered at this empty field. They said, 'Either you arrest us or kill us right here.'

"Then the deputy superintendent of police came in a jeep and asked, 'What has happened here. Now tell us what you want.' The elders of the village said they needed hospital attention. He ordered them to go back to their houses. The people said, 'We're not going back; you can arrest us if you want.' Later, some of our men went with the police to the station to call the Central Reserve Police Force (CRPF). Those whose houses were burned down went to their friends' places, and the CRPF was there for two days."

The CRPF is a separate paramilitary force under control of the central government. From Siddiqi's account it would appear none of the other forces knew in advance of the PAC attack on Maliana. There had been no clashes to attract official notice to the settlement. The killing and arson lasted less than three hours and was over by the time the other authorities learned what had happened.

Munni's Story

A characteristic of the poor in India is that few have options. Here were people whose homes had been burned and looted by their neighbors, who had seen loved ones killed, and yet they had to go on living in the same place with all the memories. Naeemuddin said there was a woman named Munni whose son was thrown into a fire. We walked through the maze of lanes and found her.

"My husband has a rickshaw," she said. "When people first heard about the riots, they got all the rickshaws of the area and collected them in a place surrounded by a wall in front of my house. On that day, when the PAC came, I heard some commotion and saw huge crowds climb on the roof of the house on the other side of my house, where the Hindu colony starts. When people saw them, they ran from here to the house on the opposite side of the lane. My son and I got separated. He was just four years old. He thought I was still at home, so he ran here to the house and called out for me. The entrance to our house was blocked by Harijans milling all around the courtyard where they had set fire to all the rickshaws. They just caught hold of him and threw him into the burning fire. I found his body the next morning. He was burned alive, but now his body was cold."

We walked to the end of the Muslim section of the Maliana. Naeemuddin wanted to show us a well where bodies had been thrown. It was outside a house where he said nine members of a Muslim family and two visitors were killed:

"Afterward, people who knew about the family wondered what had happened to them. They came and looked inside the house and found some bones but not of all the missing people. Then they looked down the well and saw pieces of bodies. They had been killed and chopped into little pieces and dropped in the well. The authorities had sprinkled some chemical down the well to speed the decomposition, so they have never been buried: the bones are still there, men, women, and children. They had a son who is the only living member of the family."

In all it is believed eighty persons were killed in the space of a few hours in Maliana.

Naeemuddin's Story

When we returned to Meerut, lunch was not ready: obviously the women of the house were preparing special dishes for the unexpected guests. While we waited, we sat on a roof watching children fly kites, and I asked Naeemuddin how he became active in neighborhood affairs.

"I wasn't active about these things earlier: it's only after going to jail that I understood how the system works," he said. "I'm twenty-six years old and have no school education, but I can read and write. I'm not afraid any more. I saw it all in jail: people were so badly beaten that some lost their arms or legs. In my barracks there were two hundred men. We became united then, and we're still united. I'm trying to learn to read better with the help of small children. I'm also trying to learn English. I'm engaged in getting ration cards and other documents the people need.

"Many Congress people have made overtures to us. There's a magistrate named Paliwal who came in his jeep and the full paraphernalia—outriders, police guards with guns, the works—to distribute blankets to widows. He told me gently, 'Do your work and don't get involved in cases against the government.' What he meant was I shouldn't take an interest in the case that has been filed against the PAC. Paliwal said, 'If there's anything you need, the government will help you but don't fight cases.'

"But he made this offer of peace to us in an armed jeep. I told Paliwal, 'One of my brothers was killed in the canal. I'm not going to forget. I can imagine how the bullet must have hit him and how showers of his blood and bits of his flesh were spattered on the ground. I can never forget the scene, never in my life.'

"They've built a police post in Hashimpura. They want Hashimpura to submit. For instance, recently a poor Bihari rickshaw man was beaten up by the police, and his watch and other belongings were taken away. We didn't know if he was a Hindu or a Muslim, but he was very poor. He was sitting on the road crying. Some people came to me and told me about the man. I went to see him. He was still crying, and suddenly I was filled with rage. I told him to come along with me and show me the policemen who beat and robbed him.

"There were some policemen and home guards sitting at the station when we arrived. I told them, 'Look here, what you're doing is not correct. He's a poor man, and you have no right to harass anyone like this. Why must you do it in our neighborhood?' There was one home guard who belongs to our locality, and he recognized me. He said satirically, 'Welcome, oh leader.' I told him, 'Cut the crap, what you're doing is wrong. It's not fair to oppress a poor person and that, too, in our area.' The home guard man told the others I was Jamaluddin's nephew, and they got worried there might be trouble, and they gave the rickshaw man back his watch and other belongings.

"We realize the smallest spark today can cause a fire, so we're anxious to keep the peace in our area, but we're not going to sit on our backsides any more."

The Story of Momin's Wife

Thinking of his anger had reminded Naeemuddin of one other person we should see. She was a woman whose baby had been killed by the PAC. She lived just behind the Imliyan mosque, amid the constant din of power looms. She was referred to, in Muslim fashion, as the wife of her husband, who was named Momin. At a corner just before her house was a small mound of earth. Naeemuddin said the baby was bashed against a wall at that spot and then was buried there.

Momin's wife, with a gray shawl over her head, remained silent as we entered a courtyard and sat before her on a low string bed. Her sister-in-law told Aditi what happened:

"Momin went out to get some medicines for the little girl. She was four months old. Suddenly, the PAC announced through a voice hailer that all young men should come out of their houses, and then they poured into the streets. One of them saw Momin and took the baby from his arms and threw her against the wall. Then they took Momin away. He never came back. He was beaten in jail so badly he died."

Momin's wife began to cry as her sister-in-law recalled the scene. The sister-in-law began to cry too. She said her grandfather had died just a week earlier.

"We lost three members of our family in eight days," she said. "How are we to protect ourselves? Perhaps Allah meant it to be this way. My brother was so fond of me. He used to tease me and pull my hair. He had broad shoulders and was so fair. Now he's gone."

After lunch Aditi and I left to return to Delhi, stopping briefly at the canal where the men had been shot. Our driver, who had visited the scene not long after the killings, said the CID burned the grass and weeds to remove the blood stains and cut down trees with bullet marks.

The People's Union for Democratic Rights, the second of India's major human rights organizations, conducted a lengthy investigation into the Meerut Massacre, taking scores of affidavits from those who suffered or who saw others being beaten and tortured in three jails where the arrested persons were taken. The affidavits were filed as part of a PUDR petition to the Supreme Court asking for the arrest and trial of PAC and police officers.

Documentation on those taken away in the vans to the Moradnagar canal and whose bodies have not been recovered was presented to the forty-fifth session of the Human Rights Commission in Geneva in February 1989. The commission has a category for the "disappeared," derived from those missing after their arrest by the military regime in Argentina.

The leader of the Indian delegation, S. S. Ahluwalia, objected to "giving credence to unsubstantiated allegations" and said the Indian constitution and judicial system "had ample protection for human rights." He said "additional safeguards existed in the form of a completely free and unfettered press . . . and healthy political institutions."

The *Economic and Political Weekly* dismissed his statement as hypocrisy, saying "ever-increasing" human rights violations were "unscrewing every nut and bolt of whatever little constitutional safeguards we enjoyed all these years."

In addition to the loss of its constitutional liberties, respect for human life is disappearing as India is consumed by the politics of passion.

47 ☀ The Politics of Passion

After independence the rising Green Revolution prosperity of Sikh farmers clashed with the existing network of Hindu traders, merchants, and industrialists. In a less structured and caste-ridden society prosperity might have eroded traditional solidarities and symbols, but in Punjab it merely heightened ethnic consciousness.

In India religion, culture, and economics form the politics of passion. The manipulation of religion of Hindus and Muslims led to the partition of the subcontinent. A similar manipulation by Hindus and Sikhs has led to the present demand of Sikh terrorists for an independent state to be called Khalistan, "Land of the Pure." But Punjab is part of traditional India's shield against invaders and is residual India's land bridge to Jammu and Kashmir. It is also the breadbasket of north India, and its waters are the lifeblood of Haryana and Rajasthan. Any political party charged with ruling India can make no other choice: Punjab must remain Indian by persuasion or force.

The founder of Sikhism was Guru Nanak, born in Punjab in 1469. He rejected Hindu idolatry, challenged Brahmin authority, and preached human equality. The essential brotherhood of man was symbolized by the *langar* (free community kitchen) in which all participated.

Ram Das, the fourth Guru, founded the holy city of Amritsar with a *gurdwara* (temple) known as the *Harmandir*. As the community grew, the Mogul empire perceived Sikhs as a political force, not just a religious sect, and during the reign of Aurangzeb, the ninth Guru, Tegh Bahadur, was decapitated and so were the two young sons of the tenth Guru, Gobind Singh.

The politics of passion was the same then as now: repression led to increased militancy. Even before his birth it was prophesied Gobind

Singh would "convert jackals into tigers and sparrows into hawks." He chose *Baisakhi*, (the north Indian Hindu New Year, observed in spring) when his followers normally gathered in large numbers at the Harmandir. He appeared from behind a curtain with a drawn sword and demanded the head of a loyal Sikh. He had to repeat the demand three times before a single volunteer stepped forward, willing to sacrifice his life for the guru. Gobind took him behind the curtain and came out with a blood-stained sword. He did this four more times, asking men for their lives. Then he opened the curtain and showed all five were alive: he had cut off the heads of goats to imitate their sacrifice.

These five formed the nucleus of a new brotherhood, the *Khalsa* (Pure). Males adopted the common surname of *Singh* (lion) and wore the five symbols of *kes* (uncut hair), *kanga* (comb), *kara* (a steel bracelet), *kirpan* (sword), and *kachcha* (type of drawers). They were further prohibited the use of tobacco and of meat slaughtered in the Muslim fashion. Before his death Gobind announced the line of personal gurus had ended, and henceforth the *Granth Sahib*, the book containing the teachings of the gurus, was to be regarded as the spiritual authority, while temporal aspects were to be vested in the *Khalsa Panth* (collective wisdom of the devout). He also fortified Amritsar and built the *Akal Takht* (Throne of the Timeless, or Immortal) opposite the Harmandir. From the Akal Takht he issued temporal orders and from the Harmandir spiritual guidance. Together they became the Golden Temple: a striking visual representation of the unity of politics and religion.

The turban and beard, steel bracelet, langar, and *akhand panth* (uninterrupted reading of the Granth Sahib) unite Sikhs. But syncretic Indians do not observe sharp distinctions. It was customary for one member of a Punjabi family to adopt Khalsa practices without being seen as any less of a Hindu. Sometimes there were more non-Khalsa worshippers at gurdwaras than Sikhs.

From Sikh Militancy to Gandhian Nonviolence

With the beginnings of the British devolution of power, English-educated Sikhs and Hindus jockeyed for jobs and identity politics came to Punjab.

Beginning in 1920 militant *Tat Khalsa* (Truly Pure) reformers pressed for the recovery of Sikh shrines from hereditary non-Khalsa mahants who had introduced idols and other non-Sikh practices. The agitation continued sporadically until 1925, by which time 30,000 Sikhs had been arrested, four hundred killed, and two thousand wounded. The agitation saw the genesis of the *Shiromani Gurdwara Prabhandak* (Central Gurdwara Management) Committee (SGPC) and its political and agitational wing, the *Akali Dal* (Army of Immortals).

In the early stages the British seized the keys of the *toshakhana* (treasury) of the Golden Temple. In May 1921 the Akalis pledged themselves to Gandhi's noncooperation movement and threatened a satyagraha in front of the temple. When the British gave the keys to the SGPC, Gandhi sent a telegram to its president: "First decisive battle for India's freedom won. Congratulations."

He thus signaled the gurdwaras were a legitimate symbol both of dignity and freedom and affirmed the struggle for a religious cause was not only a political struggle for a particular community but also part of the national struggle.

Although their tradition was armed militancy, the Sikhs in 1922 enacted one of the world's greatest dramas of nonviolent resistance. The scene was Guru-ka-Bagh (Guru's Garden), a small shrine twelve miles from Amritsar built to mark a visit of Guru Arjun. It began when some Akalis cut down a tree on land adjoining the gurdwara for use as fuel in the community kitchen. The mahant complained it was his property. A few weeks later more Akalis went and cut trees, and the British sent police to safeguard the mahant's "person and property." The Akalis persisted, and by August 24, 110 had been arrested.

The politics of passion held sway: British officials said if they backed down on this small issue they would have to back down on everything, and the Akalis thought if they lost this campaign they would lose the war.

When the SGPC dispatched Akali *jathas* (roughly, a militant procession) of fifty men, the police declared them an illegal assembly and ordered them to disperse. At first the Sikhs were simply arrested, but as jatha followed jatha, the police began to beat them with lathis and kick them with their boots. The *shaheeds* (martyrs) let themselves be beaten until they fell unconscious and were carried off to jail, only to be replaced by more men.

Fervor mounted. At daily prayer meetings at the Akal Takht volunteers took an oath to remain nonviolent and yet undeterred in fulfilling their religious duty. Their jatha then marched to the Guru-ka-Bagh, with thousands of Sikhs cheering them along the road. The jathas became larger: one hundred men, then 120. War veterans had a special jatha as did college graduates and college students. It became a *Dharam Yudh* (Holy War). Charles Andrews, the British Quaker who was Gandhi's foremost foreign propagandist, called the beatings "inhuman, brutal, foul, cowardly and incredible to an Englishman."

In November 1922, with more than four thousand Akalis in jail, the protest ended with a settlement under which a Hindu philanthropist bought the disputed land and allowed Akalis access to it.

The Birth of the Khalistan Movement

After independence, when internal boundaries were changed in 1955 to form new states, Sikhs complained that with fourteen languages recognized by the constitution, thirteen states had been formed on a linguistic basis but not one for Punjabi speakers. This was the beginning of the agitation for *Punjabi Suba* (Punjabi-speaking state) that lasted for twenty years and metamorphosed into the demand for Khalistan.

Master (an honorific) Tara Singh, the small, burly, always aggressive Sikh who epitomized Akali politics from the 1920s to the 1960s, charged Sikhs were "bound hand and foot to the slavery of an aggressively communal group." Pointing to the Sikh role in the freedom struggle, he asked, "The Muslims got Pakistan, the Hindus got Hindustan, but what did we Sikhs get out of it?"

A separate state, with a 60 percent Sikh majority, was formed in 1966 by detaching Hindi-speaking districts to form the new states of Himachal Pradesh and Haryana. But the Congress Party had the skill, money, and jobs to divide the Sikhs and win over many of their leaders, so the Akalis were never able to win a majority in the state assembly.

Two generations of toying with the Sikh identity demoralized both the Akali Dal and the Congress Party in Punjab. All politicians were branded as corrupt, self-seeking, and insincere: particularly Sikh leaders who ping-ponged from the Akali Dal to the Congress and back to the Akalis according to the rewards of office.

Then a man presented himself in the tradition of the *Panj Pyaras* (the five who offered their heads to Gobind Singh) and was acclaimed a redeemer.

Jarnail Singh Bhindranwale, the youngest of seven sons, was a boy when he entered the Damdama *Taksal* (seminary), where the fanaticism of its teachings was illustrated by the death of its fourteenth leader, *Sant* (saint) Kartar Singh, who in 1977 injured his head but refused to allow doctors to cut his hair so they could operate and so died with his Sikh identity intact.

Bhindranwale, then in his late twenties, succeeded Kartar Singh.

He had a large hooked nose and deep eyes, a chest-length beard, a black turban tied in a high, flat circle, and he wore a robe ending a little below his knees.

In September 1980 he was arrested for masterminding the murder of a rival Sikh leader but was released a month later, reportedly at the behest of Indira Gandhi. Mrs Gandhi had consistently tried to divide the opposition in all the states of India by favoring rivals to local power. It is widely believed she encouraged the rise of Bhindranwale to undercut support for the Akali Dal. If true, it was a Machiavellian gambit for which she would pay with her life.

When the idea of Khalistan was broached a few years earlier, its supporters seemed to be playacting: printing their own money and passports and installing what they proclaimed to be the radio station of free Khalistan in the Golden Temple. But in 1981 Bhindranwale cloaked the concept with Sikh mysticism and legend, traveling through Punjab conducting *amrit* (baptismal) ceremonies to induct thousands into a pure life without alcohol, tobacco, drugs, gambling, pornography, and fornication and posing for pictures with a pistol at his waist and a silver arrow in his hand. The arrow was in imitation of Maharajah Ranjit Singh who, before the extension of British rule to northern India, carved a short-lived Sikh kingdom from the remnants of the Mogul empire. Sant Bhindranwale quoted one of Guru Gobind Singh's best known couplets:

> *Koi kissi ko raaj na day hai*
> *Jo lay hai nij bal say lay hai*
> Nobody will give you power
> You have to wrest it by force.

Bhindranwale attracted a coterie of terrorists who robbed banks and killed hundreds of Hindus and those dubbed Sikh apostates. The authorities replied with random searches of anyone with a beard and turban, angering neutral Sikhs who felt their community was being humiliated: the terrorists swam in an expanding sea of sympathy. However, when the terrorists began random killings of groups of Hindus, hoping to precipitate mass flight, thereby creating a de facto Khalistan, Bhindranwale no longer could count on behind-the-scenes government support and moved to the sanctuary of the Golden Temple. There, strutting with his weapons and guards armed with illegal automatic weapons, he cowed Sikhs who opposed him into silence while former moderate Sikhs competed with shows of bravado.

The Attack on the Golden Temple

On June 3, 1984, the Akalis announced a campaign to stop the movement of food grains out of Punjab and that gave Mrs Gandhi the excuse to mobilize troops to surround and isolate Amritsar. On June 5 she unleashed heavily armed assault forces to seize the Golden Temple. In a two-day attack code-named Operation Bluestar, the Akal Takht and the *Parikrama* (the marbled corridor surrounding the sacred tank with its gold-domed temple in the center) were both heavily damaged. Some bullets grazed the temple itself.

The Sikhs put up a fierce resistance, killing 83 soldiers and wounding 253. Bhindranwale and his supporters were all killed. The government has never revealed how many other Sikhs—innocent men and women in the gurdwara at the time of a major pilgrimage—were also killed: the common estimate is one thousand. Hundreds of others were killed when the army and police simultaneously raided other gurdwaras throughout the state. In addition, at least four thousand men and women, and even some children, were arrested.

The question will always remain: why did Mrs Gandhi do it? The Golden Temple was not just another shrine: it was what Mecca and Medina are to Islamic peoples and of greater emotional value to Sikhs than the Vatican to Catholics. Was she blinded by illusions of grandeur and so determined to strengthen the Congress Party that she refused to seek a negotiated settlement that was bound to strengthen the Akalis in Punjab?

Why did she change a political confrontation into a military confrontation? How could such an experienced politician not be aware that to confront the Sikhs, with their long tradition of military service, with a military defeat, was a humiliation that could not go unavenged? The assault was guaranteed to increase terrorism, not curb it.

Sikhs believe it was neither an accident nor a blunder. They say the Congress Party wanted to demonstrate to all Indians it had the means and will to suppress a minority challenge to Brahminic hegemony.

Blood for Blood

At 9:05 on the morning of October 21, 1984, Indira Gandhi walked past the bougainvillaea at her home at One Safdarjung Road in New Delhi, moving quickly along a wide paved path to a garden to meet actor Peter Ustinov and a television camera team. At midpoint Beant Singh, a former Delhi police subinspector who had been made a member of her security guard, stepped forward, raised his service revolver, and, just as she nodded as if to return his greetings, shot five times. A second later, another security guard, Satwant Singh, fired twenty-five rounds from his carbine into her body. They then calmly gave themselves up while aides, recovering from shock, rushed her to a hospital where she died shortly after arrival.

Beant Singh and Satwant Singh were taken by members of the Indo-Tibetan Border Police to their guardhouse where half an hour later the ITBP men shot and killed Beant and critically wounded Satwant. He later recovered and was hanged, along with an uncle said to be an accomplice.

Later that afternoon the government admitted Indira Gandhi was dead, and television cameras broadcast the scene as notables came to pay their respects and crowds shouted their grief. Some also shouted, *"Khoon ka badla khoon"* (Blood for blood). Others were shown trying to hush them, but still the words were heard clearly across the nation. Soon mobs slaughtered Sikhs in Delhi, and Sikhs were dragged from trains and killed in Ghaziabad and Kanpur in Uttar Pradesh and even in Bokaro in distant Bihar. Some said the words broadcast by Doordarshan were a deliberate signal to her supporters to take revenge.

Even later, after he was hastily elected to succeed his mother, Rajiv Gandhi said at his installation: "When a big tree falls the earth must tremble." Rather than expressing remorse for the killings, his words seemed to justify them.

A Masterminded Massacre

Soon after the killings investigators for the People's Union for Democratic Rights and the People's Union for Civil Liberties interviewed survivors and eyewitnesses. In a report, *Who Are the Guilty?*, the two groups concluded:

The attacks . . . far from being a spontaneous expression of 'madness' and of popular 'grief and anger' at Mrs Gandhi's assassination, as made out to be by the authorities, were the outcome of a well-organized plan marked by acts of both deliberate commissions and omissions by important politicians of the Congress at the top and by authorities in the administration. . . . The uniformity in the sequence of events at every spot in such far flung places prove beyond doubt that the attacks were master-minded by some powerful organized groups.

It said the instigators first floated rumors Sikhs were distributing sweets and lighting lamps to celebrate Mrs Gandhi's death. Then rumors were floated that trains with hundreds of Hindu dead bodies had arrived at Old Delhi station from Punjab and that Delhi's water was poisoned by the Sikhs. Policemen in vans even toured some localities announcing the train and poisoning stories. (The same tactic—floating rumors of cutting off the breasts of Hindu or Muslim women—would later be used to provoke the killings in Meerut in 1987.)

Then, according to the PUDR and PUCL, on the night of October 31 and the morning of November 1, groups of men from surrounding villages, armed with clubs, iron bars, and *trishuls* (a three-pointed spear representing Siva's trident) and carrying cans of kerosene were taken to Sikh residential and commercial centers where they systematically set fire to Sikh houses, shops, and gurdwaras.

Despite an indefinite curfew and shoot-at-sight orders, the numbers of arsonists and looters swelled. In such cases the government is usually quick to summon the army to bolster and discipline local forces, but not in this case. Several thousand troops were mustered for Mrs Gandhi's funeral, but the army was not called out for riot duty until most of the damage was done, and even then it played a minor role in restoring order.

Many Hindus and Muslims sheltered Sikh neighbors at risk to themselves, but they were a small percentage of those living in any area. Most just watched passively, perhaps feeling too weak or too frightened to intervene, especially since the authorities were themselves passive. Some also cheered on the rioters. Ever since the emergence of Bhindranwale, newspapers had been full of stories of Sikh terrorist atrocities in Punjab. It was time, many thought, to teach the Sikhs a lesson: *khoon ka badla khoon*.

Individual Tragedies

In Trilokpuri, Nanki Bai lost fourteen members of her extended family. Most were women and young children who had locked themselves in a room for safety: the rioters tore open the ceiling, poured kerosene through the hole, and set the room on fire. When the people tried to escape, they were stoned and pushed back into the burning room.

Gurmeet Singh Gill lived near the Cantonment, once considered a haven of peace on the outskirts of Delhi. He took early retirement from the air force, got a job in a bank, and built a house with funds remitted from a relative who worked in Africa. When the attack on Sikh homes started, twenty-one persons were killed in a single nearby house, so he took shelter with a neighbor and shaved off his beard and hair. A Sikh with a beard and turban is invariably addressed as *Sardar* (an honorific that has lost meaning and simply means a male Sikh). He thought he could go out and no one would recognize him as a Sardar.

"As we were standing just near the house where I was being sheltered, we saw a child of about ten, dressed in a salwar-kameez, who was moving on the road," he told an investigator for the PUDR-PUCL. "The child was walking quite normally down the street. He was actually a young boy in the process of fleeing to safety and had been dressed as a girl. Something about the child's appearance made the mob suspect that the child was a boy and some shouted, 'It must be the son of a Sardar.' The child panicked and started running, but the mob pursued him and caught him. They asked him where the other members of his family were. The boy was really frightened, and he pointed in a certain direction and said that his father was lying there and that he was dead. To my horror the mob dragged the boy up to the father's body, threw the child on him, and burnt him saying, 'This is the son of a snake, finish him off also.'"

Some of the mobs went to the train stations to waylay arrivals. A train from Baroda in Gujarat arrived at the Tughlakabad station in New Delhi late on the morning of November 1. Passengers bolted doors and windows when they heard mobs were lynching Sikhs, but the mobs shouted they would burn an entire car unless the doors were opened, and so the passengers complied.

"They just ruthlessly hunted down the Sikhs without any mercy," a housewife named Ratnabehn told an investigator. "An old man was dragged out of the compartment by his hair and felled with an iron rod on the platform. After that they first burnt his hair, and then he was fully doused with kerosene and set on fire. It was a terrible sight. I can't describe how awful it was to watch what was going on. Two other younger men tried to run away, but they were caught and also attacked at some distance from the compartment. The old man who had been set on fire near the compartment continued to burn, screaming with agony, and remained alive right through the time the train remained halted at the station. I can't forget that scene. The crowd on the platform kept on inciting the people who were actually doing the attacking. It was horrible."

The train was at the station three hours. About twenty-five Sikhs were killed on that one train.

The Making of a Minority

Although Sikhs saw themselves as having a separate religion, they also felt they were Indians: in fact the bravest and most patriotic of Indians. Out of 121 persons hanged for fighting the British for independence, 93 were Sikhs. Out of 2,646 persons imprisoned for life during the freedom struggle, 2,147 were Sikhs. An estimated two-thirds of those killed or wounded at Jallianwalla Bagh were Sikhs. And 60 percent of the officers and soldiers who heeded Subhas Chandra Bose's call to join the Indian National Army and fight the British in World War II were Sikhs.

The attack on the Golden Temple, the slaughter of whole families in their homes, and the failure to punish those responsible for the murders turned Sikhs into a new minority, with feelings of insecurity and persecution similar to that of Muslims.

The PUDR and PUCL pamphlet *Who Are the Guilty?* specifically named fifteen Congress Party officials—including three members of Parliament and a member of the cabinet—thirteen police officers, and 198 others as instigators or participants in the killings and looting. The government appointed a number of commissions to investigate. One of these acknowledged 2,733 persons were killed. With more than seven hundred others killed in Uttar Pradesh and Bihar, total deaths were about 3,500. Yet not a single person of importance has been brought to trial.

Murder charges were registered for 1,419 deaths in Delhi, but the few cases brought to trial were dismissed for the flimsiest of reasons. Two widows who identified a local milk vendor as the man who killed their husbands had their suits dismissed when a judge ruled they were trying "to escape paying him their dues for the three months of milk supply." Another case was dismissed due to the "unreliability of the eyewitness account." The eyewitness was a woman who was the sole surviving member of a large family that had been wiped out by the mob. She saved her life by taking shelter with neighboring women. The judge found "the attitude and conduct of the witness strange. Her kith and kin were being butchered, and she had the audacity to say that she took shelter with a crowd of women."

After four years there was only one exception: six persons in a residential area were found guilty of just one of the murders. They killed a neighbor and were sentenced to life imprisonment. A few other cases that ended in sentences were trivial. One man was sentenced for three months for rioting. Another was sentenced for six months for possession of stolen property. Another, convicted of theft, was released when he promised to maintain good behavior. Ten were fined twenty-five rupees for curfew violations.

But five of the thirteen police officials named by the PUDR-PUCL were promoted, and two of the named Congress Party leaders became central cabinet ministers.

Sikh Terrorism and Police Terrorism

On May 10, 1985, forty-two persons were killed by simultaneous bomb explosions in Delhi and other parts of north India. On June 23, 1985, 329 died when an Air-India Boeing 747 crashed off Ireland following the explosion of a bomb believed to have been planted by Sikh terrorists. Two days later terrorists shot fifteen Hindu bus passengers near Muktsar in Punjab's Faridkot District. On November 30, 1986, twenty-four bus passengers were killed near Khuda in Hosiarpur District. On June 13, 1987, fourteen were killed by terrorist attacks on several homes in Delhi. On July 6 and 7, 1987, seventy bus passengers were killed in two separate attacks on buses in Punjab's Patiala District and in Haryana's Hissar District. In the first twenty-five days of January 1988, 129 persons were killed, including twenty members of three families, among them eleven women and children. In February nine members of a family mistakenly identified as informers were wiped out by terrorists said to be only fifteen years old. The following November almost 180 persons were killed in a single two-week period.

The homes of the rich and influential in New Delhi and the streets past their houses are sandbagged fortresses, with police staring at everyone who passes. At night anyone walking or driving may be stopped for questioning.

So many Sikhs have suffered that the terrorists no longer swim in a sea of sympathy. The loss was demonstrated after members of the Damdama Saheb Taksal, the seminary that nurtured Bhindranwale, took control of the Golden Temple in mid-April 1988 and flew the Khalistan flag, calling for an armed struggle against the government. This time, instead of repeating the blunders of Operation Bluestar, the government merely surrounded the temple and placed disciplined sharp shooters on higher surrounding buildings. On May 15, after weeks of sporadic gunfire, in which two police officers were wounded and thirty-three terrorists killed, the 146 persons remaining inside surrendered. Some, recognized as terrorists, killed themselves by swallowing cyanide capsules.

Later, digging into rubble left over from the rebuilding of the Akal Takht after the army's assault in 1984, authorities discovered the mutilated bodies of about three dozen alleged informers. They had been killed after tortures such as being forced to sit on hot electric plates or having their flesh torn with iron pincers. Police and paramilitary forces were praised for cleansing the shrine of defilement.

Instead of building on this sympathy by relaxing controls and cultivating the active support of the Sikh public, the government continued a savage repression that failed to distinguish between who was a terrorist and who was someone forced to give shelter and support.

In the four years since the assault on the Golden Temple, Punjab has been under virtual martial law, although without the active presence of the army. The government has never said how many men have been assigned to antiterrorist duties in Punjab: estimates range from 80,000 to 100,000. Government estimates of the number of active terrorists have ranged from as low as five hundred to as high as three thousand. And yet, in the period from May 1987 to August 1988, while claiming to have killed 508 "terrorists," the government admits an additional 5,199 persons were arrested. Obviously, many more people are being killed and arrested than even the government admits are terrorists.

Human rights activists say repressive laws hide the truth that most of those labeled as terrorists in police body counts are innocent victims of a police force.

From 1983 to 1988 eighteen special laws were passed to give greater power to the security forces in Punjab. The National Security Act, as amended in 1984, permits detention without trial or charge for a maximum of two years to prevent what are vaguely defined as activities "prejudicial to the defense or security of India."

The Terrorist Affected Areas (Special Courts) Act of August 1984 permits special courts not only for those involved in the use of violence but also for making "imputations, assertions prejudicial to national integration." The special courts can hold secret trials in jails, with the identity of witnesses kept secret, thus inhibiting cross-examinations. Even worse, the burden of proof is transferred to an accused, and a person can be presumed guilty merely be being shown to have been present at a place where firearms or explosives were used. A person can also be convicted on the uncorroborated confession of a coaccused to a police officer: this in a country where confessions are routinely extorted by torture. Even during the worst of British attempts to suppress Mahatma Gandhi's satyagrahas, the police never had such sweeping authority. Police power, down to the constable level, knows no checks.

In October 1983 the popularly elected government of Punjab was dismissed, and the state was ruled by a governor appointed from New Delhi. The man selected was Siddhartha Shankar Ray, the former Congress Party chief who had ruthlessly suppressed the Naxalites in West Bengal. He remained as the titular governor after elections were allowed in October and an Akali chief minister was installed as the head of a popular government. The Akalis were dismissed in 1985. That government was dismissed in May 1987, returning full authority to Siddhartha Shankar Ray.

There was an attempt to uncover the facts of police terrorism during the period of self-rule. In late January 1986 retired Justice C. S. Tiwana of the Punjab and Haryana High Court studied reports of thirty-five "encounter" deaths and found almost all of them fake. He also investigated practices at an isolated former "pleasure" house of the Maharajah of Patiala in Sangrur District known as Ladha Kothi: far out of earshot, it had been converted into an interrogation and torture center for detainees.

Justice Tiwana accused police of "ruthlessly indulging in apprehending innocent persons and killing some of them." He said ninety Sikh detainees had been tortured, including the "tying of fecal matter around their mouths" and the "application of electric currents on their bodies." He described two types of torture, including the dreaded "roller" used on alleged Naxalites in the 1970s:

> Either it is placed on the front side of the thighs or on the back. In the latter position, the lower parts of the legs are folded and are pressed against the log. In the former position, the victim is made to sit on the floor, with one person standing at his back, supporting his back with his knees and holding his shoulders with his hands. In this way, the person is fixed to the ground. The legs are spread on the floor and the log is placed on the thighs. One person or two persons sit or stand on the log while some other rotate it. The weight causes intense pressure on the nerves.

The second form of torture consists of stretching the legs apart to the extent it is unbearable. This is done in two different ways: in a sitting posture and in a lying posture. In the first position, the victim is made to sit on a plain surface and his hands tied-up or handcuffed with one person supporting his back with his knees. Two other persons hold his legs at the ankle level and push them apart to the maximum extent. In the other position, the individual is made to lie down on a plain surface. His shoulders are held by two persons so that he is firmly fixed to the ground and two others hold the legs at the ankle level and pull the legs apart.

Justice Tiwana ordered compensation of between ten and twenty thousand rupees (approximately $1,000 or $2,000 at the prevailing exchange rate) for each of the ninety victims, and the money was eventually paid.

The Case of Bhupinder Singh

After the popular government was dismissed, and the further possibility of penetrating the security curtain was ended, several human rights attorneys and other activists in New Delhi formed the Committee for Information and Initiative on Punjab. One case they investigated involved the death of Bhupinder Singh Sarang, eighteen, a tenth class student at the high school in the village of Muktsar.

On the evening of May 20, 1987, after Bhupinder returned home from a game of football, there was a knock on the door; when his mother answered, she found uniformed police demanding to see her son. They handcuffed him and took him away, after assuring his hysterical mother he would come back safely. When he was not returned that evening, his father sought the aid of Avtar Singh Sidhu, a leader of the town's Youth Akali Dal. The next morning they went to the police station where, after some pressure from Sidhu, they were taken to a cell where they saw Bhupinder Singh with blood stains on his face and legs, moaning with pain. Another prisoner in the cell said he had seen Bhupinder Singh tortured the previous night.

The torture continued until May 25 when Bhupinder was removed in a coma by several high-ranking police officials. A report was later entered in the records of the local police station of an encounter in which a terrorist was killed. According to the written record, the encounter occurred at one o'clock in the morning when a patrol ordered a car to stop. It did, but then three young men got out and fired at the patrol, which returned fire in self-defense, killing one. The other two were said to have fled under the cover of darkness.

The story ran in the local newspaper on May 26, without giving the name of the terrorist who had been killed. Bhupinder's father, Ujagar Singh, went to the police station and asked to be shown the body of the dead terrorist. He was told it had been sent to a hospital in a nearby town for postmortem examination. When Ujagar Singh went to the hospital, he was told the body had been returned to the police station, but he bribed a minor hospital worker and was shown the clothes removed from the body: it was the track suit his son was wearing on the night of his arrest.

Two days later Ujagar Singh himself was arrested and released after eight hours with a warning that if he told others what had happened he would meet the same fate as his son. He was arrested again on June 7 to prevent him from attending *bhog* ceremonies to appease the soul of his son and released the next morning. He was arrested for a third time in January 1988 while on his way to a religious function where he was expected to sing hymns. He was taken to a police station, again warned not to talk about his dead son in any religious congregation, and was released the next evening after the intervention of his local member of Parliament. In April 1988, when he was interviewed by a member of the Committee for Information and Initiative, he said, "I am waiting for them to kill me."

The Ordeal of an Innocent Bystander

Iqbal Singh also lives in Muktsar. His unlucky story began on June 3, 1984, when he went to the city of Patiala to see a doctor about an injured finger. The doctor told him to come back in a few days, but a curfew had suddenly been imposed, and the buses were not running, so he went, as Sikhs do in such circumstances, to stay at the local gurdwara.

The reason for the curfew was the attack on the Golden Temple. Simultaneously, the army attacked Gurdwara Dukha Niwaran in Patiala, where Iqbal Singh was staying. There was a battle in which scores of persons were killed, after which the survivors, including Iqbal Singh, were taken into military custody. Later, he was sent to a jail in the city of Nabha, and then in December he was taken to Ladha Kothi where he was questioned and tortured for ten days and then returned to Nabha for detention without trial.

In August 1985, when the cases of those swept up following the

Golden Temple attack were reviewed, the charges against Iqbal Singh were dismissed, and he was released. The story of his torture formed part of the Tiwana Commission report and made him a marked man in the eyes of police. For his safety Iqbal Singh went to live with a brother in Maharashtra.

In January 1988 he received a telegram to come home to Muktsar: his father was seriously ill. He did and so returned to a repetition of the horrors of four years earlier. On April 12, 1988, as he was standing on a street, plainclothes police, driving an unmarked car with no-see-through windows and themselves wearing tinted glasses, came up, dragged him inside, and drove him away, but not before he managed to call out he was being abducted by the Central Investigation Agency.

He was taken to a CIA interrogation center in the city of Faridkot and from there managed to smuggle out a note to his mother saying where he was. She contacted members of the Committee for Information and Initiative on Punjab, and a petition for his release was filed with the Supreme Court in New Delhi. The court granted the petition, and Iqbal Singh was freed on May 12 and later told his story:

"I was led into an office. My blindfold was removed. I was made to crouch on the floor while the Deputy Superintendent of Police Mr Joginder Singh and Police Inspector Mr Shyam Sundar sat on chairs. They immediately started to question me. . . . I told them the truth . . . but they proceeded to torture me. I was blindfolded once again. My clothes were torn off, and I was stripped naked. My turban was used to tie my hands to my back. My right leg was squeezed into a hole in a heavy block of wood which was suspended from the ceiling. I stood balancing myself on my left leg. After half an hour my leg was removed from the wooden block, and then I was hung upside down from the ceiling and beaten. After some time I was taken down. The toes of my feet were tied together and also my hands behind my back. Then I was made to lie down with my back to the floor. A heavy iron pipe was put on my legs. Four policemen got on top of it while two of them held the pipe tight across my legs from both ends and rotated it up and down. My thigh muscles ruptured. Then they started pulling my legs apart until I felt them ripping out from the pelvis. Then they started kicking me in the region of my sensitive organs. I became unconscious. I woke up in the cell. I don't know after how long."

There were several others in the cell. The next day Faridkot Senior Superintendent of Police Govind Ram came and waved his revolver, shouting if they did not confess their crimes he would personally shoot them all. Iqbal Singh said Govind Ram then stood by as his torture was resumed:

"First he ordered chili powder stuffed into my anus. Then he had petrol poured into it. Then he started working my legs all over again. I told him I was innocent and was being tortured unjustifiably. I fainted soon after."

The pattern was repeated daily for a week. One day, delirious and running a high fever, Iqbal Singh heard an officer say, "If he doesn't gain consciousness, kill him and throw him into a canal."

By that time the Committee for Information and Initiative had filed its petition to the Supreme Court, alerting police that Iqbal Singh had friends in New Delhi. He was surprised when Inspector Shyam Sundar came to the lockup and told him the interrogation had been unnecessary, saying, "You must try to recover soon. That will be in your interest. You may live if you can be on your legs."

Apparently, the police did not want to free him while he was crippled from torture, but Iqbal Singh was not aware of what was going on outside. A few days later, when he was put in a van and driven away, he thought he was being taken to be shot. Instead, he was driven to a hospital, where a doctor said he would give him an injection.

"I thought he was giving me poison," Iqbal Singh recalled. "I didn't care. I was more ready to die than live in that condition." He was also given medicine, and when he was taken back to the lockup, he began to recover, and the other detainees helped him to walk again. Only then was he released to tell the story of his ordeal.

In August 1988 Amnesty International issued *A Review of Human Rights Violations* summarizing recent evidence of abuses in India. India is believed to be the only democratic country that consistently does not allow Amnesty International researchers to probe human rights violations. Instead, the organization relies mainly on Indian civil and human rights activists.

The report said the most persistent allegations came from Punjab and cited a report by one unnamed Indian civil liberties group that seventy-three young Sikhs died in fake encounters in Amritsar District between May 12 and August 22, 1987, and the report of another unnamed group that twenty-six men were similarly killed in Faridkot District between May 12 and July 29, 1987.

A spokesman for the Indian government denounced the report as "one-sided and distorted," saying Amnesty International focused on "stray incidents of human rights," while minimizing "the numerous rights and freedoms enjoyed by Indian nationals and the independence of the press."

"We Will Keep Dying"

The government's refusal to acknowledge and halt police atrocities deepens the feeling among Sikhs that they have been reduced to the status of a persecuted minority. The horror of "blood for blood" is unending. The death of Jarnail Singh Bhindranwale in the Golden Temple gave him a claim to immortality. For several years cassettes purporting to contain the speeches of Sant Bhindranwale were sold openly in shops near the Golden Temple and other gurdwaras, but with police spies everywhere they now can only be purchased secretly. The most sought-after tape contains what is said to be the voice of Bhindranwale against the background noise said to be a helicopter. Villagers are told this proves he did not die: he was lifted away and awaits the day when the faithful are ready for his return. Even those not prepared to accept such superstition keep his photographs. The controversies surrounding his life are forgotten, and he is remembered only as the saint who created *amritdharis* (the baptized) pledged to the pure life of the Khalsa. He has become *amar shaheed* (eternal martyr).

When the government drove the terrorists out of the Golden Temple in 1988 and some surrendered instead of fighting to the death, cynics said the spirit had gone out of Sikh militancy. But a legend was found chalked on a wall: "We will keep dying but that won't finish us."

The pressures impelling Sikhs, Muslims, Dalits, and tribals to look inward arise from Brahminic Hindu claims of superiority and nationhood. In all of India there is only one religious leader boldly denouncing such claims: a Marxist professor who assumed the orange robes of a swami to use the Hindu belief in the oneness with God to foster modern, egalitarian democracy.

48 ❋ The Fiery Swami

Agni means fire, and Swami Agnivesh sees himself as a burning brand of religious rationality. He was born Vepa Shyam Rao in an Andhra Pradesh village that now is part of Orissa. In 1968, when he was twenty-seven, he resigned as a lecturer in law and business management at the exclusive St. Xavier College in Calcutta and left home for religious study. Two years later he took *sannyas* (the vow of poverty and chastity), putting on the saffron robes of an *Arya Samaj* (Aryan Assembly) swami.

The Arya Samaj was founded in 1875 by Swami Dayanand Saraswati, an ascetic from western India who preached a purified Hinduism, saying all that was good and true could be found in the Vedas and calling idol worship, caste, and the mistreatment of women later intrusions. Following his death in 1883 the Arya Samaj became an instrument in the new politics of religious passion, staging *shuddhi* (reconversion and purification) ceremonies to reclaim Muslims and Christians and eventually degenerating into an anti-Muslim, anti-Sikh defender of Hindu politics and politicians.

Agnivesh is an imposing man: about five feet ten with a deep voice and an unwrinkled face framed by a tightly wound saffron turban covering his ears and leaving only a triangle of his forehead showing. His office is in a large room at the rear of an old mansion in New Delhi, now divided into a jumble of offices and apartments. His only privacy is a small enclosed sleeping loft built into a section of the high-ceilinged room. There are no trappings of cultism: he has one full-time assistant plus a few office workers. I asked about the Arya Samaj's anti-Muslim reputation.

"When we inherit an organization, we inherit the wrong as well as the good. But when we examine the overall position, the good outweighs the liabilities. We find the Arya Samaj is the least communal of the religious organizations. I would not say there is no one in our group who is not communal in his outlook and in our one hundred year's history there have been people who have acted in communal disharmony. But remember in the 1920s when the Arya Samaj preached Hindus and Muslims were separate, there was also a separatist Muslim movement, and people who wanted to introduce reforms within Islam were resisted. Now historical circumstances are different."

To demonstrate his dislike of bigotry in all forms, Agnivesh welcomes any opportunity to join liberal, reform-minded Muslims in seminars and demonstrations. However, his consuming concern is reform of Hindu society and the struggle against secular evils.

Sati and Women in Hindu Society

In September 1987, in the Rajasthan village of Deorala, three hours drive from the state capital of Jaipur, an eighteen-year-old widow named Roop Kumar mounted the funeral pyre of her husband and was burned to death before the eyes of hundreds of spectators. In India small events have a way of suddenly bringing issues into the open, sharpening national debate. The conversions at Meenakshipuram were an example of this syndrome. So was Roop Kumar's death.

Sati (pronounced suttee, as was the earlier British phonetic spelling) has long loomed large in tales of foreign visitors to India, beginning with Marco Polo in 1293, Friar Odoric in 1321, and Friar Jordanus in 1323. The Muslim Ibn Batuta, who lived in India from 1323 to 1330, was so shocked at the burning alive of a widow he fainted. It became such a potent symbol of a backward, degraded India that the earliest stirring of the Indian renaissance in the eighteenth century focused on its abolition. It was legally banned by the British and has gradually disappeared, but there are still regular incidents to keep the practice fresh in memory.

Newspapers had reported incidents of sati in several states in 1979, 1980, 1982, and 1983, but only with Roop Kumar's death did the persistence of sati become notorious. Perhaps it was because she was so young or because she was an educated, middle-class woman. There was also the spectacle of Rajput youths circling the glowing ashes with drawn swords, praising Roop Kumar as a goddess of *sat* (truth or chastity) and her act as a renewal of a glorious tradition. Over the next few weeks, while the government hesitated, thousands of the devout made the pilgrimage to Deorala to worship at what, if let unchecked, would undoubtedly become a new temple and make the people of Deorala rich.

When Agnivesh assembled a small band of women and other activists for a protest march to Deorala, he was arrested for violating a ban on public assemblies. Although he was soon released, the protest march was effectively ended. He then took aim at Niranjan Dev Teerth, the head of the temple at Puri in Orissa, who had defended sati as justified by Hindu scripture. The Puri Temple is one of the four established by Sankara in the eighth century and is a sanctum of caste purity.

Niranjan Dev once banned the entry of Indira Gandhi, and when several thousand women demonstrated outside his *math* (monastery) in Puri, he called them "prostitutes." At another time he remarked there was nothing wrong with the constitution "excepting that it was made by an untouchable"—a reference to Bhimrao Ambedkar, the untouchable scholar who presided over the writing of the constitution. He later amended that to say the constitution contained 540 mistakes, including the belief that non-Brahmins could be equal to Brahmins.

Agnivesh challenged the Sankaracharya (teacher of Sankara's doctrines) to a *shastrarth* (an ancient form of religious debate to clarify doctrinal issues). He gathered another set of volunteers and set out on a march to confront him. Again an order was issued forbidding demonstrations, and Agnivesh was arrested and released, ending his march.

As the nearest thing to a debate, the *Illustrated Weekly of India* interviewed both men and presented their views in a single article.

For his part the Sankaracharya condemned a recently passed law banning sati as "against religion, civilization, culture, ethics, and morality" and defended Hindu practices denying equal treatment for women: "When the bodies are not equal, how can rights be equal? When the minds are not equal, how can rights be equal. . . . Our scriptures say that as compared to a man, a woman eats twice as much, is four times cleverer, six times braver and eight times more lustful. . . . It is to curb her and put her on the right path to heaven that we have these tenets."

The Sankaracharya said the scriptures permitted voluntary sati and asked what was the difference between a widow burning herself to death and a man doing the same thing as a political protest or an act of penance. But it has always been difficult to establish the voluntary nature of sati. In Roop Kumar's case a younger brother of the deceased husband, after his arrest for abetting sati, claimed the pyre lit itself "because of the divine power of sati." Her father-in-law, facing a similar charge, said he tried to hold her back but a force from inside her body threw him back and five thousand people witnessed this event.

Where there is a longing for miracles, facts will always be disputed.

For his part Agnivesh explained the Arya Samaj belief that the Vedas offered a democratic, egalitarian way of life and teachings to the contrary were later corruptions: "Sati is absolutely unthinkable. Widow persecution is also unthinkable. Caste based on birth and all the persecution that is concomitant to that type of philosophy is unthinkable. . . . Every individual has the freedom to choose."

At one point Agnivesh said the Vedas allowed a Muslim girl to marry a Brahmin boy if they felt compatible. His interviewer commented: "This is really pretty radical."

No Room for God's Children

In July 1988 I joined Agnivesh for another of his attention-getting marches: this time to allow Harijans (Children of God) to enter and worship at the Nathdwara Temple in Rajasthan, a major center for Hindu pilgrimage in northern India. He knew the march would end with his arrest, but that was part of the lesson: those who defended constitutional guarantees and liberties were silenced while those who practiced discrimination were protected.

Our march started from the city of Udaipur on a Sunday morning. Normally, shops would have been open and streets crowded, but caste Hindus had declared a strike, and no one dared oppose them. We were accompanied by files of armed police on both sides. There were about 150 men and a few women in the march, some with little placards around their necks identifying them as Dalits. After the first day crowds of men and boys who collected in small towns along the way grew openly hostile, waving black flags of protest, burning effigies of Agnivesh, and once throwing stones. The police, waving their lathis, chased them away.

At one town a group of men stood on the platform under a peepul tree and shouted, "Agnivesh down, down," and "Agnivesh will be buried, if not today, tomorrow." The marchers with Agnivesh replied with shouts of "We will go to Nathdwara and abolish untouchability" and "Swami Dayanand came to uplift women."

On the second night the district magistrate arranged a conciliation meeting at a small school. Community leaders from Nathdwara insisted anyone could enter the temple if he or she first went through a ceremony consisting of receiving a kind of necklace, eating a concoction made from leaves of the *tulsi* plant (basil, sacred to Vishnu), and reciting a formula accepting the Nathdwara deity as a savior.

The conciliation meeting was a show on the part of the district magistrate to demonstrate he had tried to keep the peace. No meeting of minds was expected, and none took place. The magistrate thereupon proclaimed a ban on demonstrations, and Agnivesh was arrested the next morning thirteen kilometers short of Nathdwara and released in Udaipur.

I did not stay for the charade. I wanted at least to see the outside of the temple and took a bus and found a room in a tiny hotel. Nathdwara was completely shut down. For two days state-owned buses and commandeered trucks had filled the town with several thousand men and boys, some armed with clubs, sticks, and chains. They jammed the narrow streets and beat their chests, vowing no one would pass except over their bodies.

The authorities had turned back Agnivesh as a threat to the peace but had done nothing to halt the thousands who blocked entry to the temple. The excuse of sacred rituals was also a farce. A month later twenty-four local Dalits went through the purification ceremonies: they accepted the necklace and the tulsi and said the *mantra* (sacred phrase). When they tried to enter the temple, they were pelted with stones, thrown out, and arrested for disturbing the peace.

Bonded Labor

After Agnivesh took sannyas, he formed a political party called the *Arya Sabha* (Aryan Assembly) to be active in the politics of Haryana (a state that surrounds the Union Territory of Delhi on three sides).

"It was hard to find money for elections, and we could see people acted according to caste and not ideology," he said. "Then the Congress Party started rigging elections in a massive way. Before the voting the Congress seemed to be defeated, but the results came through the other way around. I was sent to jail for fourteen months during the Emergency. Later, we merged the Arya Sabha with the Janata Party, which then won the national elections, and when the assembly elections were held, I was given a ticket and was easily elected from Kurukshetra district in 1977.

"Once in office I could see no difference between the Janata and the Congress people we had dislodged. There was the same old culture of sharing the loot, corruption, and masochism. Even when I became minister of education in 1979, I could see the words of the election manifesto did not mean anything. My own colleagues, who had dreamed of a new society and made sacrifices to bring that about, were also getting corrupted. I concluded elections as they were organized in this country would not provide an answer to the problems of our people."

A major factor in his decision to give up party politics was his experience in trying to liberate bonded quarry workers in an area of Haryana about thirty kilometers south of Delhi.

"They were in a helpless condition, with only a few earthen pots and scattered clothing in their huts," he said. "They were from a region of Madhya Pradesh where I had spent a large part of my childhood, so I could speak their dialect. They told me they were kept in bondage. I couldn't believe people in an open area could not run away, but they said if they tried they would be beaten or killed.

"I invited journalists from Delhi to come with me, and we took some of these bonded laborers to Delhi and gave them some food. I went to the chief minister, who was then a man named Bhajan Lal, and asked for some money from his relief fund to rehabilitate them. He was furious. He said if ever I stepped again into the quarries or brick kilns alleging there were bonded laborers he would see me finished off.

"Nevertheless, I contacted lawyer friends and went to lodge a complaint in the police station, but the police would not take it down. The next morning the police ransacked and sealed my room in the hostel for members of the state assembly. The chief minister said he would arrest me under the National Security Act because I was sabotaging the construction industry of the state by alleging there were bonded laborers."

After Agnivesh led the workers in a sit-in at a building owned by the Madhya Pradesh government, they were put on a train and sent back to their villages. Agnivesh, a former lecturer in law, then formed the *Bandhua Mukti Morcha* (Bonded Labor Liberation Campaign) and persuaded the Supreme Court to order an inquiry into bonded labor. Two young lawyers found conditions worse than the Bandhua Mukti Morcha had described.

In December 1983 the Supreme Court issued a landmark decision that not only declared bonded labor illegal but also ordered state governments to rehabilitate freed laborers and to inspect work sites to see that men, women, and children are properly paid and given adequate safety protection and medical care. Although the ruling has seldom been enforced in all its provisions, it has been the basis for actions on behalf of bonded laborers throughout the country: Surekha Dalvi used it to help Katkari charcoal burners in Maharashtra, and Champa Devi Srivastava used it to help laborers in the carpet factories of Mirzapur.

Dignity for Dalits

In Hindu mythology when the gods and demons in heaven joined to churn the pitcher (*kumbh*) of oceanic milk, they touched down on earth at four places. Every four years a huge *mela* (fair) is observed at one of these four pilgrimage sites. The largest takes place every twelve years on the outskirts of Allahabad, at the confluence of the rivers Ganga and Jumna and a third hidden river, the Saraswati. The most auspicious day of the 1989 Kumbh Mela was a night in February coinciding with a meeting of the planets that occurred, according to the pundits, only once in 144 years. It attracted, according to official count, a million and a half visitors, but probably fewer than one-fifth of that number were actually present, judging by how many could be brought by train and bus.

Just before this major day the leaders of temples and monasteries from all over India gathered for a conference sponsored by the Vishwa Hindu Parishad. A resolution was passed warning of a "major revolt" if the government did not allow the faithful to tear down the Babri Mosque and replace it with a temple to be constructed, in part, with bricks brought from each of the half million villages of India.

One day, when I called on Swami Agnivesh, he said he was going to the Kumbh Mela for a ceremony to raise the dignity of Dalits.

"Our protest is against religious obscurantism," he explained. "People feel they're poor because they're sinful, and their poverty cannot be removed unless they take a dip in the Ganges. Instead they should organize themselves into movements to fight against the exploitive structure. We will perform a yajna to provide a high position to Dalits. We don't want to be ritualistic, but that doesn't mean you fight ritualism by doing away with rituals. You have to make a sociological movement relevant to the culture of the people. People cling to something that explains life to them in times of sorrow and privation. Because our so-called socialist structure can't give solace, people seek a solution in religion. That's not bad. But obscurantist religious leaders come out with easy solutions: offer some money here, make a pilgrimage there, and all your worries will be gone. We don't believe in heaven. We believe this earth and this life must be made better."

I went with him and was surprised to find the flamboyance of his public demonstrations was missing: just the two of us went, riding in a cheap second-class railroad compartment like any villager. There was a strike of textile workers in Kanpur, and they blocked the railroad tracks for three days, dislocating train service throughout north India. Our train sat for hours at small stations as it was shunted over different tracks to bypass the blockade: a journey that should have been overnight took thirty-six hours.

When we arrived, the wide, dusty confluence area was clear of crowds, and the final tents were being taken down. About five hundred ragged sweepers and scavengers — men and women with stunted growth, sunken cheeks, and broken teeth — were brought in groups to a small fire where they poured *ghee* (clarified butter) into the flames as Arya Samaj priests chanted Vedic hymns. The Dalits wore conspicuously new sacred threads looped over one shoulder and hanging to the waist.

"Ordinarily, they're not allowed to participate or even sit anywhere near the fire ceremony," Agnivesh explained. "Women are considered impure. But Swami Dayanand opened the doors of Vedic ceremonies to all. Normally, the sacred thread sanction is reserved for the twice-born; even upper caste women are not allowed to wear it, but the Arya Samaj believes anyone who is conducting himself or herself properly in society is entitled to this sacred thread."

After the ceremony Agnivesh made a speech, and then we sat in long rows for a communal meal. Soon we left to find our way back to Delhi. It took us half a day just to get a bus to Lucknow, the state capital, and another half day to squeeze into one of the few trains running through the city. I managed to buy a black market, second-class sleeping bunk, but Agnivesh had to stand up all night. While waiting for the train, he repeated some of what he said in his speech:

"I said no such thing as karma and the sins of earlier lives exists in the Vedas. I said if anyone says you must be looked down upon because of your karma, he should be branded with a red hot iron, and if he shouts for help, he should be told whatever happens to him is because of his past life karma. I told them the caste system was abominable and should not be tolerated. I asked how can a person who is making a place dirty be called great? The person who is cleaning the place should be the great one. I gave the example of shoemakers, potters, and weavers who are also called lowly but are higher than those wearing these cloths and shoes and using the earthen pots.

"I said the best way to teach these people what really is greatness is for sweepers throughout the country to take a pledge that henceforth they will not do their traditional jobs of cleaning toilets and said that pledge should be announced from this holy fair. They raised their hands in agreement: they said they would seek other jobs for their livelihood."

I had often wondered, when I met activists who renounced the fruits of education to work for the poor, about the source of altruism in Hindu thinking. Agnivesh seemed the appropriate person to ask.

"According to Vedic philosophy," he replied, "this world and this life is a means to an end, which is *moksha*, meaning direct communion with the godhead who is all bliss, perfection, and peace. The question arises, how do you obtain moksha? The Vedic seers advocated yoga and many other methods in which one could involve himself in a process in which he or she can remain truthful, nonviolent, and just, which are attributes of God. If one wants to be truthful, one must fight against the forces of untruth, the forces of violence, and the forces of injustice. This struggle is universal: it has no bias of Hindu, Muslim, or anything like that. The Vedic teachings have the beauty of combining social consciousness and social awareness with one's personal search for moksha."

The fight against what the Swami called the forces of untruth, violence, and injustice takes place on a battlefield where Indians are at war with themselves.

49 ✺ The Triumph of Gandhi's Assassin

Gandhi created the myth of India as a land of nonviolence, but shortly before his death he had what Hugh Tinker called "a last apocalyptic vision" of the violence that lay ahead: "My eyes have now been opened. I see that what we practiced during the fight with the British under the name of nonviolence was not really nonviolence. God had purposely sealed my eyes, as He wanted me to accomplish His great purpose through me. That purpose being accomplished, He has restored my sight."

The violent reality of India is reflected in the *Mahabharata*, which some have called the only accurate book of Indian sociology: an epic of trickery, greed, and lust stemming from the unswerving pursuit of *artha* (wealth or possessions) and *kama* (desire or pleasure). It is the story of the five sons of King Pandu, known as the Pandavas; their exile by the Kauravas, a closely related clan; and the war between them for control of the kingdom.

The epic contrasts this violent world with the higher virtues of *ahimsa* (nonviolence). The negative term indicates an abstention from causing harm. Gandhi, in the myth-manipulating tradition of India, gave ahimsa an active, positive meaning. His boldest reworking of authority was his interpretation of the *Bhagavad Gita* (Song of the Adorable One), a relatively short text that appears to have been inserted in the *Mahabharata* to justify Vaishnavite doctrines embodied in the god Krishna.

Krishna and the Pandava hero Arjuna stand between the two armies on the final battlefield of Kurukshetra, and Arjuna asks why he should kill his kinsmen and teachers. Krishna tells him it is his caste duty as a Kshatriya but that he should renounce the fruits of this discipline (*yoga*) because worldly interests are of no value.

Traditionally, the Gita was seen as a text justifying the caste system and the importance of Brahminic *karma* (the word means "works" in addition to "fate"), such as worshipping god by pouring *ghee* on a fire while chanting Vedic stanzas. During the independence movement the Gita was given a new interpretation by such men as Bal Gangadhar Tilak, the Maharashtrian editor who propagated the cult of Shivaji. He insisted Karma Yoga was a warrior's duty to fight, thus cloaking opposition to the British with religious sanction.

Gandhi maintained Kurukshetra represented a symbolic struggle between light and darkness and that the Gita was concerned with renunciation or selflessness. Taking this a step further, he said nonviolence was a necessary part of selflessness: "He who would be *anasakta* (selfless) has necessarily to practice nonviolence to attain the state of selflessness." He went on to preach nonviolence as the "law of our being" and "the supreme and only way to the discovery of social truths."

Defending India's Masculinity

Nathuram Vinayak Godse, the man who killed Gandhi in 1947, had been a member of the RSS but quit because it was not militant enough. At his trial in 1948 Godse explained: "I was determined to prove to Gandhiji that the Hindu, too, could be intolerant when his honor was insulted." He accused Gandhi of denying Indian masculinity by giving way to Muslims and said it was his duty "to put an end to the life of the so-called Father of the Nation," citing Krishna's advice to Arjuna to slaughter his relatives at Kurukshetra.

Gandhi's vision of a disarmed, decentralized society died with him, and the militant, masculine vision of Nathuram Godse emerged victorious.

In December 1987 and January 1988, in an operation code-named Brass Tacks, 230,000 men, or about one-quarter of the Indian Army, were issued battle ammunition for what was said to be maneuvers in the Rajasthan desert. Simultaneously, a mountain division was sent to the border area named Jammu. Pakistan mobilized its own forces, and it seemed war was about to start. However, Pakistan's President Zia ul-Haq deflated tension by flying to India to attend a cricket match, to the disappointment of India's flamboyant chief of army staff, General Krishnaswami Sundarji.

According to *India Today*, Brass Tacks was designed "to provoke Pakistan into some action which would give the Indian Army an excuse to launch its own offensive." The action in the Rajasthan desert was a feint: the major thrust would have been to capture Gilgit in northern Pakistan. *Economic and Political Weekly* analyzed the ultimate strategy:

This attack, if successful, would have cut the Pakistan-China road link and, at the same time, given India and Russia a common frontier, since the Wakhan corridor of Afghanistan, bordering on Pakistan-occupied Kashmir, has already been "ceded" to the Soviet Union. In this way, the Russians would have achieved their age-old dream of securing a land route to the Indian Ocean, not through a hostile Afghanistan . . . but through a friendly India.

India has the world's fourth largest military force, with 1.1 million men, three thousand tanks, including new Russian battle tanks, and the latest Russian MiG-29 fighter planes. At sea it has two carrier battle groups supported by submarines, including a Russian nuclear submarine. It demands that the United States pull out of its main Indian Ocean base on the atoll of Diego Garcia, a thousand miles south of Sri Lanka. In the view of *Economic and Political Weekly* India has moved beyond "establishing a hegemony over the neighbors" and has become "a subimperialism . . . allied with the global designs of the Soviet Union."

A Carnegie Endowment for International Peace task force has reported India can assemble fifteen nuclear weapons, and there is speculation this could be increased to a hundred warheads by 1991. In June 1989 India successfully fired an Intermediate Range Ballistic Missile that can deliver a one ton weapon 1,500 miles. In contrast Pakistan is believed to have a capability of no more than five warheads and does not have an IRBM. Both nations, of course, deny they have nuclear weapons, but when India's latest missile was fired, Prime Minister Rajiv Gandhi commented: "Technological backwardness leads to subjugation."

Annual defense spending, including items generally left out of the military budget, such as pensions, border roads, and secret missile and nuclear development, amounts to $12 billion, or about 5.4 percent of the Gross National Product. Officially, the government puts defense expenditure at 3.4 percent of the GNP.

The Missing Peace Movement

India has all the familiar social movements—ecology, women's issues, education, empowerment, equality before the law—except the peace movement. There has only been one direct action: a spontaneous protest by villagers in Orissa against the taking of their lands for a missile testing range. The only hint of a peace movement—in the Western sense of actively opposing military expenditure—can be found among a scattered group of intellectuals who oppose nuclear energy. One of them is Nagesh Hegde, who formed a group called Citizens Against Nuclear Energy in Bangalore, where he makes his living as a journalist.

"I got my training in environmental sciences from Jawaharlal Nehru University in New Delhi," he said when I called on him. "When they wanted to locate a nuclear plant in a rain forest, I started writing about this, and a movement developed around the issue. We now have a broad framework of eighty people in Bangalore and work with other groups."

I asked: "Why not take up the disproportionate amount of the country's resources devoted to the military?"

"So many people are fighting the little problems of social inequality they can't think of defense spending as the real issue facing them: unemployment, poverty, and ignorance must be fought first. And the politicians want to cover up for their failures, so they call attention to the enemy without, not the enemy within. People feel they have no right to question military spending. If they do, they are traitors. If someone writes a letter to a newspaper raising doubts about military spending, the paper will hesitate to print it. And we're not given accurate information, just vague details. A member of Parliament doesn't know if something costs too much or if we need a missile."

In New Delhi, Dhirendra Sharma, who has lived abroad for twenty-two years, is an example of what will happen to anyone depending on institutional support who dares speak out. Sharma got a doctorate from London University with an abstruse thesis on "the paradox of negative judgment." After teaching in England, where he married a British woman, he returned to India to become chairman of the philosophy department of Kurukshetra University in Haryana. He then left for the United States, first teaching at Columbia University and then at Michigan State, where his subjects were the philosophy and sociology of science. He also got involved in the anti-Vietnam movement, because of which his Fulbright research scholarship was stopped. In 1974 he returned to India as an associate professor at Jawaharlal Nehru University. He was sent to jail during the Emergency, and this helped revive his social activism.

"I began to organize seminars and lectures to discuss nuclear energy," he said. "Top people who were friends warned me I was inviting trouble. And then my promotions were stopped; I was demoted from the chairmanship of the Center for Studies in Science Policies, transferred to the School of Languages, and not allowed to participate in the work of scientific organizations in the country."

"Why are Gandhians, who are supposed to advocate peace and nonviolence, silent on military spending?" I asked.

"Gandhians are a spent force. But it is more than Gandhi and Gandhians. In the Hindu ethos there is no opposition to war so long as that war is holy. The Kshatriyas were the armed forces. It was their spiritual duty to kill their opponents. I find this is the problem: How to oppose militarization in a Hindu society?"

"Why is there no strong opposition to other forms of violence, such as caste oppression and police brutality?" I asked.

"Police brutality does not reach the rich, the corrupt politicians, and the bureaucrats. There's an enormous amount of discontent in this country, and the elite have to maintain their privileged position. It's the same as in the southern states of the United States: you had to keep the blacks and the poor down, and the police had to play a role."

"There Is a Madness Here"

I said large cities were without twenty-four hour drinking water, public transportation was in shambles, and with an ever-larger population a few years of drought could bring famine and riots. "Why don't Indians see internal violence and economic decay are the real threats, not a small country like Pakistan?" I asked.

"There is a madness here," he replied. "Delhi is the most polluted city in India, yet they go on adding more cars. If we enforce certain environmental or ecological controls, it will come into conflict with the vested interests of the politicians, industrialists, militarists, and the other elite who have all the power.

"Scientists in other societies have become concerned scientists but our scientists are not critics. Most whom we call professionals are not even intellectuals. They are professional mercenaries: you pay them money and they work for you. And the traditional norms are not responding to modern challenges. There is a revival of Hindu faith. On every street corner you have two or three new temples or shrines but not two or three hospitals. People are feeling destitute and do not trust modern society and modern science and technology. It's a kind of escapism, a longing to forget their problems. They just sit and chant and feel better."

"Is the madness curable?"

"It will work itself out. In a hundred years the lower castes will get educated and come up."

"Does India have a hundred years?"

"It has been here for thousands of years: one hundred years is nothing. After the Mogul empire India went into a tremendous decline, in population and everything, but it survived."

When I said this seemed like waiting for the apocalypse, he replied:

"Perhaps it has survived too long and will kill itself. This may be a process in which nature wants to maintain its equilibrium. When Europe modernized during the Industrial Revolution, it thinned out its population by exporting people to its colonies. India and China don't have that outlet, so perhaps nature is finding another way in the disintegration of society."

Social activists believe they have a way to avert the apocalypse. Their movements are called "new," but Claus Offe says "contemporary" would be a better word:

It is this "contemporaneous" character of the underlying values of new social movements that leaves their intellectual and political proponents rather defenseless or leads them to misrepresent and often caricature these values as either romanticism . . . or as the luxurious predilections of privileged groups who have lost contact with social "realities." . . . The "modern" character of the new social movements is underlined by their evident belief in the assumption that the course of history and society is "contingent" and hence can be created and changed by people and social forces determined to do so, rather than being determined by given . . . principles of divine or natural order or, for that matter, by an inescapable road to catastrophe.

While social movement actors believe the apocalypse can be averted, they have no scenario. Theirs is street theater, not historical drama.

50 ❀ Averting the Apocalypse

Social movements are a process: interactions through which new patterns of behavior and new value systems are expressed. The actors are pragmatists, not utopians. As Ashis Nandy, a psychologist who comments on science and politics, writes:

> We are better off with negatively defined utopias than with positively defined ones. A utopia which rejects technicism or the idea of mastery over nature is often a more serious affair than a utopia which recommends a specific technoeconomic or ecological solution. . . . The latter raise problems of conflicting values; the former promises a vague, implicit negative consensus of an unheroic vision of a decent society which may not fulfill everybody's desire for a positively designed utopia but may help the diverse concepts of a tolerable society come closer to articulation.

"There's a crisis in India's concept of a desirable society," Nandy said when I called on him at his office in a rambling colonial structure in Old Delhi that houses the Center for the Study of Developing Societies.

"A growing number of Indians are looking skeptically at the given wisdom handed down by the first generation after independence. They have begun to suspect conventional economic development will not work and the existing concept of the state needs to be redefined, so we don't continually live in a paranoid world, suspicious that our neighbors are conspiring to do us in.

"The increasing entry of the state into the private lives of citizens, into all spheres of life, has destroyed much of the fabric of Indian social life. I suggest a different form of society: a different form of tolerance in the Indian tradition, whether you define that as Hindu, Muslim, Buddhist, or Christian. India has a diverse society: a lot of experiments were going on. Indians had evolved a style of living in reasonable peace with nature and with each other. I think these traditional instrumentalities have collapsed.

"Young Indian intellectuals have become skeptical of all of the sacred cows. There's a reexamination of both Gandhi and Marx. It's pointless to say to them, as one visiting scholar said here, that there are only two alternatives, capitalism and socialism, and there is no third way. They'll not accept that all other choices are preempted. They'll say, 'If we fail, the choice will be with us and not with others. Even if it seems irrational, we will explore the possibility of other philosophies.'"

Activists As Catalysts

Social movements are built on transformation: a change in values and behavior among a few who embody the vision of the new society and the passing on of this vision to those who have long been apathetic. Ideas of legitimacy must be transformed so the poor become revolutionary and not merely rebellious. As the Brazilian Paulo Freire stressed again and again, the poor must be brought to see, in the context of their own lives, how the oppressive system works. Vijay Sathe's satyagraha against the Murbad tahsildar was more revolutionary than establishing a Maoist jungle base.

While activists mobilize in a specific place and time, they are indicators of problems throughout a system. Anil Prakash was well aware of this when he set out to redress the grievances of an isolated group of fishermen in a small village on the banks of the Ganges. Parameshwara Rao, crusading for private initiatives to end illiteracy without waiting for the state to act, is widening the sphere of individual autonomy. So is Tapas Banerjee, organizing young people to fight drugs and alcohol in Tollygunge, and Sheela Patel, forming cooperatives of pavement dwellers dumped on the rocky soil of Dindoshi.

Social movements are more than the sum of their goals: the organizations themselves have meaning. The women's movement raised questions about equality and rights for women and also sent a signal proclaiming it important to recognize all differences in a complex society.

India is marked by a hierarchy of subordination. This is brutally apparent in the patriarchal family structure, where men preserve their own chances of survival in a marginal society by selling their women and children. Thus, with the branching effect of the feminist movement, Ila Pathak—fighting sexist media images, organizing consciousness-raising sessions, and exposing the male structure that covered up the rape of tribal women—is simultaneously challenging the norms of the entire society.

The same is true of the Jharkhand movement. Melucci warns against viewing ethnic social movements too narrowly as by-products of nation-building rather than as aspects of the transformation of complex societies:

> The ethno-national question must be seen . . . as containing a plu-rality of meanings that cannot be reduced to a single core. It con-tains ethnic identity, which is a weapon of revenge against centu-ries of discrimination and new forms of exploitation; it serves as an instrument of applying pressure in the political market; and it is a response to needs for personal and collective identity in highly complex societies. . . . They raise questions about the need for new rights for all members of the community, particularly the right to be different; and, second, they claim the right to autonomy, to con-trol a specific living space. . . . Difference is thereby given a voice which speaks of problems which transverse the whole society.

Toward a New Beginning

Any discussion of the difficulties confronting the formation of a demo-cratic consensus that is neither ethnic nor religious must first deal with the Orientalist construction of India as the "other"—what Kipling me-morialized as the eternal dichotomy between West and East—and the corollary that democratic institutions were doomed from the start in a society where caste is the essence of life.

Modern scholars reject both concepts. Dirks perceives the predom-inance of Brahmins as the result of foreign rule, first by the Muslims and then the British, which displaced the earlier dominance of Indian kings:

> Kings were not inferior to Brahmans [sic]; the political domain was not encompassed by a religious domain. State forms, while not fully assimilable to Western categories of the state, were powerful com-ponents in Indian civilizations. . . . Caste was embedded in the po-litical context of kingship. This meant among other things that the prevalent ideology had not to do, at least primarily, with purity and pollution, but rather with royal authority and honor, and asso-ciated notions of power, dominance and order. . . . The demise of

kingship was accompanied by the steady ascendancy of the Brahman as the maintainer of social order and the codes of caste. Brahmans reached a new high under British colonialism both in their participation in the development of Hindu law and in their preponderance in colonial administration.

Although Dalits and the other backward classes still suffer the disabilities of birth and deprivation, notions of caste purity and defilement are disappearing. Caste is seen as status in relation to "kingship" in the form of elected officials and a patron-client relationship in business and administration.

Ronald Inden notes another distortion stemming from the emphasis on caste rather than the politics of power:

Indian actions are attributed to social groups—caste, village, linguistic regions, religion, and joint family—because there are no individuals in India. . . . Caste is . . . associated with race and occupation, religion and status, land control and psychic security, with birth and death, marriage and education. Caste then is assumed to be the essence of Indian civilization. People in India are not even partially autonomous agents. They do not shape and reshape their world. Rather they are the patients of that which makes them Indians—the social, material reality of caste. The people of India are not the makers of their own history. A hidden, substantialized Agent, Caste, is the maker of it.

Inden, Dirks, and others believe nothing in Indian culture inhibits Indians in the search for solutions to the ills of their society and that an end to caste dominance will not mean an end to Indian civilization. Neither do modern scholars see anything in Indian culture that mandates false versions of institutions that have been developed elsewhere. This is not to say the Indian version must be a line-for-line duplicate. Inden, like Nandy, believes an Indian solution must grow out of Indian culture:

If I and others wish to produce a world that is more egalitarian and multi-centered, we must also at the same time transform our intellectual practices so as to make *them* more egalitarian and multi-centered. . . . We cannot claim to accord independence of action to a sovereign, independent India while still adhering (whether intentionally or not) to presuppositions that deny the very possibility of it.

Indian social movement activists shun party politics and talk in terms of grass-roots, consensual candidates. Their reluctance is not necessarily escapist: they are too concerned with changing their immediate environment to think of broader issues. They also know all previous independent movements that allied with the existing parties were eventually dominated and absorbed.

The pervasiveness of corruption, and a black-market economy that controls at least a quarter of the nation's economy, is evidence of a parallel structure that sets its own rules and takes its own toll of goods and services. Grass-roots actors seeking a place in politics would find the game is fixed.

India is a complexity that strains Western classification. It must seek its own version of a decent society and its own language of politics to recapture the traditions of a multicentered, multifaceted civilization. All Third World countries are similarly situated. The French journalist and critic Pascal Bruckner concluded:

> All remedies proposed during the last three decades for pulling the Southern hemisphere out of its rut have failed. . . . The old systems are falling apart, but no new ones have appeared. In light of this gap, the only possible course is to try tentative hypotheses, as in the sciences. . . . We must temporarily suspend judgment and develop patterns of thought that are appropriate to the challenges before our planet. History has become improvisation again.

Social movement actors believe their many experiments can act at two levels: gaining legitimacy for a new value system and then reordering society in light of these values. They rely on nonviolence and empowerment: an awakening at the bottom. The legitimizing factor is changed values, not superior force.

At the top the temptation to use force is strong. The Indian situation has a parallel with the Italian society Gramsci analyzed following World War I. He said the bourgeoisie had attained ascendancy during the long years of the nineteenth-century *risorgimento* (unification of Italy) through a passive revolution: through "hegemonic" control of civil society rather than by a direct seizure of the institutions of the state. He wrote that the bourgeoisie reinforced this control by enlisting elitist sections of the lower orders into a new middle class. In turn, this raised lower-class expectations, and with the economic dislocations following the war the dominant class felt it was losing control and the crisis could be resolved only through "direct domination" exercised by Fascism.

The revivalism of the Ram Janmabhoomi campaign to collect "sacred" bricks to build a new temple was the major impetus for the strong showing of the Bharatiya Janata Party in the November 1989 elections that brought down Rajiv Gandhi. In the weeks before the balloting more than two hundred persons were killed in Bhagalpur, Bihar, in clashes resulting from processions of Hindus carrying bricks to Ayodhya.

Militant Hinduism drives a terrified Muslim minority into the arms of equally militant and obscurantist Islamic ideologues, just as the Congress's toying with the Sikhs gave rise to Khalistan terrorism. Then, when Muslims, Sikhs, Dalits, and others claim protection or insist on their constitutional and human rights, the cry is raised they are out to destroy the Hindu basis of Indian civilization. In the process, the fabric of civil society and secular democracy is shredded.

Those who hold power in India know their history: an unraveling of their passive accession to colonial power threatens a return to the chaos that marked clan, caste, and patron-client rule before the British restored order in the eighteenth century. The fear of chaos could well lead to a new version of the Emergency. There are enough draconian antiterrorist laws on the books to allow for direct rule without a formal declaration of an emergency. A consolidation of power could be presented as a defense of Hinduism, with the RSS and its front groups ready to rally support.

Social movements have no easy solution for India's political crisis. Experience has shown participatory democracy is ineffective when confronted by the imperfect knowledge that results from greater scale and complexity. Merely recognizing the nature of a challenge in modern societies, to say nothing of making decisions, is far beyond the pristine debates of town or village meetings.

Yet social movement actors are convinced they must try. They believe caste in all its forms must end because a social order that excludes and deprives cannot assimilate into an affirmative consensus those whom it mistreats. They long for a civil society based on a consensus so powerful it can counteract the divisions and disruptions of conflicting linguistic and regional interests.

Europe, after centuries of war and with so many languages and economic regions, is evolving just that form of consensus. The men and women who have dedicated their lives to the many forms of social movements in India see no reason they too—with time and will—cannot build a similar new society.

Glossary

achkan. knee-length coat, buttoned at neck
adivasi. tribal, aboriginal
agni. fire
ahimsa. nonviolence; peace
Akali Dal. Army of Immortals
Akal Takht. spiritual center of Golden Temple
akhand panth. uninterrupted reading of Sikh holy book
amar shaheed. eternal martyr
amma. mother
amritdhari. baptized or practicing Sikh
anasakta. selfless
Annapurna. goddess of food who never says no
Antyaja. outcastes, untouchables
antyodaya. treating the last person as first
ardhanarishwara. god as half male, half female
Arjuna. Pandava hero in the *Mahabharata*
arrack. alcoholic drink distilled from various palms
artha. wealth, possessions
Aryan. nomadic settlers in India ca. 1500 B.C.
ashram. religious settlement
ashrama. stage of Hindu religious life
asuras. impious ones who churned the primeval ocean
Atman. universal self or soul
avatar. incarnation of a deity
azad. freedom
ba. mother
bagh. garden
bahadur. brave man, title of respect
Bahucharamai. goddess worshipped by hijras
Baisakhi. north Indian Hindu New Year
Bakr-Id. Muslim religious festival
baksheesh. gift, tip
bandh. bind or close, hence a strike or closure

banias. merchants, moneylenders
bapu. father
ben. sister; female honorific in Gujarat
bhadralok. upper class Bengalis
Bhagavad Gita. Song of the Adorable One
bhai. brother; male honorific in Gujarat
bhajan. hymn
bhakti. utter devotion to a personal god
bhangi. scavenger
Bharat. traditional name for India
bhog. ceremonies to appease the soul of the dead
Bhoodan. land gift movement
bhoomi. land, generally arable farm land
Bhoomi Sena. Land Army
bhoomihar. landlord, also spelled bhumihar
bidi. cheap cigarette of rolled leaf and coarse tobacco
bindi. ornamental mark on a woman's forehead
Bo tree. tree of Buddha's enlightenment
boosa. straw, cattle feed
Brahma. absolute reality, first deity of the Hindu trinity
brahmacharya. celibate stage of Hindu religious life
Brahmin. priestly caste
bund. dike, raised ground between farm plots
burqa. Muslim women's robe completely covering body
bustee. slum
cantonment. area originally for troops and officials
catamarum. boat made of flattened logs lashed together
chabutra. raised platform or terrace
chamar. leather worker
chapati. flat round unleavened bread cooked on griddle
chappal. sandal
charkha. spinning wheel, popularized by Gandhi
chat. food served at sidewalk stalls
chawl. long tenement in Bombay
chetna. awareness
chindi. cheap, cotton-stuffed quilt
chital. spotted deer
chooth. leaving, breaking up of a marriage
chotolok. lower class Bengalis
chowk. open space, often a marketplace
chowkidar. watchman, member of auxiliary police force
coolie. unskilled daily laborer
dacoit. robber, thief
dada. grandfather, gang leader
dai. midwife
daima. senior eunuch
dal. a dish made of split peas or some other gram

dalam. guerrilla band

Dalit. broken, a preferred synonym for untouchables

dana. gift

darshan. sight of an idol or holy person

dasas. bondsmen, slaves

dasyus. bandits

desam. country (Telugu)

devadasi. woman dedicated to god

Devas. heaven-born who churned primeval ocean

devi. goddess; honorific title for a Hindu woman

Dharam Yudh. righteous war

dharma. sacred law, justice, right behavior, morality

dharna. sitting in protest

dhoti. male waist garment tucked between legs

diara. land formed by shifting river bed

didi. elder sister, slang for prostitute madam

dikku. Santal designation for outsider, foreigner

Diwali. north Indian fall festival of lights

Doordarshan. television, the government-owned TV network

Dravidian. non-Aryan south Indian linguistic group

Drona. martial arts teacher in the *Mahabharata*

Duniya Dari. Way of the World

Durbar. royal court or assemblage

Durga. goddess, aspect of Kali, wife of Siva

durry. woven cotton carpet

Dwija. twice-born

Ekalavia. untouchable archer in the *Mahabharata*

ekatmata. unanimity, integration

ekta. unity

Gandharvas. minor deities, earth sprites

Ganesh. elephant-headed god of wisdom

Ganga. Ganges river; the river goddess

gaothan. tribal community land in Maharashtra

garib lok. poor people of West Bengal

gauna. second marriage for child bride

gharwali. madam, brothel keeper

ghat. steps leading to river; mountain range

ghee. clarified butter from cow or buffalo

gherao. surrounding someone as form of protest

gohar. caste gathering for revenge

goonda. petty criminal

gopuram. gateway, high tower on south Indian temple

gramdan. gift of land in Bhoodan movement

Granth Sahib. Sikh holy book

grihastha. second, householder stage of Hindu life

Gujar. shepherd caste

Gul Mohr. Flamboyant, tree with masses of red flowers
gurdwara. Sikh temple
guru. spiritual guide, teacher
gurukul. Arya Samaj school
hafta. bribe, protection money
Hanuman. monkey deity
Harijan. child of god, Gandhi's name for untouchables
Harmandir. central shrine of Golden Temple
hijra. eunuch, male dressed as female
hilsa. a favored fish found in large rivers
hookah. water pipe
iddali. steamed cake of rice and gram flour
idgah. large enclosed space for Muslim prayers
imam. Muslim prayer leader
inquilab. revolution
irunda ullagum. dark world (Tamil)
jagaran. revival or revivalist
jagir. hereditary land, previously government-owned
Jai Hind. Long Live India!
Jain. religious sect; follower of Mahavira
Jamadagni. sage in Yellamma legend
janata. the masses, peoples
jatha. procession, armed or military group
jati. occupational group, subcaste
jawan. soldier
Jharkhand. jungle place; proposed tribal state
jihad. religious war
jivandan. gift of life in Bhoodan
jogini. female Yogi, Devadasi
jotedar. medium size landholder in West Bengal
Juggernaut. temple in Puri Orissa with a huge cart used in processions
kachcha. Sikh underwear
kalasha. cauldron
Kali. goddess of destruction, consort of Siva
Kalima. phrase declaring oneself a Muslim
Kali Yuga. the present age of strife
kama. desire or pleasure
kameez. loose shirt, woman's upper garment
kangh. Sikh comb
kara. Sikh steel bracelet
karma. destiny, fate; also work or action
karmayoga. realization through action
Kaurava. one of contending clans in the *Mahabharata*
Kayastha. writer caste
kes. Sikh uncut hair
khadi. hand-spun, handwoven cloth
Khalistan. Land of the Pure, independent Sikh nation

Khalsa. pure; the Sikh community
Khatris. Sikhs converted from Kshatriya caste
khoon. blood
kirpan. Sikh sabre
kirtan. devotional song
Kisan Sabha. farmer or peasant's union
Kodumbavi. the Great Sinner
kotwali. police station
Krishna. god, eighth avatar of Vishnu
Kshatriya. warrior caste
kumbh. pitcher
Kumbh Mela. quadrennial festival
Kurukshetra. final battlefield of the *Mahabharata*
langar. free community kitchen at Sikh gurdwara
langur. slim, long-tailed monkey
lathi. brass-tipped stick used by police as a weapon
Laxmi. goddess of good fortune
Lo Bir. Hunt Council (Santal tribe)
lok. people
Lok Dal. People's Party
Lok Nayak. Leader of the People
Lok Sabha. lower house of Parliament
lok sevaks. servants of the people
lok shakti. people's power
lok umeedvars. people's candidates
lota. water pot
lungi. men's cloth extending to ankles
Mahabharata. epic of war between clans for Bharata kingdom
mahajal. large fishing net
mahamantri. chief minister
mahant. hereditary priest, head of monastery
mahila mandal. women's organization
maidan. open space or park
Malayalam. language of Kerala
malik. owner, employer
mamool. bribe, literally: custom, tradition
mandir. Hindu temple
mangalsutra. necklace worn by married Hindu woman
mantra. literally, vedic text; magic formula
Manusmriti. digest of religious teachings
Marathi. language of Maharashtra
marg. road, way
Marwar. region in Rajasthan
Marwari. banker, businessman
masjid. mosque
Mazhabis. Sikhs converted from untouchable castes
Meenakshi. south Indian goddess

megh. cloud
mehr. dowry in Islamic marriage
mela. fair
mlechha. impure, barbarian
mohalla. district of a town, neighborhood
moksha. spiritual liberation also spelled mukti
morcha. procession organized as a protest
mukadam. subcontractor
murdabad. death to, down with
murti. idol, statue
Musahars. rat eaters, Dalit caste in Bihar
mutt. Hindu monastery, also spelled math
nagar. colony, suburb
nawab. Muslim governor or high official
Naxalite. revolutionary
neem. a tree with medicinal leaves and bark
neta. leader
nirmiti. creation
nishad. fisherman in Bihar
ojha. male diviner of witches
Om. sacred syllable
Oriya. language of Orissa
Padma Shri. award of honor
padyatra. pilgrimage, walk undertaken as demonstration
paise. hundredth part of a rupee
palang. string bed
palanquin. covered couch carried on men's shoulders
pallu. the long end of a sari
pan. mixture of spices wrapped in betel leaf
panchayat. assembly of five, village council
pandal. booth, covered area for assembly
Pandava. one of contending clans in the the *Mahabharata*
Panditji. honorific for Brahmin
pani. water
Panidar. Bihari claimant to river rights
Panj Pyaras. five Sikhs who offered their heads
panth. community, sect
Pariah. untouchable caste
Parashakti. Supreme Goodness, universal energy
pargana. Santal grouping of ten or twelve panchayats
parikrama. outer circumference of temple or shrine
parishad. council
patel. village headman or official
pati parameshwar. to worship one's husband as god
patta. title deed
patwari. keeper of village land records
peepul. sacred tree, also spelled pipal

petis. boxes, girls recruited as prostitutes
petrais. fortified enclosures
pipal. sacred tree; also known as Bo tree
pir. Muslim ascetic
Pongal. rice harvest festival in Tamil Nadu
pradhan. head of council, same as pramukh
prasad. gift; coconut or other offering to deity
puja. Hindu rite of worship
pujari. priest who accepts offerings at a shrine
pukka. permanent, well built, firm
Punjabi Suba. Punjabi-speaking state
purohit. priest
qazi. Muslim judge
Raj (the). British rule in India
rajya. rule; Rajya Sabha, upper house of Parliament
Rama. god, seventh avatar of Vishnu
Ramanandi. sect of sadhus who traditionally go naked
Ramayana. epic of Rama's rescue of his wife Sita
Ramadan. Muslim month with rigid fast
Ram Janmabhoomi. birthplace of Rama
Ram Lila. pageant telling the story of Rama
Ram Rajya. Kingdom of God; era of peace
rangdaari. a tax collected by dominant persons
Rang Mela. cultural fair
rangoli. chalky decoration; muggu in Telugu
rashtra. nation, country
rath. temple cart to carry deity in procession
Ravana. Sri Lanka king who kidnapped Sita
Renuka. Sage's wife in Yellamma legend
Rig Veda. earliest book of the Vedas
rokho. halt, stoppage
sabha. assembly, society
sadhu. wandering ascetic
sahn. courtyard of a mosque
Saivite. devotee of Siva
salwar. women's loose trousers
samaj. assembly, religious organization
samiti. regional council; also spelled samithi
samyama. self-restraint
sangam. confluence of rivers
sangh. assembly, association
sanghatana. union, association
Sankaracharya. head of a Sankara monastery
sant. saint, title for ascetic
sannyasa. worldly renunciation
sarangs. tribal grave memorial stones in Bihar
Saraswati. goddess of learning

sardar. chief, leader; form of address to a Sikh
sarkar. the state or government
sarpanch. village headman
Sarvodaya. uplift for all; Gandhian concept of service
sati. widow burned on her husband's funeral pyre
satyagraha. nonviolent truth force
sena. army
seth. moneylender or banker
sevak. servant
shaheed. martyr, also spelled shahid
shakha. branch; basic brotherhood unit of RSS
shakti. the principle of feminine power
Shakuntala. heroine of Kalidasa drama of lost ring
shamiana. open-sided tent
Shariat. code of Muslim law
shastrarth. religious debate
Shia. Muslim sect
Shivaji. hero-king of Maharashtra (1627–1680)
shraddha. periodic rite after the death of a relative
shramdan. voluntary labor
shuddhi. reconversion and purification
singh. lion; last name of Sikhs and many Rajputs
sipahi. police constable
Sita. kidnapped wife of Rama in the *Ramayana*
Siva. third deity of Hindu trinity
sohrae. Santal women's harvest dance
stri shakti. women's power
stupa. Buddhist temple with solid dome
Sudra. fourth and lowest of Hindu castes
sufi. Muslim mystic
svadharma. duty
swami. Hindu religious teacher
swaraj. home rule, self-government
swayamsevak. volunteer
tahsil. subdivision of a district, also spelled tehsil
tahsildar. administrator, revenue collector of tahsil
talaq. Muslim divorce, also spelled talak
taksal. Sikh seminary
tank. pond, reservoir
tarpancha. pipe gun
Telugu. language spoken in Andhra Pradesh
tendu. leaf used to wrap bidis
thana. police station and its jurisdiction
tiffen. lunch, light meal
tirtha. place of pilgrimage
toddy. fermented palm juice
tonga. two-wheeled, horse-drawn vehicle

toplawali. sidewalk vendor in Gujarat
toshakhana. treasury of Golden Temple
Treta Yuga. second of mythological eras
trishul. trident, three-pointed weapon of Siva
tulsi. basil plant, sacred to Vishnu
upayatras. small processions
Vaishya. merchant caste
Vaishnava. worshipper of Vishnu
Varna. literally color; the four castes
Varnashrama. the code of the four castes
Vedas. the oldest Indian religious books
veer. hero
Vishnu. second deity of the Hindu trinity
vratas. fasts, vows, and visits to temples
yajna. sacrifice, offering
yatra. pilgrimage, journey, march, procession
Yellamma. goddess of the devadasi cult
yoga. a discipline of the body or mind
yuga. mythological era
Zamindar. landlord; collector of land revenues
zilla. administrative district
Zindabad. Victory!

Notes

(Full titles for acronyms provided in Bibliography.)

1 · A Longing for Freedom

Melucci (1989), pp. 12–13.

Hobsbawm on Gramsci: Henderson (1988), p. 3.

Hegemony: Boggs (1986), pp. 242–247, and Femia (1981), pp. 24–29. Gramsci maintained the hegemonic force of a civil society was a necessity for freedom. As a Communist, he had freedom from the bourgeoisie in mind, but the concept applies equally to caste domination as well as the "new class" of Communism. For general surveys of Gramsci: Bocock (1986) and Sassoon (1980). For Gramsci's own writings: Gramsci (1957) and Hoare and Smith (1971).

Sunita Narain's center: Agarwal (1987). For a total environmental assessment: Bandyopadhyay (1985).

Claus Offe, "Challenging the Boundaries of Institutional Politics," *Social Research* 52, no. 4 (Winter 1985), examines activists as a global phenomena: "The most striking aspect is that they do not rely for their self-identification on either the established political codes (left/right, liberal/conservative, etc.) nor on the partly corresponding socioeconomic codes (such as working class/middle class, poor/wealthy, rural/urban populations, etc.). The universe of political conflict is rather coded in categories taken from the movements' issues, such as gender, age, locality, etc., or, in the case of environmental and pacifist movements, the human race as a whole."

Differing traditions: Saberwal (1986), pp. 2–3, 36–57. For an extended examination of the persistence of earlier political structures: Pamela G. Price, "Kingly Models in Indian Political Behavior: Culture as a Medium of History," *Asian Survey* 29:6 (June 1989), pp. 559–572.

de Tocqueville (1945), p. 392.

2 · A Missed Tryst

Tryst with destiny: Moraes (1956), pp. 1–3.

Planning mistakes: Sukhamoy Chakravarty, "Four Decades of Planning," *Mainstream*, Sept. 5, 1987, pp. 7–9; D. N. Dhanagare, "Green Revolution and Social Inequalities in

Rural India," EPW, annual number, May 1987, pp. AN 137–144; V. K. Dhar, "Planning for Urban Poor: Issues and Options," *Mainstream*, Jan. 16, 1988, pp. 12–14, and "Catastrophic Cycle," IT (editorial), June 15, 1989, p. 4; and Sudhirendar Sharma, "Pulses, Staple No More," IT, Aug. 15, 1989, p. 77.

Kohli (1987), p. 1, writes: "[The] persistence of poverty is clearly manifest in the continuance of low per capita income. . . . Higher growth rates, and therefore higher per capita income, are not sufficient to improve the lot of the poor. New wealth has not trickled down."

The subheadings of A. M. Khusro, "Quality of Indian Growth," EPW, Sept. 3, 1988, pp. 1857–1862, summarize the failures: Quantity sans Quality, Agriculture Tapering Off, Low Quality Industry, Non-Competitive Private Sector, Small Industry on Crutches, Defaulting Public Enterprises, Jungle of Procedures, Proliferating Black Income, Inflating Real Estate, Poor Municipal Government, Low Quality Social Services, Poverty of Anti-Poverty Programs, Deficient Employment, Poor Quality Education.

Babubhai Patel, "Genesis of Agricultural Unrest," *Financial Express*, Sept. 28, 1987, says India has 165 million hectares (one hectare = 2.47 acres) under cultivation, compared to 129 million hectares in China, but China's food grains output is two and a half times India's.

Bhanu Pratap Singh, "Priorities in Development Plan," *The Hindu*, Feb. 21, 1989, disputes governmental optimism: "The claim that the country has become self-sufficient in food grains is false. . . . That the incidence of poverty is declining fast is yet another falsehood being propagated. . . . Nehru started building the pyramid from the top, which is just not possible. . . . It is now an established fact that countries like Japan, South Korea and Taiwan, which paid more attention to the basic needs of the people, have ultimately fared much better than those whose first priority was industrialization."

Prafulla Sanghvi, "Dimension of Poverty and Political Economy of Anti-Poverty Strategy," *Mainstream*, July 11, 1987, pp. 16–22, forecasts "frequent and recurrent periods of undernourishment . . . chronic malnutrition . . . unsanitary living quarters . . . inadequate access to drinking, cooking and cleaning water . . . constant exposure to communicable diseases . . . [and] stunted growth of body and mind of the children of the poor."

Cholera in Delhi: Mira Shiva and Miloon Kothari, "The Killing Fluids," IWI, Aug. 28, 1988, pp. 50–51.

Caste: André Béteille, "Caste and Social Status," in Thapar (1977), pp. 59–65, for the need to focus on status rather than ritual purity. Also see: Jose Kananaikil, "Religion, Culture and Power: The Case of the Scheduled Castes in India," *Religion and Society* 33:2 (June 1986), pp. 27–32, and V. M. Sirsikar, "Caste and Politics," in Thapar (1977), pp. 74–81.

Caste flexibility: See Sanskritization in Srinivas (1966), pp. 1–45. Srinivas (p. 6) defines Sanskritization as "the process by which a 'low' Hindu caste, or tribal or other group, changes its customs, ritual, ideology, and way of life in the direction of a high, and frequently, 'twice-born' caste. Generally such changes are followed by a claim to a higher position in the caste hierarchy than that traditionally conceded to the claimant caste by the local community. The claim is made over a period of time, in fact, a generation or two, before the 'arrival' is conceded." Critics say the 'arrival' of a lower caste is never conceded and is grudgingly granted to the extent the lower caste also achieves political power, and even so only the elite of the lower castes can hope to find acceptance.

Caste as racism: Memmi (1968), pp. 186–195. The parallels between the colonized and the colonizers in Africa and the upper caste treatment of Dalits are striking. Césaire (1972), pp. 20–23, used the equation, "colonization = thingification," and wrote in language that is repeated daily by Dalit activists: "Security? Culture? The rule of law? . . . I look around and wherever there are colonizers and colonized face to face, I see force, brutality, cruelty, sadism, conflict and, in a parody of education, the hasty manufacture of a few thousand subordinate functionaries. . . . Between colonizer and colonized there is room only for forced labor, intimidation, pressure, the police, taxation, theft, rape, compulsory crops, contempt, mistrust, arrogance, self-complacency, swinishness, brainless elites, degraded masses. . . . I am talking about societies drained of their essence, cultures trampled underfoot, institutions undermined, lands confiscated, religions smashed, magnificent artistic creations destroyed, extraordinary possibilities wiped out. . . . I am talking about natural economies that have been disrupted—harmonious and viable economies adapted to the indigenous population—about food crops destroyed, malnutrition permanently introduced, agricultural development oriented solely toward the benefit of the metropolitan countries, about the looting of products [and] the looting of raw materials."

Lack of caste improvement: Commission for Scheduled Castes and Scheduled Tribes (1985), *Seventh Report*, pp. 41–43.

Orientalism: Ralph Inden, "Orientalist Constructions of India," *Modern Asian Studies* 20:3, pp. 401–446.

The "eternal" Indian nation: Nehru (1946), pp. 50, 114, 124, 133.

Breuilly (1982), p. 144, sees British rule as more than "a negative focus of nationalism, but rather as the linchpin of a complex and changing collaborator system which positively shaped the nationalist movement."

Linguistic diversity: Pattanayak (1981), pp. 40–46.

Sense of crisis: Satish Saberwal, "The Problem," *Seminar*, July 1987, pp. 12–15.

Apocalypse: Sham Lal, "Diversity In Unity," TOI, Jan. 30, 1988.

3 · The Rich and the Poor

N. Vijay Jagannathan and Aninmesh Halder, "Income-Housing Linkages: A Case Study of Pavement Dwellers in Calcutta," EPW, June 4, 1988, pp. 1175–1178, can serve as a general description of the lower caste urban structure.

J. B. D'Souza, "The Real City-Savers," EPW, May 20, 1989, pp. 1089–1090, describes the "uncollected garbage . . . open sullage and sewage" of India's towns and cities, "reeking of human excrement" with "hundreds of improvised hovels huddled together higgledy-piggledy, ramshackle wooden stalls purveying anything from *pan* and *bidis* to sugarcane juices to narcotics [and] stray animals fouling the streets," and then enumerates the services offered by the poor "without which our urban economies would collapse."

General descriptions of Bombay: Raj Chengappa and others, "Urban Decay: A Mega Collapse," IT, Jan. 31, 1988, pp. 114–121; Michael Specter, "City of Poverty and Hope," *Far Eastern Economic Review*, July 5, 1984, pp. 20–24; Tania Midha, "White Collar Slum Dwellers," IT, April 30, 1987, pp. 96–99; Sunil Sethi and Coomi Kapoor, "City on the Brink," IT, Nov. 15, 1983, pp. 30–38.

List of Dalit trades: Fuchs (1981), pp. 67–267. This is a unique review of the genesis and rankings of Dalit castes.

Hospitals: N. H. Antia, "Big Hospitals: For Whose Benefit?" IT, June 6, 1988.

4 · We, the Invisible

General reports on SPARC: "On Housing," LB 4:5 (1986), pp. 69–81; "Women and Housing," LB, 5:3 (1987), pp. 41–50. The latter has the quotation on slum women.

Conscientization: Freire (1988). Paulo Freire's slim book, *Pedagogy of the Oppressed*, was the precursor of modern social activism in Latin America and the former colonial world. He developed his theories while teaching literacy in Brazil's impoverished northeast during the 1950s. He was jailed briefly as a subversive in 1964 and spent the next fifteen years in exile, during which he was a consultant to the World Council of Churches and a visiting professor at Harvard. He also set up literacy programs in Chile under Salvador Allende Gossens, in the newly liberated nations of Portuguese-speaking Africa, and in Nicaragua under the Sandinistas. His teachings evolved into Christian liberation theology. Freire believes revolutionary leaders should be judged by the degree to which they help people to become conscious of their oppression so they can transform the world around them: teaching them things do not happen because God wants it, or because destiny establishes it, but because there is a structure that prevents the oppressed from becoming full human beings. Without the conscious participation of the great mass of the oppressed, he says (p. 55) there is only a coup d'état: "The oppressed, who have been shaped by the death-affirming climate of oppression, must find through their struggle the way to life-affirming humanization, which does not lie simply in having more to eat (although it does involve having more to eat and cannot fail to include this aspect). The oppressed have been destroyed precisely because their situation has reduced them to things. In order to regain their humanity they must cease to be things and fight as men. . . . They cannot enter the struggle as objects in order later to become men."

Society for Promotion of Area Studies (1985) has the Pavement Dwellers Case and the survey's findings.

Sudden demolitions: Coomi Kapoor, "Squatter's Rites," IT, July 31, 1983, pp. 25–26.

Dindoshi: Rupa Chinai, "A BMC Slum in the Making," *Indian Express*, May 31, 1986; Geeta Seshu, "Asia's Largest Slum," *Indian Express*, Dec. 20, 1987.

5 · The Rescue of Bishnu and Uma

Nehru comment on sustaining resentment: Sadanand Menon, "The Marginalization of the Civil Liberties Movement," LB, 5:4–5 (1987); this volume also has the later history: Smitu Kothari, "An Interview with V. M. Tarkunde," pp. 109–124.

Passivity: Moraes (1973), p. 111, for Sarojini's comment on American troops in Calcutta. There is a debate whether India had a tradition of peasant uprisings. The evidence is slim and confined mainly to tribals. See: Dhanagare (1983) and Mridula Mukherjee, "Peasant Resistance and Peasant Consciousness in Colonial India, Subalterns and Beyond," EPW, Oct. 15, 1988, pp. 2174–2184.

SITA: Jean D'Cunha, "Prostitution in a Patriarchal Society, A Critical Review of the SIT Act," EPW, Nov. 7, 1987, pp. 1919–1925.

Anna Kurian's housing struggles: Gurbir Singh, "Bombay Slums Face Operation Demolition," EPW, April 19, 1986, pp. 684–687; "Evidence of Arson," *Indian Express*, Jan. 21, 1988.

Shabana Azmi: M. Rahman, "Eviction Problems," IT, April 30, 1986, p. 55; Jai Kumar, "Politics Are Entering Even the Kitchen: An Interview with Shabana Azmi," *Sunday*

Chronicle, Feb. 7, 1988; Tavleen Singh, "Shabana Azmi, Actress Turned Activist," *Indian Express* (magazine), Jan. 29, 1989.

6 · Sister Rita's Report

Sister Rita's book is Rozario (1988). Lagan Rai, "Each Night Is Torture," TOI, Sept. 13, 1987, interviews her.

General articles on prostitution: Ghulam Nabi Khayal, "Jammu & Kashmir Slave Trade," IT, July 15, 1984, p. 81; Sheela Barse, "Policing the Oldest Profession," *Lex Et Juris*, May 1986, pp. 34–37; Shirin Mehta, "Women of the Streets," *Bombay*, Jan. 22–Feb. 6, 1987, pp. 39–41; Asit Paul, "She Was Sold Three Times," *National Herald*, Feb. 20, 1989; Ramesh Menon, "Child Prostitutes: Nobody's Children," IT, April 14, 1989, pp. 84–87; and Dilip Awasthi, "Prostitution: The Border Trafficking," IT, Aug. 15, 1989, pp. 72–73.

The report on police bribes is in D'Cunha, "Prostitution in a Patriarchal Society."

Shakti and Sita: Madhu Kishwar and Ruth Vanita, "Traditions versus Misconceptions," *Manushi* 42–43 (Sept.–Dec. 1987), pp. 2–14.

Grandmother's remark: *Chetna News* (Ahmedabad), April–June 1988, p. 26.

7 · Devadasis and Hijras

Gilada: Rajendar Menen, "The Wretched and the Damned: An Interview with Dr. I. S. Gilada," *The Daily*, Aug. 31, 1986, and Chaya Srivatsa, "A Doctor's Crusade against Child Prostitution," *Deccan Herald*, June 6, 1986.

See Gilada and Thakur (1987); Joint Women's Program (1983); and Chitra Subramaniam, "Devadasis: God's Mistresses," IT, Sept. 30, 1983, pp. 26–27.

Hijras: Laurence Preston, "A Right to Exist: Eunuchs and the State in Nineteenth Century India," *Modern Asian Studies* 21:2 (1987), pp. 371–387.

8 · Female Feticide

Killing of newborn girls: Pankaj Pachauri, "A Murderous Tradition," IT, Oct. 31, 1988, pp. 36–39, and S. H. Venkatramani, "Born to Die," IT, July 15, 1986, pp. 26–33.

Father willing to allow girl to die: M. E. Khan and others, "Inequalities between Men and Women in Nutrition and Family Welfare Services," *Social Action* 38:4 (Oct.–Dec. 1988), pp. 388–417.

Ardhanarishwara: Srinivas (1966), p. 20. Srinivas (1978) is an overview by India's leading anthropologist of changing concepts of women.

Worshipping husband as god: P. A. Sebastian, "Upholding Ideology of Male Domination," EPW, April 8, 1989, pp. 716–718. A suit was filed challenging a Bombay movie, "Pati Parameshwar," as offensive to women. The heroine, Rekha, has a disastrous marriage with a drunkard and swindler who steals her jewels and tries to poison her. She never loses faith and takes her husband to a dancing girl who was his lover. Dismissing the suit, the court found: "The personality of Rekha is an epitome of . . . the pure spirit of Indian ethos. . . . She exemplifies the inner strength and character of Indian womanhood. Her commitment to marriage is total and supreme. . . . What is glorified is not servility but faith, compassion, courage, sacrifice and endurance."

Eve Teasing: D. N., "Student Protest against Eve Teasing at Madras Law College," EPW, Aug. 15, 1987, pp. 1384–1385.

Leela Dube, "On the Construction of Gender: Hindu Girls in Patrilineal India," EPW, April 30, 1988, pp. WS 11–19, examines the process of socialization of Hindu girls as does Kishwar and Vanita, "Traditions versus Misconceptions." Also: Modumita Mojumdar, "Land of Starving Mothers," *Seminar* 331 (March 1987), pp. 33–34, and Barbara Diane Miller, "Changing Patterns of Juvenile Sex Ratios in Rural India, 1961 to 1971," EPW, June 3, 1989, pp. 1229–1236.

Pre-ban debate: Ravindra (1986); Sonal Shukla and others, "Abuse of New Technology," *Seminar* 331 (March 1987), pp. 14–17; and Barbara D. Miller, "Female Infanticide," same issue, pp. 18–21; Amita Verma, "Mama, Don't Kill Me!" *National Herald*, Dec. 13, 1987.

Kulkarni (1986) is the official report.

Passage of the ban: "Ban on Sex Tests Major Legislation," TOI, Jan. 25, 1988; Salil Tripathi, "Paying Heed," IT, Jan. 31, 1988, p. 55.

Debate following the ban: "If Abortions Are Okay, Why Not Sex Tests?" TOI, Feb. 12, 1989; Ritu Sarin and others, "Sex Determination," *Sunday*, Jan. 24–30, 1988, pp. 13–18; and Dharma Kumar, "Ban on Sex Test Clinics Unwise," TOI, Dec. 9, 1988. Nalini Taneja, "Female Foeticide No Democratic Right," TOI, Dec. 26, 1988, is a reply to Kumar.

Ericsson clinic: Rekha Basu and Salil Tripathi, "Male Order Service," IT, Aug. 15, 1989, pp. 46–48.

Dowry deaths: Kumari (1989) is a documented account of bride burning and other brutalities. Also: David Devadas, "The Horror Spreads," IT, June 30, 1988, pp. 86–88, and Nina Kapoor, "The Ritual Murder," *Seminar* 331 (March 1987), pp. 28–32.

Suicide of three sisters: Dilip Awasthi, "Deadly Deed," IT, Feb. 29, 1988, p. 58, and Navneet Sethi and K. Anand, "A Life of Humiliation," *Manushi* 45 (March–April, 1988), pp. 45–46. Other suicides: Barbara Crossette, "India Studying 'Accidental' Deaths of Hindu Wives," *The New York Times*, Jan. 15, 1989.

Srinivas (1984) surveys dowry issues. Earlier, Srinivas (1978), pp. 21–26, discussed how education has not ended dowry. Also see: Madhu Kishwar, "Rethinking Dowry Boycott," *Manushi* 48 (Sept.–Oct. 1988), pp. 10–13.

9 · The Goddess of Food

Savara (1981) is an early study of Annapurnas. Also see: Jana Everett and Mira Savara, "Bank Loans to the Poor in Bombay: Do Women Benefit?" *Signs* 10:2 (Winter 1984), pp. 272–290. They conclude: "We have found that programs targeted for self-employed poor women may actually benefit various intermediaries as much as (or more than) they benefit the women themselves. This is because development programs do not eliminate the hierarchical structure in which poor women eixst. More program benefits flow to poor women when they are mobilized as members of grassroots organizations. Such organizations, in turn, may help challenge the hierarchical structure itself."

Vidydhar Date, "Annapurnas: Cooking for Freedom," TOI, Sept. 8, 1987, interviews Prema Purao.

10 · Tribal India

Fundamental rights: Desai (1986), p. 60.

von Furer-Haimendorf (1982) is the standard text for Indian tribal studies. Suranjit Kumar Saha, "Historical Premises of India's Tribal Problem," *Journal of Contemporary Asia* 16:3 (1986), pp. 274–319, is an exhaustive treatment stressing "the futility . . . of the classical anthropology approach putting the focus on the internal structure of tribal society rather than on external problems such as increasing economic destitution . . . accompanied by increasing levels of state violence directed against them [by] . . . the elite-controlled pan-Indian societies."

Also: André Béteille, "The Definition of Tribe," in Thapar (1977), pp. 7–14, and Jaganath Pathy, "Land Problems of Tribals," TOI, Sept. 10, 1987.

Nirmal Sengupta, "Reappraising Tribal Movements: A Myth in the Making," EPW, May 7, 1988, pp. 943–945, says the British originally discussed castes and other Indian groups in terms of race. "Tribe" denoted persons of common ancestry no matter what their status. Only in 1872 did they begin to speak of "wild" and "pastoral" tribes along with the new evolutionary category of "aborigines" and "primitives."

11 · A Truck and Some Cows

Calman (1985), pp. 175–179, has Bhoomi Sena's history.

Indra Munshi Saldanha, "Attached Labor in Thane: A Historical Overview," EPW, May 20, 1989, pp. 1121–1127, reviews the methods and aims of several groups working to free bonded labor and generate tribal militancy in Thane, including Vivek Pandit's Shramjivi Sanghatana.

12 · Creating a New Revolutionary Class

Bondurant (1967) remains the best exposition of Gandhian philosophy and tactics. In the preface (p. vii) to the revised edition of a book first published in 1958, she positioned satyagraha within the formative stage of the social movement as a method of fruitful dialogue and communication aimed at reforming democracy, not destroying it: "In satyagraha, dogma gives way to an open exploration of context. The objective is not to assert propositions but to create possibilities. . . . Satyagraha goes well beyond the pressure tactics of strike, sit-in, fasting, and other limited efforts characteristic of passive resistance. . . . There is a constellation of questions to be asked of movements which profess the use of means ethically superior to violence. These are questions about objectives, procedures, and styles of action. Does the movement seek a genuine solution? When questions of choice are forced upon an opponent, is the stress thereby generated fully recognized? Is the effort one of support and reassurance to the opponent whose change of habit and behavior is so much desired? To what degree has the encounter established (or suppressed) communications? Has the method embraced an adequate process of enquiry? In what way is the force generated through nonviolence action directed into creative channels —creative, that is for all sides and for the total situation?"

"The English have not taken India . . .": Gandhi (1984), p. 38. "This band of satyagrahis . . .": Gandhi, CW, vol. 43, p. 93.

Gramsci's hegemony and originality: Bocock (1986), pp. 7–8, 107–109.

Denzil Saldanha, "Socialization of Critical Thought," EPW, July 29, 1989, pp. PE 54–61, continues the examination of social movement groups in Thane, including Vijay Sathe's Shramik Mukti Sanghatana. Saldanha views tribal illiteracy through a Gramscian lens: "The non-party political groups . . . by mobilizing around *adivasi* [tribal] cultural identity on economic issues related to their subsistence agriculture and through critical awareness, organization and political action for social transformation, attempt to link the political with the cultural and economic. They thus offer a perspective for resolving the contradictions, between and at these levels, forced by formalized adivasi education. Above all, they create a climate of critical social awareness and political action which generates a felt-need for literacy-numeracy and functionality, in a more relevant formalized educational program."

13 • The Mutiny of the Innocents

Passive revolution: Femia (1981), p. 48.
"Whose war . . .": Dutt (1971), p. 76; "Nipped in the bud . . .": ibid., p. 235.
"What a tragedy . . .": Gramsci (1957), p. 16.
Gandhi-darshan: Shahid Amid, "Gandhi as Mahatma," in Guha (1984), p. 4.
Chauri Chaura: Gandhi, "The Crime of Chauri Chaura," CW, vol. 22, p. 415.
McLane (1977), pp. 3–18, has an equivocal answer for the question of whether the Congress was merely "the vehicle for the pursuit of parochial goals and the advancement of local careers": "The Indian founders . . . were impressed by the nobility of a nationalist vision of subordinating the interests of self, family and caste to the interests of an Indian nation. . . . [But] it is readily conceded that local politics occupied a much greater share of the time and energies of educated Indians than did national politics."

14 • Save the Western Ghats

Malhotra (1987) has the ecology of the Western Ghats. Also: Inderjit Badhwar, "Deforestation: An Environmental Holocaust," IT, Aug. 15, 1986, pp. 55–56; Raj Chengappa, "Western Ghats: The Ravages of Man," IT, Feb. 29, 1988, pp. 166–171; Sathis Nair, "Wasting Wealth of Western Ghats," in Bandyopadhyay (1985), pp. 41–51; and Sharad Kulkarni, "Forests: Laws versus Policy," EPW, April 22, 1989, pp. 859–862.

15 • The Wandering Charcoal Makers

For a background study: Madhusadan Sathe, "Katkari Labor in Charcoal-Making," EPW, July 30, 1988, pp. 1565–1567.
IRDP: N. J. Kurian, "Anti-Poverty Program: A Reappraisal," EPW, March 25, 1989, pp. A13–A20.

16 • The Failure of Charisma

Gandhi's "Last Will": CW, vol. 90, Jan. 29, 1948, p. 392.
Two articles by Ishwar Harris, "Sarvodaya in Crisis: The Gandhian Movement in India Today," *Asian Survey* 27:9 (Sept. 1987), pp. 1036–1051, and "The Bhoodan Movement:

An Investigation into Vinoba Bhave's Legacy in Contemporary India," *Asian Thought & Society* 11:32–33 (July–Nov. 1986), pp. 165–183, are overall assessments. Tilak (1984) is an analysis in terms of concepts such as *yajna*. The quotation "Ours is a . . ." is in Tilak, p. 90.

Selbourne (1985) includes critical assessments of Jayaprakash Narayan, particularly: Chadwick Alger, "The Limits of the Nation-State," pp. 77–94, which includes the quotation on trusting the people, and Geoffrey Ostergaard, "The Ambiguous Strategy of JP's Last Phase," pp. 155–180.

For idealist impressions: Tennyson (1955).

17 • The Golana Massacre

See "Golana Massacre," LB 4:3–4 (1986), pp. 74–78, and Ramesh Menon, "Caste Carnage," IT, Feb. 18, 1986, p. 29.

18 • Temples and Toilets

Manu: G. Buhler (1964), pp. 136–137.

Popular beliefs: Ashby (1974), pp. 64–70, reports a survey in which 71 percent of students questioned said they believed fate lay behind such things as success or failure in examinations or obtaining proper wives or husbands. They believed both failures despite hard work and success without endeavor were equally the result of fate. He also says education does not diminish core Indian values: "There is little indication of a determination to change existing patterns in personal, family, or community life; these have proved their worth in the past and are believed to be necessary for the present and the emerging future." There is every reason to believe his assessment is as true now as it was when he wrote almost a generation ago.

19 • A Museum of Living Fossils

Uday Mahurkar, "A Stricken Sanctuary," IT, Sept. 30, 1987, p. 164, and Ramesh Menon, "Saurashtra, Tears of Salt," IT, Feb. 15, 1986, pp. 90–91.

20 • Temples or Tombs?

B. D. Dhawan, "Indian Irrigation: An Assessment," EPW, May 7, 1988, pp. 965–971, is a comprehensive overview. Two critical articles by B. B. Vohra, chairman of the government's Advisory Board on Energy are: "Managing India's Water Resources," *Mainstream*, Sept. 5, 1987, pp. 11–16, and "Neglect of Natural Resource Management," *Mainstream*, Jan. 16, 1988, pp. 15–18.

L. C. Jain, in "Poverty, Environment, Development: A View from Gandhi's Window," EPW, Feb. 13, 1988, pp. 311–320, writes: "Seventy percent of all the available water in India is polluted. . . . Between a quarter to a half of the lands brought under irrigation can go out of cultivation permanently because of soil salinity and waterlogging. The flood-prone area has doubled over the last ten years from 20 million to 40 million hectares." Pointing to growing disparities, "The share of the bottom 10 percent of the families has plummeted from 2.5 percent in 1961 to 0.1 percent in 1981," he asks: "How does this scenario compare with the India of Gandhi's dreams? The rich seem to be getting richer; the poor more marginalized. Development priorities appear to have been reversed. The philosophy of first things first or *Antyodaya* (the principle of addressing the last person first) appears to be standing on its head."

Also: J. Kurien and T. R. Thankappan Achari, "Fisheries Development Policies and the Fishermen's Struggle in Kerala," *Social Action* 38:1 (Jan.–March 1988), pp. 15–36.

Narmada's feasibility: Salil Tripathi, "A Flood of Controversies," ɪт, Oct. 31, 1988, pp. 118–121.

21 · Pragmatic Activists

The settlement is outlined in two mimeographed papers: "Sardar Sarovar Oustees Fight Continues" (May 6, 1988) and "The 14th May, 1988, Vadgam Convention Before and After" (May 21, 1988).

World Bank: Vandana Shiva, one of India's most informed critics of Western aid, in "The Politics of Aid," ɪwɪ, Sept. 20, 1987, pp. 46–47, maintains the bank has tried to mold the Third World to suit the political ambitions of the United States and this is a growing threat to the survival of debtor countries. The argument is further developed by Jayanta Bandyopadhyay and Vandana Shiva, "Political Economy of Ecology Movements," ᴇᴘᴡ, July 11, 1988, pp. 1223–1232. They say economic development is a predatory exploitation of natural resources representing colonialism in another guise and maintain the World Bank and other international agencies further this policy by funding projects in environmentally sensitive areas, by requiring borrowing governments to pledge counterpart funds, and by linking funding with export financing.

Such criticism risks obscuring the fact that the World Bank and other foreign institutions can manipulate Third World countries because of internal social and cultural distortions. To speak of colonialism in another guise may lead to the assumption that foreign rulers are still in power in India. Social movement activists say, in effect, the indigenous hegemony must be altered before foreign influence can be lessened and to concentrate on a possible foreign enemy diverts attention from the pressing need for internal change. Hence the emphasis of pragmatists like Anil Patel on the near oppressor.

22 · Population and Sterilization

Raj Chengappa, "Family Planning, The Great Hoax," ɪт, Oct. 31, 1988, pp. 82–91, is a rebuttal of government claims to be making progress in controlling population growth and includes instances of the misuse of sterilization.

Dilip Awasthi, "Inhuman Operation," ɪт, Dec. 15, 1988, pp. 181–182, reports the sterilization of women past menopause.

Suman Dubey, "Pipli and Uttawar," in Desai (1986), pp. 274–278, describes sterilization under Sanjay Gandhi.

Rosanna Ledbetter, "Thirty Years of Family Planning in India," *Asian Survey* 24:7 (July 1984), pp. 736–758, reviews the failures to limit population growth and the frustrations felt by Mrs Gandhi and her planners.

Sundari Ravindran, "Family Health Workers," *Health Action*, Secunderabad, Andhra Pradesh, July 1988, pp. 49–52, and B. D. Verma and A. K. Singla, "A Profile of Acceptors of Terminal Methods of Family Planning in a Rural Community," *Journal of Family Wel-*

fare 34:3 (March 1988), pp. 89–93, are microsurveys of sterilization and other family planning methods.

A. M. Shah, "Parameters of Family Policy in India," EPW, March 11, 1989, pp. 513–516, says the first wave of Western educated politicians has subsided and current lawmakers are deeply involved in the traditional social order and less interested in family and marriage reform.

Malini Karkal and S. Irudaya Rajan, "Age at Marriage: How Much Change?" EPW, March 11, 1989, pp. 505–506, point out that while the Child Marriage Restraint Act of 1978 raised the legal age of marriage for women to eighteen years, and there has been a decline in the number of marriages below the age of nine or ten, consummation still takes place at menarche because the status of women remains unchanged: "At every stage in her life, a woman should be under the dominion of someone. . . . The purpose of marriage was the transference of the father's domination over her in favor of her husband. This transference should hence take place before a girl reached the age when she might question it."

23 · A Model for Community Health

For what is believed to be the first such study of rural Indian women see: R. A. Bang and others, "High Prevalence of Gynecological Diseases in Rural Indian Women," *The Lancet* (London), Jan. 14, 1989, pp. 85–88. Of 650 women studied, with a mean age of 32.11 years, 92 percent had one or more gynecological or sexual diseases with an average of 3.6 infections per woman. Half the infections were of the genital tract. Only 7.8 percent had undergone gynecological examination and treatment even though 55 percent were aware of having gynecological disorders. The team commented: "Obviously there is a large gap between the need and the care. . . . Reproductive care to women needs to be broadened beyond maternity care and family planning."

24 · Working for Women

General articles: Vimal Balasubrahmanyam, "Invisible, Underpaid and Unorganized," *Mainstream*, Aug. 16, 1986, pp. 25–27; Lalita Krishnaswami, "From Drudgery to Dignity," *Mainstream*, April 4, 1986, pp. 25–29; and Ramesh Menon, "SEWA: Working for Women," IT, Feb. 28, 1985, pp. 76–77.

25 · Slaves of Sabarmati

Ramesh Menon, "Slaves of Sabarmati," IT, Oct. 15, 1983, pp. 74–75.

26 · The Rape of Guntaben

Rape as a perk: "Middle Class Obfuscation," EPW, March 5, 1988, pp. 441–442.

Amnesty International, ASA 20/04/88 is a condensed version of the Pathak-Joseph report. The Rajiv Gandhi denial of torture is quoted on p. 7. The TOI quotation is on pp. 4–5. The CRPF quotation is on p. 6.

Amending rape law: Sunil Sethi, "Rape: Controversial Code," IT, Dec. 31, 1983, pp. 74–75, and Chitra Subramaniam, "The Rape Rap," IT, June 30, 1983, pp. 44–45.

Tyagi and Suman Rani: "The Police: Crime and Punishment," EPW, Feb. 6, 1988, p. 225; Ashwini Bhatnagar, "Maya Tyagi: Retribution," IWI, May 1, 1988, pp. 37–39; Pankaj Pachauri, "Tyagi Case: Death Penalty," IT, Feb. 15, 1988, p. 73; and Naina Kapoor, "Suman Rani Has Been Wronged," TOI, Feb. 13, 1989.

27 · The Mystic Dancer

Mrinalini Sarabhai, "Where Are We Going?" *Mainstream*, Dec. 5, 1987, pp. 12–13.

28 · Bihar: Blindings and Massacres

Blindings: Desai (1986), p. 256, and "Three Cops Jailed in Bhagalpur Blindings Case," TOI, Sept. 2, 1987.

The leading authority on Bihar is Arvind Das. See: "Agrarian Change from Above and Below: Bihar 1947–78," in Guha (1983), pp. 180–227; "Peasant Movements and Agrarian Change in Bihar," *Social Action* 38:1 (Jan.–March 1988), pp. 50–60; "Tribe-Caste Dialectic in Bihar," TOI, Oct. 25, 1985; "Caste Killings and Naxalite Alibi," *Mainstream*, June 20, 1987, pp. 7–10; and "Social Fragmentation in Bihar," TOI, June 27, 1988. He refers to *Rangdaari* in this article.

Other overviews: Sudhanshu Ranjan, "Bihar Killings in Retrospect," *Mainstream*, March 5, 1988, pp. 27–29; Shyama Nand Singh, "Roots of Caste War in Bihar," *Mainstream*, Jan. 16, 1988, pp. 28–29; and K. S. Subramanian, "Behind Rural Violence," *Mainstream*, July 25, 1987, pp. 19–26. Subramanian, a police official, refers to the Criminal Procedure Code.

Brahmin domination: Ramashray Roy, "Caste and Political Recruitment in Bihar," in Kothari (1970), pp. 228–258; Farzand Ahmed, "Transfer Spree," TOI, Dec. 15, 1988, p. 61; and Tirthankar Ghosh, "Same Tales from a Congress State," *Sunday*, Nov. 6–12, pp. 68–71.

Mass killings: Faisand Ahmed, "Murder in the Night," *Sunday*, June 14–20, pp. 36–38, and "Haunted by the Past," *Sunday*, May 22–28, 1988, p. 46; Farzand Ahmed, "Private Armies," IT, March 15, 1984, pp. 72–74, and "The Caste Carnage," IT, Dec. 15, 1985, pp. 104–105; Prabha Dutt, "Vicious Vendetta," IT, Jan. 31, 1984, pp. 54–57; and T. N. Ninan, "The Lawless State," IT, June 30, 1987, pp. 86–92.

Jallianwalla Bagh: "The Amritsar Massacre" in McLane (1970), pp. 69–74.

Arwal: Farzand Ahmed, "Deadly Division," IT, May 31, 1986, pp. 50, 55; Bernard D'Mello, "Arwal Massacre: Report of People's Tribunal," EPW, Aug. 29, 1987, pp. 1486–1488; and Smitu Kothari, "Bihar's Jallianwalla and After," LB 4: 3–4 (1986), pp. 79–95.

Fein (1977), p. xii, says a census counted over 500 victims. Leaving aside the disparities in casualties, the similarities between Jallianwalla Bagh and Arwal are revealing. Fein, pp. x–xi, says the Amritsar massacre should be seen "as crime and punishment simultaneously: it is objectively a crime against the victims but is understood by its perpetrators as a punishment. . . . The class perpetrating the crime often claims the victims deserved this punishment for a criminal act alleged to have been committed by one or more of them against the class of the perpetrators. Sometimes these punishments are frankly acknowledged by the aggressors to be reprisals or revenge. In other cases, such violence is frequently accounted for by perpetrators as acts of self-defense, and the blame is cast on the victim for provoking them. . . . Each class is excluded from the universe of moral obligation of the other, so that offenses against the other are not recognized as crimes.

Although crimes against members of the dominant class by members of the class dominated are understood by the dominant class to be crimes against all of its members, they
recognize no obligation toward the dominated." The fact that no one was punished for
Arwal, or for other massacres of minorities elsewhere, illustrates the race/caste syndrome.
However, while the Indian elite acts in the same manner as the British, it does so from
entirely indigenous impulses.

Pararia: Uttam Sengupta, "Rape of Justice," IT, May 31, 1989, pp. 44–48.

Fishermen: Rudranath Sanyal, "Bhagalpur's River of Blood," *Sunday*, Jan. 3–9, 1988,
pp. 59–60.

29 · The Role of Activists

Gramsci on a new culture: Hoare and Smith (1971), p. 325.

Similarly, on intellectual leadership, Freire (1988), pp. 162–169, writes: "Usually
[the] leadership group is made up of men who in one way or another have belonged to the
social strata of the dominators. At a certain point in their existential experience, under
certain historical conditions, these men renounce the class to which they belong and join
the oppressed, in an act of true solidarity. . . . The leaders must believe in the potentialities of the people, whom they cannot treat as mere objects of their own action. They
must believe that the people are capable of participating in the pursuit of liberation."

Philip Eldridge and Nil Ratan, "Voluntary Organizations and Popular Movements in
Bihar," LB 6:4 (1988), pp. 3–44, review activist groups other than the Ganga Mukti Andolan.

Ekalavia: von Buitenin (1973), pp. 270–272.

Kidnapping: Farzand Ahmed, "Sullied Image," IT, Jan. 31, 1989, p. 77.

30 · Nonviolent Melodrama

Freire (1988), pp. 150–151, writes: "Cultural invasion . . . is a phenomenon [in which]
the invaders penetrate the cultural context of another group, in disrespect of the latter's
potentialities; they impose their own view of the world upon those they invade and inhibit the creativity of the invaded by curbing their expression. Whether urbane or harsh,
cultural invasion is thus always an act of violence against the persons of the invaded
culture, who lose their originality or face the threat of losing it. . . . Cultural conquest
leads to the cultural inauthenticity of those who are invaded; they begin to respond to the
values, the standards and the goals of the invaders."

31 · Journalism and Its Perils

Growth of Hindi press: Suneet Vir Singh, "More Power to the Hindi Press," *Hindustan Times*, Dec. 18, 1988.

Manimala and translations of her stories: P. M. Lata, "Manimala," *Adhikar Raksha*
10:2 (April–June 1987), pp. 22–28; "Witch-Hunt," IWI, May 1, 1988, pp. 20–23, is her
story on witches.

Press bashing: see Dhavan (1987) for an extensive review of laws and judicial findings
attempting to control press activism in what Dhavan calls the "law and order" concept of
society inherited from the British. There is no constitutionally guaranteed freedom of the
press in India. The constitution only guarantees freedom of speech and expression, and

the courts have ruled the press does not enjoy rights not available to all citizens. Dhavan (pp. 1–35) writes that under Jawaharlal Nehru the press was content to be a cheering squad for his socialistic imperatives and this continued during most of the rule of Mrs Gandhi. However, as her centralism grew stronger, so did press criticism. During the Emergency, in addition to various forms of outright censorship, 253 journalists were arrested under the detention laws, fifty-one reporters, cartoonists and cameramen were disaccredited, seven foreign correspondents were expelled, and twenty-nine others were denied visas to enter India. Since then, he writes, the press has been increasingly combative: "The press is slowly coming into its own. . . . Heavily biased, greatly pressurized and manipulated, subject to enormous strains, starved of resources and riddled with varying degrees of competence and incompetence . . . the press remains a formidable weapon. With radio and television as part of the monopoly of the State, the press commands more response than the promises of politicians. [With] the emergence of a group of journalists who wish to increase the arena of bargaining to include themselves and various sections of the public, the nature of this arena itself is changing."

For specific events see: S. Nihal Singh, "The Unseen Battle," IT, Aug. 31, 1989, and "Crude Censorship," EPW, Aug. 5, 1989 (Punjab and arrest of Brahmadeo Singh Sharma); "Censorship through Guns," EPW, June 18, 1988, p. 1250 (killing of Umesh Dobhal); Ruben Banerjee, "Increasing Coercion of Newsmen," *Indian Express*, Jan. 12, 1988 (*Samaj* and other incidents in Orissa); K. Balagopal, "Pitting the Tribals against the Non-Tribal Poor," EPW, May 27, 1989, pp. 1149–1154 (torture of Sivaramkum); Balagopal's arrest: Amnesty International, ASA 20/02/86; and M. V. Desai and others, "Journalism Plus," *Vidura*, Sept.–Oct. 1987, pp. 13–21 (Dantre incident).

32 · We Have a Dream

Gandhi's vision: Selbourne (1985), p. 68.

Manthara uses a method Freire (1988), p. 52, calls dialogue, in which leaders and those whom they would lead are students, standing away from their situation to put questions to it: "Critical and liberating dialogue . . . must be carried on with the oppressed at whatever the stage of their struggle. . . . To substitute monologue, slogans, and communiqués for dialogue is to attempt to liberate the oppressed with the instruments of domestication. Attempting to liberate the oppressed without their reflective participation in the act of liberation is to treat them as objects which must be saved from a burning building; it is to . . . transform them into masses which can be manipulated."

Codes and signs: Melucci (1989), pp. 55–56.

33 · Myths and Identity

Chattopadhyay quotation: Chatterjee (1986), p. 82.

Aryan myth: Huxley (1935), pp. 146–152.

Minz (1988).

General articles: Sharit Kumar Bhowmik, "Development Perspectives for Tribals," EPW, May 14, 1988, pp. 1005–1007; Rajiv Ranjan Lal, "The Winds of War," IWI, Jan. 1, 1989, pp. 44–57; D. N., "Factors in the Jharkhand Movement," EPW, Jan. 30, 1988, pp. 185–187; and Barun Das Gupta, "Anatomy of Jharkhand Movement," *Mainstream*, Feb. 18, 1989, pp. 7–8, 34.

Gua massacre: Desai (1986), pp. 295–297, and Xavier Dias, "Not for the Love of Tribals," EPW, March 11, 1989, pp. 497–499.

34 · **The Front Paw of the Revolution**

Duyker (1987). The quotations from Radio Beijing are on pp. 72–73.

Sengupta (1983) is a reprint of a 1970 inner-party analysis of the ideological failings of Naxalism.

Ray (1988) provides an analysis of Naxalism in the context of Bengali society and the bhadralok.

The bhadralok support English-language domination despite the fact it keeps the poor as a perpetual underclass. See: Poromesh Acharya, "Is Macaulay Still Our Guru?" EPW, May 28, 1988, pp. 1124–1130. He says when a language reform committee ordered an end to teaching English at the primary level, bhadralok protests forced the Left Front government to close its eyes to widespread evasion, proving "the grip the vocal bhadraloks hold on the entire power structure and on the system of education."

Tortures: Desai (1986), pp. 238–245, 262, 271–273; Joshi, "Terror through Torture," IT, May 16–31, 1987, pp. 24–29, and A. M., "Calcutta Diary," EPW, June 20, 1987, pp. 967–968.

Present situation: Gail Omvedt, "The Left in India," *Journal of Contemporary Asia* 15:2 (1985), pp. 172–182; Ajoy Bose, "Naxalites: A Change of Focus," *Indian Express*, June 12, 1988; and Nirmal Mitra, "The Dilemma of the Reds," *Sunday*, March 27–April 2, 1988, pp. 23–26.

In Sengupta (1983), p. ii, Partha Chatterjee of the Center for Studies in Social Sciences, Calcutta, comments: "The political challenge of Naxalbari forced the state to bare its teeth to show its ugly face stripped of the facades of bourgeois legality, populist reformism and tolerance of dissent." He also comments on the ideological bankruptcy of the left: "Hitherto unquestioned orthodoxies . . . of central planning, the public sector, the mixed economy of 'non-capitalist paths of development,' of the gradual 'socialization' of the 'commanding heights of the economy' . . . [have] become the new foundations of the ideological legitimation of ruling-class power in post-colonial India. . . . One can hardly miss the significance of the increasing gap between the almost ritual theoretical pronouncements of the parties on the Left, and their day-to-day political practice, which makes it so easy for their critics to charge them with unprincipled opportunism, adhocism and numerous other crimes of this sort."

Although the Comintern created the Indian Communist Party in the early 1920s, India has proved infertile ground. Bombay, the cradle of militant trade unionism, repudiated its Communist pioneers in the 1960s. In Tamil Nadu and Andhra Pradesh, after regional parties ousted the Congress, the Communists were content to tag onto one or another of the new parties. Despite its strength in West Bengal, the CPM has not been able to make inroads in neighboring Bihar and Orissa. In Tripura the CPM has the support of Bengali-speakers but has lost favor with tribals. In Kerala the CPI and CPM are limited to the districts of Trivandrum and Cochin. Terrorists have decimated the Communists in Punjab.

35 · **From Revolt to Renewal**

The burden of alcoholism is heavy. A nationwide survey by a Bombay institute estimated industrial workers spent 60 percent of their pay on alcohol. See: *Amrita Bazar Patrika*, Jan. 23, 1989.

36 · A Civilization That Doesn't Work

Dilip and Jharna Sen, "A Man For All Seasons," *The Statesman*, Feb. 5, 1989, reviews Dasgupta's life.

37 · Death by Encounter

Calman (1985), pp. 45–48, has Satyanarayana.

Seetharamiah and Peoples War Group: Amarnath Menon, "A Dramatic Escape," IT, Jan. 31, 1984, p. 32; Venu Menon, "Fear is the Key," IWI, Jan. 24, 1988, pp. 8–21; and V. G. Prasad Rao, "Luring Them Away from Naxalites," TOI, Sept. 8 and 9, 1987.

Bhargava Commission: Desai (1986), pp. 248–252, and P. A. Sebastian, "The Shifting Modalities of Struggle—The Setting Up of the Human Rights Tribunal," LB 5:4–5 (Oct. 1987), pp. 93–99.

Murder of civil rights activists: Amnesty International, ASA 20/03/86, pp. 11–13.

Chintapalli: K. Balagopal, "A Tale of Arson," EPW, July 18, 1987, pp. 1169–1171, and "All Power Has Legal Limits," *Adhikar Raksha* 11:4 (Oct.–Dec. 1988), pp. 28–31.

Meghyam: K. Balagopal, "A Year of Encounters," EPW, Jan. 14, 1989, pp. 66–68.

In June 1989 Andhra Pradesh announced plans for a *Grama Swayam Samakshana Samati* (Self-Protection Committee) consisting of five individuals in each village who would be granted licenses to carry arms (automatically ruling out the poor who cannot afford weapons) to patrol the surrounding areas and assist police. "Encouraging Private Gangsterism," *Economic And Political Weekly*, May 6, 1989, p. 949, saw the move as a sanction for private armies loyal to the ruling party. Pointing to similar actions in Punjab and Assam, it commented: "These developments only reflect the larger breakdown of the consensus that existed in Indian society. . . . The state itself is now encouraging private gangsterism and vigilantism under the guise of fighting gangsterism. This development too was perhaps inevitable, for the criminalization of the political process had to lead, inescapably, to the criminalization of the state itself."

39 · A Man with Faith in India

A review of Dr. Rao's career: P. Prasannan, "He Lets Nothing Go Waste," *The Week*, Dec. 27–Jan. 2, 1988, pp. 8–24.

40 · Broken Promises, Broken Children

Orphans: Deenaz Damania, "Observations on the Child Welfare Scene in India," *Child Welfare* 68:2 (March–April 1989), pp. 141–144.

Antislavery Society: Sheila Rule, "British Group Finds Slavery Is Flourishing," *New York Times*, July 3, 1989.

Two extensive reviews of child labor: Neera Burra, "Exploitation of Child Workers in Lock Industry of Aligarh," EPW, July 11, 1987, pp. 1117–1121, and "Exploitation of

Children in Jaipur Gem Industry," EPW, Jan. 16, 1988, pp. 75–79, and Jan. 23, 1988, pp. 131–137.

Also: C. Prabhakaran, "The Languishing Lot," *Hindustan Times*, May 9, 1988, and Dingwaney (no date), pp. 22–23.

Carpet industry: Juyal (1987); construction industry: Mobile Crèches (1987), pp. 30–32; household workers: "Servants Exploited Up to the Hilt," TOI, Sept. 4, 1987; bidi workers: Farzand Ahmed, "Bidi Workers in the Twilight Zone," IT, Nov. 15, 1983, pp. 49–51; sugar cane cutters: D. N., "Migrant Workers, Super-Exploitation and Identity," EPW, June 4, 1988, pp. 1152–1154; knitting industry: S. H. Venkatramani, "Vested Interests," IT, July 15, 1983, pp. 26–27, and C. Krishnaswami, "Dynamics of Capitalist Labor Process: Knitting Industry in Tamil Nadu," EPW, June 17, 1989, pp. 1353–1359.

42 · The Little Match Girls

Match factories: Smitu Kothari, "Exploiting the Young," IT, Jan. 15, 1983, pp. 56–59. Nadar caste: Kothari (1970), pp. 102–126.

43 · The Riddles of Hinduism

Excrement: Amnesty International, ASA 20/02/88, p. 10; Anita Pratap, "Caste Scandal," IT, Feb. 29, 1988, p. 50.

Children not allowed on mats: M. V. Desai, "Ministering at Grassroots," *Mainstream*, July 29, 1989, pp. 29–30.

Marriage Party: "Murder of 14 of Marriage Party Recalled," TOI, May 21, 1988.

Godse/Gandhi: Rajshekar (1986), pp. 8–11, sees Gandhi as symbolizing Indian hypocrisy: "India's ruling class accepted the social and political part of Gandhism while rejecting the better part of his philosophy, namely his economic theories. . . . The Gandhian economics, laying stress on rural development, small is beautiful, cottage industry, self-reliance, simple living—all these cut at the very root of our urban-dwelling upper caste rulers. . . . Gandhi is . . . a pathetic figure. No school or college anywhere in India has a text book on Gandhi or Gandhism . . . and yet Gandhi's photo is there in every government office."

Gods to Gutters and subsequent riots: Rajshekar (1978).

Mother to Hitler: Rajshekar (1984b), pp. 4–5.

There are only two biographies in English of Ambedkar: Keer (1987) and Kuber (1987). While he lived, Western commentators, under the spell of Gandhi and Nehru, dismissed Ambedkar as an irrelevant crank. This is true of all lower caste movements. The philosophic father of Ambedkar was Mahatma (the first to be granted this honorific) Jotirao Phule, whose name is hardly known even in India. O'Hanlon (1985) is a modern scholarly study. She writes, pp. 15–16: "We may well be convinced . . . of the need for a wider definition of what constitutes 'political' activity in nineteenth-century South Asia. . . . We tend naturally to know most about the small, high caste communities of the literate; about urban societies and about those in the centers of political power. The farther we move from these narrow circles, toward the much larger groups of pre-literate peasant, artisan and small trading castes, the less information we have."

Rajshekar is evidence this is still true. His magazine, *Dalit Voice*, is seldom found on newsstands. As far as can be determined, no major newspaper foreign correspondent of any nationality has interviewed him about Dalits in India, and he has never been invited to seminars funded by major Indian or foreign institutions. He represents, in India, the "invisibility" of American racism.

Untouchables not Hindus: Ambedkar (1977), pp. 183–189. Gandhi's view: Gandhi (1973), p. 336 (Nov. 28, 1936).

The debate between Ambedkar and Gandhi is reviewed in A. M. Abraham Ayrooku-zhiel, "Religion and Culture in Dalits' Struggle for Liberation," *Religion and Society* 33:2 (June 1986), pp. 33–44.

Limitations of saintliness: Parekh (1989), pp. 207–246.

Problem not poverty: Rajshekar (1984a), pp. 5–28, and "Marxian Theory of 'Class Struggle' Falls Flat in Racist US & Castist India," *Dalit Voice*, April 1–15, 1989, pp. 3–9.

Vakil (1985) is a history of the development and application of reservations and of atrocities against Dalits. Also: D. L. Sheth, "Reservations Policy Revisited," EPW, Nov. 14, 1987, pp. 1957–1961.

Prasad and others (1987), p. 48, demanding an end to evasion of reservations, warn: "The intolerance of the upper castes and the aspirations of the lower castes are glaring indications that the Indian road to social equality is bound to be marked by bloody clashes between different castes if a definite design of policy is not attempted to achieve balance in society. The days of false promises and rosy hopes are over."

Patidars and riots: Anil Bhatt, "Caste and Political Mobilization in a Gujarat District," in Kothari (1970), pp. 299–339; Asghar Ali Engineer, "Communal Riots: A Theoretical Framework," *Mainstream*, Feb. 27, 1988, pp. 8–11, 34; Ramesh Menon, "Violence Spree," IT, Jan. 31, 1986, p. 57, "Dangerous Moves," IT, March 15, 1986, pp. 143–144, and "Ahmedabad: A Wounded City," IT, Nov. 30, 1986, pp. 155–157; Ghanshyam Shah, "Middle Class Politics: Case of Anti-Reservation Agitations in Gujarat," EPW, May 1987, pp. AN 155–173; and Achyut Yagnik and Harsad Desai, "The Wages of Populism: The Second Anti-Reservation Agitation," LB 3:2 (1985), pp. 3–18.

John R. Wood, "Reservations in Doubt: The Backlash Against Affirmative Action in Gujarat India," *Pacific Affairs* 60: 3 (Fall 1987), pp. 408–430, comments: "[The] riots reflect the success of the policy insofar as reservations have contributed to political participation by and the feeling of political efficacy among disadvantaged Gujaratis." Despite the riots, he is optimistic: "Reservation policy making in India is currently at an impasse, but time, numbers and the forces of modernizing change in India appear to be on the side of the disadvantaged."

Aftermath: Uday Mahurkar, "Police Raj," IT, Dec. 15, 1987, p. 38; Ashraf Sayed and Gautam Mehta, "Misuse of Terrorist Act in Gujarat," TOI, Sept. 30, 1987; and Ashraf Sayed, "Sanity after Bouts of Riots," TOI, Jan. 1, 1988.

Derivation of Hindu: Roy and Gidwani (1984), vol. 2, p. 186, traces the term to the Persians and Greeks. Romila Thapar, "Communalism: Historical Realities," *Mainstream*, Jan. 25, 1987, pp. 18–21, has the Arab usage and lack of all-India consciousness.

Monier-Williams (1971), pp. 12–13. D. Miller, "Six Theses on the Question of Religion and Politics in India Today," EPW, July 25, 1987, pp. PE 57–63, quoting Monier-Williams, writes: "A consciousness of being Indian . . . is a certain indifference to any labelling, it is immune to any monopoly, it is a refusal to be assumed, taken for granted, numbered. This form of Indianness is an unconscious denial of any totality, an ease with being, over time, ambivalent in one's loves and hates."

Gowalkar: quoted in George (1986), p. 35.
Ambedkar on democracy: *Dalit Voice*, Jan. 16–31, p. 2.

44 • The Conversions at Meenakshipuram

Khan (1983) is a detailed study of the conversions. Dirks (1987), pp. 269–284, has the deep caste roots of the Thevar-Pallar struggle. Durrani (1986) quotes the reaction of politicians and newspapers, including *The Organizer*.

45 • Manipulating Myths and Symbols

History of RSS and VHP: Anderson and Damle (1987).
Ekatmata Yajna: Sumit Mitra, "Road to Revival," IT, Nov. 30, 1983, pp. 34–36.
Ayodhya: Peter Van Der Veer, "God Must Be Liberated! A Hindu Liberation Movement in Ayodhya," *Modern Asian Studies* 21:2 (1987), pp. 283–301.
Cow protection: Its significance in leading to the partition of India is often overlooked. McLane (1977), pp. 271–331, saying riots in 1893 led to more than one hundred deaths, comments: "Cow protectors hoped to achieve a legislative restriction on the slaughter of kine. This stiffened Muslim resistance to the idea of majority rule and the Indian National Congress."
Liberation campaign: Farzand Ahmed, "Conflicting Claims," IT, Oct. 31, 1984, pp. 48–49, and "Unholy Row," IT, Feb. 28, 1986, pp. 66–67; Dilip Awasthi, "Ayodhya: Communal Confrontation," IT, April 30, 1987, pp. 66–67.
Hindu coup: D. R. Goyal, "Ayodhya and After," *Mainstream*, March 15, 1986, pp. 5–8.
Inder Mohan: "A Freedom Fighter's Anguish," *The Statesman*, Aug. 15, 1987, and Khushwant Singh, "Nishkam Karma," *Hindustan Times*, July 9, 1988.
Peepul Tree: "A PUCL Investigation: Communalization of the Police in the Walled City," LB 4:2 (April 1986), pp. 18–39.

46 • The Juggernaut Claims Its Victims

Growth of the RSS: Inderjit Badhwar, "Militant Revivalism," IT, May 31, 1986, pp. 30–39, and Pankaj Pachauri, "RSS, Open Offensive," IT, June 30, 1989, pp. 40–43.
Also: R. Balashankar, "The Hindu Road to Power," *The Week*, Jan. 24–30, 1988, pp. 12–19; Yogendra Malik and Dhirendra Vajpeyi, "The Rise of Hindu Militancy," *Asian Survey* 29:3 (March 1989), pp. 308–325; Ashis Nandy, "The Politics of Secularism and the Recovery of Religious Tolerance," *Alternatives* 13 (1988), pp. 177–194; and Manoranjan Mohanty, "Secularism: Hegemonic and Democratic," EPW, June 3, 1989, pp. 1219–1220.
Shah Bano: Shekar Gupta, "A Community in Turmoil," IT, Jan. 31, 1986, pp. 90–103; Inderjit Badhwar, "Anger and Hurt," IT, March 15, 1986, pp. 40–43; David Devadas, "Victims of Confusion," IT, Feb. 19, 1988, pp. 138–139; Nawaz Mody, "The Press in India: The Shah Bano Judgment and Its Aftermath," *Asian Survey* 27:8 (Aug. 1987), pp. 935–953; and Zoya Hasan, "Muslim Women Bill Campaign and the Political Process," EPW, Jan. 7, 1989, pp. 44–50.
Confrontation politics: Ajay Kumar, "A Contentious Call," IT, Jan. 31, 1987, pp. 10–13; Asghar Ali Engineer, "An Appeal to Muslims," *Mainstream*, Sept. 12, 1987, pp. 11–15; and Farzand Ahmed, "Communalism: Stirring the Cauldron," IT, Nov. 30, 1988, pp. 50–53.

Previous riots: Akbar (1988), pp. 33–44; Rajgopal (1987), pp. 75–93; and Asghar Ali Engineer, "Anatomy of Shiv Sena's Growth," *Mainstream*, Sept. 3, 1988, pp. 15–18.

Meerut riots: Engineer (1987); Patralekh Chatterjee, "Meerut's Days of the Long Night," *Sunday*, June 7–13, 1987, pp. 16–20; Prabhu Chawla, "The Agony of Meerut," IT, June 15, 1987, pp. 30–38; and Dilip Awasthi, "PAC, Questionable Conduct," IT, July 30, 1987, pp. 73–75.

Aftermath: Amnesty International, ASA 20/02/88, pp. 11–12; "Human Rights: Not at Home," EPW, March 12, 1988, pp. 497–498; "Communal Killings: Unpunished Guilty," EPW, May 27, 1989, p. 1132; "Human Rights: Guarding the Guards," EPW, June 3, 1989, pp. 1192–93; and S. D. Singh, "India Raps Human Rights Body," *Hindustan Times*, Feb. 22, 1989.

A. G. Noorani, "Amnesty International and India," EPW, June 24, 1989, p. 1373, calls India's reaction "regal arrogance" and "pompous boorishness." In the same issue (p. 1365) EPW quotes a government spokesman, in rejecting an Amnesty International report on Indian Army tortures in Sri Lanka, as saying: "India needs no lectures from the self-appointed watchdogs of human rights."

47 · The Politics of Passion

Overview: Akbar (1985), pp. 103–209; Kapur (1986); Amnesty International, ASA 20/11/86, pp. 1–7; Satwinder Dhillon, "Akali Politics: Role of Symbols," *Mainstream*, June 11, 1988, pp. 11–13, 26; Dipankar Gupta and others, "Communalized Beyond Politics," EPW, Aug. 13, 1988, pp. 1677–1684; and Cynthia Keppley Mahmood, "Sikh Rebellion and the Hindu Concept of Order," *Asian Survey* 29:3 (March 1989), pp. 326–340.

A retired police officer, N. S. Saksena, "The Price of Peace in Punjab," *Indian Express*, Feb. 8, 1988, traces terrorist gangs to smuggling and corruption that "traveled upwards to the levels of chief ministers and police chiefs."

Bhindranwale: Akbar (1985), pp. 185–200; Khushwant Singh, "The Rise of Bhindranwale," *Sunday*, Jan. 17–23, 1988, p. 26; and Kuldeep Kumar, "The Ghost of Bhindranwale," *Sunday*, Dec. 20–26, 1987, pp. 58–60.

Attack on Golden Temple: Akbar (1985), pp. 201–209.

Arthur Helweg, "India's Sikhs: Problems and Prospects," *Journal of Contemporary Asia* 17:2 (1987), pp. 140–159, says 1,200 persons were killed in the attack.

Assassination of Indira Gandhi and Sikh killings: Mukhoty and Kothari (1984); Harish Sethi and Smitu Kothari (eds.), "Voices from a Scarred City," LB 3:1 (Jan. 1985); and Ritu Sarin, "Cracking the Conspiracy," *Sunday*, Nov. 20–26, 1988, pp. 25–31.

Chakravarti and Haksar (1987) is a compilation of eyewitness accounts. Quoted are Nanki Bai (p. 33), Gurmeet Singh (pp. 151–155), and Ratnabehn (pp. 448–454). Amrit Srinivasan, reviewing the Chakravarti-Haksar book in EPW, Sept. 5–12, pp. 1543–1544, commented: "Partition now appears as a precursor of the contemporary crisis which in turn may foreshadow others. . . . And what theory of statehood is this which builds on an original mistake? . . . In such a context, the colonial claims of having united us against the barbarity of our political past begin to appear suspicious."

Sikhs in freedom movement: Singh (1988), inside cover.

Punishing the guilty: Pankaj Pachauri, "A Reluctant Inquiry," IT, Aug. 31, 1987, p. 58; "Powerful Protectors," EPW, Oct. 29, 1988, p. 2244; and "In Sorrow and Anguish," EPW, Dec. 3, 1988, pp. 2568–2569.

Terrorism: Ritu Sarin, "Delhi, Where No One is Safe," *Sunday*, June 28–July 4, 1987, pp. 27–30; Dilip Bobb and others, "The Specter of Terrorism," IT, July 31, 1987, pp. 30–41; Inderjit Badhwar, "A Time of Reckoning," IT, April 30, 1988, pp. 58–69; and N. S. Saksena, "Changes in Punjab but No Gains," TOI, Dec. 17, 1988.

Second clearing of Golden Temple: K. Gopalakrishnan and G. K. Singh, "Better Armed, Better Prepared," *The Week*, May 22–28, 1988, pp. 32–40; Rahul Bedi, "Chamber of Horrors," *The Week*, June 26–July 2, 1988, p. 8; and Vipul Mudgal, "Grave Deeds," IT, June 30, 1988, p. 49.

Anti-terrorist laws: Amnesty International, ASA 20/11/86, pp. 8–12, and "A Lid on Liberty," IT, April 15, 1988, p. 11.

Police terrorism: The Tiwana Commission report was never officially released, but a summary, with no date or source, has been circulated. Comments quoting portions: "Tiwana Commission's Findings," EPW, April 23, 1988, p. 813, and Amnesty International, ASA 20/02/88, p. 9. This describes tortures in Punjab.

Nitya/Ashok (1989) has the story of Bhupinder Singh, pp. 16–21, and Iqbal Singh, pp. 40–47.

Official reaction to Amnesty International: *New York Times*, Aug. 10, 1988.

Punishment in Gandhi conspiracy: Ritu Sarin, *Sunday*, "Cracking the Conspiracy," Nov. 20–26, 1988, pp. 25–31, and "In Tandem," EPW, Jan. 7, 1989, p. 3.

48 · The Fiery Swami

Arya Samaj: Jones (1976), pp. 30–66.

Sati: Madhu Kishwar and Ruth Vanita, "The Burning of Roop Kumar," *Manushi* 42–43 (Sept.–Dec. 1987), pp. 15–34, and Sanjeev Srivastava, "Deorala Revisited," IWI, May 22, 1988, pp. 20–23. This has the claim the pyre lighted itself.

Nandy (1980), pp. 1–31, mentions underlying causes "less amenable to conscious control." Even when the first Indian demands were heard in the nineteenth century to ban sati, "the rite became popular in groups made psychologically marginal by their exposure to Western impact. These groups felt the pressure to demonstrate, to others as well as to themselves, their ritual purity and allegiance to traditional high culture. To many sati became an important proof of conformity to older norms at a time when these norms had become shaky within." It is this psychological insecurity that thwarts reform in India, whether of sati, dowry, or rape.

March to Deorala: Milap Chand Dandia, "Stopped in Their Tracks," *Sunday*, July 24–30, pp. 62–63.

Debate: Anuradha Dutt, "When Bodies Are Not Equal, How Can Rights Be Equal?" IWI, May 1, 1988, pp. 26–33, and Nirmal Mitra, "The Swami and the Sankaracharya," *Sunday*, April 10–16, 1988, pp. 12–15. This has the story of the miracle that prevented her rescue.

Veerendra Sangar, "Government Abets Sati Campaign," *Mainstream*, April 9, 1988, pp. 2–3, has the Sankaracharya's reference to the demonstrators as prostitutes.

Nathdwara: Rita Manchanda, "Balance-Sheet of a Padyatra," *Mainstream*, July 23, 1988, pp. 13–14, 33, and Nilanjan Mukhopadhyay, "Govt. Not on Our Side: Agnivesh," *Sunday Mail*, July 17–23, 1988.

VHP at Kumbh Mela: Gautam Navlakha, "A Show of Hindu Power," EPW, April 1, 1989, p. 658.

49 · The Triumph of Gandhi's Assassin

Gandhi's apocalyptic vision: Hugh Tinker, "Even As Unto Thee," in Ray (1970), pp. 233–234.

Gandhi's opposition to a literal interpretation of the Gita: Thomas (1987), pp. 92–99.

Karma as cultic practices: Agehananda Bharati, "Gandhi's Interpretation of the Gita," in Ray (1970), pp. 57–80. Bolle (1979), p. 39, translates karmayoga in Gita III.3 as "the way of Cultic Work." Bolle translates II.47 as: "You are entitled to perform rituals,/but not at all to their results./ The results of rituals should not be your motive./Nor should you abstain from ritual." Compare this to Dayananda (1988), a distinguished commentator on the Gita: "You have a choice over your action but not over the results at any time. Do not (take yourself to) be the author of the results of action; neither be attached to inaction."

Godse: Nandy (1980), pp. 70–98. Godse was convinced posterity would vindicate him. Nandy, p. 92, quotes the judge who presided when Godse made his final plea: "Many women were in tears and men were coughing and searching for their handkerchiefs . . . I have . . . no doubt that had the audience of that day been constituted into a jury and entrusted with the task of deciding Godse's appeal, they would have brought in a verdict of 'not guilty' by an overwhelming majority."

Godse on intolerant Hindu: Dilip Simeon, "Communalism in Modern India," *Mainstream*, Dec. 13, 1986, pp. 7–17.

Operation Brass Tacks: Inderjit Badhwar and Dilip Bobb, "A Disputed Legacy," IT, May 15, 1988, pp. 78–87; Dilip Bobb, "Back from the Edge," IT, Feb. 28, 1987, pp. 40–43; and D. N., "India's Role in South Asia," EPW, July 23, 1988, pp. 1512–1513. This speaks of subimperialism.

Nuclear weapons and missiles: Sharma (1986); Rita Manchanda, "Brinkmanship," *Indian Post*, Jan. 24, 1988; Rod Nordland, "The Nuclear Club," *Newsweek*, July 11, 1988, pp. 22–31; and Dilip Bobb and Amarnath Menon, "Agni, Chariot of Fire," IT, June 15, 1989, pp. 10–15.

Military budget: Gautam Navlakha, "Layers of Camouflage," EPW, June 13, 1987, pp. 928–929, and "Indian Defense Budget: Fact and Fiction," EPW, April 29, 1989, pp. 905–908.

A. M., "Calcutta Diary," EPW, March 12, 1988, pp. 501–502, comments: "One-half of this nation may every night go to bed—or to the apology of a bed—hungry and horrendously under-nourished, the nation's military expenditure must nonetheless mount year by year. . . . As long as the nation does not learn to protest, defense expenditure will continue to expand and word and figures will continue to be so woven as to demonstrate to the neighborhood innocents that retrogression is progress and across-the-border aggression is genteel peace-keeping."

Bharat Wariavwalla, "The Price of Primacy," *Mainstream*, July 15, 1989, pp. 7–8, 29–30, comments: "It is the beastly face power that we have turned on our neighbors in recent years. In the Maldives and Sri Lanka we have used force and we periodically show the glint of steel to Nepal and Pakistan. . . . Sikkim was integrated by force into the Indian Union in 1975. . . . Military power is all we have to help us realize our ambition to be a great power: the world's fourth largest army, perhaps the seventh largest air force and the largest navy among the Indian Ocean littoral countries. This . . . is supported by a GDP slightly larger than Spain's."

Claus Offe: "Challenging the Boundaries of Institutional Politics," *Social Research* 52:4 (Winter 1985), pp. 831–835, 846–855.

50 · **Averting the Apocalypse**

Decent society: Nandy (1987), pp. 1–19. Also: Nandy, "Cultural Frames for Social Transformation: A Credo," *Alternatives* 12 (1987), pp. 113–123.

Social movements: M. S. Gore, "Social Movements and the Paradigm of Functional Analysis," EPW, April 29, 1989, pp. 928–935.

Ethnic movements: Melucci (1989), pp. 91–92.

Brahmin ascendancy: Dirks (1987), pp. 4–10.

Overemphasis on caste: Ronald Inden, "Orientalist Constructions of India," *Modern Asian Studies* 20:2 (1986), pp. 401–446.

Third World: Bruckner (1986), pp. 218–219.

Bibliography

Books

Agarwal, Anil, and others. 1987. *The Wrath of Nature: The Impact of Environmental Destruction on Floods and Droughts*. Delhi: Center for Science and Environment.

Akbar, M. J. 1985. *India: The Siege Within*. Harmondsworth: Penguin Books.

———. 1988. *Riot After Riot*. New Delhi: Penguin Books.

Ambedkar, B. R. 1977 reprint. *What Congress and Gandhi Have Done to the Untouchables*. Lahore: Agha Amir Hussain.

———. 1987 reprint. *Annihilation of Caste*. Bangalore: Dalit Sahitya Akademy.

Andersen, Walter K., and Shridhar Damle. 1987. *The Brotherhood of Saffron*. Delhi: Vistaar Publications.

Ashby, Philip H. 1974. *Modern Trends in Hinduism*. New York: Columbia University Press.

Bandyopadhyay, Jayanta, ed. 1985. *India's Environment: Crises and Responses*. Dehra Dun: Natraj Publishers.

Bocock, Robert. 1986. *Hegemony*. London: Ellis Horwood.

Boggs, Carl. 1986. *Social Movements and Political Power*. Philadelphia: Temple University Press.

Bolle, Kees. 1979. *The Bhagavadgita*. Berkeley: University of California Press.

Bondurant, Joan. 1967 revised ed. *Conquest of Violence*. Berkeley: University of California Press.

Breuilly, John. 1982. *Nationalism and the State*. New York: St. Martin's Press.

Bruckner, Pascal. 1986. *The Tears of the White Man: Compassion as Contempt*. New York: Free Press.

Buhler, G., trans. 1967 reprint. *The Laws of Manu*. Delhi: Motilal Banarsidass.

von Buitenin, J. A. B., trans. 1973. *Mahabharata*. Chicago: University of Chicago Press.

Calman, Leslie J. 1985. *Protest in Democratic India*. Boulder, Colo.: Westview Press.

Césaire, Aime. 1972. *Discourse on Colonialism*. New York: Monthly Review Press.

Chakravarti, Uma, and Nandita Haksar. 1987. *The Delhi Riots*. Delhi: Lancer International.

Chatterjee, Partha. 1986. *Nationalist Thought and the Colonial World*. Delhi: Oxford University Press.

Dayananda, Swami. 1988. *The Teachings of the Bhagavad Gita*. Delhi: Vision Books.

D'Cruz, Emil. 1988. *Indian Secularism: A Fragile Myth*. Delhi: Indian Social Institute.

Desai, A. R., ed. 1986. *Violation of Democratic Rights in India*. Bombay: Popular Prakashan.

Dhanagare, D. N. 1983. *Peasant Movements in India, 1920–1950*. Delhi: Oxford University Press.

Dhavan, Rajeev. 1987. *Only the Good News: On the Law of the Press in India*. Delhi: Manohar Publications.

Dirks, Nicholas. 1987. *The Hollow Crown: Ethnohistory of an Indian Kingdom*. Cambridge: Cambridge University Press.

Dutt, B. C. 1971. *Mutiny of the Innocents*. Bombay: Sindhu Publications.

Duyker, Edward. 1987. *Tribal Guerrillas*. Delhi: Oxford University Press.

Engineer, Asghar Ali., ed. 1987. *Delhi-Meerut Riots: Analysis, Compilation, and Documentation*. Delhi: Ajanta Publications.

Fein, Helen. 1977. *Imperial Crime and Punishment: The Massacre at Jallianwala Bagh and British Judgment, 1919–1920*. Honolulu: University Press of Hawaii.

Femia, Joseph V. 1981. *Gramsci's Political Thought: Hegemony, Consciousness and the Revolutionary Process*. Oxford: Clarendon Press.

Freire, Paulo. 1988 reprint. *Pedagogy of the Oppressed*. New York: Continuum.

Fuchs, Stephen. 1981. *At the Bottom of Indian Society*. Delhi: Munshiram Manoharlal Publishers.

von Furer-Haimendorf, Christoph. 1982. *Tribes of India*. Delhi: Oxford University Press.

Gandhi, Mohandas K. 1949. *Nonviolence in Peace and War*. Ahmedabad: Navajivan Press.

———. 1958–1983. *The Collected Works of Mahatma Gandhi*. Ahmedabad: Navajivan Press, 1958–1983. (In citations this will be abbreviated as cw.)

———. 1973. *Harijan: A Journal of Applied Gandhiism 1933–1955*. Vol. 4. New York: Garland Publishing.

———. 1984 reprint. *Hind Swaraj or Indian Home Rule*. Ahmedabad: Navajivan Publishing House.

George, Alexandra. 1986. *Social Ferment in India*. Delhi: Orient Longman.

Gramsci, Antonio. 1957. *The Modern Prince and Other Writings*. New York: International Publishers.

Guha, Ranajit, ed. 1983. *Subaltern Studies*. Vol. 2. Delhi: Oxford University Press.

———, ed. 1984. *Subaltern Studies*. Vol. 3. Delhi: Oxford University Press.

Henderson, Hamish, trans. 1988. *Gramsci's Prison Letters*. London: Zwan Publications.

Hoare, Quintin, and Geoffrey Nowell Smith, eds. 1971. *Selections from the Prison Notebooks of Antonio Gramsci*. New York: International Publishers.

Huxley, Julian. 1935. *We Europeans*. London: Jonathan Cape.

Jones, Kenneth W. 1976. *Arya Dharm: Hindu Consciousness in 19th-Century Punjab*. Berkeley: University of California Press.

Kananaikil, Jose, ed. 1983. *Scheduled Castes and the Struggle Against Inequality*. Delhi: Indian Social Institute.

Kapur, Rajiv A. 1986. *Sikh Separatism: The Politics of Faith*. London: Allen and Unwin.

Keer, Dhananjoy. 1987 reprint. *Dr. Ambedkar: Life and Mission*. Bombay: Popular Prakashan.

Khan, Mumtaz Ali. 1983. *Mass Conversions of Meenakshipuram*. Madras: Christian Literature Society.

Kohli, Atul. 1987. *The State and Poverty in India*. Cambridge: Cambridge University Press.

Kothari, Rajni, ed. 1970. *Caste in Indian Politics*. Delhi: Orient Longman.

———. 1987. *State Against Democracy*. Delhi: Ajanta Publications.

Kuber, W. N. 1987. *B. R. Ambedkar*. Delhi: Publications Division, Government of India.

Kumari, Ranjana. 1989. *Bridges Are Not for Burning: Dowry Victims in India*. Delhi: Radiant Publishers.

McLane, John R., ed. 1970. *The Political Awakening in India*. Englewood Cliffs, N.J.: Prentice-Hall.

———. 1977. *Indian Nationalism and the Early Congress*. Princeton, N.J.: Princeton University Press.

Melucci, Albert. 1989. *Nomads of the Present*. Philadelphia: Temple University Press.

Memmi, Albert. 1968. *Dominated Man*. New York: Orion Press.

Monier-Williams, Monier. 1971 reprint. *Hinduism*. Delhi: Rare Books.

Moraes, Frank. 1956. *Jawaharlal Nehru: A Biography*. New York: Macmillan.

———. 1973. *Witness to an Era*. New York: Holt, Rinehart and Winston.

Nandy, Ashis. 1980. *At the Edge of Psychology: Essays in Politics and Culture*. Delhi: Oxford University Press.

———. 1987. *Traditions, Tyranny, and Utopias: Essays in the Politics of Awareness*. Delhi: Oxford University Press.

Nehru, Jawaharlal. 1946. *The Discovery of India*. New York: John Day Company.

O'Hanlon, Rosalind. 1985. *Caste, Conflict and Ideology*. Cambridge: Cambridge University Press.

Parekh, Bhikhu. 1989. *Colonialism, Tradition and Reform*. Delhi: Sage Publications.

Pattanayak, D. P. 1981. *Multilingualism and Mother-Tongue Education*. Delhi: Oxford University Press.

Powell, G. B. 1982. *Contemporary Democracies*. Cambridge, Mass.: Harvard University Press.

Prabhakar, M. E., ed. 1988. *Towards a Dalit Theology*. Delhi: Indian Society for Promoting Christian Knowledge.

Prasad, Ishwari, and others. 1987. *Caste Merit and Reservations*. Delhi: Samata Era Publications.

Rajgopal, P. R. 1987. *Communal Violence in India*. Delhi: Uppal Publishing House.

Rajshekar, V. T. 1978. *Dalit Movement in Karnataka*. Madras: Christian Literature Society.

Ray, Rabindra. 1988. *The Naxalites and Their Ideology*. Delhi: Oxford University Press.

Ray, Sibnarayan, ed. 1970. *Gandhi, India and the World*. Philadelphia: Temple University Press.

Roy, Ashim Kumar, and N. N. Gidwani. 1984. *A Dictionary of Indology*. Atlantic Highlands, N.J.: Humanities Press.

Rozario, Sr. M. Rita. 1988. *Trafficking in Women and Children in India*. Delhi: Uppal Publishing House.

Saberwal, Satish. 1986. *India: The Roots of Crisis*. Delhi: Oxford University Press.

Sassoon, Anne Showstack. 1980. *Gramsci's Politics*. London: Croom Helm.

Selbourne, David, ed. 1985. *In Theory and in Practice: Essays on the Politics of Jayaprakash Narayan*. Delhi: Oxford University Press.

Sengupta, Promode. 1983. *Naxalbari and Indian Revolution*. Calcutta: Research India Publications.

Sharma, Dhirendra, ed. 1986. *The Indian Atom: Power and Proliferation*. Delhi: Philosophy and Social Action.

Srinivas, M. N. 1966. *Social Change in Modern India*. Berkeley: University of California Press.

Tennyson, Hallam. 1955. *Saint on the March*. London: Victor Gollancz.

Thapar, Romesh, ed. 1977. *Tribe Caste and Religion in India*. Delhi: Macmillan India.

Thomas, P. M. 1987. *Twentieth Century Indian Interpretations of Bhagavadgita: Tilak, Gandhi and Aurobindo*. Delhi: Indian Society for Promoting Christian Knowledge.

Tilak, Shrinivas. 1984. *The Myth of Sarvodaya: A Study of Vinoba's Concept*. Delhi: Breakthrough Publications.

de Tocqueville, Alexis. 1945 reprint. *Democracy in America*. Vol. 1. New York: Alfred Knopf.

Vakil, A. K. 1985. *Reservation Policy and Scheduled Castes in India*. Delhi: Ashish Publishing House.

Pamphlets, Mimeographs, Offsets

Amnesty International. Jan. 15, 1986. *Arrest of Dr. K. Balagopal, General Secretary of the Andhra Pradesh Civil Liberties Committee*. London: ASA 20/02/86.

———. Jan. 29, 1986. *Some Reports Concerning Deaths in Police Custody Allegedly as a Result of Torture or Shooting during 1985*. London: ASA 20/03/86.

———. Dec. 1, 1986. *Sikh Detainees from the Punjab Held since June 1984: Background to Their Arrest and Detention*. London: ASA 20/11/86.

———. Nov. 1, 1987. *Allegations of Extrajudicial Killings by the Provincial Armed Constabulary in and around Meerut, 22–23 May 1987*. London: ASA 20/06/87.

———. March 1988. *Allegations of Rape by Police: The Case of a Tribal Woman in Gujarat, Gunta Behn*. London: ASA 20/04/88.

———. Aug. 1988. *A Review of Human Rights Violations, August 1988*. London: ASA 20/09/88.

Commission for Scheduled Castes and Scheduled Tribes. 1985. *Seventh Report*. Delhi: Government of India.

Dingwaney, M., and others. No date. *Bonded Labor in India*. Delhi: Rural Labor Cell.

Durrani, Suraiyya. 1986. *Image of Islam and Muslims in Indian National Press*. Mimeographed. Bombay: Institute of Islamic Studies.

Gilada, I. S., and Vijay Thakur. 1987. *Devadasis, a Link Between Religious Culture and Child Prostitution*. Mimeographed. Paper at the 29th International Congress of International Abolitionist Federation, Stuttgart, Germany.

Joint Women's Program. 1983. *Banhi 1981/2: The Devadasi Problem*. Delhi: Christian Institute for the Study of Religion and Society.

Juyal, B. N. 1987. *Child Labor and Exploitation in the Carpet Industry*. Delhi: Indian Social Institute.

Kulkarni, Sanjeev. 1986. *Prenatal Sex Determination Tests and Female Feticide in Bombay City*. Mimeographed. Bombay: Foundation for Research in Community Health.

Malhotra, Kailash C., ed. 1987. *Save the Western Ghats*. Ponda, Goa: Central Organizing Committee to Save the Western Ghats.

Minz, Bishop Nirmal. 1988. *A Responsible Christian Task for Lok Mukti in Chotanagpur*. Ranchi: Dasak Jubilee Publication.

Mobile Crèches. 1987. *In the Shadow of the Scaffolding: A Study of Migrant Construction Workers*. Bombay: Indu Balagopal.

Mukhoty, Gobind, and Rajni Kothari. 1984. *Who Are the Guilty?* Delhi: People's Union for Democratic Rights/People's Union for Civil Liberties.

Nitya/Ashok. 1989. *State Terrorism in Punjab: An Investigative Report*. Delhi: Committee for Information and Initiative on Punjab.

Rajshekar, V. T. 1984a. *The Dilemma of Class and Caste in India*. Bangalore: Dalit Sahitya Akademy.

———.1984b. *Who Is the Mother of Hitler?* Bangalore: Dalit Sahitya Akademy.

———. 1986. *Why Godse Killed Gandhi?* Bangalore: Dalit Sahitya Akademy.

———. 1987. *Merit, My Foot*. Bangalore: Dalit Sahitya Akademy.

———. 1988. *Aggression on Indian Culture*. Bangalore: Dalit Sahitya Akademy.

Ravindra, R. P. 1986. *The Scarcer Half: A Report on Amniocentesis and Other Sex Determination Techniques*. Bombay: Center for Education and Documentation.

Savara, Mira. 1981. *Organizing Women in the Informal Sector: A Case Study of the Annapurnas in India*. Mimeographed. Bombay: Feminist Resource Center.

Singh, Partap. 1988. *Genesis and Solution of Punjab Problem: The Sikh Case*. Delhi: Bharat Mukti Morcha.

Society for Promotion of Area Resource Centers. 1985. *We, the Invisible*. Mimeographed. Bombay.

Srinivas, M. N. 1978. *The Changing Position of Indian Women*. Delhi: Oxford University Press.

———. 1984. *Some Reflections on Dowry*. Delhi: Oxford University Press.

Vahini-Arch. May 6, 1988. *Sardar Sarovar Oustees Fight Continues*. Mimeographed.

———. May 21, 1988. *The 14th May, 1988 Vadgam Convention Before and After*. Mimeographed. Mongrol, Gujarat.

Periodicals

(The acronyms in parentheses will be used for frequently cited sources.)

Three national English-language magazines stand out for investigative and interpretive coverage: *India Today* (IT), published every two weeks from Delhi, *Economic and Political Weekly* (EPW), and the *Illustrated Weekly of India* (IWI), both weeklies published from Bombay. Two other national weeklies are *Sunday*, from Bombay, and *The Week*, from Madras. *Mainstream*, a weekly published from Delhi, has original and reprinted articles on political and economic affairs. *Seminar*, a Delhi monthly, is a "symposium" of opinion on a major topic. *Manushi*, a Delhi monthly, is a widely circulated magazine expressing women's views. In Bombay *Adhikar Raksha* is the bulletin of the Committee for the Protection of Democratic Rights; *Bombay* is a weekly of general city interest; *Imprint* is a monthly of social and political affairs; *Lex Et Juris* is a monthly on legal affairs and *Vidura* is a bimonthly of comment.

Lokayan Bulletin (LB) is a Delhi journal of human and women's rights, the environment, and generally an organ for nonparty political activists. *Religion and Society* is the bulletin of the Bangalore-based Christian Institute for the Study of Religion and Society. *Social Action* is the bulletin of the Roman Catholic Indian Social Institute.

Newspapers

Amrita Bazar Patrika, Calcutta
The Daily, Bombay
Deccan Herald, Bangalore
Economic Times, Delhi
Financial Express, Delhi

The Hindu, Madras
Hindustan Times, Delhi
Indian Express, Delhi
Indian Post, Bombay
National Herald, Lucknow
The Statesman, Calcutta
Sunday Chronicle, Bombay
Sunday Mail, Delhi
Times of India (TOI), Bombay

All interviews were tape-recorded, often at different times. They were condensed to eliminate questions and digressions and transposed to arrange in sequence. Nothing was eliminated to alter tenor or substance.

Index

About the Author

Arthur Bonner was born in 1922 and began a lifelong journalistic career in the early 1940s as a copyboy for the *Daily News* of New York. In 1945 he moved to CBS as a radio news writer. In 1953 he went to India as a free-lance radio and television correspondent and cameraman for CBS. With New Delhi as his base he reported from almost every state and region in India and from Pakistan, Afghanistan, Nepal, Sri Lanka, Burma, Thailand, Laos, and Vietnam.

He also wrote for the *Atlantic*, the *Saturday Evening Post*, the *Wall Street Journal*, and the *Reporter*.

He returned to the United States in 1961 as a documentary producer and was associate producer of *A Tour of the White House with Mrs. John F. Kennedy*. He also continued as a foreign correspondent, covering the war between India and China, and the United Nations action in the Congo in 1962, and later current events in South America.

He left CBS in 1966 to write and publish *Jerry McAuley and His Mission*, on the man who, in 1870, founded the first religious rescue mission to rehabilitate alcoholics.

From 1968 to 1984 he was a producer and news writer for WNBC-TV in New York.

At the end of December 1984, when he was sixty-two, he took early retirement to become a special correspondent for the *New York Times*. During a cumulative eight months over the next two years, he made seven separate trips into Afghanistan with the mujahidin. He returned to the United States in 1986 to write *Among the Afghans*, published in 1987 by Duke University as part of the Central Asia Book Series of Columbia University.

Before the book came out, Mr. Bonner returned to India, where he had lived for almost eight years during the optimistic days of Jawaharlal Nehru and five-year planning, to begin research on *Averting the Apocalypse: Social Movements in India*. He made four research trips, traveled almost twenty thousand miles within India, and recorded interviews with more than sixty men and women.

Mr. Bonner and his wife, formerly senior producer of the soap opera "Another World," have three children.

Library of Congress Cataloging-in-Publication Data

Bonner, Arthur.

Averting the Apocalypse : social movements in India today /

Arthur Bonner.

Includes bibliographical references.

ISBN 0-8223-1029-5

1. India—Social conditions—1947–   2. Social movements—India.

I. Title.

HN683.5.B58   1990

303.48'4'0954—dc20   89-28006 CIP